Labor of Dionysus

Edited by

Sandra Buckley,

Brian Massumi,

Michael Hardt

THEORY OUT OF BOUNDS

...UNCONTAINED

BY

THE

DISCIPLINES,

INSUBORDINATE

PRACTICES OF RESISTANCE

...Inventing,

excessively,

in the between...

PROCESSES

OF

HYBRIDIZATION

Labor of Dionysus

A Critique of the State-Form

Michael Hardt

&

Antonio Negri

Theory out of Bounds   *Volume 4*

University of Minnesota Press

Minneapolis • London

Chapter 2
originally appeared in *Operai e Stato*
(Giangiacomo Feltrinelli Editore, Milan, 1972).
Chapters 3, 4, and 5
originally appeared in *La Forma Stato*
(Giangiacomo Feltrinelli Editore, Milan, 1977).
Copyright Antonio Negri.

Published by the University of Minnesota Press
2037 University Avenue Southeast,
Minneapolis, MN 55455-3092
Printed in the United States of America on acid-free paper

Second printing 2003

LIBRARY OF CONGRESS CATALOGING-IN-PUBLICATION DATA
Negri, Antonio, 1933–
Labor of Dionysus : a critique of the
state-form / Michael Hardt and Antonio Negri.
p.   cm. — (Theory out of bounds ; 4)
Includes bibliographical references and index.
ISBN 0-8166-2086-5 (acid-free paper)
1. Communism.   2. State, The.   I. Hardt, Michael.   II. Title.
III. Series: Theory out of bounds ; v. 4.
HX73.N448   1994
320.5'32 — dc20
93-23422
CIP

For Félix Guattari

Contents

Acknowledgments

THE AUTHORS would like to thank Kenneth Surin, Michael Ryan, and Nick Witheford for commenting on drafts of this manuscript. For the present translation of the essay "Keynes and the Capitalist Theory of the State," which appears as chapter 2, we consulted the English version that is included in Toni Negri, *Revolution Retrieved: Writings on Marx, Keynes, Capitalist Crisis and New Social Subjects* (1967–83) (London: Red Notes, 1988). We are grateful to the Red Notes collective for their generous collaboration.

Preface

Dionysus

THIS BOOK is aimed toward the proposition of a practice of joy—joy in the sense of the increasing power of an expansive social subject. The living labor of this subject is its joy, the affirmation of its own power. "Labour is the living, form-giving fire," Marx wrote, "it is the transitoriness of things, their temporality, as their formation by living time" (*Grundrisse*, p. 361). The affirmation of labor in this sense is the affirmation of life itself.

We recognize perfectly well, however, that the work we are faced with in contemporary society, day in and day out, is seldom so joyful, but rather is characterized most often by boredom and tedium for some, and pain and misery for others. The endless repetition of the same of capitalist work presents itself as a prison that enslaves our power, stealing away our time, and the time it leaves us, our leisure time, seems to be filled merely with our passivity, our unproductivity. The labor we affirm must be grasped on a different plane, in a different time. Living labor produces life and constitutes society in a time that cuts across the division posed by the workday, inside and outside the prisons of capitalist work and its wage relation, in both the realm of work and that of nonwork. It is a seed that lies waiting under the snow, or more accurately, the life force always already active in the dynamic networks of cooperation, in the production and reproduction of society, that courses in and out of the time posed by capital. Dionysus is the god of living labor, creation on its own time. Throughout this study we will focus on the evolving practices and effective theories by which capital succeeds in corralling and domesticating the savage energies of living labor in order to put it to work. Our analyses of the State's elaborate practical and theoretical apparatuses of control and exploitation, however, are oriented not toward inspiring awe at its terrific deployments, but rather at recognizing ever more clearly the powers that subvert and pose a radical alternative to its order. Under the increasingly powerful and subtle yoke of contemporary capitalist relations, living labor grows ever stronger and continually shows that it is finally indomitable. "Modern bourgeois society with its relations of production, of exchange and of property, a society that has conjured up such gigantic means of production and of exchange, is like the sorcerer who is no longer able to control the powers of the nether world whom he has called up by his spells" (*Manifesto of the Communist Party*, p. 39). Our work is dedicated to the creative, Dionysian powers of the netherworld.

PART I

O N E

Communism as Critique

Dinosaurs

IN THE following pages — perhaps to the surprise or dismay of some of our readers — we will speak not only of <u>labor, exploitation, and capitalism, but also of class conflict, proletarian struggles, and even communist futures.</u> Do dinosaurs still walk the earth?! We cast our discussions in these terms not from obstinacy or any obscure orthodoxy, but simply because we believe that, when submitted to a continual process of reconsideration so as to be in line with our desires and our interpretation of the contemporary world, these are the most useful categories for political and social analysis.

These terminological problems are not completely new. Many years ago when one of the authors of this book, then an active Marxist militant, engaged in a debate with an important European proponent of liberal democracy over the question of whether or not there is a Marxist theory of the State, the polemic quickly degenerated.[1] The problem was that the object of discussion was not the same, neither for the two participants, nor for the spectators, nor for the supporters of the two sides. For Norberto Bobbio, a Marxist theory of the State could only be what one could eventually derive from careful reading of Marx's own work, and he found nothing. For the radical Marxist author, however, a Marxist theory of the State was the practical critique of law and State institutions from the perspective of the revolutionary movement—a practice that had little to do with Marxist philology, but pertained rather to the Marxist hermeneutic of the construction of a revolutionary subject and the expression of its power. For the first author, therefore, there was no Marxist theory of law and the State, and what was passed off under this banner was only an eclectic and vulgar construction, produced by "real socialism," that is, by the Soviet Union and the other socialist countries of Eastern Europe. The second author found in Marx the basis of a very radical critique of law and the State, which had over the years been developed by the workers' movement in the course of the revolutionary process and which had in fact been repressed in the codifications and the constitutions of the Soviet Union and "real socialism."

If fifteen years ago that confusion blocked the discussion from being productive, and if the quarrel over the very terms of the debate became utterly impossible, the reader and we ourselves should have no difficulty understanding how today confronting the theme of law and the State from the perspective of communism might appear an impossible task. Today, in fact, Marxism, socialism, and communism are terms that are so compromised in dark historical developments it seems that they cannot be rescued from their polemical reductions and that any attempt to repropose a significant usage, rediscover the pregnancy of the terms, or develop a new theory appears perfectly delirious. It is certainly not the first time in history, nor even in recent history, however, that research beyond the shadows of the propaganda and nightmares of a specific period can produce important results. In the final analysis, if there was something in common between Bobbio and his interlocutor it was that both considered real socialism as a development largely external to Marxian thought: the reduction of Marxism to the history of real socialism makes no sense whatsoever. It does not make sense either to reduce to the history and the semantics of real socialism the set of struggles for liberation that the proletarians have developed against capitalist work, its law, and its State in the long historical season that stretches from the Parisian uprising in 1789 to the fall of the Berlin Wall.

These presuppositions and this desire to investigate beyond the idols of knowledge are at the basis of this book, a series of texts oriented toward a theory of juridical *communism*. This attempt has nothing to do with the juridical *socialism* of the former Soviet world, but very much to do with Marx and the critique of capitalism he developed, and moreover with the communist desire that has been expressed through more than two centuries of struggles against the capitalist exploitation of the working class and all humans. This communism is perhaps a dinosaur in the sense of the term's Greek etymology, a fearful beast—but this monster was never extinct and continues to express its power throughout our modern and postmodern history.

Communism

A theory of juridical communism takes communism as both the point of departure and the end point of the critique of the State-form. Many have pointed out, along with Bobbio, that a Marxist analysis of the State-form, that is, of the complex of legal and economic apparatuses that support and constitute the State, is virtually impossible because Marx focused little attention on the State as such and really developed no theory of the State. It is true, in fact, that Marx presented no *positive* theory of the State and its law. This does not mean, however, that a Marxist analysis has nothing to say about the State; it means rather that the point of departure for a Marxist critique of the State is, properly speaking, negative. "Communism," Marx wrote, "is the real movement that destroys the present state of things." This is the sense in which we take communism as our point of departure.

There are two closely related elements of the communist theoretical practice proposed by this quote from Marx. First is the analysis of "the present state of things," or in our case, the analysis of the theories of law and the State that are *effectively existent*. These are the theories of rule that adequately correspond with the disciplinary figures of the organization of labor and the coercive forms of the social division of labor, be they capitalist or socialist, that serve to steal away the brains and bodies of the citizens and workers for the despotism these forms imply. To this end, then, we will examine the work of authors such as John Maynard Keynes, Hans Kelsen, John Rawls, Richard Rorty, and Niklas Luhmann to discern how they adequately theorize the contemporary practices and figures of rule. We take up these authors in the same spirit that Marx in his time took up Adam Smith, David Ricardo, and Henry Carey—namely, because we think that in certain respects their work has grasped and pertains to the present state of rule.

The second element of this Marxist method, along with recognizing the present state of things, is grasping what Marx calls "the real movement that destroys" that present state. The Marxist critique of the State, in other words, must grasp the real social forces in motion that sabotage and subvert the structures and mechanisms of rule. At the base of this critique, we assume, as Marx did, the idea and the experience of living labor, always subjugated but always liberating itself. Living labor inheres in capital; it is closed in the very institutions where it is born, but continually it manages to destroy them. The critique must thus reach the level of antagonism and revolutionary subjectivities, defining and redefining their changing figures, showing how their movement and their progressive transformations continually conflict with and destroy the new arrangements of law and the State. These are the two faces of a critique of the State-form that takes communism, "the real movement that destroys the present state of things," as its point of departure. As a first hypothesis, then, we could pose juridical communism as a method of thought outside of any dimension of the instrumental rationality of law and the State, a method that destroys that rationality.

A negative method, however, is not enough. The critique must also pose a project. Communism must be conceived as a total critique in the Nietzschean sense: not only a destruction of the present values, but also a creation of new values; not only a negation of what exists, but also an affirmation of what springs forth. Critique of the State-form thus means also proposing an effective alternative. This positive aspect of a Marxist critique must also assume as its basis the idea and experience of living labor. Living labor is the internal force that constantly poses not only the subversion of the capitalist process of production but also the construction of an alternative. In other words, living labor not only refuses its abstraction in the process of capitalist valorization and the production of surplus value, but also poses an alternative schema of valorization, the self-valorization of labor. Living labor is thus an active force, not only of negation but also of affirmation. The subjectivities produced in the processes of the self-valorization of living labor are the agents that create an alternative sociality. (In chapter 7 we will examine what we call "the prerequisites of communism" already existing in contemporary society.) The expression and affirmation of the power of the collectivity, the multitude, as an unstoppable movement of the material transformation of the social organization of labor and the norms that guarantee its effectiveness are the animating force in the transcendental schema of juridical communism. This schema is transcendental in the strong sense. In other words, it is not formal but ontological, not teleological but pragmatic; it does not point toward any necessity nor trust in any transition, but rather presupposes always new processes of struggle, always new configurations of productivity, and new expressions of constituent power. As we said, in its negative aspect the critique of the State-form takes communism as its point of departure, but now in its affirmative aspect, the critique realizes communism as its end point.

As juridical communism is cast as a total critique, it should also be recognized as an immanent critique. This destructive and creative machine that we hope to grasp with a Marxist critical method is the very same one that is defined by the real level of social struggles and the quality of the composition of revolutionary subjectivities. We mean by that, first of all, that law and the State can only be defined as a relationship, a constantly open horizon, that can certainly be overdetermined but the essence of which can always be, and is, brought back to the dynamic and the phenomenology of the relationship of force between social subjects. In the second place, we mean that there is nothing in the realm of law and the State that can be pulled away from the plane of the most absolute immanence — neither a first foundation, nor a table of natural rights, nor an ideological schema, nor even a constitutional paradigm. Just like money, law (which repeats in the capitalist system many of the figures assumed by money) carries no values that are proper to it, but only those that social conflicts and the necessities of the reproduction of capitalist society, its division of labor, and exploitation produce every day. The invariable element of the ideological function of law and the State is always less real than the variable elements that constitute its present consistency, its continual contingency. In this sense, it is completely unreal. The task of the communist critique is to demonstrate this unreality and clarify the affirmative, productive figures that continually emerge from the struggles between the two classes, between domination and the desire for liberation, on the border of this void.

Labor

In recent years, the concept of labor has fallen into disuse not only in philosophical discussions, but also in juridical theory, politics, and even economics. Labor is too often defined narrowly in the realm of a capitalist work ethic that denies pleasures and desires. Our analysis has to open up the concept of labor across the spectrum of social production to include even the productive sphere that Marx called the horizon of nonwork.[2] This opening of the concept cannot be accomplished simply through a reference to its usage in the Marxist tradition but must look also to other sources in an effort to grasp the contemporary processes of the production of social subjectivities, sociality, and society itself.

The concept of labor refers primarily to a problematic of value. In our usage, in fact, the concepts of labor and value mutually imply one another: by labor we understand a value-creating practice. In this sense labor functions as a social analytic that interprets the production of value across an entire social spectrum, equally in economic and cultural terms. This conception of labor should be distinguished first of all from the many contemporary attempts to employ "performance" or "performativity" as a paradigm for social analysis and social practice:

although performance highlights the social importance of *signifying or discursive practices*, we use labor instead to focus on *value-creating practices*.[3] Focusing thus on the processes of valorization seems to us the clearest lens through which to see the production not simply of knowledges and identities, but of society and the subjectivities that animate it—to see, in effect, the *production of production itself.*

The relationship between labor and value, however, can be posed in several different ways. In capitalist society, labor points to a primary and radical alternative: an alternative that allows the analysis of labor to be posed not only as a destructive force against capitalist society but also as the proposition or affirmation of another society. Marx thus conceived the labor theory of value in two forms, from two perspectives—one negative and one affirmative. The first perspective begins with the theory of abstract labor. Marx, following the major economic currents of his time, recognized that labor is present in all commodities and is the substance common to all activities of production. From this perspective, all labor can be traced to abstract labor, which allows us to grasp, behind all the particular forms that labor takes in determinate circumstances, a global social labor-power that can be transferred from one usage to another according to social needs. Marx passed from this qualitative vision to a quantitative conception centered on the problem of the measure of the value of labor. The quantity of value expresses the existing relationship between a certain good and the proportion of social labor time necessary for its production. The principal task posed by this theory is the investigation of the social and economic laws that govern the deployment of labor-power among the different sectors of social production and thus bring to light the capitalist processes of valorization. One of the principal functions of this law of value is to make clear that in a society of producers of commodities, while there is no centralization or coordination, there is the means of making social choices—there is an order. The law of value reveals the rationality that underlies the operations that capitalists conduct blindly in the market. It thus attempts to explain the maintenance of social equilibrium within the tumult of accidental fluctuations. In this first labor theory of value, Marx essentially furthered and refined the analyses of the capitalist economists who were his contemporaries.

In Marx's work, however, the labor theory of value is also presented in another form, which departs radically from the capitalist theories and focuses not on the capitalist processes of valorization but rather on the processes of self-valorization (*Selbstverwertung*).[4] In this form, Marx considered the value of labor not as a figure of equilibrium but as an antagonistic figure, as the subject of a dynamic rupture of the system. The concept of labor-power is thus considered as a valorizing element of production relatively independent of the functioning of the capitalist law of value. This means that the unity of value is primarily identified in its relation to "necessary labor," which is not a fixed quantity but a dynamic element of the system. Necessary labor is historically determined by the struggles of the working class against waged labor in the effort to transform labor itself. This means that although in the first theory value was fixed in the structures of capital, in this second theory labor and value are both variable elements.

The relationship between labor and value is thus not unidirectional. As numerous scholars have recognized over the last thirty years, it is not sufficient to pose the economic structure of labor as the source of a cultural superstructure of value; this notion of base and superstructure must be overturned. If labor is the basis of value, then value is equally the basis of labor.[5] What counts as labor, or value-creating practice, always depends on the existing values of a given social and historical context; in other words, labor should not simply be defined as activity, any activity, but specifically activity that is socially recognized as productive of value. The definition of what practices comprise labor is not given or fixed, but rather historically and socially determined, and thus the definition itself constitutes a mobile site of social contestation. For example, certain lines of feminist inquiry and practice, setting out from an analysis of the gender division of labor, have brought into focus the different forms of affective labor, caring labor, and kin work that have been traditionally defined as women's work.[6] These studies have clearly demonstrated the ways in which such forms of activity produce social networks and produce society itself. As a result of these efforts, today such value-creating practices can and must be recognized as labor. The point again is that the very concept of labor is mobile and historically defined through contestation. In this sense the labor theory of value is equally a value theory of labor.

To conduct a critique using the category of labor from this second perspective, then, one must be attuned continuously to its contemporary sociohistorical instances. The most important general phenomenon of the transformation of labor that we have witnessed in recent years is the passage toward what we call the factory-society. The factory can no longer be conceived as the paradigmatic site or the concentration of labor and production; laboring processes have moved outside the factory walls to invest the entire society. In other words, the apparent decline of the factory as site of production does not mean a decline of the regime and discipline of factory production, but means rather that it is no longer limited to a particular site in society. It has insinuated itself throughout all forms of social production, spreading like a virus. All of society is now permeated through and through with the regime of the factory, that is, with the rules of the specifically capitalist relations of production. In this light, a series of Marxian distinctions need to be reviewed and reconsidered. For example, in the factory-society the traditional conceptual distinction between productive and unproductive labor and between production and reproduction, which even in other periods had dubious validity, should today be considered defunct.[7]

The generalization of the factory regime has been accompanied by a change in the nature and quality of the laboring processes. To an ever-greater extent, labor in our societies is tending toward immaterial labor—intellectual, affective, and technico-scientific labor, the labor of the cyborg. The increasingly complex networks of laboring cooperation, the integration of caring labor across the spectrum of production, and the computerization of a wide range of laboring processes characterize the contemporary passage in the nature of labor. Marx tried to capture this transformation in terms of a "General Intellect," but it should be clear that while tending toward immateriality, this labor is no less corporeal than intellectual. Cybernetic appendages are incorporated into the technologized body, becoming part of its nature. These new forms of labor are immediately social in that they directly determine the networks of productive cooperation that create and re-create society.

It seems, then, that just when the concept of labor is being marginalized in the dominant discourses it reasserts itself at the center of the discussion. That the industrial working class has lost its central position in society, that the nature and conditions of labor have been profoundly modified, and even that what is recognized as labor has greatly changed—all this seems obvious. Precisely these transformations, however, far from marginalizing the concept of labor, repropose its accentuated centrality. Although the first law of labor-value, which tried to make sense of our history in the name of the centrality of proletarian labor and its quantitative reduction in step with capitalist development, is completely bankrupt, that does not negate a series of facts, determinations, and historical consistencies: the fact, for example, that the organization of the State and its law are in large part tied to the necessity of constructing an order of social reproduction based on labor, and that the form of the State and its law are transformed according to the modifications of the nature of labor. The monetary, symbolic, and political horizons that occasionally are presented in the place of the law of value as constitutive elements of the social bond do manage to cast labor outside the realm of theory, but certainly cannot cast it outside of reality. In fact, in the postindustrial era, in the globalization of the capitalist system, of the factory-society, and in the phase of the triumph of computerized production, the presence of labor at the center of the life world and the extension of social cooperation across society become total. This leads us to a paradox: in the same moment when theory no longer sees labor, labor has everywhere become *the* common substance. The theoretical emptying of the problem of labor corresponds to its maximum pregnancy as the substance of human action across the globe. Although it is obvious that in this totality of reference — given the impossibility of considering labor as actually (or even simply conceptually) transcendent — the law of value is blown apart, it is equally obvious that this immersion in labor constitutes the fundamental problem not only of economics and politics but also of philosophy. The world is labor. When Marx posed labor as the substance of human history, then, he erred perhaps not by going too far, but rather by not going far enough.

Subject

In response to the recent and massive transformations of contemporary society, many authors (often grouped vaguely under the banner of postmodernism) have argued that we abandon theories of social subjects, recognizing subjectivities in purely individualistic terms, if at all! Such arguments, we believe, may have recognized a real transformation but have drawn from it a mistaken conclusion. In other words, the victory of the capitalist project and the real subsumption of society under capital have indeed generalized capital's rule and its forms of exploitation, oppressively delimiting the bounds of real possibility, closing the world of discipline and control, and, as Foucault might say, making society a system "sans dehors." This same fact, however, directs subjectivities and critical thought toward a new task: the construction of themselves, as new machines of a positive production of being that have no means of expression but a new constitution, a radical revolution. The crisis of socialism, the crisis of modernity, and the crisis of the law of value do not negate the processes of social valorization and the constitution of subjectivity, nor do they leave these processes (with unpardonable hypocrisy) to the unique destiny of exploitation. Rather, these transformations impose new processes of subjective constitution — not outside but *within the crisis* that we are experiencing, the crisis, that is, that the organization of old subjectivities is experiencing. In this new critical and reflective space, then, a new theory of subjectivity has room to be expressed — and this new definition of subjectivity is also a great theoretical innovation in the design of communism.

The problem of subjectivity does in fact appear in Marx's work.

Marx theorized about a process of class constitution that was already historically fixed. In his major works, such as *Capital* and the *Grundrisse*, his interest in subjective practices was in large part regulated by two needs: first, to highlight the objective necessity of the processes of subjectivity; and second, consequently, to exclude any reference to utopia from the horizon of proletarian action. In practice, however, both of these needs betray a paradox that runs throughout Marx's thought: the paradox of confiding the liberation of the revolutionary subjectivity to a "process without subject." It can seem that Marx thus ended up showing the birth and development of revolutionary subjectivity and the advent of communism as products of a sort of "natural history of capital." It is obvious that there is something wrong in the development of this Marxian analysis. In reality, the same Marx who posed the struggle against transcendence and alienation as the origin of his philosophy and who configured the movement of human history as the struggle against all exploitation presented also, on the contrary, history in the figure of scientific positivism, in the order of economico-naturalistic necessity. Materialism is thus denied that absolute immanentism that in modern philosophy is its dignity and its foundation.

Subjectivity must be grasped in terms of the social processes that animate the production of subjectivity. The subject, as Foucault clearly understood, is at the same time a product and productive, constituted in and constitutive of the vast networks of social labor. Labor is both subjection and subjectivation — "le travail de soi sur soi" — in such a way that all notions of either the free will or the determinism of the subject must be discarded. Subjectivity is defined simultaneously and equally by its productivity and its producibility, its aptitudes to produce and to be produced.

When we look at the new qualities of laboring processes in society and examine the new instances of immaterial labor and social cooperation in their different forms, we can begin to recognize the alternative circuits of social valorization and the new subjectivities that arise from these processes. A few examples might help clarify this point. In a coherent set of studies developed in France on the basis of the recent political struggles of female workers in the hospitals and other health institutions, several authors have spoken of a "specific use value of female labor."[8] These analyses show how the labor in hospitals and public assistance institutions, carried out in large part by women, presupposes, creates, and reproduces specific values — or better, a focus on this type of labor highlights a terrain of the production of value on which both the highly technical and affective components of their work seem to have become essential and irreplaceable for the production and reproduction of society. In the course of their struggles, the nurses have not only posed the problem of their work conditions but at the same time brought into debate the quality of their labor, both in relation to the patient (addressing the needs of a human being confronted with sickness and death) and in relation to society (performing the technological practices of modern medicine). What is fascinating is that in the course of the nurses' struggles these specific forms of labor and the terrain of valorization have produced new forms of self-organization and a completely original subjective figure: the "coordinations." The specificity of the form of the nurses' labor, affective and technico-scientific, far from being closed onto itself, is exemplary of how laboring processes constitute the production of subjectivity.

The struggles involving AIDS activism enter onto this same terrain. One component of ACT-UP and the other elements of the AIDS movement in the United States has been not only critiquing the actions of the scientific and medical establishment with respect to AIDS research and treatment, but also intervening directly within the technical realm and participating in scientific endeavors. "They seek not only to reform science by exerting pressure from the outside," Steven Epstein writes, "but also to perform science by locating themselves on the inside. They question not just the *uses* of science, not just the *control* over science, but sometimes even the very *contents* of science and the *processes* by which it is produced" ("Democratic Science? AIDS Activism and the Contested Construction of Knowledge," p. 37). A large segment of the AIDS movement has become expert in scientific and medical issues and procedures related to the illness, to the point where they can not only accurately monitor the state of their own bodies but also insist that specific treatments be tested, specific drugs be made available, and specific procedures be employed in the complex effort to prevent, cure, and cope with the disease. The extremely high level of the technico-scientific labor that characterizes the movement opens the terrain of a new subjective figure, a subjectivity that has not only developed the affective capacities necessary to live with the disease and nurture others, but also incorporated the advanced scientific capacities within its figure. When labor is recognized as immaterial, highly scientific, affective, and cooperative (when, in other words, its relationship to existence and to forms of life is revealed and when it is defined as a social function of the community), we can see that from laboring processes follow the elaboration of networks of social valorization and the production of alternative subjectivities.

The production of subjectivity is always a process of hybridization, border crossing, and in contemporary history this subjective hybrid is produced increasingly at the interface between the human and the machine. Today subjectivity, stripped of all its seemingly organic qualities, arises out of the factory as a brilliant technological assemblage. "There was a time when people grew naturally into the conditions they found waiting for them," Robert Musil wrote decades ago, "and that was a very sound way of becoming oneself. But nowadays, with all this shaking up of things, when everything is becoming detached from the soil it grew in, even where the production of soul is concerned one really ought, as it were, to replace the traditional handicrafts by the sort of intelligence that goes with the machine and the factory" (*The Man Without Qualities*, vol. 2, p. 367). The machine is integral to the subject, not as an appendage, a sort of prosthesis—as just another of its qualities; rather, the subject is both human and machine throughout its core, its nature. The technico-scientific character of the AIDS movement and the increasingly immaterial character of social labor in general point toward the new human nature coursing through our bodies. The cyborg is now the only model available for theorizing subjectivity.[9] Bodies without organs, humans without qualities, cyborgs: these are the subjective figures produced and producing on the contemporary horizon, the subjective figures today capable of communism.

Actually, grasping the real historical process is what liberates us from any illusion about "the disappearance of the subject." When capital has completely absorbed society within itself, when the modern history of capital has come to an end, then it is subjectivity, as the motor of the action of transformation of the world by means of labor and as a metaphysical index of the power of being, that tells us loudly that history is not over. Or better, it is this border that the theory of subjectivity links closely and necessarily to that revolution, when it crosses the desolate territory of the real subsumption and undergoes the enchantment, be it playful or anguished, of postmodernism, recognizing them nonetheless not as insuperable limits but as necessary passages of a reactivation of the power of being by means of subjectivity.

Postmodern

By now nearly everyone has recognized that it is useless to continue debates "for" or "against" postmodernism, as if we were standing at the threshold of a new era choosing whether or not to dive in. We are irrevocably part of this new era, and if we are to pose a critique of or an alternative to the present state of things, we must do so from within. Postmodernism—or whatever one wants to call the period we are now living—does exist, and although of course it shares many common elements of previous periods, it does constitute a significant change from our recent past. The discussion of postmodernism has involved so much confusion, we believe, partly because so many theorists (even those who analyze the changing forms of capitalism) neglect to cast their analyses in terms of the antagonisms and the lines of class conflict that define it. When recognizing postmodernism as the present state of things, in other words, one should not only focus on the new forms of domination and exploitation but also highlight the new forms of antagonism that refuse this exploitation and affirmatively propose alternatives of social organization. This means recognizing the antagonisms that arise in what today constitute the dominant laboring processes and developing them toward an alternative project. Too often authors assume that in the modern era social and political analysis subordinated culture to economics (superstructure to base), and as some sort of compensation the postmodern era requires that we invert this and subordinate economics to culture. This only adds a mistaken image of postmodernism to a false conception of modernism. The focus we propose on value-creating activities and processes of valorization, however, breaks down these boundaries between the social, the economic, the juridical, and the political and obviates what was really in the first place a poorly posed problem.

Postmodern capitalism should be understood first, or as a first approximation, in terms of what Marx called the phase of the real subsumption of society under capital. In the previous phase (that of the formal subsumption), capital operated a hegemony over social production, but there still remained numerous production processes that originated outside of capital as leftovers from the pre-capitalist era. Capital subsumes these foreign processes formally, bringing them under the reign of capitalist relations. In the phase of the real subsumption, capital no longer has an outside in the sense that these foreign processes of production have disappeared. All productive processes arise within capital itself and thus the production and reproduction of the entire social world take place within capital. The specifically capitalist rules of productive relations and capitalist exploitation that were developed in the factory have now seeped outside the factory walls to permeate and define all social relations — this is the sense in which we insist that contemporary society should now be recognized as a factory-society. (We will return to the real subsumption and its relevance for the theory of law and the State in chapter 6, "Postmodern Law and the Ghost of Labor in the Constitution.")

Capitalist relations of production appear in the postmodern era to be a sort of social transcendental. Capital seems to have no other. Social capital is no longer merely the orchestrator but actually appears as the producer on the terrain of social production. It has always been the dream of capital to gain autonomy and separate itself from labor once and for all. "The political history of capital," Mario Tronti wrote in the early 1960s, is "a sequence of attempts by capital to withdraw from the class relationship," or more properly, "attempts of the capitalist class to emancipate itself from the working class, through the medium of the various forms of capital's political domination over the working class" ("Strategy of Refusal," p. 32). In postmodernism, in the phase of the real subsumption of labor under capital, capital seems to have realized its dream and achieved its independence. With the expansion of its productive bases in the Third World, the shift of certain types of production from North to South, the greater compatibility and permeability of markets, and the facilitated networks of monetary flows, capital has achieved a truly global position. The postmodern generalization of capitalist relations, however, also carries with it another face. As the specifically capitalist form of exploitation moves outside the factory and invests all forms of social production, the refusal of this exploitation is equally generalized across the social terrain. While the postmodern era presents a capitalist society of control on a global scale, then, it also presents the antagonism of living labor to these relations of production and the potential of communism on a level never before experienced. Discerning these new forms of antagonism and the alternatives they present will be our major concern in this study.

We will by no means, however, attempt a general analysis of postmodernism, but rather limit our focus primarily to the juridical structures of the contemporary State-form (see chapters 6 and 7). In the postmodern era, juridical practices have painted a caricature of the Marxist definition of the liberal State as a "totalitarian regime" of the "rights of Man." Juridical theories of postmodernism are to a large extent variations on this theme. On the other hand, our task will be to recognize laboring processes and the production of subjectivities in the strict relation that puts in motion their continual transformation and represents the transformation of the structures of power that rule them. This task, we have said, should be conceived in the form of a total critique. In other words, we believe that by critiquing the contemporary misery of the world, confirmed and overdetermined by law and the structures of the State, one can in the course of critique free up intellectual and ethical energies capable of opening toward communism, as a political regime of radical democracy, as a form of what Spinoza calls the absolute government of democracy. Critique opens the process of constituting new subjectivities; critique is the construction of a space of freedom inhabited by new subjects, enabled by the maturation and the crisis of capitalism to pose the problematic of finally bringing its rule to an end.

Recognizing postmodernism as the present state of things does not, of course, mean that all of modern practice and thought is now somehow used up and invalid. We will argue that it is more accurate and more useful to claim that it is not modern society but civil society that has withered away, so that our world might be characterized not as postmodern but as postcivil (see chapter 6, "The Real Subsumption of Society in the State"). In any case, modernity remains open and alive today insofar as it is characterized by the current of Western thought that has continually, in the centuries leading up to our times, presented against triumphant capitalism the idea of a radical democracy. This is the line that in the modern era goes from Machiavelli and Spinoza to Marx, and in the contemporary period from Nietzsche and Heidegger to Foucault and Deleuze. This is not a philological reference but the affirmation of an alternative terrain of critique and constitutive thought: the terrain on which subjectivities are formed that are adequate to radical democracy and, through labor, capable of communism.

Marxisms

We do not refer to an alternative current in modern and contemporary thought in terms of communism merely for the sake of philological elegance. We do so because we are convinced that communism is definable not only in Marxist terms, that is, that Marxism is only one of the variants, though a particularly effective one, that define that profound and ineluctable desire that runs throughout the history of humanity. When we say communism here we refer primarily to the materialist method. Materialism too, of course, is not only Marxian. It is not by chance that in the Marxist tradition, or the Marxist traditions, beginning with Engels, we can find, on the contrary, forms of thought and methods of research that to our thinking have little to do with an immanent materialism and communism. (Later we will deal with the terrible misunderstanding or distortion of materialism represented by "Diamat," the dialectical version of materialism officially produced and imposed by the Stalinist Soviet Union. See chapter 4, "The Revisionist Tradition and Its Conception of the State.") We would therefore like to situate our Marxism and our communism rather in the great modern current of materialist critique.

We feel little need to refer to the work of other Marxist authors merely because they call themselves Marxists. Or rather, we are interested only in those authors who apply themselves to the critique of the existent, and in our specific case to the critique of the State-form. What does not interest us is the tiresome practice of constantly referring to the developments of the tradition of Marxist theory and the obligatory procedure of taking positions with regard to the other Marxist authors who have addressed this or that question. In Scholasticism, and in all dogmatic scholastic traditions, the *Quaestiones* follow one after another, boring and intact; each author must be prepared to respond to them, and the value of her or his thought is reduced to the logical relationship it establishes with the preceding response. The tradition of Marxist State theory perhaps lends itself too easily to this type of sterile procedure. When we try to extricate ourselves from these questions of orthodoxy, however, we do not mean to suggest that we have simply thrown out the entire tradition of Marxist reflection on the State developed in the nineteenth and twentieth centuries. It is obvious to us, and will also be to our readers, that we are profoundly indebted to many thinkers in the Marxist tradition even when we do not refer to them directly. For example, we adopt and develop E. B. Pashukanis's thought and his clear formula "right equals market"; we have assimilated the Gramscian conception of the relationship between structure and superstructure, its overturning in the concept of hegemony, and the reflections on the "passive revolution"; although we refute Louis Althusser's theory of the "State ideological apparatuses" in its specifics, we nonetheless try to recuperate it in the definition and critique of the State's use of ideology in the postmodern era (and Althusser himself took this approach in his final work); we both accept and critique certain classifications of Nicos Poulantzas and Mario Tronti on the "autonomy of the political" when we speak of the crisis of the concept of civil society; and so forth.

All this, however, does not make us particularly attentive curators of the tradition, and we do not hide our discomfort when asked to situate ourselves in the tradition and be part of the parade. We recognize ourselves more comfortably in the tradition of materialist critique, absolute immanentism, and communism. We are interested in critiquing the "present state of things." Our method is entirely and exclusively that of attacking the substance of things — attacking the State-form rather than attacking what has been said about it by other Marxist authors. And even when we speak explicitly about theoretical currents in Marxism, as we will at length in chapters 4 and 5, what interests us is not so much our position with respect to the various authors but the emergence, through the collective critique, of the present state of things, and specifically the new figure of the State-form. In short, what we find productive is not the relationship of one theory to another but the synergy of efforts in grasping and critiquing the object of our study.

In this context, it should not seem paradoxical that often we prefer reading the bourgeois theoreticians of the State. John Maynard Keynes, John Rawls, and the other authors critiqued in this book bring to light the critical moments of the life of the bourgeois State, from the inside. While the Marxist tradition sometimes flattens and categorizes the phenomena under study (and the tradition has really been powerful in the operation of empty sublimation), the devotion of bourgeois theoreticians to their beloved object and their immersion in the hegemonic culture allow us to understand the phenomena from within. Marx once said that reactionaries often teach us more about revolution than revolutionaries do. The reactionaries tell the truth about the object they love, be it the Indian Office or the Bank of England for Keynes, or constitutional jurisprudence for Rawls. Their critique raises the veils from that reality that critical reason wants to understand in order to subvert. Authors such as Keynes and Rawls are integrally and inseparably part of the object of revolutionary critique. Marx proceeded in this same way. Adam Smith and the market, David Ricardo and the grain business, Tooke and Fullerton and the Bank, Carey and Yankee industry are the same thing for Marx. His study of these authors only led to the definition of the contradictions in their thought to the extent that these were also contradictions of the thing. The materialist is always ruled by the love of the thing, and true thought is only nominal thought, part of the thing, concrete like the thing. In this sense, critique does not divide concepts but cuts into the thing.

If this book were to carry a message or a call, it would have to be this: Let us return to speaking about things, and about theories as part of things; let us enter the linguistic sphere not to make it a game, but to see how much reality it grasps.

Passages

This book contains essays written over a thirty-year period. The unity of its design should, however, be clear: liberate the power of living labor from the prisons that the State and the right construct to make exploitation possible. The single conceptual key that guides this set of essays is the critique of the nexus, both creative and monstrous, dynamic and repressive, that links labor and politics, and at the same time separates them. The fundamental course that we follow, which is not always explicit but should in any case be obvious, involves producing the critical and substantial elements that can allow us finally to write those two chapters of *Capital* that were projected in the *Grundrisse* but never written: the chapter on the subjective dynamics of the wage (as a mode of existence of the working class) and the chapter on the State (as a site of class conflict).

If the unity of the design of this book is clear to the reader, however, it should be equally clear that this arc of discourse is marked and fractured by historical developments and ontological revolutions. Across the thirty years of the composition of this work, we can witness the most important passage of the twentieth century: the revolution of the 1960s and the unfolding of its effects up to the collapse of the Soviet Empire in 1989. In other words, in this book we witness the passage from the "mass worker" to the "social worker," from Fordist society to computerized and automated society, from regulated labor to autonomous and cooperative labor, immaterial and creative labor. This is the same social passage, in the very composition of the general productivity of systems, that has produced new subjectivities, determined new cultural and political relationships, and consequently defined a shift in the course of history. This radical break in the history of modernity and the apparition of the new paradigm of postmodernism are at the heart of this book and dictate the rhythm of the themes it confronts. It unfolds through the transformation of the objects and subjective determinations that the revolutionary methodology of materialism addresses.

Chapters 2 and 3 in Part I of this book were written by Antonio Negri in the 1960s. Through readings of prominent capitalist economic and juridical theorists, these essays seek to define the primary elements of the modern State-form and the dialectical relationship between capital and labor on which it stands. The chapters in Part II, written by Antonio Negri in the 1970s, address the nature of the crisis of the modern State, particularly in terms of the State mechanisms of legitimation and accumulation involved in the problematic of public spending. These essays focus on the various Marxist and communist interpretations of the State and on the social movements that propose a practical critique of the State. Part III was written by the two authors together over the past three years. These final chapters address the passage outlined by the entire arc of this book, by both detailing the logics and structures that define the postmodern capitalist State and analyzing the potentialities of alternative forms of social expression outside the framework of the State that emerge on this new terrain.

Throughout these essays, we have attempted to apply the materialist method to the transformation of modernity, in a manner corresponding to the way in which the materialist method was posed and developed at the beginning of modernity. Materialism should never be confused with the development of modernity; materialism persisted throughout the development of modernity as an alternative—an alternative that was continually suppressed but always sprang up again. The Renaissance discovered the freedom of labor, the *vis viva*: materialism interpreted it and capitalist modernity subjugated it. Today the refusal of waged labor and the development of intellectual productive forces repropose intact that alternative that at the dawn of modernity was crushed and expelled. The *vis viva* of the materialist alternative to the domination of capitalist idealism and spiritualism was never completely extinguished. It has even less chance of being extinguished today when the postmodern ideologies of the dominant bourgeoisie—worn-out ideologies at their very first appearance—try to weave new networks of domination around the emergence of new antagonistic subjectivities, around the mass intellectuality of productive labor. Living labor, that indomitable Dionysus of freedom and communism, does not play this game. If the form of labor is tending toward being completely immaterial, if the world of production is now describable in terms of what Marx called "General Intellect," then living labor points toward the space on this terrain for the political recomposition of antagonism. Why not reappropriate the immaterial nature of living labor? Why not call the private property of the means of production theft—a thousand times over because exercised also on our immaterial labor, on the most profound and indomitable nature of humanity? Why not, in any case, operate scientifically on this plane, reconstructing the dynamics of domination, the functioning of the State and law, as functions of the absurd and wretched machinations of that which is dead? Vampires and zombies seem more than ever the appropriate metaphors for the rule of capital.

Through the continuous application of this method, we will address our object as it passes through these historical passages, critiquing the world of capital that tries in the postmodern era to renew the domination it exercised over the modern era. Our critique of the postmodern, postindustrial, and post-Fordist State is still and always a communist critique—a total, affirmative, Dionysian critique. Communism is the only Dionysian creator.

T   W   O

Keynes and the Capitalist Theory of the State

This essay was written by Antonio Negri in 1967 and it served in subsequent years as a fundamental reference point for the various political groups in Italy and elsewhere in Europe that adopted "workerism" as the theory of the revolutionary movement. (For historical background, see Yann Moulier's Introduction to *The Politics of Subversion* by Antonio Negri.) The economic, institutional, and political analyses of these groups all flowed from one central claim: that the developments of capital are determined by and follow behind the struggles of the working class. This analytical claim carried with it an ontological affirmation of the power of collective subjectivity as the key not only to the development of history but also—and this is the most important element—to the determinate functioning of the institutions. Politics was seen as the product of social activity, or better, social struggles. The institutions and social structures could thus be read from below, from the point of view of the revolution. This position was obviously at variance with the positions maintained by the "official" workers' movements, especially in their most extreme institutional attachments, such as the claim that it was necessary to act through parliamentary means to achieve reforms. The analysis of Keynes's thought and the politics of the New Deal demonstrated that, well beyond the ludicrous claims of bourgeois representation, reforms could indeed be attained, but in order to achieve them it is necessary to struggle for revolution.

1929 as a Fundamental Moment for a Periodization of the Modern State

FIFTY YEARS have passed since the events of Red October 1917. Those events were the climax of a historical movement that began with the June 1848 insurrection on the streets of Paris, when the modern industrial proletariat first discovered its class autonomy, its independent antagonism to the capitalist system. A further decisive turning point came again in Paris, with the Commune of 1871, the defeat of which led to the generalization of the slogan of the party and the awareness of the need to organize class autonomy politically.

The years 1848 to 1871 and 1871 to 1917: this periodization seems to provide the only adequate framework for the theorization of the contemporary State. Such a definition must take into account the total change in relations of class power that was revealed in the revolutionary crises spanning the latter half of the nineteenth century. The problem imposed for political thought and action by the class challenge of 1848 led to a new critical awareness — mystified to a greater or lesser degree — of the central role now assumed by the working class in the capitalist system. Unless we grasp this class determinant behind the transformation of capital and the State, we remain trapped within bourgeois theory; we end up with a formalized sphere of "politics" separated from capital as a dynamic class relation. We must go beyond banal descriptions of "the process of industrialization." Our starting point is the identification of a secular phase of capitalist development in which the dialectic of exploitation (the inherent subordination and antagonism of the wage-work relation) was socialized, leading to its extension over the entire fabric of political and institutional relations of the modern State. Any definition of the contemporary State that does not encompass these understandings is like Hegel's "dark night in which all cows appear gray."

The year 1917 is a crucial point of rupture in this process: at this point, history becomes contemporary. The truth already demonstrated in 1848—the possibility that the working class can appear as an independent variable in the process of capitalist development, even to the extent of imposing its own political autonomy—now achieved its full realization, its *Durchbruch ins Freie*. The land of the Soviets stood as the point where the working-class antagonism was now structured in the independent form of a State. As such, it became a focus of internal political identification for the working class internationally, because it was a present, immediately real, objective class possibility. At this point, socialism took the step from utopia into reality. From now on, theories of the State would have to take into account more than simply the problems involved in the further socialization of exploitation. They would have to come to terms with a working class that had achieved political identity, and had become a historical protagonist in its own right. The State would now have to face the subversive potential of a whole series of class movements, which in their material content already carried revolutionary connotations. In other words, the enormous political potential of this first leap in the working-class world revolution was internalized within the given composition of the class. At every level of capitalist organization there was now a deeper, more threatening and contradictory presence of the working class: a class that was now autonomous and politically consistent. In this sense the originality of 1917, the unique character of the challenge it presented compared to preceding cycles of working-class struggle, towers supreme. Henceforth, all problems took on new perspectives and an entirely new dimension; the working-class viewpoint could now find its full independent expression.

The real impact of the October Revolution, of course, penetrated the awareness of the capitalist class only slowly. At first it was seen as an essentially *external* fact. The initial response was the attempt—successful in varying degrees—to externalize the danger, to isolate the Soviet republic militarily and diplomatically, to turn the revolution into a foreign issue. Then there was the *internal* threat. What was the general response of capital to the international wave of workers' struggles in the period that immediately followed—that is, the creation of powerful new mass trade unions and the explosion of the Factory Council movement challenging control over production?[1] In this period, only backward, immature ruling classes responded with fascist repression. The more general response, however, the reproduction of reformist models of containment, only scratched the surface of the new political reality. The overall goal of capital in the period that followed was to defeat the working-class vanguards and, more specifically, to undermine the material basis of their leadership role in this phase: namely, a class composition that contained a relatively highly "professionalized" sector with its corollary ideology of self-management. In other words, the primary objective was to destroy the basis of the alliance between workers' vanguards and the proletarian masses, the alliance on which Bolshevik organization was premised. To cut the vanguard off from the factory, and the factory from the class — to eradicate that party from within the class: this was the aim of capitalist reorganization, the specific form of counterattack against 1917 in the West.

Taylorism and Fordism had precisely this function: to isolate the Bolshevik vanguards from the class and expel them from their hegemonic producer role, by means of a massification of the productive process and a deskilling of the labor force. This in turn accelerated the injection of new proletarian forces into production, breaking the striking power of the old working-class aristocracies, neutralizing their political potential, and preventing their regroupment. Just as earlier, in the mid-nineteenth century, capital had attempted to break the nascent proletarian front by means of a new industrial structure that fostered the creation of labor aristocracies, so, after 1917, with the increasing political fusion of this differentiation within the class and after the political recomposition that the working class had achieved in the wake of that break point in the cycle, capital once again turned to the technological path of repression. As always, this technological attack (including a leap in organic composition of new sectors, assembly-line organization, flow production, scientific organization of work, subdivision and fragmentation of jobs, and so forth) was capital's first and almost instinctive response to the rigidity of the existing class composition and the threat to capitalist control that this engendered.

It is precisely here, however, that the qualitatively new situation after 1917 imposed limits. The possibilities for recomposition of the labor force in the phase of postwar reconversion certainly existed in the short run, but the capitalist class soon realized that this reorganization would open up an even more threatening situation in the long term. Not only would capital have to contend with the enlarged reproduction of the class that these changes would inevitably bring about; it would have to face its immediate *political* recomposition at a higher level of massification and socialization of the work force. The October Revolution had once and for all introduced a political quality of subversion into the material needs and struggles of the working class, a specter that could not be exorcised. Given this new situation, the technological solution would backfire in the

end. It would only relaunch the political recomposition of the class at a higher
level. At the same time, this response/counterattack was not sufficient to confront
the real problem facing capital: how to recognize the political emergence of the
working class while finding new means (through a complete restructuring of the
social mechanism for the extraction of relative surplus value) of politically controlling this new class within the workings of the system. The admission of working-
class autonomy had to be accompanied by the ability to control it politically. The
recognition of the originality of 1917, of the fact that the entire existing material
structure of capital had been thrown out of gear and that there was no turning
back, would sooner or later become a political necessity for capital.

In fact, the day of reckoning was not long in coming. As always,
capital's political initiative has to be forced into freeing itself. Soon after the defeat
of the 1926 General Strike in Britain—the event that seemed to mark the outer
limit of the expanding revolutionary process of the postwar period—the specter of
1917 returned in a new and more threatening guise. The collapse following 1929
was all the more critical owing to this potential threat. Capitalism now faced a
working class that had been socially leveled by the repression brought against it,
that had become massified to the point where its autonomy had to be recognized,
and that simultaneously had to be both recognized in its subversive potential and
grasped as the decisive element and motive power behind any future model of
development. The great crisis post-1929 was the moment of truth, a rebounding
on capital's structure of the previous technological attack on the working class, and
the proof of its limitations. The lesson of 1917 now imposed itself by this "delayed
reaction" on the system as a whole. The working-class political initiative of 1917
with all its precise and ferocious destructiveness, controllable only in the short
run, now manifested itself in a crisis of the entire system, showing that it could not
be ignored or evaded. The earlier attempts to avoid the problem, to ignore the
effective reality of the working class's specific political impingement on the system, now boomeranged on the system itself. The crisis struck deepest precisely
where capital was the strongest.

In this sense the crisis post-1929 represents a moment of decisive importance in the emergence of the contemporary State. The chief casualty of
the crisis was the material basis of the liberal constitutional State. Nineteen
twenty-nine swept away even residual nostalgia for the values that 1917 had
destroyed. The Wall Street crash of "Black Thursday" 1929 destroyed the political
and State mythologies of a century of bourgeois domination. It marked the his-

toric end of the rights State, understood as an apparatus of State power aimed at formally protecting individual rights through the bourgeois safeguards of "due process," a State power established to guarantee bourgeois social hegemony. It was the final burial of the classic liberal myth of the separation of State and market, the end of laissez-faire.

Here, however, it is not simply a question of an overthrow of the classic relation between the State and civil society and the coming of an "interventionist" State. The period after 1871 had, after all, also seen a growing State intervention and a socialization of the mode of production. What was new, and what marks this moment as decisive, was the recognition of the emergence of the working class and of the ineluctable antagonism it represented within the system as a necessary feature of the system that State power would have to accommodate. Too often (and not only in Italy with the limited perspective that Fascism allowed), the novelty of the new State that emerged from the great crisis has been defined in terms of a transition from a "liberal" to a "totalitarian" form of State power.[2] This is a distorted view. It mistakes the immediate and local recourse to fascist and corporatist solutions, the form of regime, for the central, overriding feature that distinguishes the new historical form of the capitalist State: the reconstruction of a State based on the discovery of the inherent antagonism of the working class. To be sure, this reconstruction has possible totalitarian implications, but only in the sense that it involved an awareness of intrinsic antagonism and struggle at all levels of the State.

Paradoxically, capital turned to Marx, or at least learned to read *Das Kapital* (from its own viewpoint, naturally, which, however mystified, is nonetheless efficacious). Once the antagonism was recognized, the problem was to make it function in such a way as to prevent one pole of the antagonism from breaking free into independent destructive action. Working-class political revolution could only be avoided by recognizing and accepting the new relation of class forces, while making the working class function within an overall mechanism that would "sublimate" its continuous struggle for power into a dynamic element within the system. The working class was to be controlled functionally within a series of mechanisms of equilibrium that would be dynamically readjusted from time to time by a regulated phasing of the "incomes revolution." The State was now prepared, as it were, to descend into civil society, to re-create continuously the source of its legitimacy in a process of permanent readjustment of the conditions of equilibrium. Soon this mechanism for reequilibrating incomes between the forces in play was articulated in the form of planning. The new material basis of the constitution became the State as planner, or better still, the State as the plan. The model of equilibrium assumed for a plan over a given period meant that every initiative, every readjustment of equilibrium to a new level, opened up a process of revision in the constitutional State itself. In other words, the path to stability now seemed to depend on the recognition of this new, precarious basis of State power: the dynamic of State planning implied acceptance of a sort of "permanent revolution" as its object—a paradoxical *Aufhebung* of the slogan on the part of capital.

The science of capital, however, necessarily mystifies as much as it reveals. It revealed the new relation of class forces, and it registered both the painful process whereby the working class became internalized within the life of the State and its central dynamic role as the mainspring of capitalist development. At the same time, however, it mystified and hid not so much the antagonistic nature of this emergence of the working class as the generality of its effects on the system. It concealed the violence that was required to maintain this precarious controlled equilibrium as the new form of the State. Indeed, it even powerfully exalted the new society and its violent sphere of action as the realization of the Common Good, the General Will in action. In this interplay between mystification and critical awareness of the new relation of class forces, the science of capital once again revealed the necessary copresence of contradictory elements. As always, it was forced to carry out the laborious task of analysis and apologetics, to steer the narrow path between critical awareness of the precariousness of the existing framework and a determination to achieve stability. Ultimately, the only possible solution to this contradiction is to place one's faith in an independent political will: a sort of "political miracle" capable of reuniting the various necessary but opposing elements of the capitalist system—socialization of the mode of production and the socialization of exploitation; organization and violence; organization of society for the exploitation of the working class.

It is not that the basic nature of the capitalist process had changed, but rather the framework, the dimensions within which exploitation now had to operate, and the class protagonist over which capital was obliged to assert itself. A political miracle seemed all the more necessary since the antagonistic presence of the class meant that every sign of friction was cause for alarm, every mistake was likely to prove catastrophic, and every movement could denote a dramatic change in the power balance between the two classes locked in struggle. It was the extraordinary strength of the working class, backed by the revolutionary experience it had undergone, that made its mark and imposed those disequilibria that constantly required intervention at all levels of the system.

Capitalist science had to register this fact. The extent to which it did so is the measure, so to speak, of its grasp and understanding of the new situation. To follow this complex process, unmasking it and distinguishing its scientific and ideological components, is the task of working-class critique. In this essay I trace the development of Keynes's thought and reflection on the overall crisis of the capitalist system from the October Revolution to the Depression years. He is the one who showed the greatest awareness and the most refined political intuition in confronting the new situation facing capital at this crucial turning point. It was Keynes whose disenchanted diagnosis indicated for the international capitalist class the therapy to be applied. Keynes was perhaps the most penetrating theorist of capitalist reconstruction, of the new form of the capitalist State that emerged in reaction to the revolutionary working-class impact of 1917.

Keynes and the Period 1917 to 1929: Understanding the Impact of the October Revolution on the Structure of Capitalism

How, then, can we trace the development of capitalist awareness in this period? In what form and to what extent did capital grasp the radical implication of the 1929 crisis? And above all, to what extent did capital become aware of the links between 1917 and 1929?

As we noted earlier, the October Revolution was seen in two ways: internationally, as a problem of counterrevolution (or at least a problem of isolating Soviet Russia), and domestically, as a problem of repressing the powerful trade-union and political movement of the working class, which extended this revolutionary experience to the whole capitalist world. The experience showed itself to be homogeneous. Both where the movement took the form of workers' councils (1918–26) and where it was more straightforwardly trade unionist the common reference point was a certain type of class vanguard and the demand for self-management of production.[3] It is remarkable how these two aspects of the problem were kept rigidly separate by the international capitalist leadership at the time. Different techniques were used to respond to the two revolutionary challenges. Capitalist thinking was not yet convinced of the internally unified presence of the working class. Its separation of these two aspects at least partially explains its catastrophic incomprehension of the real situation.

This, at least, was the view of John Maynard Keynes. If the key moment for capitalist reconstruction of the international order was the Versailles peace settlement, then this was an opportunity lost. In this last act of a centuries-old tradition of power relations between nation-states, there was, he argued, a total failure to understand the new dimensions of class struggle, which became evident in the separation of the two aspects of the problem. How otherwise could the folly of Versailles be explained? The treaty, instead of setting up a plan to save Europe from ruin, merely expressed the frustrations and vendetta of centuries of power politics. With revolution beating at the gates, the leaders of the victorious powers merely set up a punitive system incapable of rebuilding the European order. Diplomatic hypocrisy even triumphed over the commitments made in the armistice agreements.

This was no way to defend the system and give it a new structure. On the contrary, it could only lead to a deepening of the crisis. In particular, the economic folly of the reparations imposed on Germany insured that the effects of the peace treaty would be disastrously prolonged, not just in Germany but cumulatively throughout the integrated network of the world market:

> *If we aim deliberately at the impoverishment of Central Europe, vengeance, I dare predict, will not limp. Nothing can then delay for very long that final civil war between the forces of reaction and the despairing convulsions of revolution, before which the horrors of the late German war will fade into nothing, and which will destroy, whoever is victor, the civilization and the progress of our generation. (Keynes,* The Economic Consequences of the Peace, *p. 170)*

What, then, was the correct course? There is one and only one: to consolidate the economy of Central Europe as a bulwark against the Soviet threat from the East and as a check against internal revolutionary movements — to reunite, in short, the two fronts in the capitalist defense system.

> *Lenin is said to have declared that the best way to destroy the capitalist system was to debauch the currency.... Lenin was certainly right. There is no subtler, no surer means of overturning the existing basis of society.... By combining a popular hatred of the class of entrepreneurs with the blow already given to social security by the violent and arbitrary disturbance of contract and of the established equilibrium of wealth which is the inevitable result of inflation, these governments are fast rendering impossible a continuance of the social and economic order of the nineteenth century. (pp. 148-50)*[4]

This was Keynes's position in 1919. By tracing his thought from this polemic to the *General Theory*, we may perhaps be able to grasp the difficult transition of overall capitalist strategy in the period of the interwar crisis. At this early stage, Keynes was warning against the treaty's disastrous consequences and the implicit illusion that class relations had not been changed by the working class's break with the prewar system. We are still far from any precise theoretical grasp of the new political cycle of the contemporary State. There is scarcely a hint of Keynes's later capacity to transform his awareness of the working class's rupture with the system into a very raison d'être of capitalist economic growth. Yet this intuition of the new class situation, primitive but fundamental, already illuminates the central problem of the years to come: how to block, how to control the impact of the October Revolution on the capitalist order. In order to discuss the question of the continuity of Keynes's thought and its theoretical coherence, we must go beyond the literal meaning of his writings and uncover the general problematic underlying them.[5]

At this stage, we are dealing with a political intuition. It is still far from becoming a scientific system. Indeed, from the perspective of the mature system, Bertil Ohlin was probably more Keynesian than Keynes when he argued, in 1925, against Keynes's view of the effect of reparations, pointing out that the payment of reparations could make a dynamic contribution to a new level of international economic equilibrium.[6] In any case, by 1922 Keynes's own position had changed. The "intolerable anguish and fury"[7] that had forced him to leave the treaty negotiating table in Paris was now placated. His vision was now more superficially optimistic:

If I look back two years and read again what I wrote then, I see that perils which were ahead are now past safely. The patience of the common people of Europe and the stability of its institutions have survived the worst shocks they will receive. Two years ago, the Treaty, which outraged justice, mercy and wisdom, represented the momentary will of the victorious countries. Would the victims be patient? Or would they be driven by despair and privation to shake society's foundations? We have the answer now. They have been patient. (A Revision of the Treaty, pp. 115–16)

Keynes's basic political intuition, however, already implied a radical new appreciation of the major dimensions of capitalist development. Dennis Holme Robertson recognized this with extreme lucidity: "Now the startling thing about this analysis of the economic structure of Europe is that it is in some respects very different from, and indeed diametrically opposed to, that of pre-War optimistic, free-trade, pacific philosophy, and represents much more nearly that upon which, consciously or unconsciously, the edifices of protectionism, militarism and imperialism are reared" ("Review of *The Economic Consequences of the Peace*"). Robertson goes on to point out that this implicitly goes against the concept of laissez-faire and that here questions of international politics are seen in terms of the organization of the relation of forces internally.

Aside from its public notoriety, Keynes's warning of 1919 appears to have had little influence. It was rejected by the press: "Indeed one of the most striking features of Mr. Keynes's book is the political inexperience, not to say ingenuousness, which it reveals" (London *Times*, December 4, 1919, quoted by E. A. G. Robinson in "John Maynard Keynes 1883–1946," p. 35). Politicians young and old responded with one voice of derision, and basically in univocal terms. Clemenceau reportedly said: "Strong in economic argument, Mr. Keynes ... challenges without any moderation the abusive demands of the Allies (read: 'of France').... These reproaches are made with such brutal violence that I would not comment upon them, if the author had not shamelessly thought to serve his cause by giving them publicity. This demonstrates all too clearly how unbalanced certain minds have become" (reported by Keynes in *A Revision of the Treaty*, pp. 69–70 n. 1). Winston Churchill wrote:

With an indisputable common sense Keynes illustrated the monstrousness of the financial and economic clauses. On all these points his opinion is good. But, dragged on by his natural distaste for the economic terms which were to be solemnly dictated, he made a wholesale condemnation of the entire edifice of the peace treaties. That he is qualified to speak of the economic aspects, one cannot doubt; but on the other and more important side of the problem, he could judge no better than others. (The World Crisis, *vol. 5, p. 155*)[8]

As for capital, its response was the old one, as old as 1848 or 1870, albeit pursued more drastically. It wielded repressive force to defeat the political movements of the working class and, in a second instance, it made fresh advances in the reabsorption of labor power through a technological leap and a refinement of the mechanisms for the extraction of relative surplus value. The workers' councils and the powerful current of revolutionary syndicalism of the early 1920s were defeated— or rather were denied the possibility of any revolutionary dialectic between the class vanguard and proletarian masses, which had been their organizational basis. They were simply undermined by the recomposition of the work force in key sectors, by new techniques for rationalizing labor, by deskilling, and by generalizing the mass assembly line. As always, the first response imposed on capital by the working-class wave of struggle was reformist. In this case, in the early 1920s, this became a generalized process of technological innovation. Capital was forced to absorb the thrust of the working class through an expansion in new sectors, through a radical reorganization of the factors of production.

How far, though, was it possible to pursue this old path? Had not the situation totally altered? Keynes's position, against the classic liberal separation of politics, was a generic insistence on the interiorization of the political element within the economy. Even this generic truth, however, was forgotten by the capitalist class. There was a refusal — grave in its consequences — to face the fact that Soviet Russia now offered the working class an inescapable political point of reference. If its project of containment was going to succeed, the capitalist system would have to prove itself capable of recuperating the working class as a *political* entity. The mechanism of relative surplus value was not sufficient. Indeed, its only effect was to enlarge the contradictions of capitalist development, creating a further massification of the class and accentuating the propensity toward cyclical crisis. The expansion of supply (growth in productive capacity and mass production industries) did not effectively call forth the corresponding pressure of demand. "Demand" was not yet recognized as an effective subject.

Keynes's position, still only a political intuition, was also insufficient from a different standpoint: it needed to be worked out scientifically. His strength lay in the fact that he had laid down the methodological conditions for a solution; he had identified the problem correctly. To follow his scientific and political activity in the 1920s is to follow a voice crying in the wilderness, in the bitter tones of a prophet unarmed. At the same time, however, we witness a gradual transformation of political intuition into scientific discourse. This took place throughout under the continuous impact of political events, under the pressure of the working class and the political necessities dictated for capital.[9] We have noted how, according to Robertson, laissez-faire was already abandoned as early as *The Economic Consequences of the Peace*. This was only implicitly the case, however, in Keynes's sense of the precariousness of the international order following the destructiveness of the world war and the revolutionary upsurge that followed. From now on, the problem of the crisis of the old order was to be focused primarily on the British political scene.

Say's Law was no longer valid because it did not recognize that the maintenance of the capitalist system might be a problem. It postulated the system as entirely self-regulating and spontaneous. In other words, it denied the existence of the working class as a potential negation of the system. Now it is true that as the problem of the working class gradually assumed a scientific formulation in

Keynes's writings, so it tended to be defined according to the mystified professional tradition of economic science: as a problem of employment in the crude objectivist tradition of classical economics.[10] During this early phase of his political approach to the problem, however, it is the class struggle that is given the upper hand and called forth to historicize the categories of economic science. Science is referred back to historical reality. The British working class appears in these writings in all its revolutionary autonomy.[11] To his university colleagues and liberal-minded friends, to those who clamored that the 1926 General Strike was illegal and stepped outside the limits of constitutional action, Keynes gave a short reply: That may be, but so what? Class movements may appear illegal, but this is only because the balance of forces conditioning the previous system and determining the previous legality, has disappeared. The relations of force have changed, and legality must be adjusted to fit the new situation.[12] Say's Law was no longer valid because the variables of political and economic equilibrium had altered. The new factor in the situation was the autonomy of the working class. "The trade unions are strong enough to interfere with the free play of the forces of supply and demand, and public opinion, albeit with a grumble and with more than a suspicion that the trade unions are growing dangerous, supports the trade unions in their main contention that coal-miners ought not to be the victims of cruel economic forces which *they* never put in motion" (Keynes, "Am I Liberal?" p. 305). To create a new political equilibrium thus meant taking account of this new situation, these new relations of force. If Say's equations of supply and demand no longer functioned, it was because new unknowns had been introduced. It was now necessary to integrate these unknowns into economic science:

The idea of the old-world party, that you can, for example, alter the value of money and then leave the consequential adjustments to be brought about by the forces of supply and demand, belong to the days of fifty or a hundred years ago when trade unions were powerless, and when the economic juggernaut was allowed to crash along the highway of progress without obstruction and even with applause. ("Am I Liberal?" p. 305)

One should not underestimate the depth and importance of this critique in the period of the 1920s, from a scientific point of view too. This attack on Say's Law implied the destruction of a century-old ideology, a deeply rooted mental attitude that became all the more solid the less it corresponded to reality. It implied the demystification of a set of fundamental values and norms that had guided bourgeois political science in the nineteenth century. Marx wrote:

The same bourgeois consciousness which celebrates the division of labour in the workshop, the lifelong annexation of the worker to a partial operation, and his complete subjection to capital, as an organization of labour that increases its productive power, denounces with equal vigour every conscious attempt to control and regulate the process of production socially, as an inroad upon such sacred things as the rights of property, freedom and the self-determining "genius" of the individual capitalist. It is very characteristic that the enthusiastic apologists of the factory system have nothing more damning to urge against a general organization of labour in society than that it would turn the whole of society into a factory. (Capital, vol. 1, p. 477)

The Keynesian critique of Say's Law was thus a radical destruction of the object of economic science, insofar as political economy was premised—structurally—on the theory of economic equilibrium, on an integrated and functional symbiosis of elements allowing an infinite, free access to the world of wealth. Economic science had been constructed on the notion that these presuppositions were somehow "natural." Once they were subjected to a fundamental critique, the risk that Marx referred to, that the whole of society would be transformed into one gigantic factory, was implicitly accepted.

This, however, was as far as Keynes's critique went. The destruction of the object served only for its reconstruction. Later he would even state that the neoclassical laws of economic equilibrium would again come into their own, once conditions of full employment were reached.[13] The bourgeois dialectic knows no sublation, it cannot overthrow its object. Whenever Keynes reaches the extreme limits of his critique, he is paralyzed by a philosophy that stops him in his tracks. Even when renouncing the more vulgar mystifications, he remains trapped within the arcane world of commodity fetishism; he falls back on formal schemas and sets about reconstructing the conditions for a balanced economy. Apart from equilibrium, the reaffirmation of the mystified form of general equivalence, there is no other goal to aim for. There is nothing left but the "Party of Catastrophe" (*Essays in Persuasion*, pp. 299ff.), the despairing conviction that history—in other words, everything beyond the equilibrium—is nothing but the work of imbeciles: "Neither profound causes nor inevitable fate, nor magnificent wickedness" (*Essays in Biography*, p. 429). "The problem of want and poverty and the economic struggle between classes and nations is nothing but a frightful muddle, a transitory and *unnecessary* muddle" (*Essays in Persuasion*, p. xviii). Hence the formal equilibrium that the scientist attempts to restore at the very limit of the possibilities of bourgeois knowledge. There is not even a sense of full and secure conviction: he is consciously disguising what is basically—and necessarily—an irrational obligation, an obscure substitute for any content of rationality.[14]

Clearly, then, Keynes's object, following this first attack on the nineteenth-century ideology of laissez-faire, this instinctive appreciation of the new situation created by the irruption of working-class autonomy, would be that of reconstructing a new model of equilibrium. It was only, however, with the *General Theory*, published in 1936, that this achieved definitive form. In the 1920s his work remained primarily critical: he attacked the restoration of the gold standard,[15] and identified the new phase of socialization that capitalist production had entered.[16] Above all, he insisted on the need for State intervention to mediate class conflict and guarantee economic equilibrium. (See E. A. G. Robinson, "John Maynard Keynes 1883–1946.") This work was essentially of a critical rather than systematic nature. The terms of the new class relationship are not yet integrated within Keynes's analysis in any systematic way; they have not yet become a constitutive part of the notion of effective demand, of growing risk, of the new theory regarding interest rates: they have not yet become a system.

If we examine the most significant element of this preparatory phase in Keynes's work, his argument for State interventionism, it is evident that this is simply a corollary of his critique of laissez-faire. This critique implied an awareness of the massification of the working class and the consequent difficulty of ensuring equilibrium. What is still lacking is the definition of the new qualitative implications of this irruption of the working class for capitalist development as a whole. The State intervention that is proposed is still only theorized in political terms: it is derived from the need to ensure a wider basis for development by an alliance between the progressive bourgeoisie and socialists. It is not yet argued on the basis of a clear scientific appreciation of the new dynamic of class relations and the role of the working class within it.[17]

In making this distinction, one more theoretical factor needs to be stressed. Simply to register the fact of the socialization and massification of capitalist production and hence to argue for increased State intervention was neither original nor sufficient. This could only partially grasp the character of the new form of State that emerged through the crisis, and it corresponded historically to the initial concrete instantiations of the State organized against the working class. The Bonapartist type of regime, the Fascist regime in the case of Italian backwardness, or certain variants of Prussian State socialism in the phase of struggle following 1870, are examples of this genre. The specific characteristic of the new form of State that emerged from 1929 was rather the type of class dynamic at work within the framework of State interventionism, on which interventionism was premised. Only the experience of the great crisis of 1929 would allow capitalist science to make this further step toward a new definition of the State. For this to be possible, in other words, the 1917 revolution had to triumph historically over the isolation into which these regimes had sought to constrict it.

Keynes's Shift from Politics to Science: 1929 and the Working Class within Capital

It would seem obvious to suppose that the events of 1917 had no bearing on those of 1929. Behind the obviousness of this statement, however, lies a fabric of historical relations that, if we can identify them, will give a greater overall meaning to the crisis of 1929, even if they do not wholly explain it. Although on the one hand the 1929 crisis was a direct product of the nature of the United States' economic system, at the same time it was created by an accumulation of contradictions within the system, dating from the beginning of the century, and in particular by their accentuation, by the fact that the massification of production in the 1920s had been made necessary by the impact of the working class within individual capitalist countries, at the political and trade-union level. A further reason for the way the crisis immediately took on international dimensions was the series of instabilities in trade relations that war, peace, revolution, and attempted counterrevolution had brought about.[18] Even capitalist understandings of the crisis accept this chain of causes — at least at the political level, where 1917 is seen as one of the causes by reason of the looming potential alternative that it represents.[19]

As an external explanation, that is alright as far as it goes. The role played by Keynes was to make this explanation work within an analysis of the crisis — to make it scientific. An ongoing problem finally finds a possible solution, spurred by the rigors of the crisis:

While Keynes did much for the Great Depression, it is no less true that the Great Depression did much for Keynes. It provided challenge, drama, experimental confirmation. He entered it the sort of man who might be expected to embrace the General Theory *if it were explained to him. From the previous record, one cannot say more. Before it was over, he had emerged with the prize in hand, the system of thought for which he will be remembered. (Samuelson, "The General Theory," p. 329)*

In fact, the crisis revealed the dialectical functioning of the individual elements that his analysis had identified. What, in his view, were the factors underlying the

1929 crisis? It was a buildup of an excess of supply, which had a direct effect on the level of net investment, lowering it, and therefore also led to lower values in capital's schedule of marginal efficiency. In other words, we can only understand the specificity of the 1929 crisis if we understand the conditions of economic development in the 1920s, when a broadening of the supply base (in the course of reconversion of war industry, via technological innovation and an extraordinary increase in the productivity of labor, and via the consequent growth in the production of durable goods) was not accompanied by a change in the relationship of supply to demand. The political class of the period held virtuously to notions of "financial prudence" that were simply a crude mask for dyed-in-the-wool conservatism. They would not accept that the massification of supply should be matched by an equivalent massification of demand—in fact they went out of their way to seek and defend political guarantees for the independence of supply. An increasing socialization of capital was matched by misguided claims on the part of capital to a political autonomy. And now, Keynes concludes, we are paying the price of our lack of understanding.[20]

This is the origin of *The General Theory*, Keynes's political manifesto. It is a manifesto of conservative political thinking, in which a sense of present depression and anxiety for a doubtful future paradoxically combine to force a systematic revolutionizing of the whole of capitalist economics. It has been said that "the vision of capitalism as a system always in imminent danger of falling into a state of stagnation ... permeates and, in a certain sense, dominates the *General Theory*" (Sweezy, "The First Quarter Century," p. 307). This is true if we understand that imminent crisis as a political fact that Keynes registers as such, and against which he pits himself in order to reverse it. In the *General Theory* his references to theories of stagnation are polemical, an implication that a capitalist destiny that may have been unavoidable yesterday is clearly unacceptable today, if the system is to have any hope of saving itself. To refer to "demand" is to refer to the working class, to a mass movement that has found a political identity, to a possibility of insurrection and subversion of the system. Keynes is a clear-sighted, intelligent conservative preparing to fight what he knows is coming. It is from this tension born of desperation that political will gains the strength to offer itself as a complete and systematic ideological proposition. Herein lies the necessity of Keynesian ideology.

Right from the early sections of the *General Theory*, we see how the relationship with the future is an essential part of Keynes's analysis of the inner workings of capital. The notion of expectations unites the present and the future:

expectations have a direct influence on levels of employment inasmuch as they have a direct effect on determining capital's level of marginal efficiency. (See *The General Theory*, pp. 46–51 and 135-46.) Up to this point, Keynes is with the classical economists. Today, however, the situation is different: those expectations that must be based on entrepreneurial confidence if they are to produce positive values have now been knocked off balance by a whole gamut of uncontrollable risks — and this at a time when the high organic composition of capital permits even less tolerance of large areas of uncertainty. The crisis has destroyed confidence and certainty in the future, has destroyed capital's fundamental convention that results and consequences must match up to expectations. So Keynes's first imperative is to remove fear of the future. The future must be fixed as present. The convention must be guaranteed. (See pp. 147–64.)

 Here we have our first precise definition of interventionism. It is no longer a question of political convenience, but a technical necessity; it is not just a question of registering the socialization of economic development, but the establishment of a substantial reference point for the forms and rhythms of development.[21] Investment risks must be eliminated, or reduced to the convention, and the State must take on the function of guaranteeing this basic convention of economics. The State has to defend the present from the future. If the only way to do this is to project the future from within the present, to plan the future according to present expectations, then the State must extend its intervention to take up the role of planner, and the economic thus becomes incorporated in the juridical.[22] In its intervention, the State will act according to a series of norms; it will dictate what is to be. It will not guarantee the certainty of future events, but it will guarantee the certainty of the convention. It will seek the certainty of the present projected into the future. This is the first step, a first form for the bringing together of capital's productive and political ruling classes — a form that is still indirect, but extremely necessary. In effect, the life of the system no longer depends on the spirit of entrepreneurialism, but on liberation from the fear of the future. On this the juridical basis of the State, by definition, stands or falls.

 Defense against the future, an urgent desire to stabilize the power of capitalism in the face of the future: this is Keynes's frame of reference, and its class nature is self-evident. It is another way of saying what the critique of Say's Law had already said. Here, however, the situation — of a relationship with new variables, which science has to study and understand — takes on a new dramatic urgency because of the crisis. What is this "future" that Keynes is so eager to call to account? Once again, it is catastrophe, the catastrophe that haunts him and his kind, that "Party of Catastrophe" that he sees represented before him in the living form of the working class. This sheds a new light on Keynes's statement, so often repeated as a superficial witticism: "In the long run, we are all dead." Here it feels more like a premonition for the fate of his own class. We should see Keynes's oft-criticized determination to lead his whole analysis back within static parameters as yet another attempt to rule out a range of catastrophic possibilities and to cancel out the future by prolonging the present.

Here, too, Keynes's project for capitalist reconstruction has to take account of working-class struggle. Faced with this fact, his analysis goes deeper. A second element is added to the definition of interventionism: here the State is seen as the exclusive collective representative of productive capital.[23] Specific political necessities brought Keynes to this conclusion. Already, in his analysis of expectation, he had identified a number of structural elements that (together with pathological elements such as speculation) were liable to bring the system crashing down, such as patterns of competition, expectational forecasting errors, and so forth. It is not enough that the pathological elements can be eliminated by rule of law; both the pathological and the structural elements have to be eliminated de facto. In any event, they cannot be allowed to jeopardize the security of the system's future. "For my own part, I am now somewhat sceptical of the success of a merely monetary policy directed towards influencing the rate of interest. I expect to see the State ... taking an ever-greater responsibility for directly organizing investment" (*The General Theory*, p. 164). More solidly deep-rooted overall guarantees for the future are required. Juridical and indirect forms of State intervention will not suffice. It is not sufficient for the State to guarantee the fundamental economic convention that links present and future. Something further is required. The State itself has to become an economic structure, and, by virtue of being an economic structure, a productive subject. The State has to become the center of imputation for all economic activity. This is a major step forward! As Marx says, "To the extent that it seizes control of social production, the technique and social organisation of the labour-process are revolutionised, and with them the economico-historical type of society" (*Capital*, vol. 2, p. 57). Not to mention the State! In guaranteeing the convention that links the present to the future, the State is still a structure at the service of capitalists. When it poses itself directly as productive capital, however, the State seeks also to overcome the structural frictions that a market economy and its indirect relationship with individual capitalists may bring about. Thus it becomes a new form of State: the State of social capital.[24]

For the moment, let us pass over the more obvious examples of this new definition of interventionism, or rather, of this new kind of State. We will return to them later. Let us instead look at a particular and fundamental theoretical moment that both illustrates and specifies this further step forward in Keynes's thinking: the postulate of an equivalence between savings and investment. We know that this equivalence was not postulated in *A Treatise on Money*; there, the relation between savings and investment was seen as an objective of economic policy aimed at maintaining stable price levels. Between *A Treatise on Money* (1930) and the *General Theory* (1936), however, Keynes changed his mind and postulated a concept of a measurable equivalence, within the system, between savings and investment. (See *The General Theory*, pp. 52–65 and 74–85.) The reasons for this change of heart become apparent from the period in which it happened: between 1930 and 1936, that is, the height of the crisis. At this point the political imperatives were becoming more pressing and were pushing Keynes to adopt a more radical position. In short, the new economic model had to eliminate every trace and possibility of nonconsumed, noninvested income, every overproduction of capital, that is, every dysfunction of circulation. Note that this model no longer describes forms of behavior — it is prescriptive, it lays down necessary preconditions. It is prescriptive because only if these preconditions can be guaranteed by and within the person of the State will there be any hope of confronting (or rather, preventing and controlling) the depressive moments of the economic cycle, and, in general, enabling a political maneuverability of the overall economic order. Otherwise this would remain an impossibility. Hence the unit of account makes its appearance as a budgeting device, and becomes a basic element of State activity; thus armed, the State is confirmed in its role of acting as the center of imputation for social production.[25]

Obviously, this definition of the State as a figure of imputation of social productive capital raises more problems than it solves. In the first place, given that Keynes does not conceive of State socialism as the necessary outcome of his premises, he then inevitably has to face the problem of the relationship between capital's economic ruling strata and the State/political strata, of communication and articulation between the two of them, and of the institutions that are to guarantee and develop this relationship. Here Keynes balances his abuse of speculators and private capitalists with declarations of loyalty to private capital — and the problem remains unresolved. In the second place, Keynes's intention with this equation is to mark the transition from a phase in which the banks tend to dominate investment, to a new phase in which the productive sphere itself directly determines investment; more generally he seeks to "push monetary theory back to becoming a theory of output as a whole" (*The General Theory*, p. vi). But all this is only hinted at.[26] One could go on to identify a whole series of problems that are raised but not solved. Nonetheless, despite the fact that it is tentative and couched in allusion, the equivalence that Keynes poses between savings and investment gives a definitively new configuration to the State. It is no longer merely a source of economic support and incentive, of stabilization and innovation. It has become a prime mover of economic activity. Here the critique of laissez-faire is pushed to the limit: society itself is cast in the mold of the factory—and the last vestiges of individual capitalism come increasingly under pressure.

Thus far, the relationship with the future—insofar as it represents a relationship of struggle with the working class—is established in terms internal to the structure of capital, strictly defined. Thus far, Keynes has set out to explain the necessity for a capitalist reform of the State, with a view to lessening (and if possible eliminating) the fears weighing on the future. Thus far, working-class struggle has imposed a movement of reformism *of* capital. But how does it locate itself *within* capital? How do we find the contradiction-loaded presence of the working class reexpressing itself at this advanced level of restructuring? The evolution of interventionism had been imposed on the capitalist State since the early 1920s, as a response to the political and trade-union movement of that period; now, after the crisis and the restructuring, it becomes decisive. What is the nature and quality of the relationship with the working class that is posed *within* capital?

With Keynes, capitalist science takes a remarkable leap forward. It recognizes the working class as an autonomous moment within capital. With his theory of effective demand, Keynes introduces into political economy the political notion of a balance of power between classes in struggle.[27] Obviously, the ideological (but also necessary) aim of Keynes's argument is toward shoring up the system. For Keynes the problem is how to establish a balance of effective demand, in a context where the various balances of power making up effective demand are conceived of as unchanging. This political objective, however, which would require working-class autonomy to be forever constrained within a given existing power structure, is precisely the paradox of Keynesianism. It is forced to recognize that the working class is the driving motor of development, and that therefore Keynes's statically defined notions of equilibrium can in fact never be attained in static terms. Any attempt to define an equation of static equilibrium is, and will remain, a laborious search for equilibrium within what has to be a developing situation. In effect, as Keynes appears to recognize, the system functions not because the working class is always inside capital, but because it is also capable of stepping outside it, because there is the continual threat that it will in fact do so. The problem for science, and the aim of politics, must be to contain and absorb this threat, this refusal, and absorb it at ever new levels. Capital must ensure that the dynamic factors of growth are controlled, in such a way that the balance of power remains the same. The problem, in other words, is never resolved, only postponed. Looking closely, one can see that capital's dynamism at this point only results from a continuous struggle, in which the thrust of the working class is accepted, and new weapons are forged in order to prevent the class from acting outside capital, and to make it act within a framework whose outlines are continually being drawn anew.

To what extent is this possible? The concept of effective demand contains within it a decades-long experience of how the working class has made its impact on capital—and that impact shows no sign of diminishing. In Keynes, though, there is only the awareness that the political situation is dramatic, which is then transformed into an attempt to turn the crisis, the struggle, into the driving motor of development. How far could this be taken? "In the long run, we are all dead."

Let us look at the situation in more detail. The reasons underlying the great crisis were that an excess of supply became evident in a political situation where demand, the propensity to consume, was under pressure. This caused major imbalances in the broad economic front, which then had a deleterious effect on net investment. The diagnosis itself offers a remedy—increase the volume of demand, raise the propensity to consume. Since variations in the propensity to consume, however, are essentially variations in income, measured in wage-units (*The General Theory*, pp. 91–92 and 110), this means that the equilibrium corresponding to a given stage of effectively realized demand will be that value at which the level of working-class employment determines the price of aggregate supply of output and the entrepreneur's expectations of gain. It has to be said that when we read Keynes in this way—revealing an almost circular interdependence of the various internal parts of the system, which Keynes tries to pin down and finalize—it is not easy to locate the political quality of his thinking.[28] A closer look, however, shows that his entire system of interrelationships rests on a single postulate: the downward rigidity of wages.[29] The "ultimate independent variable" that underlies his thinking is "the wage-unit as determined by the bargains reached between employers and employed" (*The General Theory*, pp. 375–76). It is here, around this motif, that Keynes's theory reveals itself for what it is; it recognizes and makes use of the power of the working class, in all its autonomy. The class can be neither put down nor removed. The only option is to understand the way it moves, and regulate its revolution.

At this point, Keynes's intervention—made dialectical by the principle of effective demand—becomes completely political, inasmuch as it becomes an attempt at conscious control of the movements of the class, movements that have to be accepted as given, as necessary and valid elements of the process. The whole conceptual content of Keynes's thinking is colored by the notion of the balance of forces.[30] Thus the task of economic policy is to dictate a continual revolution of incomes and the propensity to consume, which will maintain global production and investment and will thus bring about the only form of political equilibrium that is possible—which will only be effective if it is prepared to take on board all the risk and precariousness of a balance of power that is and remains open-ended. This, then, is how we can sum up the spirit of the theory of effective demand: it assumes class struggle, and sets out to resolve it, on a day-to-day basis, in ways that are favorable to capitalist development.

Capitalist Reconstruction and the Social State

If we now take a closer look at the problem in hand, that is, how the experience of 1929 led to changes in the structure of the State, we can see how radical was Keynes's contribution. The transformation of the capitalist State lay not only in the way its capacity for intervention was extended throughout the whole of society, but also in the way that its structures had to reflect the impact of the working class. After 1929, the State took on a general organizational structure, characterized not so much by interventionism as by the particular type of class dynamic that it embodies. Thus the only way to understand the specificity of our present State-form is to highlight the dramatic impact of the working class on the structures of capitalism.

Given that the State-form has to register the impact of the working class in society, it is now precisely at the social level that the State constructs—within the fabric of the State itself—a specific form of control of the movements of the working class. Moving from the earlier antithesis of despotism in the factory and anarchy in society (and from the first attempt to organize the contradiction-loaded relationship in the form of the rights State), capital is now obliged to move to the *social* organization of that despotism, to diffuse the organization of exploitation throughout society, in the new form of a planning-based State that—in the particular way in which it articulates organization and repression throughout society—directly reproduces the figure of the factory.

Thus Keynes makes a decisive contribution to the new definition of the State. So far we have studied a number of separate strands in his thinking that go to make up this final overall picture. This is not, however, to say that Keynes lacks an overall perspective going beyond the mere sum of individual partial strands of analysis. This overall perspective springs ready-made from his theory of the rate of interest.

This aspect of Keynesian theory is polemical in relation to neoclassical economic thought, since the latter sees the interest rate as being determined by anarchic factors operating outside of the sphere of production, in a nonsocialized phase of capitalism (rather than as a reward for abstinence and a natural balancing factor between the supply and demand of capital goods). For Keynes it derives from liquidity preference and the quantity of money on the market. If this is true, however, then once again capitalist society is prey to intolerable risks. The individual capitalist and the rentier are endowed with functions that should not be entrusted to them. This can only lead to disaster. Why do we have to accept such a disaster? Do we really have to leave the inevitable dissolution of that anarchic order to the objective forces of the process of production? As well as destroying the rentier, such a course risked sending the whole system toppling — and the day of reckoning was near at hand. Keynes concluded that if we want to take action to save the system, we have to aim at the "euthanasia of the rentier" (which, apart from being politically urgent, is also morally legitimate). This would enable collective capital to embark on maneuvering interest rates downward toward "that point relative to the schedule of marginal efficiency of capital at which there is full employment" (*The General Theory*, pp. 375–76). The whole of Keynes's prescriptive remedy is summed up in this single proposition. This aims to provide a definitive guarantee, in the crucial sphere of the circulation of money, that imbalances can be controlled.[31]

At first sight, all this seems to indicate simply a further refinement of Keynes's arguments, toward an integration of monetary theory and the theory of production at the level where capital has become social capital. On close inspection, however, we see that subordinating interest rates to the schedule of capital's marginal efficiency relative to full employment has further effects: in particular, the paradoxical effect of linking Keynesian theory back to the classical doctrine of labor value.[32] This follows to such an extent that here the reactivation of the law of value ends up providing the sinew and substance of the Keynesian perspective. All factors heterogeneous to the full functioning and direct control of the law of value are to be eliminated. Most particularly, the system — that is, the new system, the new State — is thus strengthened, in that it becomes more fully a product of the realization of the law of labor value. Here, indeed, we can say that the equation "social State equals State based on labor" begins to apply. This is a final and necessary conclusion of Keynes's bourgeois utopianism and his apologetics for capital![33]

If we now examine this theoretical tendency in a critical light, we will see how it is articulated. One might say that Keynes seeks to test a number of classical (or preclassical, as he would put it) intuitions in the context of social capital. In fact, returning to the relationship between the monetary and the productive aspects of social capital, he introduces two tendential laws: the law of average profit, and the law stating that money wages and real wages tend to converge.[34] Here he approaches the purity of the classical economists' description of the law of value. One could almost say that having developed to the point where it becomes social capital, capital becomes Marxist. Obviously, this is an optical illusion, but at the same time there are historical similarities. Whereas the theory of the individual firm effectively ignored the problem of the law of value, now the necessity of considering capital's collective identity reinstates it. It reappears in terms that are not Marxist, but rather a reformist and social-democratic version of Marxism. It reappears not only as a means of describing the process (the implicit and tendential law of how it functions) but also, above all, as a political norm and as one of the central objectives of economic strategy.

This is why Keynes's renewed utilization of the law of value introduces into his thinking the mystified notion of the social interest, the common good. With his reduction of monetary theory to the theory of production and with his analysis of both the political necessity of this reduction and the controlled forms within which it was to be realized, Keynes attempts to represent an end situation that could be attained "without revolution": a situation in which profit and interest are reduced to zero, and in which the monetary relation (this being the sphere of autonomy within capitalist power) would disappear, since money would be reduced to a mere accounting unit, simply a general symbol of equivalence between commodities produced, and thus all reasons for preferring money would disappear.[35] Social interest, stripped of intermediary and subsidiary elements, and the law of value would come to govern the entirety of development. Capital becomes communist: this is precisely what Marx terms the communism of capital (see *Capital*, vol. 3, pp. 436ff.).

This, however, is a curious way for Keynes to proceed — to forget, in the course of his argument, the premises on which his analysis had been based. To put one's faith in the full realization of the law of value is effectively to put one's faith in the full realization of the capitalist law of the extraction of surplus value. Profit and interest, unified and reduced to zero, are in reality no different from the expression of the average rate of surplus value in capital's social production (see *Capital*, vol. 3, pp. 154ff. and 358ff.). Exploitation is not eliminated, only its anarchic and competitive aspects. Profit and interest are not eliminated either; they are merely prevented from exceeding the average. Marx's antithesis remains intact—even if this fact would be of little interest to Keynes.[36] What is more interesting is the fact that Keynes's conclusion here is in open contradiction with other significant parts of his system—in particular, as regards the theory of effective demand. His assertion of a social interest untouched by class contradictions, by struggle, by power relations between two counterposed classes, negates that theory. Not only is the social reality described earlier now mystified, but there is also a contradiction in his science, because he had constructed his law of development precisely on that reality whose existence he now denies. Furthermore, Keynes (unusually, for him, but perhaps inspired by the Cambridge school of moral philosophy)[37] here ventures onto the terrain of utopianism.

This notion of capital is indeed utopian—a capital so totally social that it does not so much refuse to articulate itself via the monetary mechanism[38] as refuse to pose itself as a social force for exploitation, and thus to make itself autonomous, to pose itself as a separate essence and hegemonic power. It is a short-term utopia, up until the point where capitalism takes advantage of the qualitative leap imposed by the struggles and the crisis to abolish the most evident distortions in the process of profit-realization through the market. Then, once this has been done, there ensues an immediate mystification of the relationship of domination and exploitation that exists at the social level.[39] The necessity for this mystification is the reconstruction of capitalism within a power balance that, since 1917, has changed in favor of the working class.

Such a project, however, is completely determined within the framework of the history of capital. It reflects necessities that are immediately political, as well as being theoretical: theoretical to the extent that they are politically pressing and effective. Identical necessities, provoked by similar reflections on crisis, are at the basis of the New Deal, as of any experience of reconstruction within mature capitalism. Certainly, if we were to research the New Deal to see how faithfully Keynesian it was, we would be quickly disabused—in fact, the activities of Schacht were far more in line with Cambridge thinking. Keynes himself noted something to this effect: "It seems politically impossible for a capitalist democracy to organize expenditure on a scale necessary to make the grand experiment which would prove my case—except in war conditions" (Keynes, "The United States and Keynes Plan," as cited by R. Hofstadter, *The Age of Reform*, p. 307). Equally disappointing would be any analysis of Keynes's personal relationship with the U.S. political scene, particularly with Roosevelt.[40]

And yet all the theoretical elements that we have identified as making up the Keynesian system also play their part—and are put into effect in similar, if not identical, ways—in the experiment of the New Deal: from the recognition of the impact of the working class on the structure of capitalism to political and economic techniques aimed at stimulating effective demand via new and publicly funded investment; from emphasis on the urgency of a radical capitalist reconstruction of society to the particular kind of State that then ensues.[41] In fact, we could say that in relation to changing State-forms, only the experience of the New Deal makes explicit what we have seen as a fundamental characteristic of Keynesianism: the recognition of a changed relationship between the economic forces in play, and a matching restructuring of capital's hegemony in this new context. It makes it explicit by radically altering the "rules of the game," by a striking synthesis between the enthusiasm for reconstruction on the part of capital's ruling elite, and long-standing constitutional practices of "due process," now updated. Here, finally, we have a capitalist State audaciously adopting and recuperating the notion of "permanent revolution," for its own self-preservation. It does so with no reservations, asserting its own class essence as a capitalist State, shunning the taint of populist or traditional progressive ideologies. What is imposed is a capitalist reformism that is a long way from social-democratic whinings about imbalances in the system, and is supremely confident of being able to resolve its problems via a reproduction of itself.[42]

How could Keynes fail to see how close this radical historical experiment was to the essentials of his own theoretical and political thinking? How could he fail to see the possibility of his utopia, and the mystification that was its necessary concomitant? In the event, he fails on both counts. This mystification is revealed as such by one final aspect that is characteristic of the mature capitalist State: the increased use of violence. This violence may be direct or indirect, but it is nonetheless always present in the development of the overall promotional and regulative activity that the modern State undertakes. Once again, this fundamental truth arises in Keynes only in passing. Not only in the despairing philosophy of history that accompanies his scientific activity,[43] but also within his system itself. Precisely at the point where he is outlining a capitalist reconstruction that verges on utopia, we find Keynes going back on himself and defining the basic problem as capital's weakness within the class relation that defines it (and thus not forgetting the realities that were his starting point, nor placing his faith exclusively in the models he had proposed for capitalist reconstruction). The illustration of this comes at a decisive point in the *General Theory*—the rediscovery of the law of the tendential fall in the rate of interest.

It is not a matter here of passing judgment on the scientific validity or otherwise of this Keynesian proposition. Suffice it to say that its present formulation appears more convincing than the classic Marxian formulation, because it is based on forecasting not of an overproduction of capital but of "a drop in the discounted return to additional capital and an increase in the supply price of new capital goods."[44] In using this formulation, Keynes draws conclusions that are much more down-to-earth than his utopian schemas, and that arise from the basic situation that was his starting point. He uses the schema provided by the theory of effective demand no longer just as an index for policies aimed at achieving stability, but as an instrument for forecasting and prediction. This prediction, derived from the application of policies of effective demand, is that demand will outstrip supply, and that the deflationary tendencies of the preceding period will give way to a continual danger of inflation. In short, it is based on the definitive and irreversible appearance of all the effects that the massive pressure of the working class was objectively to produce—within this modified relationship between the classes—on the new machinery of capital. This, in fact, was what happened in the development of class relations in the immediate sphere of productive activity after the capitalist reforms imposed by the events of 1929. We can already see this happening, even under the New Deal, in the shape of the recession of 1937.[45]

At the end of all this scientific effort designed to set aside fear, however, the fear for the future still remains, the fear of catastrophe and the Party of Catastrophe. For Keynes the fears arise precisely from a combination of the necessity of reconstructing capital and a recognition of the tendency of the power balance to consolidate in favor of the working class. In a situation where the relationship between the classes has become dynamic, any attempt to create a new equilibrium is bound to be insecure, and it becomes impossible to stabilize movement around a fixed point. The only option in such a situation is to place one's faith in power, as a separate and distinct reality. Is this perhaps how we should read Keynes's elevation of the general interest to an absolute? And likewise his emancipation from his own theoretical schema of effective demand? Is it perhaps possible to see in the twofold movement of Keynes's thinking (on the one hand, open to an identification of the State's structure with the socioeconomic process, and, on the other hand, inclined to recognize a general interest of the State that is separate and distinct from the particularities of social movement) a contradiction that is necessary to the new life of the system? What is certain is that this sense of precariousness is not going to diminish. Perhaps its only adequate translation in institutional terms is the extreme violence characteristic of the modern State — *State*, meaning, once again, fear, the need for repression, violence. Perhaps this is the way that Keynes's utopianism and mystification dissolve. The settling of accounts with the "Party of Catastrophe" becomes a daily event. The communism of capital can absorb all values within its movement, and can represent to the fullest the general social goal of development, but it can never expropriate that particularity of the working class that is its hatred of exploitation, its uncontainability at any given level of equilibrium — because the working class is also a project for the destruction of the capitalist mode of production.

T H R E E

Labor in the Constitution

This essay has a strange history. It was written by Antonio Negri in 1964, but remained unpublished for over thirteen years. The author attempted to have it published, but in Italy in the 1960s there was no book publisher nor even journal editor who would dare promote a critique of socialism from a leftist, workerist, and revolutionary point of view. The essay circulated nonetheless in manuscript form. This essay develops a Marxist argument from within the tradition of European public law, not through a generic ideological confrontation but through precise interpretations of the juridical texts and institutions. The essay proposes a Marxian paradox: it carries out a critique of the discipline and exploitation of labor while at the same time recognizing labor as not only the basis of the social processes of valorization but also the specific source of institutional and constitutional structures. The recognition and development of the depth of this paradox served in the 1960s, particularly in Italy and Germany, to demystify the supposed "humanism" of capital, perhaps in a more effective, and at least different, way than the structuralist Marxist schools in France and England managed to accomplish during the same period. This essay has a great deal in common, on the one hand, with the work of Johannes Agnoli, professor of the Berlin Freie Universität, with what he called the transformations of democracy, and, on the other hand, with Gilles Deleuze and Félix Guattari's *A Thousand Plateaus,* where the struggle of the working class is situated on the horizon of the war machines that challenge and destroy the institutional apparatuses of capture set in motion by capital.

I. Introduction to the Problematic

All revolutions have only perfected this machine instead of smashing it.

Karl Marx, *The Eighteenth Brumaire of Louis Bonaparte,* p. 122

From the future of the workers. —Workers should learn to feel like soldiers. An honorarium, an income, but no *payment* [Bezahlung]!

Frederick Nietzsche, *The Will to Power,* #763

THIS STUDY addresses several problems of constitutional law and the general theory of right, problems connected to the redefinition of the contemporary State as a "social State," a "planned State," and a "State of labor." It seeks to account for several transformations that have taken place in the juridical system of sources, the structure of the State, and the connected conceptions of juridical norm and authority. The fundamental thesis is that these institutional changes, produced by underlying political changes, do not alter the class nature of the bourgeois State, but rather perfect it, making it adequate to the new needs of the development of capital. The conviction that runs throughout the essay and sustains the analysis is that Marx's projections about the development of capital have been verified to a large extent: this fact confirms the theoretical relevance of his method and justifies its use in this study.

The Constitutional Relevance of Labor

From the "socialist" battle to the "social" State: or rather, the Aufhebung *of socialism*

Let us begin by briefly analyzing a specific example that will serve as an introduction to our general problematic and consider the history of the interpretation and constitutional positioning of the founding principles of the Italian Constitution of 1948. "Italy," the first article of the Constitution announces, "is a democratic republic founded on labor." Faced with this solemn proclamation at the very foundation of the new order, no one could deny that a strongly subversive influence had managed to creep into the most fortified citadel of the already too-threatened fortress of bourgeois economic and political power. Actually, however, this statement appeared to be so general that it was practically innocuous. It would indeed have been continually crushed by the inevitable rhetoricians of the Constitution, by the ineluctable Victor Hugos of the moment, and its subversive political potential would thus have been quickly isolated had it not been linked with other elements of the Constitution. Instead, it was complemented by similar statements in articles 3, 4, and numerous others.[1] This was cause enough to rekindle preoccupations and fears. The interpretation that prevailed at the time of the drafting of the Constitution was the following: such generic statements, even though posed at the head of the Constitution, could not have any normative value. It was only a matter of recognizing the importance of labor in modern society — more a recognition of fact than an evaluation, more a sociological assertion than a program. If, then, one wants to speak of a program, one cannot, strictly speaking, go beyond the generic social tonality of the Constitution. At the time, there were no norms of application that would give concrete efficacy to such constitutional statements — and this was a field *de jure condendo*, a field of debate, unresolved and open to the play of political forces.[2]

Today, at a distance of fifteen years, the interpretative "climate" has shifted substantially. Anyone who still detects a misguided "breeze from the North" in the preamble of the Constitution is oversensitive; anyone who is still angered hearing the usual rhetoricians repeat worn-out declarations is too irritable. Constitutional (or, inevitably, political) battles have turned in a different direction and the victors have emerged as those who, with the rigidity of the constitutional arrangement, have emphasized the normativity of all the norms included in it—and few doubt this. If such norms are called programmatic, this is only because they presuppose a series of conditions preliminary to their full implementation. The normativity will not be diluted on account of this; on the contrary, the precepts posed by these norms will gain their efficacy, going beyond the legislative function to invest the entire orientation of political discourse. (See Vezio Crisafulli, *La Costituzione e le sue disposizioni di principio*, in particular pp. 66–68.) The interpretative climate is, in turn, the product of a profoundly changed political climate and a constitutional custom that manages, even if very slowly, to affirm its own hegemony. The entire implementation of the Constitution rests on the votes of everyone—unless (and this is not improbable) the ends themselves require different means. In short, if we were inclined to doubt, at this point we would doubt the adequacy of the means to the ends. Paradoxically, in the last fifteen years, the Constitution has become so firmly embedded in the consciousness of Italians, juridicists and politicians alike, that today we consider as solid bases what yesterday were most suspect: its ideological and political foundations. If ever they believed there were a need to go beyond the Constitution, they would do so in the service of those foundations![3]

Articles 1, 3, and 4 have been, implicitly or explicitly, at the center of this long constitutional battle. They touch the very heart of the matter, expressing an immediately ideological and directly political content. Today, the normative character of these articles is recognized generally. From the most learned to the most naive constitutionalists, the lesson is the same: labor should be the constitutive principle of the State-form.[4] Articles 1, 3, and 4 contain not only an "attribution of the constitutional relevance of labor" (Giannini, "Rilevanza costituzionale," p. 3), but also a characterization of the very "regime of the State community and consequently the regime of the institutional ends and tasks of the person of the State" (Crisafulli, "Appunti preliminari," p. 163). In short, labor-value contains "the fundamental element of the informative political ideology of the entire State arrangement, and thus it is the constitutive element of the regime" (Mortati, "Il lavoro nella Costituzione," p. 153). If, in fact, the analysis is extended to address all the articles that deal with this material, reconstructing systematically their constitutional rigor, one can see that articles 1, 3, and 4 constitute the basis of a coherent normative set: the prefiguration of a concrete system of social relationships and consequent political equilibria.

Does this mean that some of the fundamental ideological principles of socialism have penetrated to the heart of the Constitution and now flourish there? In our opinion, the answer to this question cannot but be positive. In fact, the substance of the Constitution would not be changed (only given a bit more color) if the present formulation were to be substituted with a more ideological one, such as the formulation long credited to the Constitution, "the Italian State is a republic of workers," or even the traditional slogan, "a republic of manual and mental workers." In spite of all the ambiguities (and we will see later how they can be resolved, in the section titled "From the Constitutionalization of Labor to Its Model"), there is no doubt that the concept of the Constitution that is principally acknowledged is that of productive labor, as a fundamental component of the structure of society, and therefore as a basis of social production. It is a polemical concept, then, both in the face of privileged social positions and in the face of capitalist exploitation aimed at private accumulation. These, rightly or wrongly, are considered to be the concepts proper to socialist ideology. It is true, then, that here we are seeing "the liberation movement of labor forces from their exploitation."[5]

At this point, however, arises the problem that interests us. Given the generally recognized presence and relevance of a typically ideological and specifically socialist concept of labor, given the centrality and influence of this concept within the entire constitutional arrangement, can the Italian Constitution be called a socialist Constitution? It is not sufficient to respond with a reference to the pluralism of constituent political forces that would have set up the constitutional arrangement dualistically. Such a claim is only useful in historiography when it refers to the determinacy of a conflict between parties or ideologies that, as such, is effective in the birth of a juridical configuration. This claim, then, is formally incorrect if it is intended to deny that the conflict gives rise to a unitary juridical norm that functions beyond the adversities embedded in its formulation. Scholarship and interpretation should thus grasp this unity and articulate it systematically. One might respond: precisely because the Constitution was dualistic, it was held captive by the political forces that emerged and its practical application was guided by these ideological principles. The contradiction was resolved in this case because the socialists were not strong enough to impose their interpretation. Even if this resolute skepticism were to explain adequately the past, however, and that is doubtful, it does not in any way explain the present. Or rather, it simply refers us to another fact: that today this dualism is effectively closed and the Constitution is and must be presented as a sufficiently unitary and coherent ordering. This is the context in which the problem that interests us appears.

It is obvious that we are not merely dealing with terminology here. If that were the problem it would be sufficient to accept the suggestion of the theory that defines as "social" the Constitution and State that came out of the Second World War,[6] seeing the socialist ideology *aufgehoben*, that is, recuperated and at the same time sublimated, not in a more vast and comprehensive but in a "new" category, in a new ideology (precisely, a "social" ideology). In this new ideology it would cohabit organically with principles that at other times were opposed to it, such as the formal guarantee of freedom and the hegemony of productive interests. Furthermore, such a suggestion can only be accepted when the conceptual recomposition of the contradiction serves to bring the investigation back to the level of reality, finding justification there.

Allow us, then, to propose the first approximation of an alternative theory. We are faced with the constitutional celebration of productive labor and the subsequent proletarian interests, and then the constitutional refiguration of a clearly bourgeois ordering in the affirmation of formal freedom and equality and in the hegemony of the productive interests of capital: a few fundamental socialist principles and then a social Constitution. What is the specific relationship between these two sets of elements? Saying that the first have been *aufgehoben* in the second is only a philosophical sleight of hand. In reality, there are two possibilities. Perhaps the first were absorbed in the second — but then, given the radicality of their effect and their totalizing capacity, the Constitution is undoubtedly a socialist constitution. This interpretation should be rejected in principle. On the other hand, perhaps these principles, common to the socialist tradition, have been transfigured by the new reality in which they are situated and there, far from representing a subversive force, serve to ground and guarantee some of the primary needs of the economic and social development of the bourgeoisie. The real *Aufhebung* in this case is superimposed on the terminological *Aufhebung*.

Social Capital and Social Labor

The definition of capitalist reformism and its present form

The configuration of the problem defined above should be explained by an analysis of the real relationships that condition it and are presupposed by it. To this end, allow us a brief historical digression. There was a point in the middle of the nineteenth century when the concept of labor, which, in its individual definition, had supported the long process of the bourgeois revolution, began to break apart. The naturalness of the originary capitalist ordering came under considerable criticism and the rationality of its project of indefinite accumulation came to be contested. The universal system of needs, described by classical economics as the creation of freedom and the immediate satisfaction of the most universal human needs, gradually disclosed itself, as Hegel might say, as a system of the most radical poverty.

The more labor generated wealth in the social complex of production, the more inept the system became at distributing this wealth, at compensating labor for its toil. "Labor continually becomes more absolutely dead," Hegel writes.

The ability of individuals continually becomes more infinitely limited, and the consciousness of the workers lowers to the point of extreme obtuseness. The connection between the various types of labor and the entire infinite mass of needs becomes completely ungraspable, and a blind dependence develops such that a distant operation suddenly blocks the labor of an entire class of men, that therefore cannot satisfy its needs and makes this labor useless and superfluous. Even though the assimilation of nature is accomplished more easily with the intervention of the intermediate rings, these levels of assimilation are infinitely divisible and the majority of factors that bring ease to the operation contribute a difficulty that is equally absolute.
(Jenenser Realphilosophie, *vol. 1, p. 239*)

Hegel reveals the consciousness of an entire age. From this point on, the organic growth of the bourgeoisie in its society, in its capital, was disrupted. To the extent that the capitalist thrust of accumulation continually invested new zones of society, the enjoyment of labor and the enjoyment of its fruits were separated and abstracted to a greater degree. The mode of production determined the relations of production, extended them and consolidated them at a social level. To the general socialization of labor corresponded, with an abstraction of its value, the most general alienation.

What the bourgeois consciousness reveals in a philosophical form, however, simply derives from the knowledge of a new real relationship, a new political relationship. In fact, as Hegel continues, "need and labor, raised to this level of universality, construct for themselves ... an enormous system of commonality and reciprocal dependence, a life of the dead that moves about, that stumbles blindly this way and that, and that like a wild beast must be constantly subjugated and tamed [*Beherrschung und Bezähmung*]" (*Jenenser Realphilosophie*, vol. 1, pp. 239–40).[7] Even though capital's own essential negation arises from the capitalist process itself, capital cannot destroy that negative force but must tame it. The negation inheres within capital as a necessary product, which continually grows

larger as capital extends across society, and which continually grows more antagonistic as the social accumulation of capital abstracts the value of labor and con-
solidates it in the dead substance of its own power. An uninterrupted process of
struggle is thus initiated. On one hand, the class of capitalists, the managers of
abstract labor, in order to survive, must rationalize the forms of its management so
as greater to unify itself and greater to dominate that class of proletarians that its
own process of concentration reproduces and enlarges. On the other hand, the
working class assumes the entire weight of social exploitation upon itself: its very
existence is the sign of a latent dissociation; each of its movements is a potential
subversion; and its internal unification is both a negative function of the capitalist
process of development and a positive function of the experience of struggles. It is
essential here to emphasize that the relationship between capitalist reformism and
workers' struggles develops from this point on in a permanent way. The relationship is a double movement: on one side, capital, with its primary goal of politically
combating the working class, has to make itself open to concessions that organize
the working class (as labor-power) internal and homogeneous to the process of
social production; on the other side, the working class, while conceding to capital
the partial and transitory moment of economic affirmation, always recomposes that
moment later in the continuity of its own political reunification and in the next bid
at revolutionary power, always within but always beyond the single determinations of development. The double relationship between capitalist reformism and
workers' struggles, therefore, is born within capital. It imposes on capital a continual process of restructuring, designed to contain its negation.

  We should further highlight the specific character of this dynamic. Capital is constrained to reabsorb continually the determinate levels of the
workers' refusal of alienation. Capital's internal restructuring is at once a demand
of development and a mystification of the workers' response. Let us look at one
example. In 1848 in France, the bourgeois republic, surrounded by social institutions, was born as a solution to a problem internal to the bourgeoisie, driven by
the necessity of a development that had been previously blocked by residual aristo-
cratic privileges. It was born also, however, as a form of the bourgeois integration
of the instances of proletarian self-government, as a force to contain the revolutionary monster that had appeared on the scene. (See Karl Marx, *The Civil War in
France*.) Since then, every bourgeois revolution has had a proletarian face, and
every political mediation of bourgeois forces has been brought on, almost imposed,
by the current level of workers' refusal and struggle—it has been directed toward

necessary solutions to further the concentration and rationalization of the collective power of capitalists. Every crisis and every capitalist restructuring thus reveals the subversive potential that had to be contained, but at the same time, inevitably, was thrust forward. Even when the organized movement of the working class was born — in its historical forms, its unions and parties — it took form within the development of capital and its political and economic institutions. And it can only be born there.

As an organized movement the working class is completely within the organization of capital, which is the organization of society. Its watchwords and its ideological and bureaucratic apparatuses are all elements that are situated within the dialectic of bourgeois development. The relationship, therefore, between the working class and its organized movement is double and ambiguous, just like the relationship between the working class and capital. It varies between moments of absolute coincidence and moments in which the present form of organization, its slogans, and its ideology are all liquidated along with the single levels of the reformist development of capital — even though they were imposed by the working class. Because the class continually sets forth its revolutionary struggle, it goes beyond the single stages of capitalist development and, in going beyond them, also goes beyond the historically determined forms of its own organization that are congruent with these stages — so as to create new, more advanced, more comprehensive forms, and determine new objectives for the working-class struggle. The capitalist *Aufhebung* burns the watchwords and the historical organizations of the proletariat, freezing them at single levels of its own development; the *Aufhebung* of the working class subsequently burns the successive levels of capital's development, reproposing its rupture and its supersession.

The workers' refusal of capitalist exploitation has come to cover the entire breadth of social production. This refusal has spread across the social field exactly to the same degree that capital, which has made the modern factory the most typical instrument of its own accumulation, has extended its material dimensions to cover the entire society. The specific effects of this situation are easily recognized. Here we should focus only on those effects that are particularly relevant to the goals of our study. In the factory-society, the distinction between economic constitution and political constitution drops out; social unification in the collective capitalist, or in social capital, no longer demands any kind of mediation; the logic of accumulation — its internal hierarchy (in this objective sense), its discipline, in short, labor as a laboring process and as a process of the valorization of capital—is thus assumed within the supporting scaffolding of the entire social organization of power. All the privatistic alternatives that single capitalists could express are negated, not by the laws of development but by the directly expressed and directly effective political law of collective capital. The State is configured as the executive organ of collective capital, as the direct manager of social production.

More specifically, however, if the antagonism between collective capitalist and collective worker is presented as immediate and can no longer be absorbed within the political mediation of the bourgeoisie, then in order to envelop and directly control the working class at a social level, and thus reduce it to being only social labor-power, capital has to organize the working class as such—and paradoxically, it has to organize itself within the working class. The "democracy of labor" and "social democracy" both reside here: they consist of the hypothesis of a form of labor-power that negates itself as the working class and autonomously manages itself within the structures of capitalist production as labor-power. At this point, capitalist social interest, which has already eliminated the privatistic and egotistic expressions of single capitalists, attempts to configure itself as a comprehensive, objective social interest. The celebration of sociality and the common good, and the renaissance of a natural right of equality and socialization are ideological hypotheses of the capitalist repression of class antagonism. The models of humanitarian socialism are assumed as emblems of reunification. The patriotism of common well-being in social production is the ultimate slogan of the capitalist effort at solidarity. Like soldiers, all producers are equally employed in the common sacrifice of production in order to win the battle of accumulation.[8]

Now we are in a position to bring this digression to a conclusion, returning to the problem proposed at the outset: the paradoxical *Aufhebung* of socialism in the social ordering. The definition of the dynamic of the development of capital in its relationship with working-class struggles (an analysis we will continue in the section titled "The Historical Process of the Constitutionalization of Labor-Power in Capitalist Development") allows us to grasp the mechanism by which socialist principles have passed into the Italian Constitution, with an indisputable effect on its ordering. Furthermore, the definition of the present level of capitalist reformism in its confrontation with the level of social capital, and therefore in its proposal of a democratic management of social labor-power, allows us to understand the annulment of the revolutionary import of these socialist principles in the Constitution. This seems to be the reality of the political relationships that the class struggle has produced in Italy in the past fifteen years; consequently, in the course of the struggle the institutions have been restructured and the ideologies transformed. In this process, too, the relationship between the working class and its historical organizations has been modified.

In the subsequent sections we will study the single determinations of this phenomenon, always within the framework of the general theory of the State. It is sufficient for now to have seen how the socialist principles of the democracy of labor can be made adequate — and even at times seem obsolete — to the goals of the accumulation of social capital.

First Consequence: Labor as a Bourgeois Category

Or rather, from a formal conception to a substantial, "laborist"
conception of the material constitution

In order to introduce our problematic more fully we should address other premises, along with their explanations and consequences, that we have only briefly mentioned until now. In general, we would like to reveal the particular role of science in this new social and political reality, and, for our specific purposes, juridical science. We will argue that juridical science succeeds in correctly reflecting capitalist development to the same extent that the reunification of society and the State within the constitution of the factory-society imposes an extenuated, if sometimes conclusive, process seeking to make the formal models of ordering adequate to the reality of productive relationships that are directly in force on a State level.

At this point, taking up again the example of the role and the constitutional restructuring of "labor," we can make a useful clarification of what we have said thus far. Constitutional modifications follow the contemporary maturation of the material conditions of development. The laborist elements of the Constitution can only be raised up and celebrated in the context of this material relationship. These elements contained in the Constitution are indicative of the present nature of the State regime, even if they are *aufgehoben* with respect to their previous generic definition. This new characterization of the problematic presents us not with a normal rearrangement of the formal elements with respect to their material conditioning, but rather with a problem central to constitutional science: the problem of the relationship between the material foundation and the formal constitution of order. Constitutional science has long been conscious of the centrality of this problem. In practice, therefore, it has very closely followed the modifications of the social and political context of ordering. It did not hide the importance of its discovery, then, when it succeeded in reaching definitions of the material constitution, rigorously understood as a historically determined and historically caused point of contact between right and fact, and between the juridical organization of power and its social structuring—or rather, when it has grasped the constitutive form of the State in labor, precisely in the sense that the structure of the ordering and the power that organizes labor are traced in the expression of labor on a social level.

One might say that Italian constitutional theorists were in the best position to develop this project. Perhaps because of the particular type of organicist statism in which it has been traditionally embroiled, Italian constitutional science has always been suspicious of dualistic positions in the definition of the relationship between form and matter, noting on the contrary that such positions—whether of idealist-critical or realist origin—end up paradoxically negating themselves by means of the absoluteness of the original point of view.[9] When these theorists addressed the project to redefine the material constitution in laborist terms, then, they already had a solidly monistic perspective that, even though it was heavily formalized, provided a useful point of departure. The development proceeded from the following premises. In coherence with the vigorous refusal of the dualism between norm and fact, this theory developed by a method of exclusion in order to individuate "the material constitution in a fundamental political end, which is given normative value insofar as it is sustained and put into effect by the dominant political force."[10] The material constitution, therefore, is not rooted in a merely existential entity, but rather in a reality already ordered toward an end. This affords from the beginning the possibility of a nondualistic conception of constitution. These theorists, then, wanted to envelop in an original unity both the moments of existential conditioning of the ordering and the elements with normative relevance that result from this conditioning. The concept of "dominant political force" seems to respond to these conditions to the extent that, imposing a special order and guaranteeing the constancy and effectiveness of the exercise of power, it reveals and sublimates a normative specification from the existential level, "a specification, in other words, in the position of the associated members of society, on the basis of which some succeed in exercising a power over the others so as to obtain obedience" (Mortati, *Costituzione in senso materiale*, p. 75).[11] Is this notion, however, sufficient to satisfy the conditions that have been posed? Undoubtedly, the method used is correct: it does not impose any bizarre mediation and the notion is not presented in an ideological form; rather it is traced, with its adequate criterion, in reality. Nonetheless, it does not seem sufficient, because the political category does not itself engender a criterion but rather is maintained by a theory of the origin of power and its legitimation. Furthermore, the problem of the legitimation of the formal ordering cannot be resolved with a simple reference to a normatively defined reality. This merely defers the problem as long as it lacks a historical specification of the fundamental normative fact; it is a solution that is still captive of the indefinite deferral, typical of the formalist method. We are moving in a vicious circle here. Even though we began with the recognition that the juridical norm is not sufficient to constitute the ordering that gave rise to it, we end up using precisely this norm to define the political fact, in this case the dominant political force, which has been employed as the sufficient foundation.[12] A strong residue of formalism still dominates this position.

It is no coincidence, on the other hand, that a deepening (from this point of view) of the concept of dominant political force, a deepening understood as the exclusion of any possible relativist interpretation, ends up by developing it as a concept of the integrity of the acting political forces in the ordering. It concludes, then, by consciously annulling any remaining determination of the existential relationship—insofar as this is now posed as an indeterminate totality of the acting political forces—and therefore by configuring the material constitution as a simple foundation and a limit to the formal legitimation of power. Furthermore, the risk of repetition, or doubling, is still present by virtue of a definition of the dominant political force that is no longer extensive but intensive (an application in which the accent falls on the specificity of the rule of a political force). The sociological model of the foundation of the constitution, therefore, duplicates the concept of dominant political force and runs the risk of an extreme relativism.

It is necessary, therefore, to go beyond this approach and define the reference to the sociopolitical dimension in a substantial way, specifically, revealing its content. A new approach should naturally follow the internal tendency of science to resolve its own problem, which is that of correctly defining the point of contact between norm and fact, materially connecting the juridical organization of power with the social structuring of power, while avoiding both formalist and relativist deviations. We should also always keep in mind, after the critique of its insufficiency, the necessary and correct premises offered to the analysis of the theory of the material constitution.

When the Italian Constitution introduces the concept of labor and traces its centrality in social reality, then, it offers constitutionalist science the possibility of going beyond its impasse. The analysis reveals that the concept of labor entirely covers social reality, repeating its existential and normative articulations. Now we can give an adequate response the question posed earlier, because labor provides an existential foundation of the order of power that can be juridically organized in the formal constitution, animate this constitution as a motor in its implementation (and as a limit to its revision), and give meaning and unity to this ordering. When labor comes to be seen as a productive force at a social level and its organization invests the totality of the social-factory, then the necessary prerequisites can be satisfied. They can no longer appear dualistic in any way because if laboring processes invest the totality of society, then right resides entirely within labor. In this way the limitations of the genericness and relativism of the conception from which we set out can now be definitively eliminated, because laboring processes—insofar as they are combined with the process of the capitalist valorization of labor—offer both a schema of the articulation of power and an immanent legitimation of its exercise, along with a relative theory of material inequality in society. Without this foundation these phenomena would have to be mystified or simply assumed acritically.

Proceeding in such a way, following and penetrating the development of capital, constitutionalist science has thus realized that paradoxical *Aufhebung* of the socialist notion of labor that we initially described. It should come as no surprise that such a notion has been adopted, transformed, and instrumentalized in a juridical system of capitalism directed toward social accumulation. That was the master line, because labor, as capitalist social production, was revealed as abstract labor at a social level, and therefore it determined the entire series of relationships of subordination that are implicit in its nature. While the permanence of a substantially capitalist structure of power is redefined as democratic and egalitarian, labor's exclusivity as social value (in which we find the expression and realization of the old socialist motto: "He who doesn't work, doesn't eat") accentuates instead the abstract character of labor and bases the conceptions of democracy and egalitarianism on this abstract labor.

We do not mean to negate the profound internal transformation, the restructuring, and the progress represented by capital assuming labor as its own constitutive category on a social level, and therefore (as we have seen) as a scientific category. In light of this, we might even ask ourselves if one could properly speak of a change in the political regime, but that will not prove useful for us here. What we would like to highlight is that this reform is still always internal to capital, which integrates the elements of socialist reformism at the point when it signals the historical affirmation of the factory-society. Even if all of this is very important for the bourgeois process of the emancipation of labor, therefore, it has nothing to do with the liberation of the working class.

Second Consequence: The Science of Capital

Or really, the legitimacy of a Marxian approach

We were talking about science. In the practice of the constitutionalists we saw science follow and sustain the reformist movement of capital to the point of revealing and posing the bases for ordering the articulation of its power at a social level in labor. Now we should ask ourselves if this particular constitutionalist practice, which is not an isolated phenomenon, is not a symptom or a manifestation of a more general movement of the restructuring of juridical science in the contemporary social and political world, capable of modifying the methods and characteristics of juridical science. We should ask ourselves further if the passage from a formal-political conception of the material constitution to a substantial-laborist conception can be described in the field of juridical science as a development common to several diverse contexts and during a significantly extended period of time.[13]

As we have seen, when capitalist production invests the entire society, considering this a necessary mediation in the process of accumulation, capital tends to be presented as a general social interest. This generality appears at all levels, dissolving the old antithesis between the particular interests of the accumulation of the capitalist and the general interests of society; capitalist production and society are presented in perfect mediation. At a social level, then, the appearance of generality is proposed as spontaneous and immediate, and it is reproposed by all the demands of economic and political life. The terms of the social restructuring are given by capital itself, and equality and democracy are the forms in which the appearance of the general interest of capital is celebrated. As for labor, it represents not only the keystone to the interpretation of the nexus between production and society, but also the value by which that nexus is defined and organized, in the inverted form given by the capitalist appearance of generality. The exclusivity of labor as productive value is defined in the appearance of the totality of labor as a criterion of social valorization.

Given this situation, science can move in the uniform realm of social appearance established by capital, devoid of lines of division. Its universalizing vocation has no need for "troublesome" contrasts in order to affirm itself. This science recognizes the immediate appearance of capitalist society, sees it as the totality of the process of social organization, and thus is able to exercise a correct analytical function, considering only appearances, referring only to the given phenomena of society, and avoiding the alternative between the brutal mystification at the service of particular capitalist interests and the sweet utopia in defense of general social interests. Since it is internal to society, science becomes internal to capital itself. Capital unifies the science of its own accumulation and the science of society—and science is willing to operate in capital without renouncing its own scientific character.

It is true, however, that this unification is a process, within the capitalist process of reform, within the general movement of the class struggle. It is a process that, even though there are moments of clear emergence, must still be regarded as a tendency. The analysis, therefore, has to be conducted by looking to the future. As Lenin said, anyone who wants to represent a living phenomenon in its development inevitably has to face a dilemma: either run with the times or fall behind. It should come as no surprise, then, that in reflecting the given reality constitutionalist science appears as ambiguous, and at times clearly still involved in the old methodological alternatives.[14] In general, however, the process, the necessary implementation of the tendency, does take place. We can recognize it not only when labor is determined as the element that constitutes the material ordering basis of the constitutional arrangement and not only when (as an anticipation, consequence, or generalization of the laborist hypothesis) the so-called ontological consideration of constitutional right is set forth (see Loewenstein, *Beiträge zur Staatssoziologie*, pp. 331ff.), but also and principally when, on a vast methodological and theoretical level, the long path of the reunification of economics and right is brought to an end, clarifying how the intermediary phase of the formalization of the economic relationship in the juridical norm gives way to the recognition of the mutual inherence of economic activity and juridical activity. In short, the assumption of labor by constitutionalist science as a constitutive element of the material constitution and therefore of the State regime represents a general condition of juridical science. Situating itself in a society reconstructed by the totalizing function of the accumulation of collective capital, juridical science (as a social science) adequately follows the constitutive rhythm of power, identifying its developments and accompanying them in the double discipline of interpreting society and creating a system.

As we proceed, then, the legitimacy of a Marxian approach to the constitutionalist theories is, in our opinion, clearly demonstrated. Aside from any interpretative choice on our part, constitutionalist science itself, through its development, prepares a terrain for Marxist analysis. In this case there is no risk of Marxian theory appearing as a generic philosophy that can be applied anywhere, always reducing and ignoring its problems. Here the fundamental premises of its own approach have already been verified by the juridical analysis, from the consideration of the unifying tendency of economy and right to the identification of the process of the capitalist valorization of labor as a model and a foundation for the social articulation of power. The Marxian approach, therefore, can be applied to the specificity of a series of unchallenged premises in the development of right at this phase of social accumulation.

There remain, however, some objections to consider, objections that were at one time brought against Marxism when it defined the relationship between economy and right, but that now, given the coincidence we have noted in the positions in this respect, can be brought against any science that presumes to see right developing in a way that is adequate to the environment of the social production of capital, or more generically in the economic realm. The more general objection is that the relationship between economic development and the development of juridical structures is not univocal but rather equivocal and thus that this relationship cannot be grasped by science. In particular, some maintain that the development of capitalism toward forms of social management, which have come to be substantially homogeneous, has instead engendered diverse institutional developments: on one hand there are the forms of the formalist rationalization of right, and on the other there is instead an accentuation of juridical traditionalism and the forms of its juridical production. They maintain, contrary to Marx's view, that when there have been conflicts between rationalism and traditionalism at an advanced capitalist level, traditionalism has won out. (See Max Weber, *Economy and Society*, vol. 1, pp. 500–517.)

This critique seems to take as its adversary only a caricature of the Marxist argument.[15] The unilateral reconfiguration of capitalist development in a rationalist and formal sense — a development that instead responds with continually greater mobility to the demands of the workers' struggle — carries with it an equally unilateral reconfiguration of the process of juridical rationalization, which also is protected from the demands and the specific determinations of the class struggle. Instead of the real development that Marxist inquiry follows and that juridical practice itself cannot obliterate, it wants to substitute a world of formal connections, and in the articulation of these connections it encounters contradictions and ambiguities that it attributes to Marx. Actually, the univocity of the relationship can hold only if we insert the series of connections between phenomena of capitalist development and juridical phenomena into the context of the relations of production, and only if we recognize how capitalist development moves in reaction to the demands of class struggle—only, that is, if we recognize that the class struggle is the origin and the motor of capitalist development. From this perspective the univocity and the determination of the relationship are not generic but specific. It is typical of the development of the laborist conception of the Italian Constitution, for example, that it is determined precisely by means of an effort to go beyond the lacunae and the contradictions of the formal constitution, precisely by recognizing that the formal constitution as such does not and cannot contain the diverse pressures of political forces and reflect their diverse equilibria except through a process of adequation.[16]

Paradoxically, the objection just mentioned does not end up contradicting the correct formulation of the problem, but rather confirming it, insofar as it stands against those positions, so frequent these days, that statically determine the relationship between right and economy, outside and independent of the modifications imposed by the social struggle. From this point of view, we can confirm the ineluctable formalization of right, considered generically, either optimistically or pessimistically, as a technocratic instrument of capitalist rationalization and homogenization. In the optimistic current, such tendencies lead to conclusions that are always contradicted by the reality of the development of right at the point when the wide adaptability of right as an instrument of power and a scientific function is brought to light. In the pessimistic current, on the other hand, these tendencies come to define the relationship as a universal process of pure and simple alienation. In any case, the lack of attention to the specificity of the relationship and the modifications it continually undergoes in the context of the class struggle ends up by outlining a scene of mechanically univocal relationships that, be it heavenly or apocalyptic, is always mystifying in its hypotheses of development and always contradicted by practice. This approach is perhaps simply an acritical reflection of the capitalist need to configure the entire society exploited by capital as a simple object of its own production. In the factory-society, instead, right substantially and directly inheres within economics, when this is properly understood as the world of the relations of production and the struggles that configure them.

The definition of the specific relationship between economics and right that the Marxist method allows us to illuminate will now permit us to undertake an ordered analysis of the subsequent problems caused by the laborist sublimation in the Italian Constitution and in general posed by this relationship.

The Rights State and the Social State

Proposal for a study of the formal problems posed by the laborist conception of the material constitution

Pulling together the various topics we have considered up to this point around the theme of our investigation, we are now prepared to propose a further plan of study that will deal with the formal modifications of constitutionalist thought, their theoretical reflections, and more generally the formal problems posed by the laborist conception of the material constitution. We will work, therefore, toward some description, even an emblematic and general description, of the consequences of the paradoxical *Aufhebung* of the socialist conception of labor, so that we can pull from it an approximate image of the social State: the State in which the *Aufhebung* is realized. Keeping this image in mind as a research hypothesis, we will be able to identify the profiles of the subsequent studies or, in other words, the planes on which we will have to examine our proposed hypothesis.

In this framework, we could never highlight strongly enough the importance of the laborist emphasis in the definition of the material constitution. Its relevance is not only ideological, but also — given what we have said about the position of the science of capital — it brings with it a series of substantial and technically relevant consequences. The explicit reference of the constitutional arrangement to the material dimension is in fact immediately polemical with respect to the formal conceptions of the constitution and the juridical ordering, to the point of inverting their premises. By means of such a reference, the juridical ordering seeks to intervene in the reality of social relationships, by directly controlling and reconfiguring those relationships. It does not seek only to adopt them as the inevitable basis of juridical consideration, or follow them to "guarantee" the effectiveness and certainty of their autonomous development.

The spirit and history of the rights State (*Rechtsstaat*) have revolved around the word "guarantee." The economic and social order, entrusted to the free expression and coordination of individual capitalist energies, must simply be guaranteed by the rights State, the guardian of individual rights and the means of their explanation. All of its instruments are directed toward this end: The fundamental rights are the sublimation, and yet the substance, of the individual interests that must be guaranteed; the division of powers is the means by which the coordination of these interests is developed in an autonomous way, at a social level, against the interference of the State itself; and the concept of law as a general and abstract norm — and the consequent subordination of the administration and jurisdiction of the law — is the means by which the State can guarantee the social life of economic individuals, abstracting social life as if it had entirely completed its own process of self-regulation, assuring its certainty and continuity. The ordering is formal because it appears as a negative rule of the social interests in which the State is guarantor, and because it assumes individual actions and their free coordination as the autonomous and "natural" content of its own action. The function of repressing the struggle of the working class, which the rights State so gladly assumes, is not contradictory, as some would like it to seem, but rather is a logical consequence of the guarantorist spirit of economic individuality and the conditions of the self-regulation of the process — even if actually it is not very formal.[17]

When the materiality of the constitutional premises is revealed, however, we are presented with a new image of the relationship between society and the State. The social State is not a guarantor and it does not assume a formal ordering, isolated from its propositions. It does not negatively register social reality, but rather puts social reality into question and actually negates its capacities of self-regulation. It thus considers fundamental rights not as single interests that it should guard but as social interests it should win; it rules positively and intervenes actively in social reality in order to construct directly its own order. Law, as a means of intervention, is restructured by the State's needs and configured as a "plan" of the construction of social order and the repartition of what is produced in society. Law is cast as a means toward the recomposition of contrasting interests. Subordinated to the necessity of administration, law assumes determinate validity and effectiveness, concrete contents and special functions. The division of powers, insofar as it is still in effect, is transfigured and tends to be considered as a means toward the articulation or repartition of powers among social groups, which can subsequently be incorporated into the unity of the State in an uninterrupted process of recomposition. Hence the relationship between legislation and administration is inverted, while jurisdiction continually discovers a greater creative function at the limit between the legal validity and the concrete truth of the process of the recomposition of contrasting and converging interests.[18]

When the State, then, reveals its nature even more, defining itself in laborist terms, its primary characteristics are radicalized: the material character of the legislative process is accentuated, the transformation from the division of powers to the division of power in society is made necessary, and the division of the public from the private, if it ever resisted its first redimensioning in society, now reaches a further reduction. Most of all, however, in the social State, with all its laborist connotations, the economic elements of the social constitution assume an even greater importance. The political and juridical constitution tends to repeat the economic constitution of society to the extent that the material dimension of social production identifies State and society. In contrast to the rights State, then, the social State assumes the entire class relationship at its heart. In place of the guarantee of the conditions for the economic self-regulation of capital, it substitutes the project to integrate the classes and regulate capital globally. In this framework, then, the laborist definition of the constitution emphasizes the modality of the management of social capital and the necessity of making it pass its political control into the hands of social labor-power, by means of a functional and efficient democratic system. Precisely from this point of view, the social State is not a guarantor State—or, if you wish, it is a guarantor State precisely from this new point of view, from the perspective of the new demands for the management of social capital. If the State makes use of repressive force, it does so against those who do not accept the integration, those opposed to the capitalist objectivity of the rule dictating the partition of the social product, and those who contest the plan, refusing to work within it.

This is the specific difference between the rights State and the social State, but we also must look at its next of kin. In the first place, we should repeat that the rights State presupposed its own economic material constitution: the self-regulation of individual capitalist interests. The rights State, however, masked that material constitution to the extent that it formalized the State and right. The formal science of the liberal era reflected this situation and thus found itself involved in the absurd, insoluble dilemma of the rationality of its development and the irrationality of its premises. Facts, series of facts, developments of facts were all preconstituted, but still had to be adopted and constituted in the rational rhythm of the formal mediations of right—the rationality of the law and the irrationality of capitalist accumulation, social universality and private particularity. Can this contradiction, which was unavoidable in the rights State, now actually be eliminated in the social State? Capitalist development says it can, and we have seen how—by making the entire society the domain of appropriation and making the object of exploitation into the subject of the management of social accumulation. This, however, is only an apparent solution. We have seen how such a new structuring is located completely within the development of capital and how in this development the irrational nature of capitalist growth is simply repeated and masked. All this is nothing but a reformist moment of capital. This capitalist reformism is thus the next of kin of the two types of State. It should come as no surprise, then, that in the social State there is an attempt to save some of the most typical principles of the rights State, such as the formal principles of freedom and equality, and make them cohabit with the principles of sociality. It should come as no surprise, finally, that the sociality that constitutes the ideological axis of all the reformist goals is paradoxically defined using the terminology of natural right. Italy's Constitution, then, from this point of view, is an extremely significant document.

It is also a significant document, however, in light of the transformative efforts by which the entire reality of the State has been constrained by innumerable and constant pressures. We might say, on the other hand, that the phenomenon we are studying is a tendency, but not for that any less real. These considerations, then, do not stop us from attempting an autonomous portrayal of the social State and an isolation of its characteristics. The appearance of the social State is, in fact, sufficiently substantial to afford us an adequate and conclusive object of study.

Our study will pass through several stages. With the proposition to investigate how the social dynamism, the material domain of the constitutional foundation, influences the formal configuration of ordering, we will initially strive to see how the process of constitutionalization comes to be materially unified in a new system of the productive sources of right. In a second stage, we will propose an analysis of the development of the constitutionalization of labor, defining its model and raising a series of problems with respect to the form of the State, the relationship between economic constitution and juridical constitution, and the theory and practice of planning as an articulation of that relationship. Finally, we will investigate the capitalist character of the sociality proposed by this model, which is justified by a new theory of authority that presents the foundation and intrinsic limit of any capitalist ordering and any general normative theory.

The allusions to possible solutions to these various problems that we have offered up to this point as hypotheses will thus be clarified and critically evaluated. It will then be necessary, however, to arrive at a new level of study—the "worker critique" of the Marxist tradition—in order to sustain the central theses of our study: namely, that labor, in the framework of the constitution of the factory-society, is a bourgeois category and that the transformations of the formal constitution resulting from the new laborist definition of the material constitution, far from suppressing, actually reveal the consolidated class nature of the system.

II. Process of the Constitutionalization of Labor

The capital, which in itself rests on a social mode of production and presupposes a social concentration of means of production and labour-power, is here directly endowed with the form of social capital ... as distinct from private capital, and its undertakings assume the form of social undertakings as distinct from private undertakings. It is the abolition of capital as private property within the framework of capitalist production itself.

Karl Marx, *Capital*, vol. 3, p. 436

Through this rediscovery of himself by himself, the bondsman realizes that it is precisely in his labor, wherein he seemed to have only an alienated consciousness [*fremder Sinn*], that he acquires a mind of his own [*eigener Sinn*].

G. W. F. Hegel, *Phenomenology of Spirit*, pp. 118–19, translation modified

The Historical Process of the Constitutionalization of Labor-Power in Capitalist Development

The exclusivity of labor as criterion of social valorization

In the second section of the first part of this essay ("Social Capital and Social Labor") we gave a rather summary description of the different role of the workers' struggle and its relationship with capitalist reformism. We saw how the antagonism between the classes, implicit in the process of accumulation, concurs with the determination of the individual phases of the workers' struggle and how the workers' struggle continually imposes and goes beyond the particular phases of capitalist reformism. That, however, was a conclusion, not a premise. Now we need to study the process more closely in order to understand what are the material bases on which capital carries out—and is constrained to carry out—the constitutionalization of labor, and assumes it therefore as the exclusive crite-rion of the valorization of social organization. We must see how the relationship between organization and the capitalist subordination of labor-power is positively articulated, because that articulation materially conditions the development and the perfecting of the political and juridical organization of the State.

The problem of the relationship between organization and sub-ordination is—if we look closely—a traditional problem of the theory of right and the theory of the State, ever since these theories recuperated the varying rela-tionship posed between these two elements and hypothesized theoretical formulas for the solution of what seems to be (and is) a paradox: namely, the accentuation of the elements of subordination to the same extent that social organization is ex-tended and perfected. In the natural right tradition, for example, the alternation and articulation between contracts of union and contracts of subjugation are philo-sophical attempts to hypothesize a formal explanation of a real problem: that is, the enucleation of the associationism of a power over spontaneity, *superpositum et abstractum*, and the perpetual deepening of this connection. Only the capitalist organization of labor, however, exemplifies the paradox in a historically definite form and reveals its nature in daily practice—precisely when capital makes this process the technical key that carries out its own organization.

The natural appetite of humans insofar as they are social ani-mals already plays a significant role in the convergence of producers in simple pro-ductive cooperation, but not only in that activity. The fact of association and social contact heightens the productivity of labor itself, giving rise to a "stimulation of the 'animal spirits'" (*Capital*, vol. 1, p. 443). "When the worker co-operates in a planned way with others, he strips off the fetters of his individuality, and develops the capabilities of his species" (p. 447). We find therefore the same spontaneity of associationism that constitutes one of the two parts of the problem also at the base of the development of capitalist mass production. The other part of the problem is represented by the command of capital over labor, which, however, is immediately reconfigured as "only a formal result of the fact that the worker, instead of working for himself, works for, and consequently under, the capitalist" (p. 448). And yet, already in cooperation, this recognition of fact becomes something the capitalist must put to use; it becomes the ineluctable condition of accumulation. As they say, the paradox becomes the technical form of the self-valorization of capital. This is how the quality of command is transformed. In the first place, "through the co-operation of numerous wage-labourers, the command of capital develops into a requirement for carrying on the labour process itself, into a real condition of production. That a capitalist should command in the field of production is now as indispensable as that a general should command on the field of battle" (p. 448). "The work of directing, superintending and adjusting becomes one of the functions of capital, from the moment that the labour under capital's control becomes co-operative" (p. 449). It seems therefore that the decisive element in the transformation is represented by a new type of organization of labor. This, however, is only the necessary condition: the subjugation of workers is made possible by the organization of labor, but it is realized by the structure of capital, the driving motive of which is the maximum of self-valorization. Thus "the control exercised by the capitalist is not only a special function arising from the nature of the social labour process, and peculiar to that process, but it is at the same time a function of the exploitation of a social labour process, and is consequently conditioned by the unavoidable antagonism between the exploiter and the raw material of his exploitation" (p. 449). The subjugation of workers, in this context, grows with the extension of the means of production "that confront the wage-labourer as the property of another" (p. 449); it grows in the second place with "the number of workers simultaneously employed" (p. 448) insofar as "the interconnection between their various labours confronts them, in the realm of ideas, as a plan drawn up by the capitalist, and, in practice, as his authority, as the powerful will of a being outside them, who subjects their activity to his purpose" (p. 450). In short, "if capitalist direction is thus twofold in content, owing to the twofold nature of the process of production which has to be directed—on the one hand a social labour process for the creation of a product, and on the other hand capital's process of valorization—in form it is purely despotic. As co-operation extends its scale, this despotism develops the forms that are peculiar to it" (p. 450).

Since the socially productive power of labor "costs capital nothing, while on the other hand it is not developed by the worker until his labour itself belongs to capital, it appears as a power which capital possesses by its nature—a productive power inherent in capital" (p. 451). The formal relationship of succession between organization and subordination is completely inverted here:

subordination is the condition of organization. When we pass from simple cooperation to manufacture, this relationship becomes even clearer. In this context the interpenetration between the organization of labor and the process of capitalist valorization becomes even more intimate and the relationship begins to show its inverted face: "The collective working organism is a form of existence of capital.... the productive power which results from the combination of various kinds of labour appears as the productive power of capital. Manufacture proper not only subjects the previously independent worker to the discipline and command of capital, but creates in addition a hierarchical structure amongst the workers themselves" (p. 481). What the partial workers lose is concentrated in capital, against them: it configures the power of capital and articulates it in the productive organism itself as a function of valorization. And in large-scale industry the process is completed. (See pp. 553ff.)

The general design of the relationship between organization and subordination is thus specified in the capitalist system. It is a relationship completely intrinsic to capital, and the elementary and spontaneous elements that pre-exist its configuration are qualitatively changed by the mode of production. At this point, however, we can clarify another element of the relationship. Up until now we have seen how, in the realm of production, organization is immanent to subordination and vice versa. What we should recognize next is that this condition of mutual implication is expressed on a social level to the extent that capital extends its productive existence across society. The process of the socialization of capital, in fact, develops the relationships implicit in the capitalist definition of the single productive relationship—and foremost is the relationship between organization and subordination.

Marx elaborates this development at length. "Accumulation is the conquest of the world of social wealth. It is the extension of the area of exploited human material and, at the same time, the extension of the direct and indirect sway of the capitalist" (pp. 739–40). If "the worker himself constantly produces objective wealth, in the form of capital, an alien power that dominates and exploits him,... the capitalist just as constantly produces labour-power, in the form of a subjective source of wealth which is abstract, exists merely in the physical body of the worker, and is separated from its own means of objectification and realization; in short, the capitalist produces the worker as a wage-labourer. This incessant reproduction, this perpetuation of the worker, is the absolutely necessary condition for capitalist production" (p. 716). "The capitalist process of production, therefore, seen as a total, connected process, i.e. a process of reproduction, produces not only commodities, not only surplus-value, but it also produces and reproduces the capital-relation itself; on the one hand the capitalist, on the other the wage-laborer" (p. 724).

This process of the social organization of capital, however, should not be understood only in quantitative terms; it is not simply the reproduction of the class antagonism at a social level—it also involves the deepening and redefinition of subordination. If within the process, in fact, the intensification and the massification of production at a social level imply a growing concentration of capital, this only comes about in such a way that increases both

the power of capital [and] the alienation of the conditions of social production personified in the capitalist from the real producers. Capital comes more and more to the fore as a social power, whose agent is the capitalist. This social power no longer stands in any possible relation to that which the labour of a single individual can create. It becomes an alienated, independent, social power, which stands opposed to society as an object, and as an object that is the capitalist's source of power. The contradiction between the general social power into which capital develops, on the one hand, and the private power of the individual capitalist over these social conditions of production, on the other, becomes ever more irreconcilable, and yet contains the solution of the problem, because it implies at the same time the transformation of the conditions of production into general, common, social, conditions. (Capital, vol. 3, p. 264) (See also vol. 1, pp. 781ff. and vol. 2, pp. 108-9.)

The conditions of the social organization of capital thus directly characterize the conditions of the subordination of labor power at a social level: a subordination objectively tied to the objective organization of capital, which is socially extended and qualitatively deepened through reference to a continually more generalized abstraction of labor. The social objectivization of capital is complete. The factory and large-scale industry define the productive process in the entire society. The despotism of the factory, which corresponds in social terms to libertarian anarchy, represents a phase that has now been completely superseded in the mode of production. If the factory has been extended across the social plane, then organization and subordination, in their varying relationship of interpenetration, are equally spread across the entire society.

Given this development, we are now able to define exactly the forms of the relationship between organization and subordination in the factory-society. The relationship is dialectical: it celebrates on one hand capitalist organization, and on the other the subordination to capital. It celebrates capitalist organization to the extent that the factory-society remolds all of the conditions of social life. This organization is a concrete *reductio ad unam*, a reduction of all the forms of exploitation to industrial exploitation. This is not simply "the appropriation of surplus-value, or surplus-product, but simultaneously its creation is a function of capital." All the preceding forms of exploitation are cleared away: "The other kinds of capital, which appeared before industrial capital amid conditions of social production that have receded into the past or are now succumbing, are not only subordinated to it and the mechanism of their functions altered in conformity with it, but move solely with it as their basis, hence live and die, stand and fall with this basis" (*Capital*, vol. 2, p. 57). From this point of view, labor, as a source of the creation of wealth, is assumed as the exclusive criterion of social valorization insofar as the factory-society eliminates every other competing criterion, every other source of the production of wealth.

In the relationship, however, subordination is also celebrated, as a condition and an effect of capitalist organization. Industrial capital is creative because it continually revolutionizes the forms of production, reproducing the antagonism and subordinating it to new levels of organization. The social unity of capital is an end, not a premise; it is a victory and a construction over the class antagonism that continually reappears; it is the continual recomposition of labor-power within itself, to the limit of its constitutional situation in the social structure of capital. (See *Capital*, vol. 1, pp. 477–80, 636–39.) Because this is the end point of the process.

If, in fact, in covering all of society, the economic constitution of capital cannot but become a State constitution, then capitalist organization and subordination must be restructured in this context. Labor-power, which appears as a social totality, is configured as the people within the mechanism of the reproduction of capital: the people are labor-power constitutionalized in the State of the factory-society. As labor-power, the people therefore come to be called to participate in the production of the social product, organized in the general process of capitalist production in society; equally they are subordinated and forced to yield to the demands of social accumulation, and thus the continual reproduction of the relationship of waged labor. At this level of capitalist organization, the people, as social labor-power, are thus called upon to manage their own social exploitation, to guarantee the continuation and reproduction of the general movement of accumulation.

This is a long way from the idyllic image of a continual process of development from democracy to socialism! In reality, when capital, at the social level of its development, dons the cloak of sociality and represses within itself private irrationality, it must also, in the generality of its own development, adopt social labor-power, as variable capital, as the people. The democratic management of the reproduction of the capitalist relationship of production thus becomes a natural development at the highest level of capitalist expansion — when, that is, industrial capital adopts the general interest within the mechanism of its own social accumulation. The configuration of the organization of labor-power in this mechanism is now a form of activity and production that is not only economic but rather directly political. Subordination increases to the extent that the participation of labor-power in the reproduction of capitalist relations at a social level is increased and perfected. Industrial capital, therefore, not only eliminates every criterion of social valorization except labor, it also positively constitutionalizes labor-power in the democratic management of its own growth. It thus represents at a social level the entire antagonism that was implicit in the phase of primitive accumulation. It is constrained to organize productive social forces within itself to a continually greater degree, and to the extent that it does organize them and thus grows larger, it is increasingly separated from them as an extraneous, objective, and abstract power.

Anyone who follows the historical development of the process of the constitutionalization of labor-power in capitalist society cannot but recognize the validity of these theoretical claims. There are two fundamental phases to this process. The first is the phase of primitive accumulation and of the expansion of capital in a competitive regime. The organization of labor-power within capital is here at a minimum: both from the technical, productive point of view and from the political point of view. The factory regime entrusts its own survival to the coercive mediation of conflicts. Capital itself, on the other hand, is constrained to struggle in society to confirm itself as the exclusive actor in the economic and political domains; and yet, in this struggle, it does not scorn the alliance of the working class. In any case, social legislation does not go beyond the phase of repressive action on one side, and preventive intervention on the other. In this phase we cannot properly speak of labor right.[19] When industrial capitalism becomes hegemonic in contemporary society, however, and when capital is structured at a social level, developing the process of accumulation in equally general terms, we begin to see the concept of right yielding to these demands: first preventive legislation tied to a productivist conception is proposed and then legislation actually for social protection is put forth.[20] The organization of labor-power in capital is generalized and to a continually greater degree the factory extends outside its material limits and the mediation of conflicts is carried out on a social and political plane. Labor right is thus born and continually renewed. If this concept does not manage to acquire a stable definition and remains provisory, this is only because the material and the methods of labor right are continually recuperated by general public law, by the State, which is ever more invested by this realm of labor and posed as its guardian.[21]

Certainly, this process is not automatic. Alongside capitalist reformism there is always the struggle of the working class. It is the workers' struggle that materially imposes reformism on capital; it is the workers' struggle that practically casts aside the fears, uneasiness, and regressive tendencies of the capitalist class.[22] We have already seen, and we will see in more detail, how the working class plays a double role in this process, imposing it and superseding it. On the other hand, the workers' interest in capitalist reformism lies in the fact that along with the concentration of capitalist power over society there is a parallel concentration — first the formation and then the organization — of labor-power in the working class, and therefore the maximum point of capitalist organization corresponds to the maximum potential of worker insubordination. For the moment, however, we will look at the capitalist face of the process and limit ourselves to that.

Corresponding to the complex process of the extension of the power of capital over the entire society and the socialization and integration of labor-power within capital, then, there is a heightening and expansion of the constitutional function of labor. Labor, as a source of complete social production, becomes a source of the State; the constitution is a constitution of labor, that is, of the relationship of waged labor. This is the foundation on which every social and political development is based. Not even right and law can escape its power.

First Juridical Consequence: Crisis of the System of Sources

*The capitalist integration and the historicopositivist integration
of the sources*

The disruption of social relationships is reflected in the realm of right and law in a very direct way; to the extent that right and law participate in the transformation of reality they cannot but be directly involved. Furthermore, a series of juridical phenomena, which would otherwise be difficult to understand, are clearly explained from this perspective. This parallelism of transformations, this implicit reference between social phenomena and juridical institutions, constitutes the only possible horizon for a scientific understanding of juridical developments.

The eminence and celebration of labor as the exclusive criterion of social valorization has various effects in the realm of right and we will trace them in the following sections. The consequences that interest us initially are those that deal with the modes of production of right. We should recognize, in fact, that this is the most important of the various points of contact between right and society. Practices of interpretation and jurisdiction, which are continually obliged to settle accounts with reality, insofar as they are inserted at different levels in the system, have an existence that is less exposed, or rather, more protected, by premises that are already juridically significant. Juridical production opens onto a world foreign to right that nonetheless must be appreciated on the basis of right. This relationship involves a struggle between unequal forces, from which right often comes out subjugated, or rather made to conform to the reality from which it was produced. Juridical science, on the other hand, has suffered so much from this precarious situation of juridical production that it often attempts to exclude the problems of production as irrelevant—but always in vain. There is no formalism so pure that it does not have to at least presuppose a fundamental norm materially characterized by the historical context of the social arrangement. Consequently, that material presupposition eventually reappears, inevitably, at various levels of the formal ordering as an uncontrollable residue. Having recognized this fact, contemporary juridical science prefers to follow and gradually make itself adequate to the new situation. It is a difficult and complex process that has not yet been completely accomplished. We will interpret it, then, keeping in mind its present limits but also attempting to identify its tendency. Initially, the exclusivity of the material laborist foundation on the production of right is experienced in two principal ways: insofar as the foundation is exclusive, it demands the unification of the system of the production of right; and insofar as it is materially defined and historically determined, it imposes specific models on the system of production. First, therefore, we must study the general form that the unification of the laborist foundation imposes on the production of right, and then we will turn to the particular models of this production.

For the moment, let us focus on the first point. One should note that in recent times juridical science has accelerated the process of the unification of sources, and thus it has been receptive—sometimes despite itself—to the tendency of the movement of social reality. In this way it has contributed to the demystification of the traditional formulation of the problem. The tradition, in fact, presented a cluster of propositions referring to the foundation of right that brought into play, in the form of a series of material definitions, a tangled complex of problems—and subsequently eliminated them, acritically confusing them. In particular, then, as Norberto Bobbio has noted (*Lezioni di filosofia di diritto*, pp. 51ff.), there are three profiles under which the problem of the sources of right has been presented: as a problem of the origin of juridical norms; as a problem of the formations of the juridical arrangement; and finally, in a subordinate and hidden position, often surreptitiously eliminated, as a problem of the formation of a social authority that could contribute legitimacy and effectiveness to the norms, thus supporting their arrangement. We should note, however, that this did not come about by chance. The problem of the formation and legitimation of social authority did not need to be posed at all, in fact, as long as the juridical system adopted the given social order without doubts or regrets. We could give the period of juridical positivism the label, adopted from political historiography, of "the era of security"—secure faith in the social and political presuppositions of the ordering, certainty in the present perfection, or, if you like, the indefinite perfectibility of the juridical system. Hegel and Kant, in two different cases, are the guardian spirits of this era. The so-called problem of sources, then, is born not before but after the construction of the system and is related to the need not to found the system but rather to define it in a conclusive way. It is not insignificant to recall here that the unity of the bourgeois scientific world remained formal and ideological until the development of the factory-society brought science within the realm of capital. As a result, the system prefigured its own material substrate and the sources were defined by the arrangement, not only in the obvious sense that every system defines its own productive mechanism, but rather in the sense that such a mechanism was adopted only because it was functional to the preconceived interest of the system, which leads us to believe that those sources, though functional, were not specific. To pose it in extreme terms, the system seemed to invent the sources.[23] On the other hand, the "practical" jurists did not seem to doubt that the reference to sources, after the definition of the arrangement and the valorization of its different levels, was, if not merely an elegant decoration, certainly a result of dressing up a system that could appear as unfounded. For their part, they stayed off to the side, happy with what they already had.

We should look more closely at these sources. Are they all within the system, or can they no longer be found, or can they be found everywhere? Material and formal sources, internal and external sources, written and unwritten sources, primary and secondary, immediate and mediate, legitimate and illegitimate, legal and customary, and so forth: the confusion crowns the imposition of the problem on the system. The differences that separate these sources in subtle ways are said to be "specific manifestations of the difference among a real cause, a principle of value, and a cognitive principle of the system" (Horvath, "Les sources du droit positif," p. 134). It is only that they forgot to recognize that these distinctions cannot be grasped so long as they are still wrestling not with the real principle of the production of right but with the principle of the system. It is useless to try to make the foundation of the system appear as a problem while at the same time you try to locate it within the system itself. At this point the most dignified way out is still the classic exit of idealist philosophy: make jurisprudence the foundation of right. Science thus appears, in agreement with the premises, as the self-conscious and ontological foundation of right: *Recht kann nur aus Recht werden*, while the facticity of production is irrelevant, or at least subordinated, as far as science is concerned.[24]

Some say, however, that today juridical science has abandoned this perspective. When capital recuperated science within itself there was no longer room for a problematic that avoided confronting reality. On the other hand, capitalist integration and the resulting restructuring of social authority proposed as central precisely this relationship among social authority, the foundation of norms, and their situation within the arrangement. The other problem, that of the origin of the single norm, was subsumed in the larger question of the relationship between authority and norms. Beyond the question of the unification of sources — and their unification in an existential structure that also configures an expression of authority — there is still the recognition that the problem is not that of projecting over reality what science has autonomously decided, but rather founding within reality every creative, modifying, or destructive effect of juridical norms.[25] It is the very image of reality that is, finally, modified. The capitalist unification stamps a meaning and direction on the norms; the unification is not simply quantitative but also defining. Even though this discussion is reopened when one tries to define the nature of this facticity that generically determines the juridical arrangement — and reopened in a confused way, determining, for example, an alternative between theories attentive to the definition of sources as real powers and theories attentive instead to the procedure according to which these powers are developed — nonetheless the discussion makes clear that the foundation has to be defined as a real, productive, and defining act. If the arrangement is a system of determining normative values, then a source can only be that from which those values and their system derive, that group of social forces that construct through right the system of their own manifestation, the hierarchy of their own essence.[26] Certainly this unification is still formal, but it is a formalism that in grasping the productive moment of the foundation opens onto a development, and thus alludes and tends toward a positive historical content. To start with, it inverts the traditional theory of sources. We must therefore push further forward and, before anything else, analyze the nature of this productive act.

This can be done, for example, by confronting and demystifying the distinction between productive sources and cognitive sources.[27] By means of this decisive duplication of the concept of source, a conspicuous margin of self-determination of the system is maintained and the definition of the productive act is closed between the very narrow limits of the simple moment of the origin of the norms and the arrangement. The norms, invested by the social authority in the process of their construction, are then transferred and connected in a merely formal fashion. In fact, the ordering is duplicated insofar as, in this form, the founding authoritarian ordering does not repeat the founding positive ordering.[28] With this distinction between two sources, the deepening of the investigation with respect to the unification of sources and the nature of the productive act is in danger of becoming useless, because — given the margin of autonomy conceded to the system by virtue of the autonomy of the cognitive process — the system could recover its footing on the material foundation, neutralizing or at least prejudicing its effect. It is only a risk, but we should add that it is a calculated risk that is consciously run; in fact, beyond all of its specific functions, the distinction is put in force principally because it is the final resistance to calling juridical positivity historical positivity and leading the formal framework back to its historical foundation.[29] But how could such a distinction be maintained in such a profoundly unified juridical configuration, in its origin and its development, by the categories of the unity of capitalist integration? Even though the theory has clung to the distinction to save its tradition of scientific autonomy, at this point, practice was charged with the role of provoking the definitive crisis of this position. In the practice of interpretation, particularly when different orderings were confronted, superimposed, or confused, it became clear that the concept and the system of sources were purely relative, and that it was not possible to identify them outside of the historical context of a single ordering. Even for the continual tasks of definition, however, on the limited basis of a single ordering, the traditional formal chronological and hierarchical criteria were insufficient. They were distorted by the relative nature of the system. Only the material foundation of the ordering could save it from chaos and uncertainty, insofar as that foundation is presented as existentially determinate and normatively determinant.[30]

From this point of view, one can anticipate an initial and partial conclusion regarding the distinction between productive sources and cognitive sources. This distinction must be redefined in light of what has been said thus far, so that one has to recognize that "between the two types of sources there is a relationship not of interdependence but, on the contrary, of strict connection. The connection is given from the fact that if the productive source is the juridical act in its most fundamental moment, the cognitive source is the same act seen from another perspective: that of the document." Beyond this technical usage of the distinction, one can also recognize that "cognitive sources do not exist as an autonomous juridical category. It would be better to speak of modes or means of cognition" (Carlassare Caiani, "Sulla natura giuridica dei testi unici," pp. 50–54). It could not be otherwise if it is true that the productive act that founds the ordering embraces and contains everything. The nature of such an act is clarified and explained as exclusive, and from this perspective every margin of autonomy of the system is eliminated.

This conclusion, however, even though it may be convincing with respect to the particular problem we have discussed thus far, is nonetheless still partial. The ordered connection of the system on the basis of a source that is materially determined and primary in authority, even if it manages to achieve unity, runs the risk of dissolving the key to the articulation of the arrangement and the system that the plurality of the formal sources—once conceded—designated in various ways. Arrangement and system are presented as one compact block. To reintroduce articulation, would one not have to reintroduce distinctions within the system? Or is there instead the possibility of grasping the real unity as a real articulation? These questions must be answered if the problem is to be resolved completely.

We find a response, in fact, when we look to this second possibility. The same analysis that demystified the autonomy of the system of formal sources and identified the historicopositive nature of the real foundation also grasps the historicopositive articulation of the fundamental productive act of the arrangement. This is the first and foremost meaning of the claim that the constitution is above right. This principle proposes that the productive act is given and historically consolidated as a specific articulation of normative contents, and that it thus reveals an order of normative contents that is not formal but material. The constitution, as the first incarnation of the fundamental productive act, develops an arrangement that is not formal but rather adequate to the materiality of the productive act. The very concept of hierarchy, though it could be conceived in formal terms, is at this point profoundly redefined; one speaks rather of competence, referring to the differentiation of normative contents with respect to the various materials. (See Crisafulli, "Gerarchia e competenza," pp. 808–10.) In short, the analysis ends up devouring the very concept of source, insofar as that notion is formally defined. The real problems alluded to by the concept of source, the problems of unity and articulation, are recuperated and in this sense reproposed in the discussion on the material constitution. The unification of the system is complete. It is realized in the form of the material constitution that by itself makes exclusive and organizes all juridical productivity.

This seems to be the first important effect of the assumption of labor in the material constitution as the exclusive criterion of social valorization. Its exclusivity manifests itself as the unification of juridical production, as the preordered organization of its development. Now we must see, from a material point of view, the second meaning of the assumption of labor: no longer as an "exclusive" criterion, but as a determinate material foundation.

Second Juridical Consequence: Crisis of the Theory of the Sovereignty of Law

From integration to conflictuality; or rather, the form of the constitutionalization of labor

Our focus in this section will be on the progression from the problem of the material unification of sources to the description of the form in which the laborist connotation of the constitution is developed in the global movement of the arrangement. We have already presented a series of premises, and at this point we must investigate their consequences. First, therefore, we will summarize the premises in an elaborated, articulated form.

The constitutionalization of labor-power and capitalist relations of organization and subordination is, as we have seen, an exclusive and totalizing process. Integration immediately reveals its positive face: it brings the totality of social relations to light, positivizes them, takes away any nostalgia for spontaneity, and finally, identifies and uniquely configures the material act of producing right. Having said this, however, we have said everything and nothing, because the analysis does not explain the form of this constitutionalization, which is always an integration of struggle and a supersession of conflict, raising to higher levels their resolution and organization. It is easy, in fact, to conceive the integration as entrusted to a comforting faith in a decisive objectivity; it is more difficult, though absolutely necessary, to recognize the other fact, that of struggle. Sometimes it remains subterranean and sometimes it emerges in violent and indistinct form, but the clear scientific conscience of capital resists considering it. Practice, however — or rather the experience of real relationships — forces capital to confront it every day: not only is it forced to give political consideration, but also (and this is what primarily interests us) juridical and technical consideration, to the problem.

From this perspective, in order to understand the coherence and importance of this point, it is sufficient to look at a problem that is typical of contemporary juridical science: the problem of the positioning of law within the system of sources. It is useful to remember at this point that the process of capitalist integration has long been presented as a process of integration within the law. Law gradually became the exclusive source of right, the juridical system became a system of law, and, at the beginning of this century, juridical positivism was proposed and imposed as legalism. Today, however, none of this edifice is still standing — not one stone. Just when positivism seemed to be victorious, there arose critics from all quarters, and for fifty years now currents of thought have contested its ability to serve as an exclusive ideology and a sufficient method for juridical science. This came about principally because integration within the law represented one moment, but only one moment, in the vast process of the juridicalization of social relations. It did unify, but, precisely insofar as it was a unilateral unifying force, it was unable to account for the struggle and the real articulation that sprang up within the unified system. Struggle sprang up and imposed its force all the more because the integration had brought difference into the system. This difference had not been recognized, however, and it demanded recognition — it refused to be flattened into unity. The phases of the scientific movement and the solution of the debate were also defined by this situation. Despite what so many claimed, the alternative to the positivism that was in crisis was not its simple negation — and thus some sort of revival of natural right — but rather the development of positivism in an open conception of the historical positivity of the arrangement, an identification of its material foundation, and an appreciation of the dialectical content of the process of unification. It is no accident that the crisis of positivism was conceived, in some important cases, as a problem of the crisis of sources: a crisis of law principally insofar as law could not adequately contain or describe within its system the movements and the characteristics of the process of the constitutionalization of social labor.[31]

The crisis of positivism, then, can be described correctly as a crisis of the dogma of the exclusivity of law. It is, however, at the same time a restructuring or a positive reworking of positivism in the context of the constitution of the social State.[32] We should dwell for a moment on these two points.

Why does the law turn out to be unable to found the process of the constitutionalization of social labor? We have already indicated some of the more general reasons, and now it is time to look into the particular aspects of the problem. First, one should note that law represents a long tradition of nonsociality. It occupies an ambiguous position, either as a "norm of objective right" or as an "act of the State's will directed toward posing the norm." (See Carnelutti, *Sistema di diritto processuale civile*, vol. 1, p. 97.) The objectivity of the norm that is posed is connected to a procedure that defines the law fundamentally as the will of the sovereign and an expression of the State machine. The ambiguity is only theoretical; historically, law is burdened with unilaterality by the position of its traditional procedure. As we have seen, however, that does not take away from the fact that this univocal expression of the sovereign will, embodied in the law, can serve to found, sustain, and guide the process of the constitutionalization of labor. There is a moment when the new democratic foundation of sovereignty seems to allow all of this to become a stable form of development—and the importance of this fact should not be underestimated.

This, however, is only one moment. Right away, in fact, the inadequacy of this solution too becomes clear: on one hand, it is only an apparent solution and, on the other, it is ineffective. It is only an apparent solution because the democratic techniques detach the moment of the constitutionalization of labor-power from the concrete determinations of the socialization of labor-power, and they suspend this nexus, abstracting it and configuring it as a separate moment in the middle of the process. These techniques only reconstruct this nexus a posteriori, after having situated law within a State system of the expression of authority. It is an ineffective solution because the socialization of labor-power is a real fact, even if one does not want to recognize it, and therefore it imposes a series of conditions through the dialectical configuration of social relations that it brings to light. Law is general and abstract; the social management of labor-power imposes material and concrete measures. Law legislates over the immutable and typical continuity; sociality is a continuously mobile situation and requires commands that are adequate to this situation. If one still wanted to speak of generality and abstraction, in an effort to preserve this nexus, one would have to say that the first moment simply contemplates "the generality of the temporal order, or rather the possibility of repeated applications of the precepts" and that the second moment, articulated with some heterogeneous criterion such as equality, serves to represent the impersonality of command. (See Crisafulli, *Lezioni di diritto costituzionale*, vol. 1, pp. 249ff., in particular pp. 256-57.) It would be better, however, to take the bull by the horns and recognize "the end of the predominance of the classical concept of State law" (Forsthoff, "Über Massnahme-Gesetze," p. 223). Normativity is expressed in the social State as concrete command: the constitutive realm is opposed by provision as *actio*, that is, a "specific relation between means and ends," "action that need not and cannot constitute but that rather grasps the rules that are ordered and serves to realize an end" (Forsthoff, "Über Massnahme-Gesetze," pp. 225–26; see also Fechner, *Rechtsphilosophie*, pp. 26ff.).

All of this comes about because the constitutionalization of labor-power is conditioned by the socialization of labor-power. The legal relationship is immediately social, and in this sociality the relationship is continually reconsidered and renovated, measuring itself against the concreteness of the cases to be solved, making itself adequate to their plurality.[33] In addition to the crisis of law in the realm of sociality (we will have to come back to this point repeatedly), there are other elements that make the theory of the exclusivity of law as source frail and untenable. Namely, the conditions for the relevance of the theory have ceased to exist: first, with the disappearance of the division of powers, whose function was practically that of "leaving a complete independence to legislative power," and second, with the progressive erosion of the division between public and private. (See Bobbio, *Lezioni di filosofia del diritto*, pp. 58-60.) It is precisely the process of the constitutionalization of labor that produces this effect, insofar as it determines not only the unification of the foundation but also the unity of the development of law. The elevation of labor-power to the social level here reproduces the unification of the process of capitalist production, and thus all of the powers are unified. In this configuration, the socialization and the constitutionalization of labor-power are found in planning, which is their true summit, the true unification of all powers, the continual spilling over of the public onto the private, and the real socialization of the private realm. (See Guarino, *Scritti di diritto pubblico dell'economia*, in particular pp. 341ff.) Juridical theorists, particularly in constitutional law and administrative law, have been quick to grasp this development.[34]

The conditions of the sovereignty of law disappear, and at the same time the juridical world is completely redefined. Insofar as it is unified and integrated, the juridical world imposes a series of negative determinations by virtue of which the formal horizon of the existence of law is destroyed, moving back toward a new positivity of law.[35] This is the time, therefore, to address the definition of this positivity, in which juridical positivism is revived and renewed.

If law proves to be incapable of founding the process of the constitutionalization of social labor, then, what is the positive form assumed by this process? The same factors that deposed the law as sovereign are those that shape the new positivity. We have already recognized the central feature: while the development of the capitalist mode of production on a social level unifies the entire society in the factory, it also reproduces class antagonism on an extended scale. Where abstract labor acquires its greatest density, there class antagonism is socialized at its highest level. Capital discovers this fact when, by its own intrinsic necessity, it pushes the process of integration to its extreme, and thus discovers that its determinate positivity resides in this relationship. If parallel to the push toward integration there is an accentuation of struggle and social conflict, then capitalist integration can only exist to the extent that such conflict is first grasped and then regulated. Here we have the new reality of juridical positivity. It is expressed in the responses to these two demands: one negative demand of integration and one positive demand of the integration of conflictuality.

The negative demand of integration is explained, as we have seen, by the decline of the system of sources insofar as that system represents a duplication of the juridical world and insofar as it functions as a static mechanism to adjust the relationship between social reality and juridical reality. The positive demand of the integration of conflictuality can be explained only when conflictuality and the practices of labor-power at a social level are made the dynamic basis of the adjustment — and here one could say not adjustment but creation — of continually new, more intrinsic relationships between society and law. Conflictuality must characterize the model of integration. Here, then, the norm would have to yield to conflictuality, to the positive and negative moments that it organizes. It does, in fact, adapt in this way. The norm is put at the service of economic and political ends, functioning as a means to such ends, even while it is defined as a concrete and individual act. As the level of socialization increases, this capacity to make the norm adequate to social reality must also increase, and equally there is a growing need for provisory syntheses between the legal imperative and social consensus. Grasping the tendencies of development, interpreting them, and maintaining them demand constant attention, and it is continually more perfectly achieved.

This is also the condition by which the positivity can be grasped and reconstructed, not according to a preconstituted design, but precisely on the basis of particular moments of the conflictuality itself. The sociality of law is completely disclosed here: the constitutionalization of labor is made autonomous, and integration is configured as a continuous process of "the formation of community" (Ballerstedt, "Über wirtschaftliche Massnahnegesetze," p. 379).

In summary form, then, this is the positive context of the constitutionalization of labor, which is determined by the socialization of labor-power. It will be necessary to keep this generic framework in mind to be able to proceed in our investigation and define the specific way in which right is produced in the social State.

The Configuration of a Specific Mode of Production of Right in the Social State

The capitalist Aufhebung *of the "withering away of the State"*

"Through this rediscovery of himself by himself, the bondsman realizes that it is precisely in his labor, wherein he seemed to have only an alienated consciousness [*fremder Sinn*], that he acquires a mind of his own [*eigener Sinn*]" (Hegel, *Phenomenology of Spirit*, pp. 118–19, translation modified). In other words, there where integration seemed to have flattened the entire complex of social relationships to the point of configuring them as mere mechanical objectivity, positivity is rediscovered as generalized insubordination, as struggle. It is characteristic of the nature of integration that each integrated element is at the foundation of all elements. The general equivalence of subjects is inverted in the valorization of each subject so that the more the singular subject can be validly integrated, the more it can recognize the entire movement of integration and situate itself within that movement, insisting on its own presence. For precisely the same reason, however, this insistence implies a confrontation: the determination of the singularity in the face of the totality. In labor, whose socialization allows for the integration of labor-power, singular labor-power discovers a general commonality, but at the same time discovers the sense of its own position. The intersection of the two recognitions is the confrontation that is the only basis for the process of integration.

That is the formal image of the process of integration. Its importance lies in the fact that it describes the process of integration as a process of the recognition of various parties, as the organization of dissent and consent,

of one of the parties, but rather as an instance of mediation, of a real agreement. The higher the level of conflictuality, then, the more difficult it will be to achieve an agreement. At this point the process must be bilateral; it must be a collective contract, or actually a bilateral normative process that tends, in a context of ineluctable conflictual repetitions, to rediscover moments of partial agreement and harness the conflictuality within a process.

It is interesting to investigate how the collective contract, for example, tends to be eliminated or transfigured in this process. This happens to the extent that the contract is intended substantially to discipline the conflict. The reference of the normative process to an indeterminate and indeterminable series of successive relationships, which distinguishes the collective contract from the private contract, has to be dissolved here into the formulas of the bilateral normative process—so that every privatist residue is eliminated from the traditional conception of the collective contract. Gradually, the collective contractual process gives way to an indefinite contractual procedure that remains continually open or that closes on single moments only to open up again. The avenues of the further expansion of this process are thus quickly defined. In the place of a substantial normative process there is a code of procedures for the solution of singular and continually more unforeseeable conflicts. In the place of a collective contractual process there is a collective administration that makes the normative process permanent, and in order to guarantee this normative process it establishes a collective jurisdiction of industrial conflictuality, so that the unification of powers in a continuous normative process is fully realized.[37] Even with this image of the unification of the process of the production of right, we still need to investigate the specific modes of production. The fact that the ordering as a totality produces right, however, is already a specification of the production. The contractual forces constitute a "community capable of normative activity" precisely because they are unified, or rather because they are insistent on their own existence, in other words, contestational, and consensual only at the end of the process.[38] Their capacity to produce right thus derives from the fact that at the same time that they are distinguished from each other in conflict, they are still tied together by the reciprocal recognition that conflict cannot be avoided and their counterpart cannot be suppressed. This determines the mode of production: a production in the state of parity, organization in parity, and "ordering whereby contract and obligation are redefined in the particular light of organizational instruments of social power in the state of parity" (Gino Giugni, *Introduzione allo studio dell'autonomia collettiva*, p.

116). Right, as norm and as plan of development, is born here from the agreement, which (to the extent that the mechanism is perfected) constitutes, above all, a continually more perfect set of procedures for reaching agreement.

At this point the process of the production of right is entirely a bilateral normative process; it is the definition of a command based on consensus, on the social agreement of conflicting parties. It thus reveals ever more clearly the tendency to determine not substantial norms, but procedures of conflict resolution designed to make the norm adequate to the concrete case, and thereby produce right in a complex and continual synthesis of legislative, administrative, and jurisdictional acts.

Clearly, all of this comes about in a very particular context, and we have purposefully proceeded in our analysis only through examples. We should not forget also that these manifestations of autonomy are still subordinated. The value of this experience, however, consists fundamentally in this fact: it recognizes and adopts the conflictual, dialectical character of social relationships in industrial society, and, consequently, configures or models a specific tension and modality of production. This experience is also valuable because, insofar as it does away with all residual privatist and corporatist illusions, it is potentially capable of investing the entire society and thus the entire right of society. Even if it is true that labor legislation is only a phase, one should not forget that in a society that has adopted labor as the exclusive criterion of social valorization, such a phase cannot be limited within a particular consideration; on the contrary, it reveals a central tendency and is endowed with an exceptional, expansive force.

There have been many attempts, on the other hand, to reformulate the experiences of labor right on a general level. One could note, parenthetically, that the uproar announcing the crisis of legalism was accompanied precisely by the attempt to generalize certain models of the social foundation of right, rediscovered in the world of labor. (See primarily the *Recueil d'études sur les sources du droit en l'honneur de François Geny*.) They were insufficient attempts, in any case, which (for ideological and technical reasons) could not grasp the complexity and the specific nature of the phenomena. "Professional right" and "corporative right," in fact, raised up to a social level the normative autonomy of groups in which we perceived the basis of social self-government. The dialectical and conflictual element of the experience of self-government, however, still escaped this framework, so that it risked ending up (and this has happened in particular historical circumstances) as the perfected mystification of the relationship between right and soci-

tion, supported in this case by a communitarian utopia and susceptible to authoritarian tendencies. In reality, only a further deepening of the process of socialization could provide a resolution to this contradiction.

It is interesting to see how the generalization of the laborist experience at a social level was imposed precisely as a product of the most accentuated socialization of labor as soon as that level of development was reached—and this was independent of the various efforts that each of the ideological groups made to negate that development. For example, when the corporative ordering was destroyed there was a resuscitation of the attempt to ground the collective contractual process in the sphere of private relationships.[43] This appears to be simply a regression, or at least a unilateral polemical position just as tawdry as the corporative theory of a strictly public relationship. In fact, however, it was not a regression, precisely because a new reality was pushing it forward, despite all the circumspection that the privatist formula elicits. Beyond any opposition with the proposition of a strictly public relationship, and actually insisting on that perspective as a corresponding element of its unilaterality, the private theory was gradually socialized. All of the effects of the collective agreement—the process of normative production and the preparation of instruments for labor guarantees—assumed a social dimension in which the distinction between public and private dropped out.[44] This is also demonstrated by the fact that, on another front, those who remained tied to a public conception of the collective contract now had to recognize the privatist view of the essentiality of the contractual instance and strictly articulate it with the moment of normative production.[45] In this case too, therefore, the most prominent position is given to the socialization of the relationship. From this point, then, from this stage of development and at this level of awareness, the mechanism develops to make the production of right procedural and constitute its specific mode in the social State. Thus it seems possible to identify, beyond the breaks in development and the difficulties in comprehension, the real tendency of the passage from particular experience to the production of labor right and finally to the general phase in which the process of socialization of labor is fully established in a proper constitution with proper modes of juridical production. We still need to investigate how this passage came to appear obvious to the juridical consciousness, no longer as a passage but rather as a realized tendency, as the new context and the new modality of juridical production.

In reality, even this was difficult for the jurists. Just as they recognized the passage, now they recognized the new problematic situation, but did not yet have the conceptual instruments to grasp it fully or define it systematically. The downfall of the distinction between public and private seemed a catastrophe to them and the affirmation of the category of specialty seemed to open the gates of chaos. These were real phenomena, however, that in the long term could not be ignored. They attempted the usual way out of the problem: clothe the new reality in old concepts and refurbish the outdated system for the present context. The paradoxes that resulted were in some cases amusing, but in all cases significant.

Perhaps, from this point of view, the most exemplary paradox is that tied to the rebirth of custom. It is, in fact, a positive paradox that opens up the possibility of large developments — more than the analytical framework can manage to close. Everyone is aware that the claim of any spontaneous reconciliation in the relationship between right and fact is today, more than ever, outdated; on the other hand, for a long time it has been claimed that custom can no longer have any properly normative value.[46] There are still, however, attempts to revive custom, directed not so much toward the specific definition of custom as a source of right, but rather toward the general meaning that the reference to custom has often supplied in juridical history: a reference to the material foundation of the ordering, its social configuration, and the wide diffusion of juridical production. This brings with it, therefore, a reevaluation of the decentered and procedural nature of juridical production. The new reality, not the traditional concept, demands this. In this way, then, theorists simply allude, with an old juridical armory, to the new life of right and, on the basis of this allusion to reality, custom itself (for whoever still wants to use that concept) comes out transfigured. From this perspective, in fact, the reference to custom is not only the proposition of the need to reconstruct completely the system of sources, but also the fulfillment of this need — in the sense that, by virtue of this transfigured conception of custom, juridical production is nothing but a social process of normative production and control. (See Ascarelli, "Ordinamento giuridico e processo economico," pp. 64ff.) It is no coincidence, then, that the reference to custom is tied in particular to the experience of custom in international law. In this context, in fact, its functioning as a decentered source of right, the procedural character of production, and the consequent passage from the negotiation of agreements to a procedural institutionalization of agreements, forcefully indicate the same framework that they wanted to define for the processes imposed by the socialization of labor.[47] It is difficult not to recognize that there are many analogous cases.

Would it not be better, though, to stop talking about custom?

This entire section of our study is dedicated to the definition of the model, and thus we will respond to these questions in the course of our investigation. Before we set out, however, we should ask ourselves why social capital needs to elaborate a model, how it creates this model, and how it makes it work. These are preliminary questions, but they are important for the goals of our subsequent treatment, at least insofar as the model is born and functions within the entire process. It is in fact an ideal model, but it is objectively rooted and functions within the mechanism of capitalist accumulation.

By inventing and proposing the current model of development and the model of the forms in which development must be implemented, social capital is not proposing an innovation but rather confirming an existing constitutional tendency. Capital, in fact, is always born and developed on the basis of exploitation, transforming the concreteness of that social relationship into the abstraction of its own configuration. From the very beginning, the unity of capital is abstract since it is born and established as a configuration of abstract labor at a social level. The entire history of capital could be conceived as the history of successive approximations of a general model of abstraction — as a long path to defeat every possible alternative model for development and, in that way, totalize the abstraction. The realization of the complete alienation of labor at a social level is the permanent goal of the capitalist process. In this context, the process or production and the process of circulation make their relationship real, while the creative moments and the reproduction of capital are firmly grounded.

With respect to the structure of capital and its permanent project, the current "social" model is only distinguished, then, by a certain intensity. This intensity derives not from the fact that the model is simply a projection of the general needs of development, but rather from the fact that it is commensurate with the concrete historicopolitical possibilities for the realization of these needs. The model thus configures itself as an analysis of the equilibria that allow the contemporary subsistence and development, while excluding the crisis, of the system of exploitation. In the case at hand, if the forces contesting the capitalist project, which are always present and continually renewed, are within capital, then the capitalist project must mold itself to them and construct itself on the basis of their mapping. The different intensities of the project of the expansion of alienation are defined in this way. Hence the current "social" model gains its intensity from the current "social" level of the capitalist project and the current "social" level of contestation.

Let us pause a moment to examine this last point: the current level of contestation. We have repeatedly claimed in the preceding sections (specifically in "Social Capital and Social Labor" and "The Configuration of a Specific Mode of Production of Right in the Social State") that corresponding to the socialization of the relationship of capitalist exploitation there is a "social" contestation of the capitalist project. Today the special intensity of the model comes to be distinguished from this general spread of contestation in operation here. The model thus has to be perfected formally, up to its very limit, in the moment when one grasps at its base the exclusivity of the relationship. The model must be defined, projected onto the development, and from time to time controlled. The intensity of the contestation (it is worth repeating this) is precisely the factor that imposes the exclusivity of the problem. The current level of development, which the model expresses and pushes forward, is a product of this situation, so that the process of positioning models of reunification, which is a physiological process for capital, turns out to be singularly specified and totally extended.

For the same reason we should add that here the formal intensity of the project has to become subject to a material determination. The celebration of formalism can only end up, at the limit, inverted in the adoption of a totality of content. If the unity of the project is to be rigorously understood, then, given the conditions of its development and application, it cannot be defined materially except with a concept equally unitary and absolute: in the case at hand, the concept of labor as the exclusive criterion of social valorization. There is no alternative. Perhaps some other concept would have sufficed if the project of unification had not proceeded so far. Today it is impossible to oppose a vanguard with a retroguard. Capital is constrained by the intensity of contestation to pose itself completely as productive capital. The constitutionalization of labor is not only objectively given by the socialization of labor-power, but also subjectively imposed by it. Following the maximum formal intensity of the unification of development in the model, there cannot but be a maximum unification around labor-value.

If capital needs in general to elaborate its own model of the unification of development, then today in particular it has no other alternative than defining that model as a model of labor, with respect to the current "social" level of contestation. We have already seen, on the other hand, in the preceding sections (in particular, "First Juridical Consequence," "Second Juridical Consequence," and "The Historical Process of the Constitutionalization of Labor-Power in Capitalist Development") how labor is concretely adopted as a content of the material constitution and how, consequently, science has come to be internal to capital. Here, however, we still need to grasp and emphasize the dynamic and totalizing function of the adoption of labor. It is adopted not so much in the sense that its real unifying presence in some particular matter is recognized, but rather in that its position is seen as the entirety and the end of development.

From this point of view, the adoption of the concept of labor has to respond on the material plane to the demands that the definition of the model posed on a formal plane: the demands of the continuity, the radicality, and the totalizing capacity of value into which the formal totality is inverted. It is true, therefore, that the capitalist project is rooted in the past in order to sublimate in that perspective what appears to it as imperfect in the present. Such a development, then, is dialectic only in its form, in its response to social pressures and contestations, while in substance it simply reconfigures the continuity of the process of accumulation, indefinitely developed at a social level, and here consolidated in the organization of the State. This only means, however, that the concept of labor also has to be adopted in such a way as to satisfy these conditions.

It is no coincidence, then, that in the juridical world the concept of labor has the definition it has. It too is presented in the model as a reaffirmation of what is contested in the present: as abstract labor—in other words, mere production that excludes the analysis of the conditions of production itself while confirming those conditions at a social level.[48] If the unification has to come about in the continuity of development, then, what would be the purpose of establishing "abstractly egalitarian and classist" notions of labor that would block that very development? The definition instead has to be general and able to apply itself to the totality. In the model, labor simply means "activity" (Esposito, pp. 62–66), any activity related to the production and exchange of goods and services (Riva Sanseverino, p. 105), or any "juridically relevant activity that demonstrates the human capacity to modify the external world (in order to satisfy the needs of oneself and others), assumed constitutionally to be the right/duty of the citizen" (Balzarini, pp. 20–22). The obvious preoccupation about excluding from the notion of labor the attribution of simple subordination is so strong that it produces a general celebration of productive labor, which, in its spread and growth throughout society, affirms the freedom of everyone. The sociality that results from this growth and the general attribution of value to that sociality and to every citizen insofar as the growth moves forward are the objectives that were firmly supported and imposed.

This also shows us how the model works. The functioning of the model definitively demonstrates its demands and the modality of its origin.

The fundamental characteristic of this functioning is really a premise, so that in it the result and the process are equivalent: the totality of the abstraction of labor, which is the result, must be found in its entirety in the single moments of the life of the State, which constituted the process. The particular intensity that the "social" State of mature capitalism has with respect to preceding political forms of the State becomes clear principally in the moment when the process unfolds. At that moment the intensity of contestation is articulated and developed to the point of producing an equivalent intensity in a reconciling and conclusive mediation. To the extent that the contestation is generalized, the possibility of its mediation must also be generalized; to the extent that the law covers the entire social field, the social field has to be configured in conformity with its reconciliation in law, in right, and in the "will of the State." In this way, the chance or hazardous quality that class contestation would be able to throw into the process is eliminated a priori, and thus the process avoids all possible surprises. There has to be a coincidence of form and matter, ends and intentions. And this coincidence reveals the mode of the functioning of the model. The totality and the intensity of the design of capitalist abstraction make good on the laws of formal logic.

If this is true, the event of the birth of social capital already configures the condition of its perfection. The golden age is inaugurated along with the capitalist project to consolidate its own social being. The model reaches the threshold of utopia — it can do that, it is only a model. When it comes back to settle accounts with reality, things will be different. Therefore, postponing the "irony" that could destroy it, we conclude by repeating what all this means: it is a project for capitalist unification, the unification and the capitalist socialization of labor-power that become conscious in the theory of capital. It is worth taking this hypothesis seriously for the moment. This will be useful at least to the extent that the analysis of the model will allow us to penetrate the development in its scientific dimension, which is essential to it.

The General Theory of Right and the Construction of the Model

The development and deepening of the definition of the rights State; or rather, the affirmation of unity

What is the image that social capital gives itself in the figure of the State? We have seen what demands social capital is responding to by posing a model and what characteristics that model must have. Now we will investigate what materially constitutes its definition. First, let us pause to define a series of formal and abstract characteristics that condition the further development of the definition. This is still the moment of unity in the process of the definition, and juridical science, which more than any other science has had an interest in the social specification of capital, gives us an introduction into the heart of this definitional process in its initial phase. When juridical science was attracted by the perception of an irresistible unifying movement in society, in fact, it quickly sought to define the categories of the comprehension and articulation of its discourse in terms of the formal demands and material characteristics of the movement. By proceeding in this direction, juridical science moved forward on the basis of what it already firmly had; in other words, it set out from the definition of the rights State, leaving it behind as a scientific model of yesterday's world, straining its limits, prolonging it, and sublimating it in a model of the new State that it foresaw. In this way, juridical theory responded to the typical necessities of a science within capital: to demonstrate and found the differences upon the uninterrupted continuity of the process of accumulation. In doing so, it made itself a general theory of right, developing and defining itself around this task.

It was very difficult, however, to go beyond the rights State, impressing on its theory a dynamic that would invest and resolve in itself the social totality. And yet, when the material conditions of the ordering were mature to the point of permitting it, the link this movement led toward was already there. The rights State can assume the social form that capital always produces, whatever the modalities of its empirical development. The rights State is already, in this sense, a social State because in it the form of juridical guarantee is only social. Other than that, however, the social form of the rights State is directly contradictory with its particular content. The rights State is a State of private guarantees, a State that receives and guarantees, in the form of right, all that the social-economic world spontaneously produces. The formal conditions, in other words, the eminence of the "social" modality of mediation, which could allow the analysis to go beyond the rights State, have existed, but the historical conditions, that is, the adequation of the regulated material content to the social form of regulation, have been lacking. If these conditions were to have existed, the rights State would have been particularly well placed to reabsorb and restructure the new material; the heavy task of guaranteeing that which is received would have been transformed into the fascinating job of guaranteeing while prefiguring, and transforming reality on the basis of the juridical form (insofar as it is a social form), refiguring it, and reconstructing it. In that way, the rights State, maintaining its proper function, would have inverted its own dynamic, raising to the level of truth the continuity of the development that would have defined its new meaning.

The first echo of this encounter of the changed historical conditions of the development of capital (which reaches the social level of its own development), with the predisposition of the theory of the rights State to give them form, seems to be grasped in the work of Hans Kelsen. Now, it would be undoubtedly paradoxical to want to find in Kelsen the first moment of the process of the constitution of the social State—and that is not what we want to do. When we look closely, however, it is not so paradoxical to consider his work as a first step along that path. A heterogenesis of ends, certainly, but this is still within the continuity of the process. Kelsen's discovery of the "basic norm," the *Grundnorm*, represents a development of incredible importance in the theory of right from the perspective of capital. For the first time, the idea was posed that the entire social normation could derive from, be deduced from, and be validated by a fundamental norm that unified everything in itself. (See Kelsen, *General Theory of Law and State*, pp. 110ff.) In the new historical situation determined by the workers' movement and in the perspective that it opened up, this was the condition whereby the exclusivity of the laborist foundation of the social constitution could, in due time, be received. For the first time, through a resolute formalization unifying the State horizon as an objective normative ordering, as the unity of this ordering, the entirety of social life could be reduced to a common denominator. The reduction of the State to a mere "point of imputation," to a mere "personified expression of the normative ordering," corresponds positively to the fact that the State is configured also as a final common point of reference of all the State actions, qualified as specifically normative, the common reference point of intersection of all the facts, qualified as State actions. (See p. 191.) One could never emphasize strongly enough the importance of this resolute inversion of the perspective.[49] Without this twist, none of the contemporary developments in State theory would be imaginable. The very foundation of the general theory of right as a science of the unity of the juridical ordering comes out of this theoretical decision. Along with the general theory, a new model of the State begins to take shape to the extent at least that an exasperation of its juridical conception puts pressure on the very figure of the rights State. Kelsen conceives all the problems of the general theory of the State as problems concerning the *validity* and the *formation* of the juridical ordering, and therefore as *juridical problems*. From this panjuridicalization of the theory of the

What interests us, in any case, is the fact that both want to grasp in its fullness the procedural development of the system, beyond any dualistic residue, or specifically any hierarchical or merely deductive residue.

It is true that in the formalist school and in the work of its major exponent, Adolf Merkl, there remain gradualist elements: the theory of the formation of right by levels is still the condition of the definition of right as a normative ordering. With respect to the early work of Kelsen, however, which we have discussed up to this point, that gradualism has undergone an extremely pertinent qualitative modification. The acts that constitute every level of the ordering are in fact both executive acts and creative acts, between a maximum of mere execution and a maximum of mere creativity (maximums that always remain ideal).[50] As F. Wehr explains, Merkl thus "replaces the traditional conception of the normative set in only one dimension ... with a juridical ordering (a totality of rules of right) in several dimensions" (p. 221)—and Merkl adds that in this multidimensional system the coordination of the acts is quickly substituted for the schema of their hierarchical reference. (See *Allgemeines Verwaltungsrecht*, pp. 68–77, 140–57, and 177ff.) It is no coincidence that in the final results of this school the procedural character of the development of the ordering comes to be conceded with no reticence; the creativity of the ordering, in every point of its development, is assured in its entire extension. The equivalence of the single moments of the ordering, in the process of its concretization, or rather of its effective realization, becomes the key to the very movement of the system.[51] The new configuration of the model seems, then, to come out of the critical deepening of the Kelsenian framework. The procedural character of the development is clearly defined. Even in this case, however, at certain moments the emphasis on the procedural character of the ordering does not seem to be expressed full-heartedly. The formalist methodology of these authors, instead of grasping the richness of the social articulations in the juridical schema, seems to want to distill it through formalism, obliterating its specificity in order to show simply the formal connections. In this substantially neutral context, gradualism seems thus to overflow the limits of the procedural character and hold on to hierarchical schemas in order to survive— surviving, that is, as formal gradualism. Really, in a theory that actually wants to be "more" formalistic (with respect to Kelsen), there are not large margins for the possibility of not ending up absorbed, as abstracted and infected, by the inevitable internal logic of every axiological system. From this point of view, the procedural character and gradualism end up opposing and contradicting one another.

It was necessary to go beyond this type of formalism. This is what Alf Ross did, independent and critical of these formalist schools but still as a development of Kelsenism. (See *Theorie der Rechtsquellen*, pp. 328ff.) His juridical realism was a successful attempt to arrive at the unification of the juridical ordering by eliminating every form of gradualism and refiguring the procedural character of the ordering as the circularity of the ordering. "The reality of rights lies in the correlation among them [*der durchgehenden Korrelation*]" (p. 281). There do exist various stages in the development and concretization of the ordering, but this is not a *Stufenbau* (a fixed stage), but rather a *Stufenfolge* (a sequence of stages). "In the system none is first in an absolute sense" (p. 331). There do exist gaps and systematic defects in the ordering, but it would be illusory to look for their solution in a vertical reference to the most abstract norms. The incompleteness of the law serves only continually to put in play and in motion the ordering in its circular totality, and thus consolidate the horizon of the creative connections. (See pp. 347–49.) Nonetheless, only beyond the infinite systematic subdivisions is located that rights truth (*rechtliche Wahrheit*) that is born of the parallelism of facts, acts, and norms that "lies in the joint ordering among them [*der durchgehenden Zusammenordnung*]" (p. 309). Only the entire system is the decisive and ultimate source of right. Gradualism, which up until this point has represented the form characteristic of the entire process of ordering, is definitively liquidated. The fundamental norm itself, insofar as it is a logical norm, insofar as it is an index of the totality of the system, must now be subordinated to the general movement of the ordering. Consequently, the norms are related in a mutually dependent relationship: the higher norms are conditioned, in their realization, by the lower ones; creation and execution are not different moments of inclusion in a deductive system, but rather elements that perpetually interact with one another, and thus configure the movement of the system. (See pp. 360ff.)

We have now arrived at the point of seeing theoretically developed that figure of the juridical ordering in which the new model can properly situate itself. Its characteristics include the accentuation of the formal (and thus social) characteristics of the rights State, the instance of the unification of the ordering (and thus the destruction of every dualism present in the ordering), and finally, the recognition that in this process the equivalence of the single moments has to be posed completely, realizing the unity of the ordering thanks to the circular articulation of these same moments — to the point of creating an image of a self-propelling totality that contains in itself the standard and the logic of its own development. At this point the conditions for the definition of a unitary process of valorization are all given.

The Conditions of the Concretization of the Model of Abstract Labor

Negation and the project to transvalue it

What we have discussed thus far — that is, the process of unification in the theory of right — clarifies several conditions of what we call the new model of the State, the State of social capital that assumes productive labor as the only criterion of valorization. At this level of extreme formalization, the model can be overturned — or really must be overturned — in a totality of content. Keeping in mind only these conditions, however, one still remains on the plane of possibility, of conditions — precisely, on the terrain of formal speculation. It is no coincidence that after Ross has arrived at the end of the process of the formal totalization of the ordering, which has been overturned into the material totality of the ordering, and the consequent equalization of the systematic process of the production of right with the customary process of the production of right, his claim remains merely a claim. (See p. 311.) In any case, the problem is still open, and its solution can only come from the discovery of further specific conditions of concretization. We must thus investigate now how the formal model of the juridical totality can succeed concretely in articulating itself, including and being included in the materiality of the social totality. On the other hand, although the systematic totality — already at a formal level — is shown to be open with respect to reality, social reality is presented instead as divided and mobile, and it almost seems substantially incapable of weaving itself back into the system. Labor-value, which, taken at the formal and abstract level, is a unifying force in its real, living movement, is portrayed here as divided, disarticulated, and ferociously polemical. The unitary affirmation that labor creates through its agreement in the abstract form is confronted by the negation carried by the concrete form of labor: what the abstract unifies, the concrete separates. The elementary and spontaneous movements of labor-power possess — to take up the Hegelian imagery — the blind power of physical necessity, and are charged with every potential of insubordination to the point of open revolt. This negation increases — quantitatively and qualitatively — in step with the increase of separation at a social level, and in step with the unification and increase of the power of abstract labor itself. A sort of neurosis of the mobility and the rupture of the law of development that abstract labor accumulated at a social level determines and takes hold of the entire society. This mobility is implicitly insubordination, and in any case functions as such at the point where the necessity of capitalist development wants instead to impose strict discipline. The bourgeois world warns of this experience and protests loudly against alienation. (See earlier, the section titled "Social Capital and Social Labor.")

How, then, is it possible for the theoretical project to incorporate reality? How is it possible for the new model to weave reality back into its own framework and re-form it in the design of a full, composed totality?

We should point out that all of that does indeed come about. Capital cannot dwell on lamenting alienation; it must move along the path of unification because the conditions of its own existence reside only in this unification. It cannot be blamed for ingenuousness in revealing its own conditions of existence; it must instead push every experience, even antagonistic ones, to completion. Hence a capitalist use of mobility must quickly be found. The roles must change: as a response to the external imposition of labor-power constituted and potentially insubordinate at a social level, mobility must become a moment of the life of capital itself. Capital must restructure itself along with and according to that same mobility expressed by concrete labor. It must also open itself quickly to the proposals that emanate from its material base. Have we not seen, on the other hand, that the same, perfected juridical model of the State wants to promote the maximum of mobility in its abstract unity? What seemed a theoretical demand now shows itself as a practical necessity. (See Ross, *Theorie der Rechtsquellen*, pp. 366ff.)

All of that, however, still sounds rather generic. We must now investigate how this process of unification plays out, starting from negation, but recognizing it and paradoxically revaluing it. Let us look at this process by proposing the common exemplification of labor right, aware of the general validity of such an exemplification and the tendential force of development of this "special right." Labor right can be defined historically, in fact, as a continual attempt to reveal and control precisely the negation that inheres in concrete labor. The more the process of the socialization of labor-power proceeds, the more labor right refers ever more directly to the State.

From this point of view, the path that moves across labor right (and we refer in an overly schematic way to a process tragically charged with responsibility and struggles) is the very same path that proceeds through a series of negations — from the first declarations of labor right to the need to promote the right to work freely, and from the foundation of the active instruments of the contractualization of labor to the definition of the project of the democracy of labor.[52] It is a path traveled by those who are forced to take it, only subsequently to negate it and contain it in turn in order to make it functional, thus controlled and contained, in the general arrangement of power. Such a claim might appear paradoxical. If we look closely, however, we see that it is not, because it is certainly true that here we find ourselves faced with a series of positive claims of the right of concrete labor. It is true, for example, that the "right to work" has first the negative content of the worker refusal of the blind dynamic of a freely exchanging capital rather than the positive content of a call to participate in the mechanism of production. The so-called right to work freely means, above all, a refusal of the use of the worker as a piece of machinery, and the refusal of the worker to be assigned to production as a blind process, rather than a search for the qualification of concrete labor in the capitalist mobility of production. From the perspective of right and power, however, these rights simply express the positive contents mentioned above and, in this their positive function, come to be assumed as necessary elements for the creation of a free market of labor-power and its definition as adequate to the needs of development.

This is equally true for the subsequent phases that labor right goes through: the phases in which the principles of the collective contracting of labor become fundamental and the democracy of labor is imagined and approached. Here the negation that concrete labor produces is made collective, general. It is organized first in syndicalist forms, then political forms, and it spreads its effective subversion from limited environments to the entire arrangement of society. From the perspective of right and power, recognizing the negation as such must mean transvaluing it positively, and putting it in position to make it function positively in the process of accumulation. Negativity is transvalued in positivity, made to act, with the carrot or the stick, as a positive element of development.[53] This transvaluation can be made only by the State, that is, at the level of a structure so general that it is able to envelop within itself the generality of contestation.

We should emphasize this conclusion. It indicates the resolute direction of conflictual social reality, but also demonstrates that the negative force remains potent as long as labor right remains a particular, special right, not recuperable in toto in the entire State structure. The positivization of the negation, that is, the negation of the negation, can come about only when the totality of social life and its effective relationships are invested. Only then can one say that "State right can lose, at least in the field of labor relations, the character of a superstructure imposed by diverse prevailing interests and thus assume a form intrinsic to the explanation of interests, resulting from the organization and the equilibrium of those same interests" (Prosperetti, "Lo sviluppo del diritto del lavoro in relazione alle modificazioni della vita economical," p. 45). This still means that without specific attention to the moments of the negation, the ideal model cannot make itself real. Negation is the keystone to its translation into reality. Only by recognizing negation is it possible to attempt the reconstruction—a reconstruction that can only be characterized by the meaning of the totality that the same negation presents, one that imposes a precise structure and specific modalities on the synthesis.

The Enlightenment of Capital

Negation of negation and the apotheosis of concrete labor
in the process

We have seen how capital, through the recognition and transvaluation of negation, has set out to determine the model of its own mature existence. Now we will see capital, in its fullness and splendor, pose the project of its own accomplished arrangement. The negation is negated and the formal schema, negating the negation, can sink down into reality, or better, sublimate reality in itself. The enlightenment of capital is all here: the hope and effort to resolve every phenomenon, every opposition within itself, and the project to illuminate by itself every reality. In this way, every opposition must be expressed and concrete labor must act in capitalist development as free labor, beyond any horizon of alienation, raising itself to the level of truth.

As we will see, the conditions whereby this comes about refer, on one hand, to the assumption of a formal schema of procedural mediations in a perspective of rigid unification and abstraction, and, on the other hand, to a material determinacy, recognized in its content of real and always present opposition but, as such, made functional in the totality of the project of mediation. The model will be the accomplished synthesis. Let us look, then, at the characteristics of this accomplished schema. The first is defined by the unity of the process: a unity of the resolute design of the real contradictions, which must precisely grasp in its heart the complex system of relationships that constitute the basis of capitalist production at a social level. The unity is imposed by development and remains also the condition of its further perfectioning; it is thus the most universal characteristic of the model, and also the most formal. Without this there cannot be capitalist development. Negatively, then, this characteristic of the model, insofar as it is the condition of further development, serves to support the claim that a moment of the pure and simple negation of mediation can no longer be given within the model. It is a minimum condition, but a necessary one. (See earlier, "From the Constitutionalization of Labor to Its Model," and below, "The Social State.")

This last specification, however, leads to the consideration of the second characteristic of the model. Although in the final instance negation cannot be given within the model, negation can nonetheless be present at every moment. In order to resolve the negation, the model assumes a procedural character. We are no longer dealing with the procedural character of the formal refiguration of the model, but rather with a real, concrete, and determined procedural character of the continuous, specific, and positive reconstruction of an equilibrium on the basis of an equally continuous series of contestations. At this point, without recognition of the parties involved and their contestation, right cannot exist — that is, there is no acceptance of valid and effective norms. Whether this be an adaptation to an old ordering or the creation of a new one, the decision of the equilibrium is only achieved in a procedural way, from the recognition and mediation of the parties involved.[54]

We should insist further on this second characteristic of the model. The spread of the process to address all of the ordering could appear only as a generic indication, an analogical refiguration, or a maximum program, depending on one's point of view. (See Herz, pp. 12–13.) It is instead a fact, without which the model — and more important, contemporary capitalist development — could not be achieved. In this sense, the process does not integrate but substitutes the traditional image of the formation and validity of the ordering. The process is thus substituted for the procedure while "the progressive formation of volitions, operation and decisions, the subjects of which are not predetermined [and] the succession of which is not predetermined or necessitated by a juridical norm" is opposed to the "preordered and causative succession of acts of determinate subjects and offices, acts predetermined in their sequence by normative acts aimed at obtaining the formation of a decision or final act" (Alberto Predieri, *Pianificazione e costituzione*, p. 430). While the procedure thus has a preexisting logical reality, the process is immersed in the temporal succession. (See F. Benvenuti, "Funzione amministrativea, procedimento, processo.") The process is completely dialectical in the sense that it envelops a contradiction. In short, it is historically configured — charged with all the determinateness that the materiality of social production brings to the schema of its formal solution. That which constitutes the juridical and constitutional process is the transvaluation of the mobility of social labor power. This is the mechanism that brings the frenetic chaos of concrete labor back into the reconciling project of abstract labor.

This mechanism is made possible by the fact that abstract labor still remains the point of reference for reconciliation. In it, punctual or procedural contestation must present itself as mediated, and therefore resolved. The path starts up again from here—from the unity arrived at through the ascending rhythm of mediations to the unity developed in the descending rhythm of the articulations: procedure in the first case, organization in the second. It is clear that the division is merely theoretical. Historically, the processes have had to bind and hold themselves together in abstract labor. The paradox of the contestation that is placated in consensus and transvalued in the unity is reproduced now, inversely, in the path that leads from unity to organization. Contestation rises up again and reopens the game. The various moments thus hold together, and it is no coincidence that, in the context of a tired juridical theory, one speaks of a spread of the process while at the same time emphasizing the contract and the institution. This alludes to the reunification that is really presented, with which theory has to settle accounts, because it exerts a pressure and explodes the old theoretical armory.

Contestation is thus placated in consensus—or better, to use juridical images, the process is resolved in the contract and moves within the institution. The different forces, after having been encountered each celebrating its own particular, concrete point of view, are found again reconciled in agreement, in assent. This assent assumes a social figure. Individualities, when they are pacified again and discover a common *quid*, also discover and are pacified in a social *quid*— and all the more so as this consenting becomes a social necessity, imposed by the elementary norms of cohabitation beyond a certain limit of conflictuality.[55]

This, then, is the model's third characteristic, which really takes the form of a condition and a hypothesis: that the unity and the procedural character will find, beyond the elements of contestation that articulate them, a basis of consensus that fixes them. The procedural character must, at this point, become organization: a procedural and articulated organization, but one that always remains within the unity of the ordering and responds to its final goal, that is, the synthesis of the social totality in abstract labor, in the project of its accumulation and development. The model thus reaches perfection. The myth is complete. The circularity of procedural mediation is its organizing guarantee; there are no longer disjoint elements. In their unity, they constitute the ordering.

We could launch into numerous examples at this point. Rather than recuperate the single movements of the theories, however, it will be better to focus on the direction of the most general tendencies of public law: toward what we call the new State, which is the planned State from the point of view of the form of procedure and the social State from the point of view of its political form.

The Social State

Democratic programming as a political arrangement of the State and as an Eden of free labor

There is no doubt, then, that the planned social State constitutes the accomplished form of the realization of this model.[56] Unity of the project, procedural articulation of its realization, and adequate organization of the entire movement: these are the elements of the model that are found concretely operating in the planned social State. The model discovers here, in short, the positive constitutional realization that historically validates its figure and celebrates that process of the constitutionalization of labor that followed from it from the beginning — expanding the forms, the efficiency, and the validity, showing in labor the exclusive value posed to unify and orient the entire normative activity of society. It is worth repeating here that, as much as capital is developed at a social level, this unity of labor-value in determining the process of valorization is affirmed completely. The unity of the process of valorization through labor reveals here the intensity of the capitalist project of social unification.

This sheds light on the juridical reality of the planned social State. The model, insofar as it is also a project, reveals the mechanism of the realization of value in the social world. The monism of the scientific horizon can only be presented as a positive environment of the development of value — without any obstacle in its path. The first consequence of this situation of the exclusivity of the process of valorization through labor and the globality of the associated project thus consists in the fact, immediately appreciated by juridical science, that labor is presented at this point, explicitly, as a collective, social mechanism aimed at valorization and organization. The entire perspective of juridical science is overturned: before its goal was to understand; now it is to reconstruct. Hence, for example, the material constitution that, as a point of juridical reference, unified in labor the entire social ordering *à rebours* is here articulated and presented as an expression of a general social purpose. It is transformed from a model of juridical reference to a project of political action, from a schema predisposed to comprehension to a constituted power in positive support of a constituent power.

This is what "planning" means: assuming labor as the unique foundation of social valorization and reconstructing the entire juridical, social, and political ordering in its likeness. We can thus understand how the planned normation produces (and this is seen in its broad damages) not only a modification of the particular elements of the structure of the State but actually a new configuration of its political form.[57] This happens because the planning activity, insofar as it realizes the unity of the process of valorization through labor, is in itself a diffusive activity, and insofar as it is diffusive, it is also global. It can only be global, and it must structure itself so as to make that globality real.

The new specific form of the State is determined by the procedural mode of formation and continual restructuring of the ordering. The procedural articulation of planning arises from the necessity to envelop the totality, in its elements of consensus and dissent, and to make these elements equally operative in the globality of the project. We are not interested in focusing at this point on the forces that are opposed to this procedural character of the movement: every form of nonproductive, speculative capital is an adversary to this project, exactly as is every form of social insubordination that presents itself as subversive to the institutions. These forces are eliminated.[58] What interests us here is the form of the procedural articulation of the global movement: a form (as we have seen) that is in a certain sense dialectical, in that it resolves oppositions as prolonged mediation in a continual movement. It is a form that, to the extent that labor establishes the continuity of the process of valorization at a social level, can only be social.

We should be clear, however, about this "sociality." Its determination must be specific, and must envelop the infinite variety of social formations, recognizing them in their individual and historically qualified instances. From this point of view, the relationship among the single instances that emerge from the world of labor, and which here have to be united in a single project, appears as a relationship among social powers. The design of the mediation must thus be developed on the basis of these concrete individualities. The theory of public law, attentive to the traditional conception of the division of powers in the State, finds here the possibility of discovering fundamental analogies and developments. Beyond any analogy, however, it should be recognized that the environment in which these categories function is already profoundly modified. In fact, here we are faced with a series of "social" powers, not "public" powers (however redefined in a social sense), while the division and the unification of the powers have a constituent function at a social level. The guarantist function (guaranteeing the private in the face of the public) that the division of powers used to exercise drops out to the extent that these categories are annulled in the "revolutionary" continuity of the process. No power can exceed its own environment so long as it is not constituted. When subsequently it is constituted in the planned State, it is thrown back again into the rhythm of the constituent modifications to seek new consensuses in the continuity of the project. The guarantee is still given by the division, but, paradoxically, only insofar as the division remains effective, insofar as it is permanent and reproduced after having reached positive, even if ephemeral, unities. This is thus the "social" figure of the form of the procedural movement; it emphasizes the social dimension of encounter, conflict, and accord. The analogy with the theory of the division of public powers does not go very far. It would be better to speak of a social articulation of "social powers," and include in that category all the broad series of constitutive moments of the social dialectic, from the individual to the public.

For an example of this, it is enough to look at what happens to the trade unions, which are very important elements of this social procedural mechanism. In fact, if one poses the problem of the nature of trade unions separate from the analysis of their functioning in the social procedural mechanism, one ends up in a blind alley. If, however, one poses the problem instead from the point of view of the social procedural mechanism, even the juridical nature of trade unions, and particularly the polemic over their public or private character, vanish into thin air. The social procedural mechanism redefines within itself, with its own valorizing movement, the subjects of conflict. When these elements are grasped, the juridical nature of the actors in the procedural mechanism is simply that which they derive from participation in the process.[59] The same thing happens when the problem of the relationship between private and public in planning is posed, because when this relationship is set in motion such distinctions fall away. The law of the process is simply its effectiveness, and in the globality of the process the effectiveness configures the true nature of the subjects, correlated to their function and, often, only to their situation. Every hierarchy that is not determined by the procedural mechanism, its rhythms, and its modes, falls away. The controls are only the correspondence of those involved, the parties exerting force on their counterparts in equal right of the reciprocal relationship — and all of this evolves in the continuity of the process of mediation.[60]

One must say that this process seems to realize that ideal of the full freedom of subjects that is both the positive myth and the original sin of bourgeois society. Do we not actually touch on a limit of anarchy, to the extent at least that it seems the State is afforded no preconceived preeminence whatsoever? And does not the assumption of this absolute horizon of social mediations seem thus to exclude the intervention of the State in the process of planning? In reality, the planner is caught here in a strange paradox, because while the resulting planning is the form of the State, permitting it a series of completely specific interventions of address and coordination, in that same moment the process is refigured as a form of the extinction of the State, as a celebration of its social definition with respect to and against its merely State definition. This is certainly a curious paradox, and yet the myth of mature capital lives on the basis of it. Without troubling this positive myth, capital risks using the State to reach, in planning, intolerable limits of oppression and power, thus excluding the possibility of recuperating at the same time the margins of consensus that are necessary for it. Planning thus wants to be, at the limit, an Eden of free labor: associated in groups, mediated in the relationship among groups, organized at a general social level, but always free labor, freely running from one mediation to the next, accepting only its own law, and thus validating its own freedom.

We can understand this more clearly by looking at the schema of democratic planning. Here we have a full and perfect circle. The planning index sets out on the basis of the State (in the fiction that imagines the State, initially, as the point of departure of the process) and returns to the State as an end result. The development of the process, however, implies the participation of numerous subjects that are subordinated to the totality of the process. The various levels of coordination, the procedures of the revision of the index, the end, and the controlled reciprocals thus create such a network of relationships, all equally relevant, or rather essential, that in reality the intermediaries of the process can be infinite, like the points that constitute the circumference of a circle. If one then wants to determine a single center of the process, this can be shown only conventionally. (See, for example, Predieri, pp. 219–20 and 417ff.) The most common convention is the State, but it is only a convention. It is a convention that is often harmful to the project, to the extent that it risks reintroducing a series of merely hierarchical elements, and thus distortions within a process of mediation that must be instead extremely mobile and continuous.

The model has thus attempted to make itself real. We will see in the next section the extent to which it has succeeded. For now it is sufficient to emphasize that its reality is certain at least within the science of capital. Mature capital thus imagines itself, thus publicly describes itself, and thus asks adhesion to the structure of power in which it is developed. This is sufficient reason for our analysis.

IV. Critique of the Model of the Bourgeois Theory of Authority

Need and labor, raised to this level of universality, construct for themselves ... an enormous system of commonality and reciprocal dependence, a life of the dead that moves about, that stumbles blindly this way and that, and that like a wild beast must be constantly subjugated and tamed [*Beherrschung und Bezähmung*].

G. W. F. Hegel, *Jenenser Realphilosophie*, vol. 1, pp. 239–40

"Of course there's something in it," Count Leinsdorf replied patiently. "But what I still don't understand is this — we always knew people should love each other and that the State needs a strong hand to make them do it, so why should this suddenly become a question of either-or?"

Robert Musil, *The Man Without Qualities*, vol. 3, p. 419

Ailments of the Dialectic

The labor of Sisyphus of reunification; or rather, capitalist self-criticism and the need for a theory of authority

Does the model we have outlined really work? We have seen the demands that drive its definition and then its accomplished figure, which often seems to have a mythic quality about it. Now the problem is no longer definitional but substantial, no longer that of scientific hypotheses but of historical verification. In short, we must show that the model does or does not work. If the model does become real, we must identify the reasons that make this possible: in other words, is this realization a response to the internal demands of the concretization of the formal totality, as it seemed from the point of view of the model, or instead a response to other, much more pressing demands, which dictate different routes?

Finally, we must see whether the model is an ideal that gradually assumes a specific historical positivity, or rather a mystification that hides and distorts in the eudaemonic myth a real social functioning of a completely different nature.

One can respond to these questions all together. To start, let us ask ourselves, does the model in question present antinomies in the process of its realization? There certainly are antinomies, and very serious ones. The first is the following: the unification of the social totality around a unique principle of valorization, specifically the concept of productive labor, continually reopens the conflict between abstract labor and concrete labor. It reopens such a conflict not in particular situations—since that is also the condition of the elaboration of the model—but in an unstoppable tension toward the totalization of conflict at a social level. When productive labor, which was itself born in the modern factory, imposes the model of the factory on the entire society, the contradiction that constitutes productive labor in the factory is not annulled but multiplied. The conflictuality inherent in single relationships of capitalist production thus expands and makes every social movement its prey—it is contagious, capable of upsetting every synthesis. What irony that this is the model of the social State! The State was entrusted to a dialectic that could resolve every contradiction, but because of this dialectic it finds itself now faced with a much larger contradiction. The dialectic of the model was supposed to provide the possibility of reconstructing a pacified horizon, but instead this dialectic has led to such ailments! Now the contradiction poses one totality against another; the entire society is refigured as a site of unresolved and unresolvable tensions. The pacification of the concrete conflictuality of the model of abstract labor is, on the plane of reality, a desire, but not one that is actually attainable—or rather, it is a sort of labor of Sisyphus, continually interrupted, always taken back up, and now more than ever, an impossible synthesis. These considerations, however, are only of preliminary interest in the context of our study. It will be more interesting to see how such a contradiction, revealed as a general situation, appears also in the single formulations of the model, in its elements—in short, in all the scientific apparatuses that, in this actual situation, have to represent control in the articulations and pacified consciousness in the resolution. The unity of the model still appears, after and despite every effort, as only theoretical. The dialectic of the unification is only abstractly in force, so that when the model is complete and it should only be necessary to lower it onto reality to see it function materially, instead its single elements appear split apart again. It seems that the process of unification has been completely useless and empty; it seems that the model holds only when standing on its head, overturned.

Although the ordering is presented, from the point of view of the production of norms, as a simple horizon of legitimation within which the unity of the process and the multiplicity of the sources established a consistent relationship, instead the relationship seems to disappear. If the conflictuality is not resolved, the validity of right is no longer tenable. The irresolvability of conflict prevents there being a coherent and valid continuity. On the other hand, from the point of view of application, the relationship between general and abstract norms and determinate ends that continually had to reconstruct the ordering in the globality and determinateness of its social functioning, disappears as well. If the conflictuality is never placated, the certainty of right, which is the irreplaceable element of provision, of rational calculation, and thus of regular development, is blocked.[61] The indefinite reference of resolution (which is a consequence of the social celebration of conflictuality) seems, in short, to make the juridical model of the social State fail, and block its functioning in a blind alley.

The model, however, is defended and continually reconstructed and reproposed by juridical science. The model manages to function; the antinomies do not annul its effectiveness. If its foundation is indeed so unstable and its configuration so abstract, though, how does it manage to work? There is no reason to be astonished. The practice of power is often more farseeing than its theory. It is clear, however, that the critique of the model must serve to clarify still further the necessity of its usage and establish that at its foundation there must be elements that somehow make its functioning possible; they must be present even if they are not spoken. On the basis of these elements, the contradiction between unity and plurality has to placate itself effectively, while maintaining itself in a broad articulation. On the basis of these elements the antinomies must become dialectical, avoiding decisive confrontation and crisis.

Such elements are all consolidated within the bourgeois theory of authority. Up until now we did not and could not speak of authority. The model seemed to be born in a world of free individualities working toward the construction of a free community, in which the use of authority as an element of cohesion and repression could and did seem odious. Instead, authority is the way out of the set of problems and contradictions that are created, and the real guarantee of the effectiveness of the model itself can only be the surreptitious insertion of authority into the model. We are certainly dealing with a mystification, but is it for that reason less effective? On the contrary, when has capitalist development ever permitted that such a significant level of social product be shared with social labor-power, and correspondingly that social labor-power be engaged directly in the distribution of the social product and the management of its production? When, therefore, within certain margins, has the path indicated by the model been so easy to follow?

On the basis, then, of the practice and theory of authority (even if it is only surreptitiously introduced) and the mystification of its effects (presented in the model as effects of the simple productive association of free labor, independent of any form of coercion), the copresence of opposites that the model held united in the permanent risk of rupture now becomes effectively possible. If someone were to denounce the mystification, one could simply respond that we are dealing with a transitory phase, a moment that sooner or later will vanish — science has such great hatred of force!

We are less optimistic. Here the theory of authority (and its practice) appears as the decisive element that, beyond any illusion, effectively sustains the model and makes it practicable. The problem, then, will be that of evaluating the vigor of this theory, identifying it in the unity (see "Subordination in Social Capital") and the multiplicity of the ordering, and in the synthesis, no less mystified, but no less real (see "The Social Organization of Capital").

Subordination in Social Capital

Juridical consequence: unity of ordering and the reasons
of normativism

Starting with the very first analyses we conducted on the capitalist development of labor-value, we have clarified the inherence of the relationship of exploitation in the global process (which is precisely both a laboring process and a process of valorization) and emphasized the always more distinct emergence of its power over society, completely invested both by the laboring process and the process of valorization. The more the capitalist process is extended at a social level, the more the coercive content of the relationship of exploitation is generally consolidated. The paradoxical fact is that its generality seems to make the relationship of exploitation disappear when instead it is being extended, because the more the elements of coordination, typical of the mature organization of capital, are extended at a social level, the more the elements of subordination emerge and are imposed (also at a social level). It is useless, however, to cry scandal if authority is the true connective element of the juridical relationship between unity and plurality. Before being the connective element in the juridical world, authority is also the product of the objective world that is social, economically integrated, and dominated by capital. Once we finish with the old ideological cloaks, we see that authority survives in reality to the extent that science understands this final correspondence between the juridical world and the social world by means of the emergence of the unity of power.

We can thus see how juridical science reflects this process correctly from within the process itself. The real paradox is repeated in the paradox of the theory, in particular in the normative-imperativist theory that, the more it is criticized on the basis of the demands of social coordination and its valorization, is instead all the more revalued on the basis of the demands of social unification; it always reappears, having lost, if you like, some of its empirical characteristics, but having, in any case, gained in its generality.

It is not difficult, in fact, to recognize that normativism and imperativism have been, in recent scientific developments of the theory of right, rather privileged objects of controversy. No theoretical position and no author has failed to contribute a critique first of imperativism and then of normativism. Despite this continuous controversy, however, normativism and imperativism are today enjoying new life and new fortune — in their central nucleus, or rather in the assumption of coercion as an actual or potential element, but in any case specific and necessary, for the definition of the juridical ordering as such.[62] It is true that the imperativist conception of law has been dismantled, but it is equally true that the imperativist conception of right has been confirmed; it is true that the normative conception has lost its value as the exclusive key in the interpretation and application of law, but it is equally true that the normative element of the general and specific reconfiguration of right has been imposed. One could say, on the contrary, that in a complex process including diverse theoretical components, the more the eminence of the radically unifying coerciveness of the ordering is imposed, the more it is considered independently of the single movements of the ordering. Theorists have arrived, in the most refined and exhaustive expression of the scientific development, at identifying imperative force in an "independent and latent" moment that is distinct but not separated from the single norms composing the ordering, and that instead coincides (on the context of its definition) with the entire ordering.[63]

This scientific process responds in a precise way to specific demands. In order to consider these, however, it is useful to look more closely at its effects. Two are fundamental: on one hand, the one that allows the maximum of unity of the ordering in the perspective of the use of coercion and also guarantees the social development against any alternative or impediment; on the other hand, the one that maintains the articulation of the relationship between coercion and ordering, and develops the latter independently of any immediate, odious, and coercive conditioning. These effects correspond fully to the demands organized by the model, which are those that grasp the single norms not in a process of emancipation from the imperative will of the State but directly in their emergence from the social process. They have to serve, on the other hand, as if they were produced by a unique source of power. From this point of view, the distance between the coercive horizon and the horizon of the procedural mediations is the guarantee that both continue to function, and thus the pure and simple guarantee of the life of the ordering. This dualism thus manages to correspond to the contemporary phase of the development of the social State. It responds to the utopian (but in large part functional) pressures toward a procedural reconciliation of conflicts, which is necessary within certain limits for the life and growth of mature capitalist society, and thus makes it possible to consider the process of social organization as a process of self-organization; and it also responds to the parallel need of guaranteeing that this conflictual process is not resolved in civil war, in the unmediable counterposition of values and interests. Within the development of the model, then, authority must be discovered. It is kept always hidden, however, and only referred to as an "independent and latent" force, with respect to the possibility of a free, autonomous development of the procedural character.

This is an elegant and efficient solution. If we turn back again from the consideration of the juridical development to the analysis of the material development with which it was first articulated and merged, we see that the description of the double horizon of coercion and procedural mechanisms also agrees with the form of socialized capital. The eminence of the relationships of exploitation is articulated here with the set of planned productive relationships. The democratic character of the management of socialized capital is subordinated to the conditions of the growth of profit that remain, in any case, the keystone of development for social capital. (This is the so-called economic criterion that has become continually more important in proposals of the constitution of labor.)

It is no accident that every conflict between the two levels must be resolved, either in a mediated or immediate way, in favor of the economic element. The content of the solution of the conflicts is conditioned and subordinated to that criterion. If the conflicts impinge on the form of accumulation only lightly, they are tolerated; or rather, as the system is perfected, conflict, as we have seen, becomes the very form of accumulation. If the conflict is transformed into antagonism, however, and impinges on accumulation in its material substance, coercion must be called on to intervene. These are the laws of capital, and no parascientific myth can pretend that they have fallen away, or been made useless in the social forms in which accumulation is developed today.[64]

We have thus seen the reasons for normativism, or rather the reasons for which — after the capitalist myth of free labor has recaptured its original humanistic flavor — a theory of authority is practically and theoretically reintroduced as a definitive guarantee of the practicability of the model. We should still consider, however, the form in which the theory of authority is reintroduced, because that will allow us to further the analysis.

The Social Organization of Capital

Unity and multiplicity in the bourgeois theory of authority

If we look closely, we can see that the problem of the relationship between the model and the theory of authority is the same problem, posed within the model, of the relationship between the unity and the multiplicity of the ordering. In the first (utopian) schema of the model, the unification of the multiplicity was configured as a simple result of the completion of the process; now, instead, the unification is imposed in the form of authority. While the first unification wanted to be immanent to the process, this second one seems to transcend it; while in the first case the process was configured as a monistic process, now it appears that its figure is dualistic. The contradiction is obvious and it seems that the modification of the model in the theory of authority would result not in perfecting but in destroying the model.

We have yet to see, however, if this contradiction and this result of the insertion of the theory of authority are not still given at a merely formal level, and if in reality things do not instead work out very differently. The consideration of this contradiction, then, must be brought back to reality. In this context, the surreptitious insertion of the concept and the practice of authority at the end of the process of development of the model, even if it seems contradictory from the theoretical point of view, is immediately congruent with the practical point of view. In fact, all the ambiguity that the formal descriptions of the process of the formation of the juridical ordering and its concreteness traced in the relationship between parts and the totality, between multiplicity and unity (both in logical and phenomenological formalism), falls away, resolved through the effectiveness of unifying authority. Is this still, then, a spare, positivist solution, marked by a blind empiricism? Not at all, since this would be precisely a step backward that would destroy every novelty brought to the science of the model. The fact is that here we abandon not only the formalist philosophical camp (that only manages to repropose contradictions at all levels), but also the camp of positivist and empiricist formalism that annuls the ambiguity and the contradictions, simply opposing them to the fact of authority. We must consequently venture onto the terrain of the social definition of juridical action and thought, the only terrain that permits the construction of an adequate framework of study. Only on this plane can the rediscovery of an authority that resolves the problem of the model and its functioning be configured in a specific way, outside of any utopianism but also outside of any factual reduction. One can therefore only discover again that element that always represents the motor of development, labor-value, which in itself (and in the process of social capitalist development) carries both the necessity of the emergence of social authority and the necessity of its pluralistic legitimation, by realizing the relationship between the form of its own emergence and the reality that subtends it. All the dualisms fall away because the final form of the process is not dualistic; only its process is. The theory of authority is a solution that, while it appears as deus ex machina and seems almost insulting to those projecting the capitalist model, is instead perfectly adequate to the model. The reinsertion of authority seems contradictory only to the limited gaze of those who remain hopeful within the process, not those who see the completion of the project with a scientific eye.

Let us return for a moment to the earlier passages on the material constitution in order to clarify our analysis and in the hope that we can now trace in the material constitution (based on labor) the entire articulation of social relationships of coordination and subordination, association and hierarchy. Earlier we found ourselves faced with analogous problems and analogous solutions. (See section I.) At this point in the analysis, however, that same image reappears and regains clarity, insofar as the wealth of new motives that the model has expressed comes to be resituated and redimensioned in that image. The initial demand of finding the motive of the real unification of the social capitalist ordering again in labor is reconfirmed here—no longer, however, only as a demand, but rather as a newly discovered figure.

If, on the basis of what has been said, we touch on the problem of the relationship between unity and multiplicity, it is not difficult to foresee that the bourgeois theory and practice of authority (precisely insofar as they are referred to the reality of the capitalist development of labor-value) far from exclude, but rather envelop, the multiplicity at their heart and there situate it correctly. Even if the mystification of multiplicity's "living on its own" falls away, and even if the hope of a reunification that only derives from the internal movement of the multiplicity, from its process and its internal mediations, vanishes, still the site that the multiplicity covers in the life of the ordering is completely eminent. The various observations we made while studying the process and the model of the constitutionalization of labor can sufficiently demonstrate this. (See sections II and III.) At this point the problem is that of determining more closely the form of the cohabitation of unity and multiplicity.

We have, in fact, a series of negative elements that allow us to avoid the illusion — present in the first definition of the model — that the synthesis of unity and plurality is given outside of the simple development of the formal demands of the process, resulting from a rhythm that is self-engendered in form. We also know, however, that despite these negative elements, one should not (through the authoritarian synthesis of the process) negate the conflictuality from which the process develops, but rather only guarantee its course and effects, and protect it from any possible antagonistic reflex. These elements, however, are either conditions or results of the process: What form does it actually assume? This is really the same as asking: How is the authoritarian perspective compatible with the single norms that do not all present, or in any case are capable of not presenting, a specific coercive content? How, furthermore, is this perspective compatible with these norms, which, on the contrary, insofar as they are formed through conflict-uality, present an accentuation of the organizational moment — or rather, a specific quality, in any case of content — rather than the disposition to be unified in the field of coercion? Many other questions could be posed, but we can quickly recognize the response if we remember the premises that posed strict authority as controlling the totality of the ordering. The organizational fact and the consequent emergence of norms that do not immediately have a coercive content, then, are not absolutely contradictory to authority. They can have a coercive content, however, as a specific technical content, but above all they must be able to have one in reference to the totality of the ordering system in which they are situated. Realism and juridical pluralism in the context of the theory of the production of right are thus perfectly compatible with the eminence of the theory of authority, when the eventuality of coercion is conceded to the single norms and the actuality of coercion to the system. At a scientific level, the problem can also be posed as a problem of the compatibility of a pluralistic theory of sources with a primary source that gives unitary organization and coherent meaning to the plurality of sources. This case can also be solved by recalling that the primary source is not so much that from which materially follows the variety of the ordering as that through the criteria of which the totality of the system is enveloped and the articulations are legitimated. It is thus the system itself. (This seems to me to be the conclusion presented by Enrico Allorio and Gino Giugni.) When one then insists on the content and on the difference that, in always new ways, the single determinations of the ordering express (that is, on the material and historically determined character of the single norms), thus revealing another aspect in which the insuppressible instances of pluralism are shown, in this case too contestation to the theory of authority is not added, but simply a new context is defined in which the unity-multiplicity relationship must be proven. (Vezio Crisafulli embarks on this terrain.)

What, then, is the form in which the process is developed? It is the form that allows and sometimes determines the copresence of opposites. The validity of the single norms will be referred to the totality of the ordering just as the effectiveness of the norms and the organizational facts will be referred to that totality. (This is Alf Ross's position.) Only at the level of the totality of the system, however, is there coercion and authority. At all the other levels, the relationship with coercion is only hypothetical. This keeps always open a broad margin between unity and multiplicity, but never allows the eventual synthesis to escape the finalization of the totality. This is the form in which the process does and must develop.

We have thus reached the point at which we can recognize the site that multiplicity occupies in the figure of the mature capitalist State. The emergence of the theory of authority situates its function in the correct way, without, however, lessening its relevance. Unity and multiplicity must live together, with certainty of their synthesis, given the authoritarian horizon that supports their movement. In this way, the juridical perspective and the real perspective, right and capital, find one of the most advanced moments of their cohabitation. The inherence of the two realities is at this point really a structural element. The single movements of the social articulation of the process of accumulation find in the juridical form a full and adequate figure.

From Contradictions to Antagonism

The impetus that launched this last phase of our investigation was the recognition that the model of the social State, maintained simply by faith in the scientific method, by the necessary connection of its internal forces, did not hold. Contradictions of every type appeared to ensnare it, and this State, which derived the rationale and the motor of its own movement from conflictuality, seemed instead, in this perspective, to have fallen prey to conflictuality. The model, in short, although it was entrusted to an immanent justification, collapsed. Only the transcendence of power can serve to give it real sustenance. Hence we have arrived at a solid, conclusive point in the analysis. Having set out from the consideration of the exclusive function exercised by labor-value in the most mature juridical system, our investigation has led us to evaluate completely the function that capital entrusts to its mystification. Multiplicity and unity thus coexist, and conflictuality, continually linked to the development of labor from the concrete to the abstract, in the rhythm of capitalist accumulation, is contained.

What price, however, is paid for all of this? The price is yielding to the transcendence of authority and reestablishing that horizon of *superpositum et tremendum*, the critique of which seemed to be the point of departure for the juridical theory of mature capitalism.

What, then, are the consequences of this? Our investigation set out from the recognition that the growth of capitalist accumulation had unified society around labor-value, but had done so around its two extremes, concreteness and abstraction. The entire juridical system of the contemporary State was born to resolve this determinate opposition. The antagonism between concrete labor and abstract labor needed to be transformed into contradictions, and the entire path of contemporary juridical thought is oriented toward determining the specific mediations of these contradictions. We have seen, however, where this ends up: mediation requires the recuperation of authority and transcendence. The scientific perspective is overturned once again and pushed toward horizons of mere factuality, just when it seemed to want to be situated happily in the fullness of synthesis, in the joy of a full historical communion. On this plane, the antagonism, whose reconciliation was our point of departure, reappears and thus makes any possible mediation useless.

The entire movement of the construction of the model of the State of labor, and the analysis that is made within it of the composition of its motives in unity, can now be seen in its inverted form: where there is unity we can see contradiction, and where there is contradiction we can see antagonism. The problem is reproposed now just as it was at our point of departure. The fact that the juridical horizon has been enriched with many new theoretical motifs, and that science has sought to find again an adequate way out of the initial problem, does not serve to hide the fact that the end point of this overworked path reproposes the same problem that stands at its beginning. This is not to say that the intermediate problems are irrelevant, that they do not constitute extremely important moments in the scientific process, since, on the contrary, the level and form of antagonism are today qualified by the forms and intensity that the effectiveness of the scientific process has marked. What does not change, however, is the content of the opposition and the figure of antagonism: abstract labor and concrete labor are irremediably contradictory, and each seeks the solution of its own problem, beyond the hope of a peaceful and gradual reconciliation, on the plane of force — where they were initially measured against one another.

At the beginning of this study we saw reformism, that is, the search for a juridical mediation of conflicts, pushed from two different sides, and both forces in play were necessary to determine development. Now we see reformism, having reached the peak of its development, find itself once again faced with the same problem — but with one less possibility, that of going back again to the instruments that allowed it to go beyond the old antagonism.

How will the story end? That is not for us, here, to say.

In Guise of a Conclusion: Is a Workerist Critique Possible?

The only conclusion that this study claims to have reached, beyond the clarification of a series of juridical processes, is the recognition of a problem and the level at which this problem is posed. This level is not simply, as some say, that of the content of the opposition, but of the form of the conflict that the end of the attempt of mediation will assume.

The dialectic is finished. Hegel is dead. What remains of Hegel is the self-consciousness of the bourgeois world. The bourgeois world is dialectical and cannot but be dialectical.

But we are not. The workerist critique is not today the restoration of the dialectic, but rather the discovery of the terrain and the form of the conflict.

Allow me a personal note. At the end of a study of formalism I completed a few years ago, *Alle origini del formalismo giuridico*, I pointed out the need for a dialectical study of right. I believed this would be able to resolve a series of problems that formalism, in the complexity of its configurations, seemed incapable of resolving. Today, however, that hope is clearly illusory. Today we see right planted firmly in reality, we see its extinction in society; right is acquiring that evolutionary rhythm that it never seemed possible to intuit. The copresence of opposites is thus made concrete. But is all of that a solution? Does not all of this repropose just what it seemed to resolve?

Through the obscurities of this task, we can only be guided today by a revolutionary critique of reality, by the critique from within things and events, and by revolutionary struggle.

PART II

F   O   U   R

Communist State Theory

This essay was written by Antonio Negri in 1974. It was circulated widely and republished

in France and Germany in the mid-seventies because it focused on what were then consid-

ered to be immediate political problems regarding the attempts of the "Eurocommunist"

parties to form "compromises" with the conservative ruling parties and thus enter into

governing coalitions. In Italy, in particular, there was a vast and active leftist political

terrain outside of the realm of the Communist party and the "official" workers' movement,

and opposed to these institutional alliances within the State. This essay reconsiders the

various Marxist and communist theories of the State both from a Marxian perspective and

from the perspective of the radical social movements active in the seventies. This

reconsideration of the literature is necessary to discern and highlight the useful aspects of

the communist tradition and, more important, to situate the problematic of State theory in terms of contemporary political conflicts. The conviction that runs throughout this essay,

buoyed by the growing political activity in Italy at the time, is the same claim that Marx

asserted in *The Eighteenth Brumaire of Louis Bonaparte*: all revolutions to this point

have only perfected the State machine; the point, however, is to smash it.

The Revisionist Tradition and Its Conception of the State

"STATE MONOPOLY capitalism consists in the subordination of the State apparatus to the capitalist monopolies." Ever since Stalin posed this definition for the Third International in the 1930s, the official current of the workers' movement has taken few steps forward in developing the theory of the State, and has thus neglected the analytical tasks necessary to adjust the political course of international communism in light of the changes at work in the capitalist State in response to the great economic crises. (See chapter 2.) The mechanical and instrumental conception of the relationship between monopoly capital and the structure of the State has remained intact. According to this view, large monopoly capital (a necessary by-product or outgrowth of capitalist development) has taken command of the movements of the State, in a continuous and precise way. The State has arrived at a fusion with large monopoly capital (as a specific and delimited part of comprehensive capital) and is subordinated to it.[1] The eventual modification of the (managerial and/or proletarian) juridical structures of the large monopoly does not interfere with the relationship of subordination imposed by the State, but on the contrary accentuates the interrelation of the elite rulers and solidifies the character and direction of monopoly command. "In reality, what appear to be conflicts between business and government are reflections of conflict within the ruling class" (Paul Baran and Paul Sweezy, *Monopoly Capital*, p. 67; see also, Pierre Jalée, *Imperialism in the Seventies*). The instrumental relationship of subordination has not changed either; rather, if anything, it has been accentuated by the development of a supernational and/or multinational organization of monopolies and State monopoly capitalism (Stamokap).

The political goals of such a refiguration of the State ("the slave of the monopolies") are immediately clear to anyone with the least experience in dealing with the tradition of the official workers' movement. They involve organizing struggles on the widest social front against the outgrowths of capitalist development and the distortions of the power of the monopolies, imposing (from the point of view of the entire society) a new model of development on the State (otherwise the seat of the mediation of power and the transmission of the will of the monopolies), struggling (through reforms that attack the monopolistic organization of the State) against the despotic character of its relationship to society, and purging (through the broadest system of social alliances) the State of the influence of monopolies; in short, opening an antagonistic dialectic between civil society and the monopoly capital State (often also called "fascist") in the name of democracy and the majority. "The State is related to the monopoly fraction as its agent/tool: this relation is understood as a conspiracy which uses personal contacts to place the State (still, however, capable of conducting the revolution from above) in the hands of a small group of monopolists. Let the people as a whole drive out these usurpers and the State will do the rest!" (Nicos Poulantzas, *Political Power and Social Classes*, p. 273).

These are the political objectives of the theory of "State monopoly capitalism." It is clear that a different and opposed conception of the State would carry different and opposed definitions, tactics, and strategies. Some objections arise, however, within the theory of State monopoly capitalism itself. One author, for example, has tried to attenuate the declaration that the State and monopolistic forces have fused: "Monopoly capitalism and the State are independent forces" that *converge*, without, however, there being a rigid and unilateral subordination of State to monopoly. (See Eugen Varga, *Politico-Economic Problems of Capitalism* and *Die Krise des Kapitalismus und ihre politischen Folgen.*) Such objections, however, do not manage to pose the essential point because they do not have the power to problematize the State-society-capital relationship, and thus repropose the thematic of the State as an independent social function. This is all the more dramatic when it is widely recognized (as we see in S. L. Wygodski's *Der gegenwärtige Kapitalismus*, the best manual on this topic available today) that we have entered into a new phase of the relationship between State and capital, a "qualitatively new" phase from the point of view of the interpenetration of the two horizons. The theories of State monopoly capitalism do not take up this recognition in their analyses of the comprehensive process of the social reproduction of capital but only in regard to some special thematics, such as technology and science.

The problems discovered by the current phase of class struggle, the theory that is born of it, and the strategic attempts that follow from it are very different. It seems that the quality of the new relationship between capital and the State — in other words, the fact that their articulation is developed on the plane of the whole society, which is entirely absorbed within the demands of the reproduction of capital — completely escapes the theory of State monopoly capitalism.

From this point of view, the theory of State monopoly capitalism appears as a variant of the elitist theories of the State, and, in the very context of analyzing what is specific to the State, it ignores several significant elements of the materiality of the State organization, such as legality, "its" justice, the call to "consensus," and the continuity and the effectiveness of mechanisms of mediation.[2] All these elements are relegated to the field of "subjectivity" in such a way that the implacable and obsessive image of large monopoly capital ends up moving on a singularly vacant and swampy terrain—and this is precisely the terrain on which social antagonisms would emerge. The base conviction of this theory, then, is that the capitalist economy of the State is a closed system of objective validity and effectiveness. From this basis follows a purely instrumental conception of the State, a relegation of political activity to a context of merely subjective autonomy, and a trivial assumption of democratic strategy as a hypothesis of the mobilization of oppressed civil society against the overarching power of the monopoly.[3]

We should take a moment to highlight certain apparently contradictory characteristics of the theory of State monopoly capitalism. The blatant opportunism that this reveals consists essentially in the ambiguity that is established between the objective aspect (the State-monopoly relationship as a mechanical, material, and necessary nexus) and the subjective aspect (the State-politics relationship as an instrumental, voluntary nexus). The State is a base structure insofar as it is subordinated to the monopoly, and it is a purely ideological and reflexive superstructure insofar as it is a political State. The same is true for civil society, which is, on one hand, subordinated in the repressive, necessary structure of monopolistic development and, on the other, voluntaristically idealized as a possible site of conflict and antagonism. In fact, the only really antagonistic element of the process resides in the contradictions of monopolistic development itself. From this point of view, the theory of State monopoly capitalism gives rise to a purely objectivist version of the theory of catastrophic collapse.

Anyone who tries to touch on the site of working-class struggle in the theory of State monopoly capitalism will end up with his or her hands empty. In fact, the problem of the nexus between the materiality of exploitation in the process of the production and reproduction of capital and the structures of capitalist development (and crisis) is never even posed—or better, it was resolved in advance when the necessity of the process of capitalist reproduction in the form of State monopolism and the completely ideological character of class struggle were conceded. On the other hand, the goal of class struggle can only be the reestablishment of the capitalist rationality of development ("socialism"?) against the deformations of the monopolistic arrangement.[4] The site of class struggle is, in the extreme and dominant conceptions of State monopoly capitalism, a site of mere ideological indetermination, and consequently analogous to the site of democratic struggle. Working-class struggle is confused with and negated by the struggle of the "great masses," dismissing all of its qualitative characteristics. Any relationship between class goals and power goals thus disappears.

Even in the less extreme versions of the theory of State monopoly capitalism, there is still a reductive conception of class struggle. In particular, as we have already noted, there have been references in recent literature to a socialization of the monopolistic articulation of power that insist on the extension and the compactness of the interrelations between the monopolistic State and the technico-scientific structure of society.[5] The ambiguity here is extreme, and the discrepancy between "objective factors" and "subjective factors" is in danger of exploding. At any rate, in this case too the relevance of class struggle is minimal. When it is not immediately led back to the dialectic of the objective contradictions of the monopoly, the contradiction is socialized merely along either revisionist lines à la Engels or technocratic lines.

From the methodological point of view, the theory of State monopoly capitalism is based on both a neutralized extreme of Marxism and Marxist categories and the extremization of the fetishism of ideology, the autonomy of ideology, and the political will of the masses. (See the Introduction by R. Ebbinghausen and R. Winkelmann to *Monopol und Staat*, pp. 9ff.) As far as we are concerned, these apparently divergent and substantially concomitant tensions are brought together in the distortions and the mystification of unity from the point of view of class. The theory of State monopoly capitalism is, in short, a theory that finds its rationale in the dysfunctions of capitalist distribution, while it is totally incapable of bringing the institutional world of social reproduction of capital together with the worker point of view that follows from the knowledge of, and the struggle against, exploitation.

Whatever the reasons that led to the development of the communist theory of State capitalism, and whatever the motives that led to its renewal in the 1960s, now we must recognize that this theory represents a rotten planet from which we must take our distance as soon as possible.[6]

Situating the Problem: Marxian Approaches

The long preamble on "Stamokap" should not seem superfluous. As we will see, despite the crudeness of its framework (or perhaps thanks to it), the theory of State monopoly capitalism has had stronger effects and more direct influence than one might think. The consequences of the theory are vast indeed. They are not limited to the general definition of the monopoly relationship (the eminent capitalist economic reality) versus the State, but also involve a normative definition of the mechanism of the production of right (normative of social action), a purely repressive, nondialectical (in the short, medium, or long term) conception of the relationship between the State and social conflict, and both a cynical and an adventurist approach to the relationship between the State and class struggles ("pessimism of the intellect, optimism of the will"). The disparity between all this and the reality of the practices of the two classes in struggle — capital and the working class — is immediately obvious. Stamokap, however, is justified and founded on a Marxist definition of the State. "The executive of the modern State is but a committee for managing the common affairs of the whole bourgeoisie"; it is "power organized in one class for the oppression of another" (*Manifesto of the Communist Party*, p. 35). This is the "orthodoxy" of Stamokap.

"Orthodoxy" does not interest us very much. While paying that obligatory homage to the tradition, however, one should note that there are at least two other more complex and comprehensive definitions of the State in the work of Marx and Engels (and this is simplifying to the extreme).[7] The first was formulated in *The German Ideology*:

By the mere fact that it is a class and no longer an estate, the bourgeoisie is forced to organise itself no longer locally, but nationally, and to give a general form to its average interests. Through the emancipation of private property from the community, the state has become a separate entity, alongside and outside civil society; but it is nothing more than the form of organisation *which the bourgeois are compelled to adopt, both for internal and external purposes, for the mutual guarantee of their property and interests. The independence of the state is only found nowadays in those countries where the estates have not yet completely developed into classes . . . , where consequently no section of the population can achieve dominance over the others. . . . Since the state is the form in which the individuals of a ruling class assert their common interests, and in which the whole civil society of an epoch is epitomized, it follows that all common institutions are set up* with the help of the state and are given a political form. *Hence the illusion that law is based on the will, and indeed on the will divorced from its real basis — on* free will. *(The German Ideology, p. 99, emphasis added)*

This definition is given its determinate formulation in the *Grundrisse* and *Capital* as the "concentration of bourgeois society in the form of the state" (*Grundrisse*, p. 108). The State thus gradually internalizes the mediation of capitalist interests to the reproduction of rule through the organization of society. The emancipation of the State from civil society is only the condition of a successive dialectical and mediatory refolding back onto or into civil society, within its conflictual fabric, according to the rhythm defined by the class struggle. The mediation of the dialectic between the repressive and organizational functions becomes the configuration, the life, and the progress of the capitalist State. (See Antonio Negri, "Rileggendo Pasukanis.") From this point of view, Marx planned to write a chapter of *Capital* dedicated to the State. "The whole will be divided into six books: 1) On capital (containing several preliminary chapters); 2) On landed property; 3) On wage labour; 4) On the state; 5) International trade; 6) World market" (Letter to Lassalle of February 22, 1858, *Selected Correspondence*, p. 96). Hence the dynamic of the State is concomitant with that of capital: from the functions of accumulation exercised by the State to the organization of credit and the monetary system, and from the legislation on the factories to the organization of the workday.

Marx and Engels also develop a further moment of this logic as another definition of the State. The State intervenes at a crucial point in capitalist development in order to maintain "private production without the control of private property" (Marx, *Capital*, vol. 3, p. 438) once the bourgeoisie has shown its "incapacity for managing any longer modern productive forces" (Engels, *Anti-Dühring*, p. 330). In this context Engels poses the figure of the State as the *ideal collective capitalist* and claims that "the more it proceeds to the taking over of productive forces, the more does it actually become the national capitalist, the more citizens does it exploit" (*Anti-Dühring*, p. 330). Engels's definition, which is commonly used and literarily felicitous, deserves closer attention. "But the transformation, either into joint-stock, or into state ownership, does not do away with the capitalistic nature of the reproductive forces. In the joint-stock companies this is obvious. And the modern state, again, is only the organization that capitalist society takes on in order to support the capitalist mode of production against the encroachments as well of the workers as of *individual capitalists*" (*Anti-Dühring*, p. 330, emphasis added). In the State-owned industries, then, "the workers remain wage-workers—proletarians. The capitalist relation is not done away with. It is rather brought to a head" (pp. 330–31). In this sense the State, "whatever its form, is an essentially capitalist machine, a State of capitalists, the ideal collective capitalist" (R. Finzi, "Lo Stato del capitale, un problema aperto," pp. 491–92).

If one were to repropose the problem of the State of capital now in the light of these definitions, one would have to emphasize a few elements that follow from the Marxian discourse.

1. The proposed definitions have a dynamic character in Marx's discourse and correspond to different phases, or qualitative leaps, of the relationship between the State and capital, and between the capitalist State and civil society. This path of the Marxian analytical project, corresponding to the real movement of the tendency, is from a minimum to a maximum of integration, with regard to both of these couples. The movement, therefore, is from a maximum of capital's instrumentalization of the State to a maximum of the capitalist State's organizational integration of civil society. In the contemporary phase of class struggle, the capitalist State shows a level of structural integration of civil society that nears the extreme foreseeable limits. The capitalist State begins to be defined *really* as an "ideal collective capitalist." In several respects it reaches the point of linking its own definitional categories with the same definitional categories of "productive capital." If this is true, the fundamental problem posed today is that of studying the structural materiality of the relationship between the collective capitalist and the contemporary State, and following its organizational articulations, in other words, the nexuses of the social reproduction of capital more and more integrated and commanded by the State. Contrary to what is done by the theory of State monopoly capitalism, there must be a structural theory of the State-capital-society relationship and a political strategy adequate to the structural character of these interrelations.

2. As Marx schematically poses it in another passage of the *Grundrisse*, the progressive dialectic of integration reveals a specific dynamic of the comprehensive mechanisms of exploitation—a dynamic that has a *direction*:

> Then the state. (State and bourgeois society. —Taxes, or the existence of the unproductive classes. —The state debt. —Population. —The state externally: colonies. External trade. Rate of exchange. Money as international coin. — Finally the world market. Encroachment of bourgeois society over the state. Crises. Dissolution of the mode of production and form of society based on exchange value. Real positing of individual labour as social and vice versa.
> (Grundrisse, p. 264)

The theory of the State is dialectically linked with the theory of the crisis of the capitalist mode of production, with the *directional* theory that leads toward breaking down the historical barrier of labor. The theory of the State is thus dialectically linked through a theory of crisis to the theory of the working class. The structural analysis of the relationship between the State and the collective capitalist is then assigned a merely preparatory role with respect to the determinate analysis of the historical development of the structural transformations and the privileging of the crisis as a fundamental moment of transformation. (See *Crisi e organizzazione operaia* by S. Bologna, P. Carpignano, and A. Negri.)

3. In the third place, given the presuppositions above, the structural analysis of the State-collective capitalist relationship and the precise determination of the modifications in the crisis should be brought back to the analysis of the class mechanisms (and the relationship of force in the struggle between the classes) that lead and give meaning to the transformations. Communist political strategy is born of the tendential unification of the theory of the structure of the State, the theory of crisis, and the theory of class — a unification that is continually reproposed at the different single levels of the political composition of the working class. Any "regional" analysis that denies the proper tendential reunification and refoundation on the basis of determinate class practice runs the risk of being meaningless, if it is true that "the real subject retains its autonomous existence outside the head just as before; namely as long as the head's conduct is merely speculative, merely theoretical. Hence, in the theoretical method, too, the subject, society, must always be kept in mind as the presupposition" (*Grundrisse*, pp. 101–2).

Recent communist State theory deals extensively with these themes. We will pick up the thread of the discussion, then, and address these themes in the order presented.

The Contemporary State of Theory: Neo-Gramscian Variations

Before directly addressing these themes, we should glance at some variations of the most recent communist State theory, which, while accentuating and insisting on the necessity of a structural approach to the definition of the new quality of the State of capital, still do not seem able to ground the analysis on the solid terrain of the critique of political economy. In the two most comprehensive, most recent, and most widely distributed works on this topic, *The State in Capitalist Society* by Ralph Miliband and *Political Power and Social Classes* by Nicos Poulantzas, there is no doubt that the intention and the approach are decisively structural. A certain pragmatism on the part of Miliband and an articulated analytical inclination on the part of Poulantzas lead the discussion, at any rate, toward the elements of the new, material consistency of the contemporary State. Both works present particularly rich treatments of the problematic. The problem, furthermore, is correctly posed: it deals with defining in what way and in which dimensions the "relative autonomy" of the contemporary State is determined with respect to the world of economic relations, keeping intact the class character of the State. We are dealing, in short, with the investigation of the dialectical articulations of the relationship between the contemporary State and the "ideal collective capitalist."

To what extent, however, are these efforts successful? In his polemic with Miliband, Poulantzas raises essentially two orders of critique, which are coherent and concomitant. First, there is a methodological critique. Miliband has difficulties, Poulantzas claims,

in comprehending social classes and the State as objective structures, *and their relations as an* objective system of regular connections, *a structure and a system whose agents, 'men',* are in the words of Marx, 'bearers' of it — träger. Miliband constantly gives the impression that for him social classes or 'groups' are in some way reducible to inter-personal relations, that the State is reducible to inter-personal relations of the members of the diverse 'group' that constitute the State apparatus, and finally that the relation between social classes and the State is itself reducible to inter-personal relations of 'individuals' composing social groups and 'individuals' composing the State apparatus. ("The Problem of the Capitalist State," p. 70)

Next, there is a substantial critique. Setting out from this perspective, Miliband has forgotten that "the fundamental contradiction of the capitalist system, according to Marx, is not at all a contradiction between its social character and its 'private purpose', but a contradiction between the socialization of productive forces and their *private appropriation*" (p. 71). The entire analysis of the system accomplished by Miliband, in its objective relations, is thus dissolved according to parameters typical of the sociological ideology of "social action" rather than Marxist analysis.[8]

Poulantzas's polemical remarks are indeed justified by a careful consideration of Miliband's work. Really, in Miliband's hands, the problem of the relationship between the "ideal collective capitalist" and the contemporary State is transformed meaninglessly, but safely, into "the empirical problem of intersecting relationships between the State, the economically dominant class, and the State elite" (Guastini, "Teoria e fenomenologia dello Stato capitalistico"). Here Miliband echoes the work of C. Wright Mills rather than that of Marx! Furthermore, the recuperation of the bourgeois theory of social action is possible for Miliband because, insisting on the socialization of productive forces and the "new element" that constitutes the contemporary State, he does not seem to grasp the fundamental fact: that this socialization of productive forces reproduces and multiplies the antagonistic dialectic between productive forces and the capitalist arrangement of production. On the contrary, for Miliband socialization is the mediation of the contradictions of forces, and only the "possible," juridically private character of appropriation reintroduces, with respect to socialization, elements of antagonism. Alessandro Serafini states this point very well:

The civil society that [Miliband] refers to is not only the Marxian "set of material relations of production," but also includes ideological and institutional relations. In short, Miliband's reference scheme is not Marxian, but Gramscian. The consequences are significant and they apply precisely to the conception of the State, its function, and its situation with respect to civil society. Between the material relations and the State a third moment is inserted, a further level of mediation, which Miliband generically calls the "political" level. In this context, the "conditions of possibility" of the State itself are posed; in this autonomous context, the bases for that consensus that makes possible the legitimation and the exercise of the monopoly of force by the State are created. This "political" level thus becomes the positive and active term: the site where capitalist power finds not only justification but also foundation. Consequently, the State is the product of this comprehensive mechanism and the institutional result of this mechanism of struggle between ideologies and between representations of interests. Contrary to Marx, then, Miliband poses the foundation of the institutions — in the broadest sense of the term — as this political level that is automatized and made active. Contrary to Lenin, then, Miliband poses the State as only restrained by the comprehensive political mechanism of the rule of capital. ("Gramsci e la conquista dello Stato," pp. 39–40)

We have seen how Poulantzas grasps in part the substantial limits of Miliband's framework. The methodological discourse and the substantial critique he speaks of are combined in the call for a more "objective" foundation of the problem of the capitalist State. To what extent, however, does Poulantzas manage to accomplish this? Up to what point does the radical critique of "elitism" and the "private juridical character" waged against Miliband make it possible to identify the real *paliers* of a communist theory of the State?

Several commentators have emphasized the confused character of Poulantzas's discourse. (See Finzi, "Lo Stato del capitale" and Guastini, "Teoria e fenomenologia dello Stato capitalistico.") Perhaps it would be better to identify the foundation and the reason for this confusion of elements: the fact that in Poulantzas the communist theory of the State tends to be configured as a "regional study" — in a specific region, even though it may be predominantly economic.[9] In the end, however, regional specificity becomes so broad that it seems almost to find itself facing a new version of the theories of the "forms of the State," while the economic predominance comes to be projected objectively in a "final instance" so far away as to appear insignificant — with not a word about laboring processes![10]

We should pause, however, and look at the problem more closely. We are not interested in dwelling on a critique of the "Althusserian" methodology employed by Poulantzas.[11] We are not interested primarily in pointing out that the defects of this methodology determine a series of "ideological self-developments" in each considered "region"; that for each of these regions "the fundamental concept of class as a *determinate relationship* that is expressed in a concrete totality" (Cardoso, p. 56) comes to be suppressed methodologically; that the preoccupation with a "formal" distinction between the various aspects of interpretation of a phenomenon ends up determining "distinct fields of human practice and distinct theoretical spheres" in the place where, for Marx, there are "levels of complexity of reality that are articulated in complex totalities of thought" (Cardoso, p. 62); and that in the end the "autonomy" of the State — as a regional field — does not find credible elements of relativity (hence "Bonapartism" is considered an "eternal" element of the bourgeois State). All of this is secondary. What is not secondary, however, is that the methodological unilaterality of Poulantzas's discourse is articulated with a substantial framework that is clearly determinate and articulated: "the autonomy of the political" is presented again, not as a dialectical nexus between productive forces and capitalist arrangements of production, but rather as a "third level" located between the other two. This means that, once again, Poulantzas's methodology is functional to a specific distortion of the Marxist conception of the State, which consists in the identification of a foundational level of the State that is not the Marxian world of relations of production but rather the fetish of a recomposed "civil society" — an indeterminate image of real class relations cast in terms of representations. This historicist and idealist cocktail of the Gramscian theory of civil society reappears unexpectedly as the basis of a theory that pretends to be resolutely antihistoricist and anti-idealist.[12] The Gramscian thematic of "hegemony" — key to the sociological interpretation of the functioning of the structures of bourgeois power — is hypostatized and fixed on an "objective" terrain, while the dialectic of hegemony is offered in terms of ideas and mere representations of interests. (See Pizzorno, "Sul metodo di Gramsci," and Poulantzas, "Préliminaires à l'étude de l'hégémonie dans l'Etat.") This, parenthetically, is also a great disservice to the Gramscian concept of hegemony, which is a hypothesis based on the activity and the victory of the proletarian party! Finally, the very theoretical objective of the analysis — identifying the relative autonomy of the State with respect to other regional terrains (the economic terrain in particular) — remains mystified since the relative autonomy is presupposed so as to constitute the result of the analysis. At the limit, "relative autonomy" seems to constitute the emblem of civil society rather than the State, the specific sign of the *foundation* of the State rather than the qualifying term of the *exercise* of State power.

If we look at the political consequences of these neo-Gramscian formulations of the communist theory of the State, we have to recognize finally that the limit we noted has been reached. Here again, as in the Stamokap theories, the State mystifies its relative autonomy with respect to the antagonism of working-class struggle. From this point of view, the workers' struggle does not and cannot be waged against the State, but must be mediated on the level of civil society. The struggle against waged labor and against the State as a direct social organizer of waged labor is opposed here and substituted by a model of struggle in the world of the distribution of goods. Since the worker foundation of the Marxian analysis is neglected, the analysis of the new form of the capitalist organization of waged labor becomes unproductive and insignificant. Once again distribution is at center stage, once again we are given the world of representations and acritical immediateness, and once again we are faced with political economy and politics *tout court* rather than the critique of political economy. In this sense, the neo-Gramscian theories of the State lead to the repetition of the theory of State monopoly capitalism, without having its gloomy dignity, the height of proletarian sectarianism.

Reproposition of the Problem: From Distribution to Production

Let us now take up the themes cited earlier in the section titled "Situating the Problem: Marxian Approaches." It is not simply a question of understanding that "capitalist development changes the nature of the State in an essential way and, since it continually expands the sphere of its intervention, the State acquires new functions and makes always more necessary, above all in political life, its insertion and control" (Rosa Luxemburg, *Politische Schriften*, vol. 1, p. 76). It is a question of understanding *how* this comes about, and a question of bringing back the single aspects of the transformation to the totality of the process of class struggle.

In the 1960s, the most recent, youthful, and (politically) heterodox Marxist critique began to pose this theme in a somewhat satisfactory way. The insistent call to the Marxian methodology of the determinate abstraction of the tendency and the concrete totality has, above all, allowed authors to redefine a correct horizon of the Marxist definition of the State—a horizon that excludes at the outset any revisionist inversions and any support of discourses extraneous to the structural perspective of the analysis. (See, for example, Roman Rosdolsky, *The Making of Marx's 'Capital,'* and Helmut Reichelt, *Zur logischen Struktur des Kapital-*

begriffs bei Karl Marx.) The analysis of the capitalist State (whatever the successive developments of the study) must, then, be founded on the level of the production of commodities, as an essential moment of capitalist antagonism.

In fact,

revisionist theories, political science, and many economic theories share the assumption that under capitalism the State can comprehensively and consciously regulate economic, social, and political processes. In this context, the State as "social State" would be independent of capitalist production in the "distribution of the social product." Allegedly, the State could use its leverage to improve capitalist society, or even to transform it gradually toward socialism. Thus, this conception also assumes that "the spheres of distribution and of production are independent, autonomous neighbours." Consequently, "distribution" should not be affected by fundamentally nonmanipulatable limitations posed by production and the laws controlling it. (Wolfgang Müller and Christel Neusüss, "The Illusion of State Socialism," pp. 18–19)

This claim, however, with all the illusions and mystifications that derive from it, is completely mistaken. "The specific element of the capitalist mode of production consists in the fact that the basis of the economic reproduction of society is the *circulation of capital* and that the sphere of the distribution of income does not represent a *moment* of the circulation of capital." The "dual character" of the productive process — as a sign of class antagonism that presides over the capitalist organization of the direct laboring process — thus invests the entire range of the circulation of capital, and no phases or moments can be defined that, in the field of the entire process, would be independent or autonomous of the initial antagonism. Some speak of the "relative autonomy" of the State, the State as a "market" of pluralistic actions (or relations of force) that are established on the level of distribution. All of this is pure and simple mystification, and nothing that really happens in the political life of the States of advanced capitalism could lend it credence. An attempt at defining the State must, then, descend again from the realm of the circulation of capital (and its socialization), as a realm of the enlarged reproduction of productive antagonisms, to the realm of direct production. This is Marx's path: Marx's analysis of the organization of the working day and the legislation of the factories points toward this methodology and this terrain of the argumentation. (See Müller and Neusüss, pp. 60ff., and Mario Tronti, *Operai e capitale.*) As in Marx's analysis, the State thus becomes the apex of a comprehensive dialectic between the organizational aspects and the repressive aspects of the presence of the working class within capital. The concept of the State emerges only dialectically from the antagonistic contrast of these functions, where both the mechanism of a continuous tendency toward the ideal unification of control and the mechanism of the process of a profound alienation of the emergence of class push the reality of the State continually toward a figure of the comprehensive organization of exploitation. At any rate, "the questions raised above all reduce themselves in the last instance to the role played by general-historical relations in production, and their relation to the movement of history generally. The question evidently belongs within the treatment and investigation of production itself" (Marx, *Grundrisse*, p. 97).

One should immediately add that this reproposition of the problem and this redefinition of its proper terrain do not in any way exhaust the thematic that interests us and, moreover, only touch on the specifics of the problem, that is, the question of *how* the State is integrated in society in capitalist development. We know that it is integrated in an antagonistic way, in the realm of circulation; and we know that the socialization of production and the extension of State command over the socialization of production are moments of the enlarged reproduction of the essential antagonism. The question to deal with now, however, is that of addressing the series of nexuses that are opened within the productive relationship, describing them in their contemporary figure and casting them in the logic of class and struggle.

In the course of the 1960s, in the ardent climate of the reconstruction of a worker political perspective and after the definitive recognition of the crisis of Stalinism, some attempts in this direction were developed. The German refoundation of the problem from distribution to production (the article by Müller and Neusüss was one of the most widely read texts in the German movement) should be compared with a series of Italian writings of this period: from Raniero Panzieri's *La ripresa del marxismo-leninismo in Italia* to the work of Mario Tronti, and from the journal *Quaderni Rossi* to the most recent experiences of the movement.[13] These Italian authors have tried to enlarge the project of the refoundation of the thematic of the State, reformulating the nexuses that were traversed in this effort. In the Italian more than the German experience, the problem was posed not only in relation to the proposition of the thematic of circulation and production against that of distribution, in other words, the thematic of the "worker" against that of the "laborer" and the "citizen," but also and above all, beyond the mere theoretical hypothesis, in relation to a political verification of the mechanism according to which the world of distribution (the forces that regulate it and the reformism that epitomizes its regulation) reacts to the insubordinate movements in the sphere of production. From this point of view, the relative autonomy of the State has reemerged — as a category and a function — to the same extent that the social development of struggles, the growth of the insubordinate practices concomitant with the extension of the dimensions of productive labor, and the deepening of its abstract character, have brought to light the real dialectic of the State in the face of the struggles.[14] Rather than being able to be defined as "autonomous" in the sense of an *internal regulator of the relationship of capital*, the figure of the State has shown how its function consists in *substituting itself for the automatic relation of capital* and regulating the increasingly antagonistic contradictory relationships that follow from the positions of force of the two classes in struggle.

From the point of view of the workers' struggles, in other words, and, that is, the point of view of the Marxian privileging of the analysis of the antagonisms of production, we are witnessing a doubly concomitant process. On one hand, the State is constrained to intervene ever more heavily in production, configure itself as a representative of social capital, and transform into reality its tendency to personify Engels's "ideal collective capitalist." On the other hand, insofar as this unfolds to the rhythm of the class struggle, the State continually gains a greater relative autonomy for its practices. We should note here, however, that this autonomy is not posed with respect to the class of capitalists, and not with respect to capitalist development's logic of exploitation, but with respect to the logics of value and progress that contradictorily legitimate capitalist development itself. The State becomes a collective representative of capital, a substitute for the automatic relation of social capital, and a party of the bourgeoisie in the full sense, when the workers' struggles, impinging on the relation of capital, setting it in crisis, and devaluing its contents, force it to be that. The new relative autonomy of the State, then, is a will to permanency and continuity of the power of exploitation and a celebration of capitalist command, *even in a situation of devaluation*. The relative autonomy of the State is not detached from the world of capitalists but is a more powerful capacity to determine crises and destroy value, and a more powerful will to control the dynamic and the consequences of a relationship of crisis in a purely repressive function. (See Antonio Negri, "Crisis of the Planner-State, Communism and Revolutionary Organisation.")

Reproposing the problem of the State in terms adequate to the workers' struggle and the present capitalist crisis thus means strongly reproposing the problem in terms of the critique of political economy and the foundation of the analysis of the world of production. Here we should keep in mind Engels's warning that "the more [the State as ideal collective capitalist] proceeds in taking over the productive forces, the more it actually becomes the national capitalist, and the greater the number of citizens it exploits," and thus the capitalist relation is not suppressed but rather pushed to its apex (*Anti-Dühring*, p. 330). We should keep in mind also that this level of extreme rupture between productive forces and relations of production multiplies the destructive capacity of capital. This mixture of the socialization of exploitation and the enlargement of the force to determine crisis, devaluation, and destruction is what today creates the figure of the State in its "relative autonomy"!

Developments of the Structural Analysis of the State:
Mechanisms of Organization

A notable contribution that, however it be valued, has marked a step forward in the structural definition of the State has come from authors who situate themselves in the Frankfurt School. Setting out from a rather traditional framework of analysis and adopting some well-known developments of juridical sociology, Jürgen Habermas insisted as early as 1962 on the disaggregation of the private principle of the market and, consequently, on the disaggregation of the conception of the juridical norm as qualified by abstraction and generality. (See *Strukturwandel der Öffentlichkeit*.) Where the dialectic of the public sphere became twisted by a unity of command primary and superior to that sphere, and where the planning of social integration and the repression of the social autonomies became structural to the development of modern societies, the guarantees put forward by the rights State became a pure mystification that masked a plebiscite form of consensus. What alternative was there to the disaggregation of the civilizing and liberal function of bourgeois public opinion? There was no alternative that was not purely subjective and utopian in a situation where every function of autonomy tended to decline under the principle of exclusion. "Critical publicness" has become by now only a "principle of hope."

A Marxist development and radicalization of this Habermasian approach does not have to waste time with the highly contested discussion about the events of 1968.[15] We are interested not so much in following the process by which the totalitarian image of power comes to be affirmed, but in the concomitant process according to which it is articulated in the structural analysis of the functions of the State. The State's capacity to make itself the representative of the comprehensive process of the social extension of surplus value is established on the basis of a completely rigid mechanism of inclusion and exclusion. Claus Offe argues that the guarantee of valorization is not determined in guaranteeing "the political privilege of a dominant minority both economically and in excluding and repressing articulations of need that could prejudice the system" ("Dominio politico e struttura di classe"; see also *Strukturprobleme des kapitalistischen Staates*). The processes of valorization, like the processes of exploitation, are thus spread out through the entire machine of the State; capitalist valorization, the reproduction of capital; circulation, and realization all tend to be identified in the category of political domination.

We must therefore abandon the perspective that — in accordance with the tradition of the sociology of power, both in its orthodox Marxist [?] and its Weberian forms — analyzed the organization of social power according to the "intentional" schema of the "interested use of the means of power." In its place, in the conditions of the regulated capitalism of the Welfare State, it seems more adequate to give a "functional" explanation of the privileging and the directions of action, which meet in the "process of valorization" of politically organized power. This change of perspective implies that as the point of reference for the analysis of systems of politico-administrative action, the structurally privileged "interest" of "a ruling class" (or of its administrative adviser) should no longer be proposed, but rather a schema of "three fundamental problems of the system," the solution of which for the political system is hypostatized in an "imperative" that is objectively obligating and specific with respect to the interests. (Offe, "Dominio politico," p. 73)

The three sets of problems are (1) "the set of economic stability that includes the problems of the guarantee of full employment and balanced economic development," (2) "the set of the relations of foreign affairs, foreign trade, and politico-military matters," and (3) "the set of the good faith of the masses that is referred to the problems of the internal integration of the population."

What should be clear from all this is that the fabric of the politico-logical analysis of the State has been created by weaving together the Marxian definitions of the reproduction of capital. The realm of the analysis, which brings in many of the contributions of American sociology on exclusion and marginalization,[16] and which at times betrays a Teutonic tone of catastrophism, is still firmly grounded on the analysis of relations of production. The fact that some conclusions lead to determining — in society — a large context of disadvantaged interests, so as to make difficult any direct reduction of these interests to class relations, does not exclude the class nature of the situation. It simply defines the particularities of the trends of capitalist socialization and extends them in terms of their class definition. The insistence on the spread of the antagonisms, in fact, accentuates the possibility of their being characterized in class terms.[17]

Up to this point, however, we are still in the realm of the relative problematic of the general definition of the relationship between State and civil society. The totalitarian character of this relationship and the quality of the relations and the dynamic should now be articulated and analyzed in their concrete dynamisms. In this regard, too, the most recent literature offers us significant contributions. In particular, Claus Offe proposes to address this problematic of the determinate articulation according to two fundamental schemas: the analysis of the mechanisms of rule in the formative system of the political will and the analysis of the functions of rule of the State apparatus.

The most significant advances have been made, in my opinion, on the basis of the first of these schemas. Johannes Agnoli has described in perhaps the most comprehensive way the process according to which the mechanisms of political representation and constitutional responsibility alternate—in a merely mystificatory function—or negate one another in the tendency by which the State becomes increasingly a direct instrument of capitalist valorization.[18] It is not a matter of denying the "relative autonomy" of the State in this case, either; it is simply a matter of defining its situation with respect to the function of rule. Hence we will see the entire State machine "filter" and "predispose" the system of needs that civil society presents according to successive integrations and necessary exclusions. The antagonisms and the polarity that the process of capitalist socialization spreads from the sphere of production to that of distribution must be (and are) dissolved in a pluralism functional to the mediatory recomposition of comprehensive capital. Comprehensive capital—in other words, the general (political) mediation of capital—articulates the logics of political participation, not giving space to the alternatives deriving from social interests but rather continuously playing on their manipulation, opposing to them the objective and necessary logics of technico-economic development. (See Walter Euchner, "Zur Lage des Parlamentarismus.")

From political representation to the organs of representation: the crisis of the parliamentary system forces other institutions (parties, trade unions, and so forth) to take up its role and assume both the function of the integration and repressive mediation of social interests and the function of destroying their potential antagonism. The State of mature capitalism extends its rigidly selective function by means of a flexible instrumentalization that calls for (but often, and continually more frequently, does not obtain) the participation of social groups. The formation of the political will is thus represented as an articulation predisposed by (or, at any rate, included in) the system of rule, through a selective mechanism that runs throughout (to the point of determining) the social plurality. (See Hans Joachim Blank and Joachim Hirsch, "Vom Elend des Gezetzgebers," and Antonio Negri, "Lo Stato dei partiti.")

Despite the enhanced performance of the processes of selective integration and the richness and articulation of the mechanisms, the State deployment of comprehensive capital finds itself always — and in an expanded way — confronted by the rise of unresolved and unresolvable antagonisms. In a completely consequent and complementary way, then, mechanisms of transmission and repression are added to the integrative-selective mechanism. Analyzing the bureaucratic machine and the processes of planning, Offe has developed the analysis of the compositive elements of the second schema, which deals with the functions of the direct rule of the State system. Obviously, here the bureaucratic administrative system is prominent. The advanced democracy of mature capitalist systems puts in play a system of surveys, pressures from above, and symbolic politicization that, while determining the same "political" legitimation of administrative action, allow it an effective development. The participatory selectivity imposed by the administrative machine permits the exercise of repressive functions that are continually more fully politically legitimated. In this realm, the relative autonomy of the State once again wins completely its essential density. In the operation of "filtering" social interests, in the evaluation of their level of organization, and in the successive decision of the alternative of integration and/or repression, the State achieves the political mediation of the process of capitalist valorization.[19] This does not function only in general and formal terms: the "planner-State" substantializes the single passages of the process of the valorization of capital with the materiality of public decision making. The flexibility of objective command tries to make itself internal to the laboring process itself; the capitalist machine becomes "political" from bottom to top; and the State becomes, in the realm of Marxist analysis, a chapter of *Capital*.

Let us pause a moment, however, to clarify this point. In the exposition of this first aspect of the structural theory of the State (relating to the mechanisms of organization), we have pushed a bit too hard, celebrating the coherence of the framework and the intelligence of the its most innovative proponents while neglecting other characteristics that the "Frankfurt School" analysis nonetheless emphasizes. A certain unilaterality and rigidity of the exposition, an excessive emphasis on the tendential quality of the process, and, again, a certain catastrophic anxiety are all present in the analysis, as its philosophical core. This would simply be a matter of "peripheral" features, however, if these elements did not produce mystificatory effects in both the analysis itself and its conclusions. It seems, in fact, that a theoretical and political distortion results precisely from this tension—in the absence of an accurate analysis of the quality, extension, and dimension of productive labor in capitalist society, or rather, in the absence of a precise definition of the level of the "subsumption of labor." In almost all the authors discussed above, the focus on the tendency toward the political unity of the process of exploitation (in the figure of the State) leads to excessive insistence on the disparity of political possibilities and undue emphasis on the formal schema of exclusion that is substituted for the criterion of inequality born of direct capitalist exploitation. In this context, when the conflicts that political rule must resolve do not lead back to class structure but rather to a horizontal schema of the inequality of life worlds, the very conception of rule, rather than being grasped as a function, risks becoming again an unmediated natural essence. The instruments of rule risk being defined and evaluated in purely ideological terms. This real tendency thus becomes a screen that blocks definition of a present reality, which is contradictory in a much more concrete and articulated way. If instead the analysis were focused on the articulations of social labor, in the guises of productive or unproductive labor, labor directly or indirectly productive, and above all with respect to the mechanisms of the reproduction of labor-power, it would afford much more decisively a realistic definition of the organizational structure of the planned capitalist State and a tendential hypothesis more adequate to the effective state of things.

The structural analyses of the planned State are increasingly moving in this direction. Joachim Hirsch has set out along this path, but almost in secret, as if he were simply repeating and developing in a particular field the initial hypothesis of the "school." (See *Wissenschaftlich-technischer Fortschritt und politisches System.*) Really, the analysis of the mechanisms of adaptation of the State administrative machine to the changing social conditions of the capitalist realization of value have shifted the accent of the discourse toward the nexus that is established—more or less directly—between the capitalist economic base and the State. State planning has revealed not only the political necessity of appearing and functioning as a criterion of the internal discrimination of the objectives in relation to the end of economic growth of the system but, above all, as an initiative fixed on continually determining a social arrangement adequate to the reproduction of capitalist relations of exploitation. In late capitalism, the relationship between civil society and the State can only be a strategy aimed at economic growth in equilibrium (where equilibrium means capitalist partition of incomes and investments, and capitalist definition of needs) and the infrastructural reproduction of labor-power and the conditions of production (profit). Capitalist socialization thus returns to being the socialization of the relationship of exploitation in the specific sense. The entire machine of the State is seen developing on the basis of the necessity to control this socialization of the capitalist relationship of exploitation. The analysis of the infrastructure of the capitalist circulation of goods once again has to yield to the definition of productive labor and confront its powerful social emergence with the State apparatus. On the other hand, the structural specificity of the relationship between the State and capitalist development is negatively verified by the new figure assumed by the crisis. The crisis, at this level of development, is always presented as a political crisis. This is not because the crisis can no longer be defined in material economic terms, but instead precisely because this specificity is so extended and presupposes such social conditions that it is able to recognize its own figure only in political terms. The correlation between capitalist socialization and the State thus finds, precisely in the celebration of the political, a determination of class that is no longer superable. (See also Joachim Hirsch, "Elemente einer materialistischen Staatstheorie.")

An analogous framework is carried even further in *The Fiscal Crisis of the State* by James O'Connor, an American author with an extensive grounding in the German literature. In advanced capitalist societies, the State must carry out both functions of accumulation and functions of legitimation. The accumulation functions tend to affirm the socialization of reproduction costs both of constant social capital and variable social capital. The legitimation functions can also be quantified in the Marxian categories of social consumption and public expenditure, that is, aimed at the determination of a linear and adequate relationship between social demand and capitalist supply. The most interesting element of this proposition is the opposition that casts instances of social accumulation against instances of legitimation. O'Connor thus pushes the powerful compatibilities established by the Frankfurt School between integrative mechanisms and repressive apparatuses to the limit of contradiction. The opposition appears at all levels of the State machine, from the financial and fiscal to the monetary mechanisms. Although all this is only allusive, however, in reality the contradiction is not abstract. It begins to reappear with the emergence of organized and antagonistic social forces. The virtuous coincidences between the mechanism of profit and the financing mechanisms of public expenditures become impossible; the legitimation of accumulation no longer holds; and the crisis is represented as a political crisis — a crisis of the State.

We are certainly still on the (rather backward) terrain of the objective analysis of the capitalist structure and the contradictions that mark it (and, in parallel, we still seem to be working with an idea of communism as planning and productive rationality). The path that goes beyond and recuperates the structural analysis of the Frankfurt School, however, seems to have been opened. Despite everything, a reference has begun to emerge — within and against that structural Moloch that is the planned State of late capitalism — that points toward determinate contradictions resulting not from the relationship between capitalists (and the struggle over the partition of profit) but from the struggle between the classes. Class struggle is thus introduced into the structural image that the Frankfurt School has given to the State.

Developments of the Structural Analysis of the State: The State in the Theory of Crisis

This is only a beginning. On other theoretical trajectories, there has been a reemergence of the structural theory of the State and its opening to the thematic of class struggle. It is as if, after having been subjected for too long to a certain materialist primitivism (in the theory of the instrumental State-monopoly relation), the theory has been turned around again, and its determinate negation has been posed in a dialectical position that tends to recuperate the specificity of the functional mechanisms of the State. At the end of this path, elements of synthesis are reproposed that go beyond and recompose the complexity of the analysis from the worker point of view. Naturally, this dialectical development only refers to a trajectory of thought, and for us simply serves as the guide for the exposition.

We can certainly verify this by pointing to the fact that gradually, in relation to the violent reemergence of the elements of capitalist crisis in the most recent cyclical phase, the centripetal unilinearity of the structural theory of the State has also gone into crisis. It has gone into crisis not in the sense of negating the qualitative leap it represented in the development of the Marxist theory of the State. The fact that the State is presented as inhering globally within development and as its internal mediation is a definitive and irreversible element. It goes into crisis rather in the sense of showing how the State — already identified as the substitute for the automatic relation of capital — is submitted to the crisis, in what form it is involved, and how it reacts.

Offe tries to elaborate, from his point of view, a first draft of a theory of crisis. (See *Strukturprobleme*, in particular pp. 169ff., and "Crisis of Crisis

Management.") After having specified that the ductility of the relationship between the State and single capitalists constitutes a fundamental condition for creating harmony over a long period of development, and that the transitive functions assumed by the State serve essentially to modify the force of the economic laws of the market—in other words, after having emphasized the complexity and the articulation of the subsumption of capitalist development in the State—Offe explains the reappearance of the crisis as a necessary effect of the transfer of the regulatory functions of the market to the State. The anarchy of the public sector is the necessary correlate of the incessant rationalization of economic development. This is true with regard to the level of the reappearance of the contradictions. Furthermore, with regard to quality of the contradictions, it should be noted (taking up the results of O'Connor's analysis) that they are determined on the aporias of the relationship between processes of accumulation and the process of legitimation, or—as Offe might say—on the asymmetry between the consequences of the process of valorization and the means by which it is regulated. On the basis of the American and German experiences, these authors are focused primarily on two parallel phenomena: on one hand, the marginalization of always higher portions of labor-power from production as a result of perfecting the productive mechanism and as an effect of the strategies of prevention set in motion; and, on the other hand, the continuous deepening, with these dialectical nexuses, of the functional chaos of the public apparatuses and the multiplication of the parasitic characteristics (or bodies) within the State of mature capitalism. All this is posed certainly not to validate the revisionist theses on the autonomy of the State and the possibility of a rationalist reform, but on the contrary to confirm the impossibility of a reformist attempt to control and transform the State of mature capitalism. (See Frances Fox Piven and Richard Cloward, *Regulating the Poor*.) The tendency of the planned capitalist State to determine a proper stability by means of achieving an adequate measure of comprehensive social surplus value, a complete administrative and planning rationality, and a system of effective and dynamic legitimation thus runs up against continually stronger critical contradictions, which are determined on the level of the planned structure of the State and which determine there an implacable series of failures.

With these drafts of a theory of crisis, the structural framework of the analysis of the State undoubtedly takes a great leap forward in the direction of making the produced image dialectically dynamic. Is this sufficient, however, to determine the effective nature of class in the crisis and the State? This question becomes so charged because attempts at an institutional and sociological closure of the theory of crisis can be developed on this very same terrain. (See, for example, Habermas, *Legitimation Crisis*.) On the other hand, is it not true that Offe's arguments only represent one point in the passage toward a presentation of the theory of crisis that is more consistent from the class perspective?

Let us look at the aspects of the problem one by one. Offe maintains expressly that "because of the fact that the process of accumulation becomes formally political, it must change the nature of class." In fact, when one adopts the perspective of an organized accumulation with essentially administrative means and forms of social mediation different from the mere production of commodities, the parameters of the definition of class must change, just as the sequences of the determination of the crisis change. (See *Strukturprobleme*, pp. 27–63.) At this point, however, Offe's discussion stops, since the call back to consciousness and its collective recompositions and reconfigurations cannot be certain to resolve the problem of the definition of class. Offe's analysis halts at the void of the determination of class — but this has an immediate consequence for the development of the analysis. The political system also rests on its stability and vacillates in the crisis in a void of material determinations. What in reality disappears, with the exclusion of the "old" conception of the antagonism between the two classes, is the logic of the movement of the system. The reproposition of the problem of the crisis within the comprehensive structures of the structure of the State and the progressive unification of political and economic processes does not solve the problem of the class nature of the process, its dynamism, its orientation, and its meaning. It simply reproposes the problem at a higher level — and this should be emphasized as an extremely important moment.[20]

What, then, rules the dynamism and the crisis? How can the problem be reproposed once the planned and global nature of the contemporary State has been established? This question has indeed been addressed — and given a response — with particular insistence on the residual relationship between the State and the dialectical set of single capitalists.[21] In particular, Elmar Altvater has shown with great skill that if, in accordance with the theses of the Frankfurt School, "the State cannot in any case be conceived as a mere political or institutional instrument to be used by capital," then the special form of the amalgam impressed by the State on the social existence of capital must envelop the entire competitive dialectic of single capitalists. (See "Notes on Some Problems of State Intervention.") In this framework, the law of value — and the effectiveness of its functioning — cannot be conceived as substituted or abolished, but rather as simply modified. It is modified in the sense that the State, while confirming and validating the functioning of the market with an infrastructural and transitive intervention, is presented, on the other hand, as a sort of vacuum, as "not capitalist in the society of capital," as a "negative limit of the process of the formation of value." This is a dialectical, biunivocal relation: the State is contemporaneously a (totalizing) condition and an effect (of the functioning of the law of value, like a law of the discrepancy and the average of single capitalists). The process of capital to become autonomous is thus intrinsic to the nature of the capitalist process but posed in a negative relationship, dialectically negative, with the tendency of capitalist development toward valorization. The State guarantees capitalist relations (guarantees them to an ever greater extent) insofar as it acts in a noncapitalist form, and thus it is not a direct element of valorization.

The theory of crisis is thus established on the basis of these premises, and from these premises—with varying intensity depending on the weight given to the dialectic of single capitalists—the foundation of the crisis is deduced. Let us take a moment to examine a few examples. In the work of Wolfgang Müller, the intensity of the subordination of State planning to the dialectic of single capitalists appears in its most extreme form. (See "Die Grenzen der Sozialpolitik in der Marktwirtschaft.") In this case, the crisis acts again like a crisis of disequilibria and circulation. For Altvater, instead, since the dialectic between the State and the law of value of the market is seen from the perspective of equality according to biunivocal tensions, the crisis is represented in qualitative terms. (See "Notes on Some Problems of State Intervention.") Stagflation is the emblem of the crisis precisely because in it come together two moments: the intervention of the State to the point of saturating the material (negative, infrastructural) conditions of production; and the crisis of the quality of the value of capitalist production, since that can only be determined by the functioning of the market. In short, the State, intervening in Keynesian fashion, can prevent collapse, but, since it is not an element of valorization, the State ends up determining stagnation or new forms of crisis. Development can only derive from the immanent forces of capital. Finally, Paul Mattick, while assuming as fundamental the relationship between the State and private capitalists and holding private capital as the driving force of the process, does not insist on the alternative and sees the interdependence increase, or at any rate intensify, in the crisis phase. (See *Marx and Keynes: the limits of the mixed economy.*)

I believe that at this point we have reached an essential alternative in our analysis. Let us take up Engels's claim that the State configured itself as the "ideal collective capitalist" in order to "maintain private production without

the control of private property." As the ideal collective capitalist, "the more it proceeds in taking over the productive forces, the more it actually becomes the
national capitalist, and the greater the number of citizens it exploits" (*Anti-
Dühring*, p. 330; see earlier, the section titled "Situating the Problem: Marxian
Approaches"). It is clear that this definition should be taken in dynamic and tendential terms, but it is also clear that, in the process, the transformation of the
State into a productive entity is determined with precision and that therefore two
lines must be taken into consideration: the decreasing importance of the relationship between the State and individual capitalists, and the widening and deepening
extension of the process of exploitation regulated by the State. We have seen how
the structural theory has followed and described the extension of the process of
exploitation and its relocation within the State — failing nonetheless to determine
the specificity of the relations of exploitation on a social terrain, "thus tending to
keep the image of the planned State of exploitation at a limit of insignificance."
How could it make sense to move from the critique of this inconclusiveness in
order to return to identifying the origins of valorization and crisis in the mechanisms of the market? How could it make sense to reduce this planned State to a
merely "conditioning" or "residual" element of the production of surplus value?
The two questions are really one: either one denies the planned nature of the contemporary State (but only the blind can do this) or, if that is admitted, it is not
possible to reintroduce surreptitiously a central dialectic with the single (and furthermore private) capitalists. The contradiction between the State and the single
capitalists should obviously be kept in mind, but considered (as the documentary
material shows) in a subordinate way. As a clear and sure alternative, the analysis
should be brought back to the "ideal and collective" complex of capital and the
State as its representation, discerning within that totality, according to class lines
and the expansion of the worker point of view, the real mechanisms of exploitation
as they emerge in this new dimension. The structural analysis of the State is perfected and completed with an analysis of the crisis, with a definition of the technical and political composition of the proletariat — redefining in this sense the
Marxian theory of value.

The theory of crisis is thus also redefined. From this point of
view, a series of definitional elements of the crisis grasped in the structural
school — but often in terms too formal and, at any rate, from an objective structural perspective — gain a material foundation and general meaning. Along with
the qualitative leap that capital and the State accomplish — according to both
Marx's prediction and the structural description — there is also a qualitative leap

by the entire structure of exploitation. The relevance of the subjective moments (in the Marxist and Leninist sense: as the relevance of the comprehensive class practices) and the emergence of the subjective class point of view thus become the most important and decisive elements from which the analysis can be developed and completed. (See Antonio Negri, "Marx on Cycle and Crisis.") This methodological point is a definitive rejection of those positions that, while searching for a dialectical path for the analysis, continue to forget that the Marxian dialectic includes the objective circuits of capital only insofar as it is based on the dialectic of exploitation and the antagonistic relationship between the two classes. (See Romano Alquati, *Sulla FIAT e altri scritti*, and Antonio Negri, "Crisis of the Planner-State.")

From the substantial point of view, the necessary modification of the class nature of a process of accumulation — which, as Offe might say, has become formally political — leads the analysis back to the definition of the new mode of posing productive labor (and its categories), to the new figure of the proletariat, and so forth.[22] There is much work to be done, but only in this way is it possible to arrive — with a correct image of the State — at the dimension and the antagonistic relationships of class.

A Parenthesis: The Quibblings, Allusions, and Self-criticisms of Bourgeois Theory

The oddest fact is that although communist State theory seems to consider the presence of the working class only in a tangential way, bourgeois theory — while having programmatically to negate or mystify or, in any case, mediate it — is attracted to the working class and forced to measure its own theoretical validity against its political efficacy. Even though bourgeois theory can never consider worker subjectivity (that is, in Marxist terms, the set of working-class practices, be they spontaneous or conscious, proper to labor power or to the party, that are in any case active in the dialectic of capital) as a theoretical fact, nonetheless its approach to the materiality of this emergence and the sequences deriving from it makes the field of bourgeois theory paradoxically more attentive to these developments than the field of working-class theory.[23] This is not the place to ask why this happens — this is only one of the many errors of revisionism! It is more interesting to consider how bourgeois theory approaches the problematic of the State, while it keeps in mind — almost as if it were a demon to exorcise — that massive worker presence.

It is now well known how the development of the theory of the State, from Keynes to the New Deal, was conditioned by a reflection on the causes of the great capitalist crisis following the Bolshevik rise to power in 1917 and lasting into the 1930s. (See chapter 2.) The conception of the State that resulted from this was based on a gigantic effort to restructure technically the composition of the working class (from the paradigm of the professional worker to that of the mass worker) and also on an attempt to make the State a dynamic machine of planned and reformist mediation of capitalist development.[24] Economics submitted to this innovation of the capitalist State, as did the other disciplines applied to social exploitation, such as sociology, human engineering, and urbanism. In Keynesianism, the fundamental hypotheses of development were nonetheless confirmed; the dualism of the fundamental perception was translated and recomposed in a continuous and stable mediation, in the restoration of the fundamental categories of capital, such as profit, development, and expanded reproduction. The "stagnationist" school does not really modify this Keynesian framework very much; the pessimism of their outlook does not change the theoretical framework.[25] More time has to pass in order to arrive at a modification of the theoretical framework — a period marked by tragic events, from the collapse of the remaining illusions of equilibrium to the emergence of a force of the working class that would be inextinguishable without such a modification.

The complete dialecticalization of the image of capital is thus the result of bourgeois economics in the period that followed the Second World War. What are the terms of this scientific development? What are its effects on the capitalist image of the State? The path taken by Piero Sraffa, the most eminent theoretical figure among the bourgeois innovators in the field of economic action, is well known. (See *Production of Commodities by Means of Commodities*.) He starts from the refusal (and critique) of every attempt of classical bourgeois economics to elaborate a theory of the market, because he claims it is impossible to pass from the formation of the rates of profit in terms of included labor-value to a theory of the general rate of profit. Keynes's optimistic conclusion on the possibility of reconstructing the categories of capital is thus destroyed through an analysis that dissolves the possibility of the capitalist mediation of all the relations among the defining elements of capital — or rather, all the relations except one: "The rate of a profit remains a *linear* function of the wage" (Claudio Napoleoni, "Sulla teoria della produzione come processo circolare," p. 52). Economic theory is thus made a conscious theory of distribution, in which any element of determination of the qualities of distribution generated internally disappears while the externality of relations of force between the classes decisively takes precedence. As Napoleoni says, from this point of view, Sraffa simply offers "the justification in principle of all the contemporary attempts to close the economic discussion within the limits of preparing the practical instruments of planning" (p. 59). Others, less generously, maintain that Sraffa's work only represents an extension of the algebra of Leontyev, the great Menshevik planner.

If we look closely now we can see that, faced with a dissolution of the categories of capital in the conflict with an uncontrolled movement of the variable wage, it was the figure of the planned State that became central: where the category "capital" was not capable of mediation, the category "State" replaced it. The State, however, is refigured implicitly here, just as it was in the Marxist structural theories—in other words, not as a mere substitute for the rule of the market but as a specific innovation and a capacity to determine the elements of valorization, even if only among the relations of force that regulate distribution. The concept of capital has been reconstructed within the figure of the State and the concept of value is no longer the substance nor the measure but simply the State's expression of the will to mediate social antagonisms. As a paradoxical confirmation of all this, one economist adds: "The best way to confront the theory of distribution, introducing again the reality of the class struggle into this fundamental problem of political economy, seems, then, to be combining Sraffa's relation among the rates of wage and profit with what little we know—mostly from Marx—about the interrelations between real and monetary phenomena" (Domenico Mario Nuti, "Economia volgare e distribuzione del reddito," p. 271). This amounts to saying "Let's force further the externality of the capital-class relationship, and let's locate it even more resolutely on the horizon of the powerful and totalitarian mystification of money and the State."

Between Keynes and Sraffa, a theoretical itinerary is thus traversed that, although confirming the planned reality of the State as the only alternative to the disaggregation of the market, reveals ever more clearly and with fewer illusions the antagonistic nature of this totalitarian State reality. Worker and proletarian subjectivity—as a total exteriority that is always present for the system—is the element that the bourgeois science of economic process and its State regulation must ever more effectively subsume and reveal.

Not only, however, is this itinerary accomplished at the highest levels of capitalist consciousness, but an analogous itinerary is also achieved, even if at times on the narrowest of paths among treacherous swamps, by the dutiful and servile bourgeois juridical science. In this case, too, the crisis following the First

World War determined important changes, culminating—within the New Deal laboratory—in a definitive dislocation of right with respect to the State. In other words, there were increasing attempts to transform right, on the institutional terrain and with the aid of realist theories, into a function of the organization of consensus to particular and concrete ends of reform. Some characterized the democratic administrativization of right as an attempt to privilege procedures with respect to norms, reformist goals with respect to normative repressiveness, and consensual processes of pluralism with respect to the authoritarianism of the centralized juridical system. (See chapter 3, in particular section IV, "Critique of the Model of the Bourgeois Theory of Authority.") New Deal democratic interventionism is, from this point of view, a Keynesian experiment in right, radically different from the traditional interventionism of both liberal and fascist regimes. Some thus called it a dislocation of right with respect to the State. In fact, in practice the rights State—that is, the State justified by the preexistence of a juridical system to guarantee and protect public and private rights—democratically reappropriates right, making right a function of the State, attempting to put the system of guarantees and protections to work, a posteriori, dynamically, not formally but substantially. The attraction of this project must have been enormous since an entire troop of formalist jurists, who were educated in Europe but through emigration came into contact with the New Deal experience in the 1930s, accepted it as the hypothesis of their discussion. We are not only talking about the Neumanns and the Friedrichs, but principally of Hans Kelsen, whose final theory was completely and tediously aimed at solving the problem of the execution of the valid act in dynamic and procedural form. (See chapter 3, "The General Theory of Right and the Construction of the Model.") The circularity of normative and executive acts became in this case the effective key to the democratization of the system. The goal of liberal guaranteeism was adopted and transfigured in the accession to a juridical ideology of power for which the elements of validity and legitimation were all internal to the system—insofar as the system covered the entire flux of the social materiality that it regulated. This was indeed a Kelsenian utopia. It was so utopian, in fact, that, as in the work of Abbé Saint-Pierre and Immanuel Kant, the investigation concluded on cosmopolitanism and the declared utopian character of an international moralizing function of right, the foundation of all social orderings and the legitimation of the work of jurists.

International ordering, however, really means Bretton Woods, which means imperialism, and so forth! (In particular, on the origin of Keynes's "idealism," see Paul Fabra, "25 ans après Bretton Woods.") With regard to this juridical tradition of Keynesianism in domestic orderings, too, the effects are paradoxical. The same type of democratic thrust that allows the rupture of the traditional connection between State and right, just as was given in the rights State, ends up in reality with an affirmation of the totalitarian character of the State, which, even though it has little to do with traditional legitimation, nonetheless renews its definitive and formal characteristics. One could say that the reformist dislocation of the right within the State—dictated by the capitalist needs to recognize and co-opt potentially subversive subjects—finally manages to identify a disproportionate eminence of the State over right and legitimation over legality, such that, once again, also with respect to this proposition, we find the lines of the figure of the State described by a structural theory. (See Ulrich Klaus Preuss, *Legalität und Pluralismus*.) We thus come to the end point of a path that, although recognizing the collapse of the rights State and the corresponding collapse of the function of the market, and while trying democratically to bring the participation of the subject into the juridical system, in reality remodels the State, accentuating its centralizing, bureaucratic, and authoritarian characteristics. Schmitt's reevaluation goes along with Kelsen's; decisionism and jurisprudential realism are wedded; and technocratic approaches and the cult of efficiency are linked with professions of faith in democracy.[26]

A step forward has, in any case, been accomplished. In the juridical mystification of the relationship between the classes, the adversary, with its new essence and its comprehensive (antagonistic) inherence within the system of power, has been recognized and newly mystified at a higher level. It seems so clear that bourgeois science, in the two strategic realms of political economy and juridical science, in addition to touching on a correct definition of the new characteristics of class antagonism, proposes a context of mediation and definitions that strangely approach the reality of the State—approaching it in order to mystify it—just when it is perceived in a tiresome way from the theoretical point of view of the proletariat. It is obviously not a matter here of calling for all to rally behind bourgeois science. It is rather a matter of arming ourselves in order to attack and destroy it. That is possible, however, only when one understands the real dimensions of the contemporary State. We should add that (except for the Marxian point of view) Stamokap-style revisionism, variants of neo-Gramscianism, and the various objectivistic and economistic waves of structural theory are all poorly equipped for this task.

Bourgeois science, on the other hand, is always animated by a secure class hatred that allows it to identify the adversary: in other words, that terrific subjective reality that is the massified proletariat of the societies of advanced capitalism. For this reason, if for no other, it touches closer to reality than do far too many "Marxists"!

Repropositions of the Problem: State, Class Struggle, and Communist Transition

There has been too much discussion of the crisis of the planner-State. It has been discussed in a confused way that risks throwing out the baby with the bathwater. In fact, the crisis of the procedures of planning, which is equally strong in the Anglo-Saxon and the Continental countries, does not mean in the least that the progression toward the figure of the State as total representative of collective capital has been halted.[27] On the contrary, the crisis of the planner-State prepares the way for a further step forward, a new qualitative leap in the relationship between the State and capitalist production. This is not, in any way, a reopening of the competition between single capitalists, the revaluing of the rules of the market, or the decline of the power of automatic intervention. On the contrary, the necessity of State intervention in the large aggregates of capitalist production is pushed to an extreme, while the determination of the conditions of production and the identification of transactive functions on the circulation of commodities are amplified and consolidated. Heralding the end of the planner-State without clarifying the meaning and the dimension of the crisis leads to two secondary and one fundamental distortion. The first distortion, typical of juridical fetishism, is to consider juridical processes on a par with structural phenomena and therefore deduce the complex of real capitalist processes from the insufficiency and the defeat of the programming procedures. A second distortion results from a blindness to how the planned State of collective capital makes use of juridical instruments, from time to time celebrating their instrumentality and their functional conditioning: the functional chaos of the programming State machine is, in any case, marked by a class logic. These, however, are secondary distortions. The fundamental distortion consists in giving credence to a false image of capitalist development; the worker objective of the destruction of the State as representative and quintessence of capitalist power is thus opposed by a collapsed image of the single capitalist, the faded flag of "socialism" is waved, and all the despised weapons of opportunism are reproposed.

What, then, does the crisis of the planner-State mean? In what sense and why is there a crisis of the procedural instruments of programming, as a complex, as a set with constitutional relevance (because singly, in fact, they often hold)? In general, crisis of the planner-State means crisis of the Keynesian State as a project of State intervention for capitalist development, based on a politics of the regulation of the large dimensions of income, an essentially financial instrumentalization, and a tendentially socialist ideology. This crisis is principally determined by the insufficient presence of the State in the economic mechanism and the insufficient automatism of the intervention. This State is faced with a high level of worker struggles that exploit the planned terrain in terms of both simple and direct political rupture (the quality of the demands) and rupture of the capitalist proportions of the processes of reproduction (the quantity of the demands). In other words, in many of the new situations of planned capital, the inherence of the instruments of participation and selection has not been sufficiently effective; the capitalist apparatus of containing and strangling the worker attack has not been able to put itself in play through a careful dosage of repressive instruments and technological innovation, of political consensus and the continual prevention of conflicts. In this situation, the working-class struggle — enjoying the massive support of the struggle of the international proletariat — has been able to put the State programming in crisis and set in motion processes involving the radical crisis of the system. The fall in the rate of profit, which typically leads to the development of the capitalist mode of production, is thus linked with a mass attack on profit that, beyond striking directly at the mechanisms of valorization, has determined the end, or at least the weakening, of all the old paths pursued to reestablish the rate and the mass of profit. For the first time in its history, capital has had to undergo an attack of such dimensions that the economic laws of development and crisis have been defeated. The classic sequences of capitalist economics — inflation, recession, unemployment, crisis, and restructuring — can now only function if reinforced by a surplus of power. The spontaneity of this sequence has been toppled; instead, what is spontaneous is the contemporaneity of contradictory sequences from the point of view of capitalist science and experience. Paradoxically, the multiplication and enlarged reproduction of the crisis by means of the structures of integration have become spontaneous, in relation to the interrelated compactness of the functions and the structure of the mature capitalist State. The "input" of the workers' struggles corresponds to a process of *conversion* that multiplies and reproduces the single logics of the crisis, determining an institutional chaos, and finally a comprehensively critical "output" that itself produces new modifications of social struggles and that, at any rate, is a condition of the communication and circulation of the struggles.

Within this type of crisis and these relations of force between the classes, the only capitalist path consists in the further deepening of the nexus between the State and comprehensive capital. The maneuver of restructuring can be carried forward only to the extent that the State, going beyond its Keynesian equilibria with comprehensive capital, accentuates its presence within the productive machine itself; in other words, it accepts the role of "reinforcing" the processes of valorization with the entire armory of its own figure. Political "valorization" makes real the valorization of capital. In this tendency, the capitalist supervision of the sector of production and the armory of its command over the productive process (technicians, managers, submanagers, and so forth) become "public officials," as an outgrowth of the power of the State and a reinforcement of the logic of productive command. This is equally true for the instruments of consensus (that is, political and/or trade-union figures of consensus). New techniques of programming are being formed on the basis of this new fabric of power: programming not by large aggregations in terms of a socialist reassumption of consensus, but programming by internal lines, through a limited search for a consensus that differentiates — in purely political terms — one stratum of workers from other strata, selects and controls to the same extent that it organizes and reorganizes social production, and so forth.

It is easiest to grasp these phenomena expressed in their most radical and tendential form in the Federal Republic of Germany, precisely on the basis of a specific political history and a series of processes of integration that are not matched in any other advanced capitalist country. Perhaps this situation has resulted essentially from the fact that in postwar Germany Keynesianism (which even has had interesting affinities with Nazism) never constituted a fundamental politics, because up until the Allied occupation a constitutional structure of the social State of labor was imposed. (See Karl Heinz Roth, *Die "andere" Arbeiterbewegung und die Entwicklung der kapitalistischen Repression von 1880 bis zur Gegenwart.*)

Let us return, though, to the problem, or better, to the reproposition of the problem — to that fact, that is, that the fundamental acquisitions of the structural theory of the State are confirmed by the phenomenology of the crisis and the analysis of the processes of restructuring (on the part of capital). That, however, only hints at the theoretical-political key to the solution of the problem. This key must be developed on both the theoretical and the political plane. It is not possible, though, to do that here. What perhaps will be useful instead will be to indicate which, in my opinion, are the terrains in which this study should be developed.

On the political terrain, first of all, there seems to be a radical divergence in the way in which the materialist analysis of the set of class relations must proceed. All the phenomena we have cited, from the perspective of both political economy and State theory, seem to push the critique toward the determination of a subject of development and crisis that can no longer simply be defined as a complex of the dialectical logics of the realization of capital. That set of logics is dissolved, it seems, and the series of phenomena regulated by capitalist development and/or crisis seem to show a radicality of the antagonism present in the process that can no longer be reduced dialectically. This substantial modification of the political process is signaled by capital and assumed as fundamental by reformism.[28] This radical modification of the relation of capital (which, in all advanced capitalist countries, shows the solidity of a new, permanent dualism of powers, as the political overdetermination of the era) is experienced primarily on the terrain of the autonomy of the working class. All the goals and all the practices of the autonomy of the working class are determined by it. This fact, however, reopens precisely the political problem, which consists in dealing with the alternative power. The capitalist and reformist perspective proposes the foundation and exercise of a State power capable of integrating the working class, in a form that is functional to the resumption of development and radically antagonistic to the emergence of worker power. We should emphasize this point: today development moves ahead only through the destruction of the autonomy of the working class, and Nazism is a necessary component of power. The other pole of the alternative is clear: no workers' struggle exists that is not immediately struggle on the terrain of the transition, struggle for communism, and struggle for the extinction of the State. The primary political task becomes that of centering the discussion on the transition, deepening the analysis of the current dualism of power, and leading every discussion on organization back to the thematic of power. (See, for example, Danilo Zolo, *La teoria comunista dell'estinzione dello Stato*.)

In the context of the contemporary political and economic crisis this type of alternative is posed with absolute urgency and intensity. The emerging figure of the State is one that shows development only as the complete destruction of worker autonomy. The reformist price of the operation — in the countries where it must be paid — is not too high. This is a problem that is solved on the sociological and electoral levels of the interchange of the political strata! The State that is defined in this crisis, on the other hand, is perhaps a figure still more structurally coherent than our German colleagues were able to realize with respect to their admittedly terrible experience. It is laughable to hear those who speak of the

State becoming fascistic while they themselves make it a practice to label the work-ers' struggles as "criminal"! We should instead consider this strongly advancing process of the restructuring of the State as a force capable of breaking the auton-omy of the working class and nullifying it through either reformist-style internal division or technological marginalization.

Some conceive of capital as essentially unplannable! They have a very feeble imagination and, moreover, a paltry, rose-colored image of social development and capitalist processes, which are processes of exploitation, destruc-tion, and domination more than anything else. Some, on the other hand, imagine the passage from capitalism to communism as a level, continuous path—but then where is the passage? In any case, capitalist planning exists and is very healthy, and the functional chaos of the ordering of the State lives, too. At these levels of indus-trial integration no capital exists that is not planned—and not for development but for rule, or rather, for development only when the working class begins to be so strong that there can be no rule without development. Here again, however, there is the struggle for the destruction of the working class and the restructuring of the State to this end, for the planning of the destruction of working-class auton-omy, and for the planning of a resumption of the rate and mass of profit.

On this directly political terrain, then, the research should be pursued and the problem reposed, but also on another contiguous terrain: that of the deepening of the critique of political economy. Marx left us an image of the State, as Engels has said, in which the public management of private property reproduces capital and deepens exploitation. Today, we move ever more on this terrain. Neither Marx nor Engels, however, could have foreseen the level of class struggle we find here. The relations opened at this point between the persistence of the situation of a duality of powers, the emergence of a workers' power antago-nistic to capitalist power, and the theory of exploitation (the theory of value) should now be developed. The State as collective capitalist is the manager of exploitation and the planner of all exploitation according to a function of the law of value that foresees a socialist transition and management in terms of the median profit (which tends to be equal to surplus value). If the State, however, is con-strained to be thus by a situation of workers' struggle never before experienced in the history of capital, and if (in the presence of these struggles) the equaling and averaging of value are lowered, then again in this case we have to reconsider the entire analysis and repropose it on the terrain of the critique of political economy. We will need to demand of the critique, in other words, a rereading of the theory of value at levels on which its zeroing begins to be presented as a real horizon and where there is a massive worker aggression against the functioning of the law of value. What is the State, as collective capitalist, at this point?

Perhaps it would be worthwhile here to carry the discussion forward by taking up and overturning the point of view expressed by Elmar Altvater (see earlier, the section titled "Developments of the Structural Analysis of the State"). In Altvater's argument there is—even if only from a rigorously objectivist point of view—a strong insistence on the "marginal" and "residual" character of State intervention in the capitalist economy. He does not deny the planning intervention of the State but defines it in extraeconomic terms. The limit of this position seems to consist in the fact that this extraeconomic reduction of the State, after the State itself has been located in its power of planning, does not grasp the political and dualistic nature of the relation of capital. If we try to reapproach Altvater's intuition from a dialectical point of view, however, we now see the parasitic and terroristic residues of the State of capitalists reappear as a direct function of the critical difficulties of producing surplus value, the level and intensity of the workers' struggles, and the new form in which the fall and flattening of the rate of profit appears today. The political analysis can follow this process, focusing on the "dual character" presented by capitalist production summarized in the figure of the mature capitalist State. "Dual character" means not only the reappearance of class antagonism at every level of the capitalist synthesis, but also today, in the context of the crisis and principally faced with its permanent worker matrix, the exacerbation of the antagonism and the divergence of the terms of the synthesis.

The highest figure that capital has succeeded in producing for its State is thus also the extreme limit of the significance of the capitalist organization of social labor. When the rationality of planned rule is attributed to the State of capital, the comprehensive goals of this rule are reduced to an operation of control and destruction. All that, if you like, is due to the insuppressible emergence of an antagonistic power. On this basis it is worthwhile to carry forward the analysis and, above all, to act.

F   I   V   E

The State and Public Spending

This essay was written by Antonio Negri in 1975 amid a situation of fiscal and political

crisis in Italy, and, like chapter 4, it was aimed at challenging the policies of the "Historic

Compromise" between the Italian Communist party and the ruling Christian Democratic

party. Beyond this immediate polemic, however, the essay is directed toward a critique of

all those who believe it is possible to back away from supporting the Welfare State and

who propose austerity measures to address the economic crises brought on by increasing

public debt. The fiscal crisis of the State is certainly not limited geographically to Italy nor

historically to the 1970s. It has become an essential function of the contemporary State to

act as an agent of both legitimation and accumulation. Techniques that reduce public

spending and the fiscal powers of the State thus also undermine the administrative powers

of the State itself. Moreover, the power of the social forces that oppose the State is such that any decrease in public expenditures, in what we call the "social wage," has become

practically unfeasible. In other words, the Welfare State is not merely one possible figure

of the contemporary State; it has become its essential and irreversible element.

This essay certainly betrays the urgency of the Italian situation in the

mid-seventies. The political struggles in this period extended across a wide spectrum of

social sectors (both within and outside the factories) and were organized in new and

powerful forms. The Italian State responded to the social unrest with emergency measures,

such as the "Legge Reale," which increased the powers of the police and the judiciary, and

which, in turn, exacerbated the state of social turmoil. (For historical background of this

period see Franco Berardi, "Anatomy of Autonomy.") In the context of these fiscal,

political, and legal crises, the problematic of public spending provided a means of defining

the lines of conflict between the social forces of contestation and the capitalist State.

The Problematic as a Whole: Conditions of Interpretation and Real Conditions

IN THE major capitalist countries, public expenditures (by the State and the public sector) approach or surpass half of the gross national income. The increasing rate of growth of public spending with respect to the growth of national income is an irreversible trend. "Yet despite this, there have been only isolated studies by Marxists which systematically examine the causes and consequences of this unprecedented growth" (Ian Gough, "State Expenditure in Advanced Capitalism," p. 53). When such studies do appear, in fact, they only rarely grasp the new specificity of the situation in general; instead they recast the explanation of the situation in terms of the old objectivism of State monopoly capitalism, with completely unsatisfying results.

In the context of the theory of State monopoly capitalism, in fact, public spending appears as a simple financing of private capital and its direct public projections. The effects of the crisis linked to the expansion of public spending remain unexplained and unexplainable. Interpretations of the crisis of advanced capitalist countries that avoid the problematic of public spending, in its indisputable individuality, seem to me to be based in either hypocrisy or denial.

Communist State theory, however, to the same extent that it has rejected the theory of State monopoly capitalism and parallel versions, has recently addressed the new relationship that is configured by the State (as center of the collective and real imputation of the ideal capitalist) and the critical contortions of political economy.[1] There no longer seems to be any doubt that the State acts as both a political and an economic force at the center of the process of the circulation of capital, not in a subordinate way but with essential functions. The tendential process indicated by Marx and Engels is now being completed, and at the same time the course of the complementary component of the tendency is being realized: the practices of the working class now have a definitively destabilizing effect on the system. The more the two-sided character of commodities and the processes that produce commodities is revealed in the antagonism that constitutes them, the more the mechanism of the circulation (that is, production plus reproduction) of capital develops and assumes a comprehensive figure in the State of advanced capitalism.

The general theoretical consciousness, however, comes to a halt at this point. If the State assumes such centrality, then its expenditure, that is, public spending, must be considered as the wage expenditure of the factory-State. When the critique of political economy violates the rules of political economy (as the communist critique must do), then the struggle *over* public spending must be seen as a fundamental terrain of conflict. Too often, however, it is not. The Statist mythology of the social-democratic and revisionist tradition takes the situation back in hand, and when it cannot avoid critique of the State, intimidates it or forces it to yield to the capitalist fetishes of equilibrium and balance! Schmidt replaces Marx and Gotha wins out over the critique.

Thus in *The Fiscal Crisis of the State* James O'Connor, who has pushed forward the linkage between wages and public spending more than anyone else, equivocates on the distinction between the State as social capital and the State as social spending—an analytically useful distinction but completely abstract, or even mistaken if this tends to support the claim that the production and reproduction of the elements of variable capital (this is today the preeminent function of public spending) must be considered unproductive expenditure. On the contrary, in the second section of Marx's schema of the structure of reproductions (*Capital*, vol. 2, chapters 20–21), this spending for the reproduction of the elements of variable capital is indirectly productive, and therefore productive of surplus value—

and this becomes even more clear as the mechanism of capitalist production extends across the entire society. (See Ian Gough, p. 57.) The gap that O'Connor rightly noted between directly productive State investments and indirectly productive State expenditures does not in itself determine an economic disequilibrium (as his schema seems to suggest). It comes to determine a disequilibrium insofar as the practice of the working class destabilizes the relationship in terms of force, in terms of continually unsatisfiable pressure, and continuous struggle.

It is even less plausible to continue to claim that the crisis induced by the rise of public spending in the State budget is internal to, and even determinant of, the crisis of the profitability of mature capitalism.[2] There is such a relation, but it is certainly not linear: the crisis does not consist in the rise of public spending, nor does it rest on the fact that this is in itself contradictory with private accumulation. Public spending becomes an element of contradiction because worker power upsets its relationship with the State's system of rule (in the capitalist relation, the State is a balancing force) and strangles it in the *irrationality* of proletarian pressure and workers' struggle.

Addressing the State-public spending question means, then, eliminating from the outset any simplification that might in any way lead to objectivisms typical of the "theory of State monopoly capitalism"; it means assuming in definitive terms that the State is both the field and the subject of the fundamental contradiction that capitalist development encounters when faced with the social emergence of the proletarian class; and it means, finally, recognizing that the mechanisms of the crisis follow in Marxist terms from the "explosion" (as Marx says) of the relation that constitutes capital, that is, the relation of the two classes in struggle. In the final instance, Marx explains, everything rests on the proportion between necessary labor and surplus value, or rather, between the different moments of objectified labor and living labor surrounding the problem of exploitation and its proportions (*Grundrisse*, pp. 359-64). Public spending is the public and State form in which the relationship of the State exploitation of the worker society of productive labor is mystified. Public spending is a social wage and the analyses and destabilizing practices of the working class should be developed on the basis of this fact.

The State-public spending question, then, must be addressed by cutting away all remnants of social-democratic and revisionist Statism, any illusion about the "neutral and mediating, relatively autonomous" State, and any notions of the supposed double nature of the State, "good" when it assists us and "bad" when it finances private capitalists! Unfortunately, the State is not Manichean, but is instead the organic structure of the power of the ruling class. "The modern state," Engels tells us, "no matter what its form, is essentially a capitalist machine, the state of capitalists, the personification of the ideal collective capitalist" (*Anti-Dühring*, p. 330). The chapter of *Capital* on the State, which Marx never wrote, has been written by subsequent capitalist development, following the lines of the tendency Marx foresaw. (See chapter 4.) Our task, then, is to critique it.

Let us begin by looking at public spending from the worker point of view. The working class has always known one revolutionary use of the direct or relative wage:

Struggle against the reduction of the relative wage also means struggle against the commodity character of the labor force, that is, against capitalist production taken as a whole. The struggle against the fall of the relative wage is no longer a battle on the terrain of mercantile economy, but a revolutionary attack on the foundations of this economy; it is the socialist movement of the proletariat. (Rosa Luxemburg, Ausgewählte Reden und Schriften, *vol. 1, p. 720)*

There is a chapter of this struggle that is unknown, however, or at any rate has not reached a sufficient level of militant consciousness, and that is the chapter that will be written on the struggle over the social wage and against the State.

This is a program that involves all the productive social labor-power at a level of capitalist development that Marx described as a phase in which the potential of the entire community of labor is opposed to capital as a simple mediator of circulation-realization (*Grundrisse*, pp. 699ff.).[3] The critique of political economy is thus transformed immediately into a "critique of politics" because the proletarian attack on the social wage casts public spending as a capitalist terrain of the organization of the relationship between production and consensus, between development and rule, and between political constitution and social proletarian struggles.

The theoretical practice of capital thus moves forward on a terrain that the proletariat confronts, in terms of struggle, only episodically and spontaneously. Certainly, worker spontaneity is massive and ferocious. In all the advanced capitalist countries there is not one budget (at the level of the relationship of the most direct mediation and control on the part of the State-boss) that holds its own. The capitalist attempt to extort social surplus value in order to mediate and contain the level of social struggles is in crisis everywhere. The mechanism of authorizations and controls, which is the fundamental key to the administrative rationalization of the State command of capital, has been put in crisis everywhere by waves of workers' struggles for reappropriation.[4] With equal strength and intensity, however, and with greater continuity, capital pushes forward the work of readjustment and concentration of control, administrative planning, and spending. Capital and its science do not anticipate the problem, but working through the passage from the worker determination of the crisis to its capitalist closure, they anticipate its solution. "They" are all working on this. Cutting the ties between the State budget and public spending has become the fundamental problem, while rearticulating the differences and symmetries between the mechanism of financial control and the demands for political intervention is the second correlated essential problem.[5] Where the principle of bureaucratic-rational legitimation has insufficient foundation and is incapable of being applied to a conflict that is so widespread and profound, recourse is made to charismatic legitimacy and the political pressures and participatory mystifications of social-democratic coalitions until the level of inputs of demand for public spending has been enveloped.

There are enormous stakes around these issues. Even though communist theorists do not lead us to the determination of the solidity of the problem, we are forced to confront it by the practices of the two classes in struggle: the proletarian insistence on this terrain and the capitalist attempt to anticipate it with repression. At this point, "public spending" becomes a central element of the debate. Around this issue we must try to understand if several important problems of analysis and proletarian struggle (problems of the quality and intensity of exploitation) are included and transfigured in this framework and if the eventual new relationships do not modify, from the point of view of a comprehensive worker theoretical practice, some assumptions with regard to the definition of the State and the communist struggle against the State.

Naturally, this issue could lead in another direction, to an analysis of the material dimensions of public spending in Italy and the workers' possibilities of attack. Many comrades are working in this direction, and we hope that soon the results of their work can be made public.

First Analytical Approach: Evaluative Elements of the Tendency toward the Social Unification of Productive Labor

To discuss public spending it is perhaps necessary, more than in any other field, to situate oneself clearly on the Marxian terrain of the analysis of the process of the circulation of capital, as a sphere of the production and reproduction (and innovation) not only of commodities but also social relations, and thus on the terrain of the tendential emergence of revolutionary antagonism and subjectivity. This becomes difficult when, as happens in the case of the authors most firmly linked to the class point of view, the neoclassical and Keynesian mystification of the mercantile system continues to dominate the horizon.

Let us adopt, for example, the categories of public expenditure proposed by James O'Connor:

Social investment *consists of projects and services that increase the productivity of a given amount of laborpower and, other factors being equal, increase the rate of profit. A good example is State-financed industrial-development parks.* Social consumption *consists of projects and services that lower the reproduction costs of labor and, other factors being equal, increase the rate of profit. An example of this is social insurance, which expands the reproductive powers of the work force while simultaneously lowering labor costs. The second category,* social expenses, *consists of projects and services which are required to maintain social harmony — to fulfill the State's "legitimization" function. (The Fiscal Crisis of the State, pp. 6–7)*[6]

This distinction — which, though analytically suspect, is still useful (see Gough, p. 71 n) — becomes dangerous when it is assumed unilaterally to define the gaps and the regions of disequilibria between the sectors of spending. In this way, disequilibria, crisis, and above all inflation come to be seen as arising objectively, à la Keynes, from the dysfunctions in the organization of distribution. The gaze does not go beyond this minute barrier; it limits itself without having dared to touch on the materiality and the force of the social relationships that rule over the diversification of the sectors and the disproportions of spending (or distribution) that are determined. "Necessarily," Hirsch notes with regard to Offe's work, "in this way the concept 'society' is reduced to a phenomenological concept of structure" and the State is stripped of the concept of class that characterizes its (politically) structural intervention in society for ruling the relationships of reproduction ("Zur Analyse des politischen Systems," pp. 87, 91, and 93).

What should be addressed, instead, is the terrain of the proletarian subject and its situation in the capitalist circulation of commodities, because this is where the modifications have been so vast as to destroy the possibility of neoclassical and Keynesian interpretations of the asymmetries and the disequilibria of public spending. In short, our hypothesis is that these do not simply consist in disequilibria of distribution but reveal a much more profound and massive structure, which is shown first by the modification of the site and nature of productive labor in mature capitalist society, and second by the level of struggle and the demand for power expressed by the proletarian subject. This is what we will try to demonstrate.

At the base of the disproportion theory of public spending and the theory of inflation as an effect of the rise of public spending (principally in the sector that O'Connor defines as "social expenses") is the conviction that workers in State-induced production are "'unproductive' from the point of view of capitalism as a whole" (Yaffe, "The Crisis of Profitability," p. 51). The claim that workers in what O'Connor calls the "social consumption" sector are unproductive workers, however, would clearly seem to be excluded by the claim, mentioned earlier, that they are subsumed in the second part of the Marxian schema of reproduction. That only leaves the employees in the third group formulated by O'Connor, "social expenses," which (surreptitiously) leads to productive labor for "luxury" spending, or at any rate spending that does not, in Marxist terms, create value (see *Capital*, vol. 1, pp. 741ff.).

What sense can this compartmentalization still have at this level of the capitalist integration of civil society through the State? Are the workers who contribute to the production of "social harmony" really unproductive? Would it not be better instead to change the very concept of productive labor, modifying its definition in the direction that Marx himself identified?[7]

With the progressive accentuation of the co-operative character of the labour process, there necessarily occurs a progressive extension of the concept of productive labour, and of the concept of the bearer of that labour, the productive worker. In order to work productively, it is no longer necessary for the individual himself to put his hand to the object; it is sufficient for him to be an organ of the collective labourer, and to perform any one of its subordinate functions.
(*Capital, vol. 1, pp. 643–44*)

Would not this modification of the definition of productive labor, enlarging its conceptual purchase, better correspond to the extension of the capitalist mode of production and its rule over contemporary society?

Reviewing the results of a long discussion of these questions among English Marxist economists, Ian Gough concludes, "all State workers producing either components of the real wage, for example social services, or elements of constant capital, for example research and development work, are indirectly productive for capital" — in other words, they produce surplus value ("State Expenditure in Advanced Capitalism," p. 83).[8] Bob Rowthorn, on the other hand, insists that it is beyond doubt·that "the educational and other [administrative] sectors of the State, even if 'unproductive', can push workers to produce surplus value, part or all of which is transferred to the capitalist sector where surplus value appears in the hands of the capitalists" ("Skilled Labour in the Marxist System," p.

36). This is true in the sense that the productive integration of capitalist develop-ment increasingly imputes the State with a totalizing support function with respect to productive activity. The State does not, in Keynesian fashion, organize mercan-tile relations, but, directly or indirectly, and in any case effectively, it organizes productive relations. It organizes relations that are productive of commodities and, above all, productive of relations of production.

The growth, and even the enormous expansion, of public spend-ing does not conflict with the development of capital, but rather is organic and necessary to the contemporary productive figure of capital. In addition, public spending today constitutes the essential prerequisite of every moment of accumu-lation. It makes no sense therefore to speak of public spending that is inflationary in itself. At this level of the socialization of production and command, one could give an essentially positive proof of the functioning of the law of value. If the law of value does malfunction and the inflationary mechanisms are set in motion, this is due not to the organic relationship established between public spending and the composition of capital (which is dominated today by State command), but rather to the rupture of this organic relationship imposed by the workers' struggles, by the antagonism that opens at this point between the organic composition of capital and the political composition of the working class (which at this level of the unifi-cation of labor-power is, at any rate, productive).

The crisis does not consist in the disproportion between the three forms of spending identified by O'Connor, and more important, does not consist in the contradiction between, on the one hand, directly productive spend-ing, including spending to reproduce labor-power (which is thus indirectly pro-ductive), and, on the other hand, the political spending of the State, which pro-duces not surplus value but social consensus and harmony. This contradiction cannot exist because if social consensus and harmony are indeed achieved, they are achieved as functions internal to the relations of direct and/or indirect production. The crisis consists in the inability to control the different components of the com-position of capital at this level of class struggle and the development of capital; it consists in the irreducible antagonistic presence of the working class.

Why, though, does collective capital run the risk of an exten-sion of the crisis from the level of direct production to that of social production? Why does capitalist development involve itself in a dimension it cannot directly control and in which the problem of public spending (otherwise completely func-tional to private capitalization)[9] is open to general contradictions, which are inev-itably effective in their social generality?[10] Although the specific Marxian definition of the concept of productive labor needs to be modified in the way we have out-lined, Marx's analysis of the tendency whereby both the definition and the site of productive labor assume another sense still holds. This tendency moves in the direction of the development of the contradiction of the rate of profit. Little by lit-tle, the private, individual logic of profit falls away, as is illustrated by the process of concentration and the continual capitalist reform of its organic composition in the direction of a greater proportion of constant capital. (See Marx, *Grundrisse*, pp. 690ff.) To the same extent that the individual logic declines, capital organizes levels of social productivity, steals surplus labor from productive cooperation, and substitutes for the lost value the value produced by general social productivity, through the permanent and direct assimilation of all productive forces (and their reduction to constant capital) and through the integration of all of society into the factory of the collective capitalist. (See Marx, *Capital*, vol. 1, p. 635.) From this point of view, public spending represents the cash flow of the factory-State and is cast entirely in the structural gap between the fall of the rate of profit of the indi-vidual businesses and the pressure toward the rise of the general productivity of the system. The fact that within this structural gap there may be inflationary ele-ments is secondary: the structural gap does not define the reality but simply the possibility of inflation, which is realized exclusively by the intensity and the level of the workers' struggles.

If this is true, there follow several immediate consequences. In the first place, public spending proves to be a real moment of productive spending and thus its consideration should be entirely brought back to the levels of the cir-culation of capital in contemporary society. In the second place, public spending, constituted by a quantity of money (means) at the disposal of the State for direct or indirect production, weighs heavily as extorted surplus value globally on the com-munity of social labor-power, and specifically on the extorted value of social coop-eration. In the third place, it follows that a public expenditure thus constituted represents a basis of asocial exploitation for capitalist accumulation and, as such, is also contracted as a wage basis and destroyed as a basis for the financing of capital: the two moments cannot be separated if Marx's analyses of the relative wage are accepted. (See Rosdolsky, pp. 293–96.) In any case, this is the fundamental terrain of class struggle at this level of the development of capitalist exploitation.

It is not by chance, then, that the "theory" of reformism focuses its effort on this terrain, trying to defend itself against the Marxian critique. The most intelligent, and thus the most dangerous, positions correctly recognize public spending as social surplus value extorted by the collective capitalist. (See, for example, Francesco Galgano, *Le istituzioni dell'economia capitalistica*, in particular pp. 33–38.) As a result, just as the economic expropriation of the worker can be transformed into a political demand of the citizen (as is obviously the case in the project of the historic compromise in Italy), so too, insofar as they are citizens, they can put their hands on what was denied them as producers! It is clear that the disproportion between the validity of the analysis and the miserable opportunism of the conclusion can only be explained by the relative inexperience of these authors. If this were not so, as, for example, in the much less adventurous proponents of the politics of reformism, we would be dealing simply with despicable ideological mystification and the vile betrayal of the masses.

Second Analytical Approach: On Social Accumulation, State Management, and the Contradictions of the Capitalist Foundation of Legitimacy

In the old days the business enterprise accumulated and the State legitimated (better if it was a "rights State," but even if it was not). The State has existed historically as a "business committee of the bourgeoisie" in the course of capitalist development and Marx's treatment of the use of public debt in the initial phases of accumulation and in the critical phases of development demonstrates this adequately. (See *Capital*, vol. 1, Parts IV and V, and vol. 3, pp. 395ff. and pp. 464ff.) At that level of capitalist development, legitimating meant grounding the claim to right (which establishes the basis of an effective and legal relationship between the exercise of power and civil consensus) on the representative forces of the capitalist business enterprise, the values of economic development, and the direct capitalist mystification of the general interests. The State legitimated insofar as it guaranteed the pursuit of the general interests of development. At the contemporary level of capitalist development, however, the situation seems to have changed. A series of developments in motion today—the totalizing socialization of capitalist production, the rampant processes of abstraction, the growth of service-industry jobs, the general absorption of the so-called productive forces (social cooperation, science, technology, and so forth) into comprehensive capital, and the tendency of the infrastructure of social and political services to be enveloped within direct production—all determine a structural deepening of the mediatory functions of the State in the comprehensive production process. In terms of both organizational functions and the mass of surplus value socially extorted, the quantity directly involving the State has enormously increased. As we have suggested, this process is paralleled by the functioning of the law of the tendential fall of the rate of profit at the level of the business enterprise. (See primarily the analysis of Altvater, "Notes on Some Problems of State Intervention.") The State accumulation of social surplus value thus appears in the first instance as compensation for the fall of profit of the business enterprise (see *Capital*, vol. 3, pp. 232–66), but in a second instance these new State functions become ever more intense and determinate. The State begins to appear as a hegemonic force in the realm of the mode of capitalist production; the State accumulates in a prevalent and determinant fashion.[11]

How is the principle of legitimacy formed at this level of capitalist development? State accumulation does not contribute to the process of the general fall of the rate of profit except in the sense (traditional to the functions of countertendency) of raising the mass of profit. This can no longer represent a principle of legitimacy. Capitalist exploitation must be directed toward general interests in the hope of economic development. The increase of the mass of profit, then, is not enough to legitimate; the rate of profit is what gives the power of command and imposes the obligation to obey in the capitalist mode of production. Even if the mature capitalist State were to succeed in transforming itself through a correct evaluation of the rate of profit — if it were to go far beyond the Keynesian functions of market regulation, if it were to be directly productive, if through quasi-oligopolist investments of public spending it were to create highly productive regimes in the management of public services, and if the State were to try to reorganize the extraction of social surplus value in terms of progressive and rational fiscal management (that is, in terms of the law of value) — it would still be far from being able to impose itself.[12] The very nature of social labor in its generality and abstraction, that is, in its specific quality at this level of development, prevents this from coming about. In this case, in other words, the very possibility of calculation (in terms of the law of value) is, on one hand, impeded, as in the case of cooperation, by the spontaneous valorizing quality of social labor and, on the other hand, surpassed when labor time becomes an inadequate basis for measuring the expression of superior productive capacities. (See *Grundrisse*, pp. 699ff.) Furthermore, indirectly productive labor, which is in large part that linked to the State, opens possibilities of extremely differentiated and complex internal planning. (See Bob Rowthorn, "Skilled Labour in the Marxist System.") At this point State intervention to maintain the mass of profit is totally "arbitrary" in terms of the law of value. We should go further, though. The econometric arbitrariness (which is, in any case, fundamental from the point of view of comprehensive capital's planning) appears as totally irrational from the point of view of class; the use of the law of value, in this retreat of capitalist resistance, is reduced (or seems to be reduced from the proletarian point of view — and that is what counts) to the simple practice of command.[13] This is all the more clear when one considers that if capital is essentially a category of relation between class forces in struggle, the fall of the rate and the accumulation of the mass of profit mean, in class terms, the fall of the quota of the valorization of capital with respect to an implacable massification of proletarian struggles.

What principle of legitimation (of both power and consensus, both discriminating and participatory force) can sustain the capitalist direction of development today? In the realm of the social accumulation of the State there is no principle of legitimacy — this is certain. The accumulation of social surplus value by the State operates on the basis of a growing antagonism. Capital mystifies this knowledge of its own structure and calls the effects of this antagonism a problem of the priorities and selections of public intervention.[14] In fact, the fiscal policy is hateful, as is the exploitation of social cooperation, indirectly productive labor, marginalization, and the mass capacities of scientific innovation. The capitalist planners of the State recognize this situation.[15] Within this comprehensive crisis of credibility, then, the only moment of real legitimation is still referred back to the principle of the business enterprise, to the highest level of the extortion of surplus value and the production of productivity on the part of the capitalist. The extension of the mode of capitalist production in the form of the State must be subjugated to these levels of productivity as essential moments of the definition of capitalist reproduction. Reachieving high rates of profit (that is, productivity and exploitation mystified in profit) becomes a condition and criterion of the development of social accumulation through the State. The characteristic situation of the initial phase of capitalist development is thus inverted: the State accumulates and the business enterprise legitimates, pulling along (in terms of productivity) consensus, the fundamental element of the legitimacy of the capitalist State at its most mature level of development. The business enterprise thus becomes a support (a *Träger* in Marx's sense) of development — its quality and definition. Productivity, as a valorizing element of the social relation of production, is the legitimating term of the comprehensive process.

If we now return to public spending, we see that if this is one of the figures (perhaps the fundamental one) of the capitalist appropriation of social surplus value, it must yield to the norms of the productivity of the business enterprise. We have already pointed out that this is certainly not possible for structural reasons, but that does not resolve the problem. In fact, the process presents itself in terms of this contradiction: the failure of the city of New York in the name of the productivity of the business enterprise does not mean an elevation of productive capacity directly recuperable in the quantities of the accumulation-reproduction of capital, but means only the reproposition of a repressive, exclusive, and terroristic logic of domination against the uncontainable quality of cooperative, intellectual, and innovative labor. The rates and the quantity of public spending must, at this level of capitalist development, be posed with the authority of the business enterprise, not because that modifies the average productivity of the system (which is already closed in the antagonism between the mass of accumulation, along with social struggles, and the fall of the rate of profit), but because that legitimately imposes, reproposes, and sanctions the logic of capitalist domination.

As always, all the contradictions of capitalist development are two-sided. This reversal of the accumulation-legitimation relationship, so that the State now determines the former and the business enterprise the latter, reveals in its worker side new aspects and possibilities for proletarian struggle. In the very moment that the business enterprise opens to the wage even to guarantee productivity and the rate of profit, giving the State the responsibility of guaranteeing socially the effectiveness of the wage itself and recuperating it in the social circulation of commodities, an enormous space of rupture is opened for proletarian struggle. This is the space, the gap that extends between the productivity of the business enterprise, as a legitimation project of developed capital, and the real terrain of accumulation, both that controlled by the State and that of comprehensive social cooperation.

Deepening and expanding the contradiction that is presented in the capitalist plan itself to the point of bringing it back to the antagonism between worker interests and capitalist development can be carried out in various ways: either by lowering the productivity of the business enterprise, as workers have always done, or by accentuating the dysfunctions of the social accumulation of the capitalist State, as proletarians are spontaneously beginning to do — or by doing both at the same time. This seems to be the master line of workerist analysis. With the tendency of worker labor-power to recognize itself as the proletarian unity of unsubordinated labor, the dualities, the ambiguities, and the crises do not count. The workerist analysis makes the process dialectical and unified, from the contradictions at the heart of the proletariat to class antagonism.

The factory wage and the social wage are two poles of the figure in which the working class is mediated and subsumed in the social and State figure of capital. Capital tends to separate itself into two figures, to play the factory wage as an element of the legitimacy of the capitalist State against the emergence of the productive unity of social labor. On the other hand, the articulation of the struggle from the factory wage to the social wage becomes a devastating power of the capitalist contradiction, which is functional to the capital's domination.

There is one final element to consider, however, which is not tactical but theoretical. In the context of this process the "relative" character of the wage negotiated by workers explodes. In fact, the "relativity" of the wage negotiated by the factory workers arrives at an equivocal relationship—dominated by capital—between the real wage and the monetary wage. Factory capital dominates the calculation of the factory wage and in the calculation makes it relative and politically functional. On the other hand, the proletarian struggle over the social wage disrupts the functioning of capitalist logic, blocking its calculation and control. It is completely clear, then, that it is not at all important whether real wages rise or fall—from a Marxist perspective there can be few illusions about this! What is important is leading the wage component back to the role of independent variable, and that is possible in the practice of the proletariat on the social terrain.[16]

Recognizing society as a factory, recognizing the State as a boss, destroying the fetish of productivity as legitimation, and bringing legitimation back to the comprehensive needs of the proletariat is, at any rate, today's subversive task. It is possible that this is enough, because when the relativity of the wage is destroyed, and when the logics of division and domination through division are broken by force, the emperor will be revealed as he was in the fable: naked and crazy.

The Crisis of Public Spending in Italy

We should pause a moment to consider the reality of the crisis in more detail. There is extensive and useful documentation of the crisis of public finances in Italy in the years following the wave of struggles in the 1960s and the resulting institutional panic. (See *La finanza pubblica*, edited by Mediobanca, and also Franco Reviglio, "La crisis della finanza pubblica [1970–1974].") In short, what happened was that the debt of the State and the public administration exploded in the early 1970s, rising from 2.5 percent of the gross national product in 1970 to 7.9 percent in 1973, subsequent to a significant expansion of spending (rising consistently faster than the gross national product) and insufficient incomes. This gave rise to the formation and consolidation of a growing deficit and a rigid structure of capital expenditures and capital transfers. The situation changed in 1974, but more in appearance than in reality. The new situation offered no possibility of structural intervention, and, given the permanent strong absorption of resources by the structural debt, it was only possible to implement conjunctural interventions to support employment levels, changes that were neither significant nor organic, even given a slight economic improvement.

There is no doubt that in this period the Italian public administration was put on the ropes by proletarian action, and that consequently the levels of exploitation of the social productivity of the system were blocked. From the capitalist point of view, this situation required an energetic response, and it is clear that, even if gropingly, a strategy of readjustment is being formulated. We can see this as one step further in the rationalization of circulation, the containment of spending and the drive for investment, the restoration of the global control of all the centers of economic decision making, the planning of the consolidation of debts, and above all the reaffirmation of the criterion of the legitimacy of public spending. This criterion has to function in the (controlled) mediation between the reduction of the deficit and the definition of a standard of productivity adequate to business regulations. At the same moment when the proletariat discovers the totality of the social terrain of its own exploitation, capital is constrained to accept this terrain, but only when the rules of business command are reproposed there. Breaking these sequences of proletarian pressure, putting its hands on the totality of control, defining rupture and control in terms of the rules of capitalist business — this is what "good government" means today. The reconsiderations and contortions of the theoreticians and officials of public finance are in this regard identical to, and by this point assimilated within, those of the theoreticians and officials of planning.

We can see, in fact, what is happening on the plane of restructuring intervention: a block on spending, new levels of austerity and provocation, a definitive disruption of the sequences of development that were poorly conceived in the last decade by the theoreticians of planning, and, most important, an active policy of displacing social labor-power and creating, on a par with the new dimensions and qualities of the labor market, a sort of "industrial reserve army" in the form of marginalization and/or abandonment of entire social strata. (See Massimo Paci, *Mercato del lavoro e classi sociali in Italia*.) In short, it is a strategy to divide internally the unity of productive labor, which is potentially revolutionary and, with its demands of recognition, completely destabilizing of the current state of politics. This is the task that the project of capitalist restructuring has to address.[17] This attack on the processes that form the new political composition of the working class is what will reestablish the rule of business and support the suffocating legitimacy of the norm of capitalist appropriation of all the surplus value, in whatever form it is produced.

The Italian situation is not unique. Although in the other mature capitalist countries the levels of public debt with respect to the gross national product have been lower than in Italy, some of them do have substantial debts, and, at any rate, the policies of readjustment and restructuring they have set in motion bear profound similarities to those in Italy. This is because it is not so much the debt that must be battled but the new political composition of the working class, which forces both public spending and the debt to grow.[18] In all the mature capitalist countries, and more so according to the larger size of the labor market, this project of consolidating social accumulation and its legitimacy in terms of business productivity is the central focus, and it is accompanied by measures to destroy the struggles of the emergent proletarian subject.[19] This capitalist tendency defines a figure of the State that is highly centralized and functional, and that dictates norms, behaviors, and procedures serving to concretize the new foundation of legitimacy in the strict relation that links it with (and derives from it) diverse moments of the process of the social accumulation of capital. In short, State intervention for realigning and directing public spending is only the mirror that reflects the consolidation of a principle of legitimacy, which is not new but now exclusive, that is, which was not ineffective before but is now given priority in its effectiveness: the principle of business productivity, for the social accumulation of capital and against the proletarian subject, which is tending toward unity and which is expropriated of that wealth.

It is no coincidence, then, that legality (the password of the validity of the juridical action of the State) should yield increasingly to the determinant material conditions for the legitimation of State action. The formal interpretation and definition of the juridical ordering are under increasing pressure to give way to functionalist theories, the most significant quality of which seems to be, if we do not misunderstand the German and American theorists, the insistence on the determinant criterion of administrative action.[20] Although this is paradoxical from the old juridical perspective, legality can now be reconstructed only ex post on the basis of the fulfillment of the substantial functions that rival the system of right's capacity of address. One could develop an interesting casuistry of this phenomenon, but this is not the place for that. It is important rather to emphasize that what is gradually established on the basis of this juridical and administrative initiative is not the old form of legality but an arrangement of new norms of behavior and intervention. In this framework, capital and its State tend to make their own and make effective the utopian efforts of the various currents of "alternative jurisprudence," demonstrating an unusual open-mindedness toward their theoretical founders.[21]

At any rate, this is only a first approximation. When the new principle of legitimacy is posed with such weight and such exclusivity, the "lacunae" of the ordering that begin to emerge are so common and continuous that even the extensive application of evolutionary and alternative criteria does not allow the recomposition of the horizon of traditional legality. What is recomposed here, in the urgency that always characterizes its functioning, is a well-known law: the intervention is cast as exceptional and extraordinary as a result of a lacuna of the ordering and the urgency of the situation. Within the crisis, these functions multiply in frequency and extension. Extraordinary administrative intervention, preventive terror, and peremptory initiatives corroborate and develop the notions of evolution and alternative, defining (this time really effectively) new horizons of legality.[22] On the basis of these horizons, these functions, and these violent ruptures, the formalist command has to extend itself across the new legislative production and its roles of legal management. After having broken the old administrative routines with a devastating intelligence, the principle of legitimacy can allow itself to rest under the same cover with the new legality.[23]

What capitalist command asks of its functionaries today is that they rationalize (that is, make consequent and continuous) the content of the jurisdictional decisions, whenever and wherever they appear, making it adequate to the new principle of legitimacy, in other words, to the determinant and material criteria of business productivity. The entire complex of social labor is submitted to this imperative, with coercive social norms when possible and, in the majority of cases, with jurisdictional normative behaviors. What still remains of the normative systems put in place by the struggles and the worker conflicts against the State? Nothing remains that cannot be bent to the will of capitalist command, here and now.

If we now turn back to the theme of public spending, we are struck by the freshness of the reflections that its problematic suggests. It is always useful to rediscover a terrain on which the Marxian and workerist analysis of the wage finds a further space for application — in the first place, to show how the science and practice of capital are constrained to the most severe repressive operations in order to negate the subject that the social wage reveals, and, in the second place, to identify a terrain of struggle on which, on the basis of the social wage, all the practices of the hostile power tend to be united from the mass point of view of the proletariat and determine a further terrain for the expression of the workers' hatred.

The New Proletarian Subject in the Period of Crisis and Restructuring

In a fundamental passage of the *Grundrisse*, Marx develops a series of notes on class composition. Even humans, insofar as they are producers, are regarded "from the standpoint of the direct production process," Marx emphasizes, "as the production of *fixed capital*," as the accumulation and perfecting of productive capacity (pp. 711–12). Little by little, the subject that enters into the process of direct production is transformed by it, so that the very same process of direct production "is then both discipline, as regards the human being in the process of becoming; and, at the same time, practice, experimental science, materially creative and objectifying science, as regards the human being who has become, in whose head exists the accumulated knowledge of society." "As the system of bourgeois economy has developed for us only by degrees," Marx concludes,

so too its negation, which is its ultimate result. We are still concerned now with the direct production process. When we consider bourgeois society in the long view and as a whole, then the final result of the process of social production always appears as the society itself, i.e. the human being itself in its social relations. Everything that has a fixed form, such as the product, etc., appears as merely a moment, a vanishing moment, in this movement. The direct production process itself here appears only as a moment. The conditions and objectifications of the process are themselves equally moments of it, and its only subjects are the individuals, but individuals in mutual relationships, which they equally reproduce and produce anew themselves even as they renew the world of wealth they create. (p. 712)

We are not interested here in the philosophical relevance of Marx's materialist definitions, but rather in bringing up to date his consideration of and his insistence on the dialectic determined between "being moved by" and "moving" capital, which is grounded in the emergence of the working class. This is where both the new quantity of the wage and the new quality of worker needs, desires, and practices are determined. If it is indeed true that, in any case, the system of needs is always given in capitalist development in the form of exchange value, and that only a utopian could hope to rupture this alienating relation in an immediate way, then the progressive socialization of labor, its abstraction, and its growing productivity can and must rupture the determinate form of social exploitation. Capital itself moves class on this terrain, and is in turn moved: this is the meaning of the extraordinary development of productive social potential. From this point of view, then, the more the form of exploitation is made social and the more the form of the wage mystification of exploitation is also made social, the more the negation is deepened and becomes determinate in the body of capitalist society.[24]

In more specific terms, it seems actually that behind the expansion of public spending (as spending for the social wage) there are practices that allude to a more advanced level, in the Marxian sense, of class composition. To an ever greater degree in advanced capitalist countries, work and pay do not correspond and the worker consciousness develops levels of wage presence that are in any case unassailable, even if they are not politically organized.[25] The process of "worker education," which has been addressed by so much of the revisionist and neo-Gramscian literature,[26] has certainly not remained in the hands of the capitalists and reformists but, reorganized by the struggles, has been structurally rooted in practices and needs that only a generalized level of the social wage and political guarantees can answer and satisfy.[27] The dialectic between capital and the working class, which is continually socialized to a higher degree, is determined at a level of political class composition that characterizes our era in an absolutely new and irreducible way.

The capitalist strategy of public spending, however, tries to negate what it reveals. As we have seen, it is forced to do so. It will have no great success, however, if it is true that, more than arriving at the lowering of levels of income and marginalizing repression, the State's action has succeeded at most in setting in place new relative differentiations (within the permanent limits of guaranteed income). The State thus plays out, as we will see again, the relationship between functions of social accumulation and functions of business enterprise legitimation. (This is the mythology of "communist" productivity and/or cooperation against lax work habits, absenteeism, and "the capacity to enjoy" that Marx spoke of.[28]) The effort to negate the new reality of class composition, however, through a compression of public spending is nonetheless effective.

This is even more clear when, beyond the living labor directly used (or momentarily not used in this form) in the laboring process, indirectly productive service labor, scientific labor, and all the components of social knowledge come into play. An enormous literature has already contributed to our knowledge of the contemporary trajectory of the Marxist tendency on this terrain.[29] Social knowledge enters in an always clearer and more certain way in the synthesis of the determinate historical formation. The mechanism of social reproduction tends to become scientific in all its fundamental structures, from economic to infrastructural, and from communicational to political. In the continuity of the process of the social reproduction of capital, social knowledges today aggregate and become real. This store of indirectly productive human activity, however, this mass of living labor that will be exchanged for commodities on the terrain of the production and reproduction of capital, is dominated, divided, differentiated, and striated by capitalist command. It is assumed as the totality from the point of view of exploitation, in other words, from the point of view of the realization of the social circulation of exchange values, but insofar as it is represented by itself as productive labor it is pushed to the margins of social insignificance. Certainly, capital must be willing to allow some conditions for the "spontaneous" reproduction of this mass of productive social labor, but it does so increasingly in terms of a "natural condition" of reproduction, the value of which is mystified and at the same time greedily sucked into the capitalist recomposition of command. (See Massimo Cacciari, "Lavoro, valorizzazione e 'cervello sociale.'") This completely objectivistic opposition reflects *one* moment of the development of relations of capitalist production, between productive forces and relations of production—when by "productive forces" one understands "science, general social knowledge, the quality of labor, the sociality of labor, nature, machinery, the organization of labor, and so forth" (Romano Alquati, *Sindacato e partito*, p. 165). This opposition, then, is completely resolved in a total subordination of productive forces to capitalist relations of production and command. In this framework, public spending is entirely capitalist spending, an investment for capitalist reproduction. The capitalist negation of the creative mass of social labor-power can no longer proceed to completion. For this very reason, in the wage dimension, in the sector of the reproduction of social labor-power as such, we again find the characteristics of capitalist action on the wage in general: a continuous attempt to reduce necessary labor and extract the highest mass of social surplus value—with the same greediness and monstrous cruelty that we recognize in every factory.

On this terrain, then, the struggle over the relative wage opens up again: from the workers' struggle over the direct wage to the workers' struggle over the social wage. Here, too, a series of traditional divisions of the struggle—economic struggle and political struggle, syndicalist struggle and struggle for power—come down even more heavily (if that is possible). On this terrain, however, something else is in play, that is, the response to the worker pressure to reappropriate social productivity against the State's expropriation, and the need to recognize the new subject of production as a revolutionary subject.[30]

This field of struggle is opened as both articulation and totality: from two points of view, that of capitalist command and that of the proletariat. From the worker point of view we have to ask the question if there is "the possibility that the working class can use the productive forces for valorizing itself against capital, as an antagonistic class. If an alternative use of highly developed productive forces is possible" (Romano Alquati, *Sindacato e partito*, pp. 165–66). It is even more important to ask ourselves at this point if the concept of class composition, beyond its use as a descriptive and analytic category, can be translated into an operative category and an organizational schema of the conscious working-class reappropriation of productive forces.[31] As always, however, these questions have, and can only have, a partial answer. This process is in motion, but the articulation only gains meaning on the terrain of the totality of relations of force, because against the successive working-class reappropriations of productive forces is unleashed all the power of the capitalist devastation of the worker vanguards and the articulations of the workers' struggle. Public spending, its articulations, its tendencies, its planned priorities, and the rationality of command that runs throughout it constitute one of the fundamental weapons of capital. Public spending has introduced into social accumulation (and the social struggle of the workers) the legitimacy of the capitalist business enterprise founded on the rate of profit and the State guarantee of an accumulation for profit. Public spending has organized the community of labor in order to destroy its possible political form and subject it entirely to the legitimacy of the rate of profit—a new worker world capable of communism is submitted to the dead fetish of a falling rate of profit.

The effects of State action against the revolutionary recomposition of the new subject of production can thus only be combated on the terrain of the totality. Only the living collective legitimation of the communist reappropriation of productive forces by the proletariat, by living labor, that unique independent productive force, can respond to the legitimacy of the capitalist State in its process of restructuring. When, necessarily, the legitimacy of the State is articulated with terror and the power of devastation against the working class, only the struggle for power—power against power, terror against terror—can give dignity to the workers' struggle. The entire capitalist restructuring is centered (at all costs) on the project to destroy the new composition of productive social labor and its political potentiality. The entire process of institutional restructuring is equally directed toward the mediation between old formal instances of legality and newly emergent functional necessities in order to make itself effective. The normative soul of these processes of capitalist rearrangement is the law of the falling rate of profit, and the recognition that, as Marx says, the death knell is sounding for the civilization of capital. The tension here between the State and the new proletarian subject cannot but be destructive. If on capital's side everything is conceived in the short term and the will to destruction stinks of pessimism and delusion, however, on the workers' side the will to destruction is terrible because it is articulated with the hope and the certainty that in the long run we will win out. Today the analysis of power from the class point of view holds less and less interest. What is fundamental is instead the attention to the practices of the new proletarian subject and the permanent illegality of its daily behavior. The analysis of power as an analysis of the political "response" to the boss only comes after this.

Further Considerations on the Accumulation and Legitimation Functions of Public Spending

"Planning is done by big business for big business": This is not true today nor was it true yesterday. Neither the *économie concertée* nor the various forms of mixed economy can ever really be reduced to this. That the logic of the business enterprise dominates and legitimates planning processes does not mean that these have ever been simply projections of the immediate interests of the big capitalist. Rather, planning involves mediating among social forces, determining the materiality of the infrastructures of production, stimulating the comprehensive productivity of the system, and ascribing the (active or passive) power of the organization of the social circulation of commodities centrally to the power of the State. Public spending is the cost of these operations together and, as a characteristic of the wage response to the State activity in the field of programming, it certainly cannot simply be subsumed under the will of big capital.[32] Planning primarily involves reproposing, by means of organizational mediation, a terrain of the composition of class conflicts. We should keep in mind that at these levels of class struggle, the dual development intrinsic to the capitalist logic of rule is completely affirmed.[33]

All of this, though, seems to be harking back to old times, when there was a reformist hope that the conflicts were really mediable and that the reorganization of the labor market through a mediation between productive social functions and social welfare could be sustained within foreseeable and controllable proportions. In fact, every highly developed capitalist country has witnessed the crisis of this project. The economic potential of the new proletarian subject has never been reined in by the planned project and where this subject has not succeeded in manifesting itself as continuous struggle, it has nonetheless been present in the form of qualitative and quantitative insubordination on the level of the wage. Keynesianism, the Keynesian utopia, and that "alternative" presented by the Keynesian left have been burned by this tendency of class struggle.[34] Social accumulation and business legitimation are thus distinguished in hostile terms: public spending finances the social struggles rather than financing the mediation between social accumulation and business legitimation.

At this point, and on the basis of these presuppositions, capital translates the crisis into restructuring, or more precisely, it casts crisis in the guise of restructuring. The fundamental element of the capitalist strategy consists in shattering the nexus between social accumulation and legitimation, and therefore transforming public spending into a schema of the destruction (when possible, otherwise the containment) of the massive proletarian presence in society, and the encouragement of productive models adequate to the necessary rates of profit. The project seeks to block the rising cost of social labor and exploit widely without paying for it (or rather paying the simple costs of the "natural" reproduction of social labor), by lowering necessary social labor and raising surplus social labor. At this point, public spending, which has been forced to grow in an extraordinary way by both the pressure of the working class and the capitalist recognition of the essential character of general social industriousness, destroys its own ambiguity. Public spending gradually transforms itself into an expression not of the theory of value but of its capitalist destruction; it must be a contemporary element of the capitalist practice of command.

If we take up the terms of the discourse more concretely, this means carrying the discussion to a higher level of abstraction, showing the essential passage of the worker (and capitalist) supersession of the barrier of the law of value at the very moment that it is being realized. (See the Epilogue of Roman Rosdolsky's *The Making of Marx's 'Capital.'*) The socialization of productive labor and the complete domination of the law of value over society, in other words, historically determine a set of State activities that negate the spontaneous levels of the law of value—and this is equally true in both the "socialist" and the highly developed capitalist societies.[35] In both cases the law of value only functions under the State's "enforced control." We call this "bureaucratization" in the socialist societies and "authoritarianism" in the capitalist, but the result is no different. We should not fall into any Weberian illusions here, as if the advent of a charismatic innovation could free the functioning of the law of value and guarantee the plan. The fact is that in the dialectic of productive relations and productive forces, the law of value acts as a fundamental term of the organization of exploitation. Its realization also realizes exploitation and determines absolutely particular conditions of insubordinate resistances in such a way that the spontaneity of the functioning of the law is heavily adjusted, because it is not a definitive productive arrangement but an obstacle to the expansion of the productive force that its own realization determines. Only command, then, improbably taking on the expression of social labor, represents at this point the continuance of the law of value, where all the practices of the new proletarian subject express instead, spontaneously, the intolerance of and rebellion against this barrier blocking productive force.

Capital and its collective rationality know all this and act on the basis of it. This is where public spending is reformed in the repressive irrationality of capitalist command. This is also, however, where the critique of political economy (which has been worn out along with the law of value) gives way to "the critique of politics" *tout court*—not a critique of politics that looks simply to political forces but one that primarily addresses the problem of command and its institutional organization, functional to social production. It is also possible here to show the functional and structural contradictions that the demise of the law of value and the substitution of the political law of planning (and restructuring) for market calculation open for the workers' struggle.[36]

The problematic of public spending now becomes the terrain of a worker critique insofar as the struggle over the relative social wage can be immediately functional to the deepening of the institutional contradictions and the struggle against the institutions. Critique of political economy versus critique of politics versus critique of administration, planning, and restructuring—this is the path we are traveling.

On the other hand, all the determinations of State practices against the working class, which develop in the specific realm of restructuring but already define tendencies for the midterm future, converge on this point: destroy every illusion of planning in terms of the realization of the law of value and, on the contrary, act on internal lines toward the devastation of the unitary potential of the proletariat as a productive and revolutionary force. Public spending must essentially guarantee a process of arbitrary segmentation of labor-power by destroying every relationship between production and qualification, and every valorizing sequence between comprehensive social formation and the value of production, and thereby determine not so much a division between labor-power and the reserve labor force but a ferocious division between different levels of labor-power, opposed in terms of wage differences.[37] The comprehensive rigidity of public spending, which has already been conceded, must here be rearticulated according to the schemas of command (in other words, restructuring), not primarily for the increase of profit but rather for the permanence of the capitalist mode of production.

In this situation every reformist operation, however conceived, loses credibility in the space of a morning. There is no more room here for opposing the State and the worker objectives on the social wage: this space has been destroyed by the subsumption of public spending entirely under the criterion of business enterprise legitimation. Every case of reform results in a capitalist attack on worker socialization and an attempt to destroy the social form of production. All the dysfunctions and disarticulations of the administration, in which reformist practice is continually more deeply rooted, are not defined on an abstractly rational terrain but on a terrain that is functional *insofar as* it is determined by specific structural necessities that are exclusively determined by the relations fixed by class struggle.[38] Administrative action is definitively irrational insofar as its rationality cannot reside in the social functioning of the law of value but simply in the practical power of capitalist command. Administrative rationality does not become terror, it is terror. Strip capitalist society of its only rationality, that which is grounded in the greediness of exploitation, and you have this baroque monster of provocation and devastation.

Restructuring does not resolve but accentuates the capitalist crisis. The analysis of public spending demonstrates this in the clearest of terms. Public spending is cast in the contradictory relationship between the pressure to maintain the standard of capitalist profitability and the necessity to respond in some way to the wage demands of an always more imposing social labor-power, thus grasping the processes of social accumulation in the form of the wage. In other words, public spending bridges the chasm between the collapse of the historic barrier of the law of value and the capitalist determination to make the law of value hold at all costs, and in determinate proportions. This relationship cannot be sustained, no matter what shaky supports reformism might offer. Between the emergence of a new mode of production—internal to a new composition of the working class—and the enforced persistence of the capitalist rule of command there is continually less possibility of mediation.

The crisis of public spending should be privileged in the analysis because it presents both the positive (worker, collective) and the negative (capitalist command) factors of the general crisis. It is clear, however, that here the analysis of the crisis brings us directly back to the figure of the State and the collapse of its dignity as mediator of capitalist production. In this case, too, the Marxian paradox is realized: the more the State resolves the conflict between civil society and the force to command social production completely within itself, the more this resolution proves to be dialectically uncertain, and the more the working class shows in real terms its hegemony over society. The revolutionary project for communism lives this contradiction and this possibility.

The Ideological Collapse of the Institutional Workers' Movement: Reformism and Repression

The workers' movement, insofar as it is an institutional movement, appears today as revisionist in ideology, reformist in project, and technocratic in practice. Let us look at the effects of this situation point by point.

In Italy, the ideological revisionism of the institutional workers' movement has a long history. In certain respects this is a Gramscian history. Gramsci's conception of hegemony within and over civil society was a real innovation with respect to the Marxian and Leninist conceptions of the State. (See Norberto Bobbio, "Gramsci and the Conception of Civil Society.") On the basis of this conception, there is first of all and fundamentally a space of ideological mediation entrusted to the social force of the workers' movement as a condition of a revolutionary process that attacks the heart of the social productive forces and according to models of comprehensive adherence. All of this has a dignity that the revisionism that afflicts the proposal cannot deny. This corresponds, furthermore, to a determinate phase of the development of productive forces in Italy (that is, the prefascist era), and consequently is reproposed as a response to the necessities of antifascist political action. The revisionism of the Gramscian proposal is not, then, what makes the thematic of the institutional workers' movement ideologically dangerous. What is dangerous is rather the contemporary usage of formulas more or less derived from Gramsci. The proposal of hegemony requires a definition of civil society, but today civil society is dead: it has been subsumed into capitalist development and reformulated by the social unity of productive labor. A hegemonic process is, in this situation, completely subordinated to the compact insistence of the social command of capital for profit—command that reorganizes civil society and makes it exist only as a projection of the production process and the structure of power. Over the collapse of the image of civil society unfold the conceptions of alliances, politics maneuvered in the "mixed economy," and the ideological pressure on the middle classes. The reality of the class struggle, however, demonstrates the continuity of the terrain of insubordination and the tendential unification of the proletarian subject in the struggle against the State.

On the other hand, what is left of the discourse that was proposed by revisionism on the terrain of institutional relations and mediations, and that is necessary and complementary to the discourse on tactics? What is left of the discourse on the continuity of the democratic struggle and the struggle for socialism, and on the predisposition of the contemporary constitutional structures to support such a continuity of struggles? The frameworks of not only social relations but also institutional relations have unraveled to such an extent in the crisis of the late-capitalist State that the terrain of the constitutional reality has necessarily been superseded and distorted by the power of the bourgeoisie, the fundamental principles of democratic cohabitation have been selected on the basis of consensus, and the problem of consensus has been systematically resolved in terms predisposed to specific lines of conduct, be they authoritarian or terroristic. Today as never before the framework of legitimacy, the authoritative sources, and the very process of the material validation of power are posed so far outside the schema of democratic legitimation that, just as Luxemburg foresaw, radical democratic struggle, far from being a first stage, becomes the fundamental material of the workers' struggle.

The working-class struggle puts the functioning of the law of value in definitive crisis, not only in the sense that its practices determine and reinforce the functioning of the law of the tendential fall of the rate of profit, but in the even more profound sense of destabilizing the very terms on which the law holds, in other words, taking away the meaning of the relation between necessary labor and surplus labor (which, as Marx says, is in the final instance the foundation of everything). At this very moment, socialism becomes impossible. Socialism and all the socialist utopias try to put forth the actual realization of the law of value, which amounts to saying the complete real subsumption of social labor into capital. This is possible, however, only in terms of the dialectic of the classes, only as a moment of class struggle. At this point, all the variants of the socialist utopia, both the objectivist ones (socialism as the socialization of the means of production and the rationalization of command) and the subjectivist ones (the new mode of production, cooperation, participation, comanagement, and so forth), are put in crisis, because the law of value is never realized except by at the same time shattering itself apart, imposing at an extremely high level the new antagonism among capitalist labor, command (however legitimated), and the set of productive social forces of the proletariat.

The collapse of the reformist model, tied to the ideology of the planned realization of the law of value, still appears, and even more heavily at this point. It is sufficient to look again at the problematic of public spending, how it is posed from a reformist perspective, and what new antagonisms the reformist will create. Public spending is seen by the reformists as spending that is either directly or indirectly productive. Correctly, they tend to rationalize its management, mold it in terms of the schemas of priorities, and use it to guide development and influence its direction. As we have seen, however, beyond these formal criteria, there is a contradiction between the form of social accumulation and the source (measure and proportion) of its legitimation — a class contradiction that demonstrates both the tendential unification of the productive social subject and the irrationality of the criterion of the proposed business enterprise legitimation *by its own standards.* As the contradiction becomes subjective in class terms it also becomes explosive. The pressure on public spending becomes a wage pressure, as the political pressure of the working class on the relative wage and — principally and specifically in the present period — the struggle against capitalist labor becomes a worker allusion to the new emerging productive force, which demands payment as such.

In this web of contradictions the attempt to rationalize public spending — a rationalization that must necessarily follow business parameters and explain the business figure of the State — becomes immediately repressive. This happens not so much because it employs the instruments of the repressive power of the State (and all its multiplying separate bodies) to this end, but because it uses them within the intensity of an unresolvable structural contradiction. If socialism is impossible, reformism is even more so. Every reformist practice, in fact, is immediately repressive.[39]

It begins to become clear here that the revisionism and reformism of the official workers' movement suffer not only the blow of the collapse of their conception of class relations. Beyond the unreasonableness of their project there is the unreasonableness of a will positively directed, whatever the costs, toward the realization of an old design. The adhesion to the project of capitalist restructuring on the part of this reformism follows from the necessity to repress actively the proletarian subject that is coming together, straining the State budget, demanding payment for extorted social labor, and putting pressure on the barrier of the order constituted to legitimate the empire of business profit over all aspects of social cooperation. Actively repressing the proletarian source, restructuring the productive social subject, segmenting the markets of labor-power, guaranteeing the processes of mobility that destroy workers' power, and marginalizing terroristically entire social strata—these operations have become, in Italy as in all capitalist countries under social-democratic management, the foundation and the content of reformism. The content of the "first phase" of reformism, which is being perpetuated all over, becomes the foundation of the will to repropose an impossible socialism! The collapse of the ideological project is here completely indistinguishable from the contemporary repressive practices of reformism.

These are the reasons, once again, for the increasing practices of class division, primarily in the sector of productive intelligence that, as it has become more social and more concentrated in the service industries, has begun to represent the true connective tissue and the central nervous system of the processes of the social accumulation of capital. Denying or masking the class nature of these new roles and sectors, and mystifying their functions by casting them back into the old dimension of the "middle classes," are fundamental operations. They are not painless operations, however, because although they are directly social functions of productive force, their operation is decreasingly legitimated *socially*, and instead the *authoritarian* legitimation of their role is ever more heavily felt. This is their proposition and imposition to be the *Träger* or supports of the bureaucratic-terroristic mediation of socialism with an authoritarian face, a productive rationality that reproduces the dead logic of the business enterprise and mystifies the social density of the process of accumulation, negating the very nature of their productive labor and reducing it to the parameters of command, the subordinated and subordinating function. As the roles of the State administration are increasingly implicated in the contradiction they create, the crisis of reformism becomes ever more serious. The technocratic figure that is increasingly attributed to State administration also experiences a crisis, subjectively, as the functionality of its rationalizing practices is shown to be directly terroristic.

In Italy, for example, the "historic compromise" entirely presents the advanced form of the social-democratic figure of the State for the management of the capitalist crisis. The entrance of the Italian Communist party (and probably of all the communist parties of Latin Mediterranean Europe) into the block of power of European social democracy changes all the political terms of the class struggle. As for the figure of the State, we have begun to see in what sense the demands of command increasingly define the class struggle.

The point of intersection of the development of reformism and the structure of the State has probably already been reached. From now on, the class point of view must keep in mind this new political synthesis. This, in the long run, is certainly the enemy to attack.

Old Tactic for a New Strategy

Why should we choose public spending as the topos for our discussion of the general problematic of the State? Because around the issue of public spending, the analysis of the objective contradictions, which constrain capitalist restructuring and the reformist State, can be transformed into a subjective terrain. This is a potentially subjective terrain in that it is the terrain of wage struggle, with all the political qualities that theorists like Rosa Luxemburg have to attribute to the struggle over the relative wage. Public spending corresponds on one hand to the social terrain of production, and on another hand to the terrain of the social wage. It corresponds, in short, to an (ever more relevant) aspect of the expression of social capital in its internal dialectic and thus poses the problem of worker antagonism within the relationship between society and the State. The problematic of public spending indicates both a form of the capitalist subsumption of labor and the fabric on which the antagonism can be determined subjectively.

It is not enough to insist on the opposition that has opened in the society of mature capitalism between the accomplished arrangement of relations of domination for exploitation and the "worker society" that, in an always more continuous and complete way, creates the totality of social wealth — between, in other words, a formed economy and a forming economy (like the ancient distinction between *natura naturata* and *natura naturans*).[40] Neither is it sufficient to insist on the enormous progress of directly and indirectly productive social labor, and pose it against the process of social accumulation, which is firmly in the capitalist hands. Marx saw this very clearly (*Grundrisse*, pp. 690–711). These discussions on machinery, Roman Rosdolsky observes while reading the *Grundrisse*, "despite the fact that they were written more than a hundred years ago, still generate a feeling of awe and excitement, containing as they do some of the boldest visions attained by the human imagination" (*The Making of Marx's 'Capital,'* p. 425). Marx already saw the end of the material barrier of the law of value, the automation of productive force, and the liberation of innovative forces as a material and immediate precondition of the construction of communism.

This, however, is not enough. Subjectivity here becomes, and cannot help but become, the keystone of the process. Within the possibility of communism is an enormous set of needs and desires that begin to be liberated. Individually, we can only achieve "rough" prefigurations of them, Marx suggests. (See the chapters titled "Private Property and Communism" in the *Economic and Philosophic Manuscripts of 1844* and "Communism" in *The German Ideology*.) The only real prefiguration we can collectively accomplish, however, is through struggle. Assuming a terrain of struggle does not, and cannot, exhaust the totality, nor can it allude to a significant set of realized needs. Assuming the struggle is assuming first of all the negative need for destruction. The wage is a terrain of struggle that, reproposed at every level, can set off the explosive potential of needs and desires. Only at this point, then, does quantity pass into quality in such a way that innovation, proposition, and a desiring restlessness are unleashed. Our task cannot be the prophecy of the future but the identification of the contradiction on which the future may be realized. With a breadth and intensity that no individual can achieve, the masses know how to produce. "The social wage against the State" is not, therefore, a strategy but the practical identification of a terrain of struggle, on the basis of the determinations of the insoluble contradictions of reformism and power, and in the theoretical certainty that every open and conscious class struggle is today immediately and necessarily a struggle for communism. On the terrain of public spending, the old tactic of the struggle over the relative wage opens the proposal that leads to the strategy of communism. Every mass space constructed by the struggle today cannot but be a breach out of which rises the mass of desires contained and repressed by the mode of social production for capitalist accumulation. We see it in everyday life: how many and how intense these desires, how impatient and how resounding their force of expression! All this is due to the form of capitalist production, the socialization of exploitation, and the weight and totality of the process of the capitalist irrationalization of social relations. It is also, however, due to the resistance and the recognition of the generality of exploitation on the part of the great mass of laborers. The wage is the category in which capital grasps and mystifies, in a fundamental form, the complex of political, social, historical, and human aspects of the proletariat. Today capital has been constrained to marshal the wage, or a large part of it, in the form of public spending. Here, primarily, the contradictions can explode again — the social wage against the State.

Some elements show that, in a new form, the contradictions are already exploding. Resistance to the expropriation of the surplus value of social production is no longer exercised simply in the old forms of trade-union defense, directly planted in the large factories; instead, new forms of political positioning and attack immediately address social levels of accumulation. The forms of struggle for "autoreduction" in Italy, for example, are primarily an expansion of the workers' wage struggle.[41] This, however, is not the only new element emerging. Gradually, as class consciousness grows, so too grows the awareness of a new terrain of struggle, across the entire social plane. The worker reappropriation of labor time and free time, which has always developed in the factories, develops today in the struggle of social reappropriation and the struggle over the social wage. Autoreduction is the last, highest form of the struggle of the mass worker, and the first figure in which the social reappropriation of wealth is determined on the basis of the new proletarian subject of the class struggle — the negation and sublation of the mass worker.[42]

The passages of the dialectic of class composition are given here in subjective form. Resistance, autoreduction, appropriation: these forms of struggle run along the same path as the transformation of class composition. This is undoubtedly and immediately the terrain of the social wage. These political initiatives are oriented toward exacerbating the contradictions that capitalist command undergoes on this terrain. The three forms of struggle dovetail in a progressive way: the second transforms into an attack on the limits of the first, and thus the third with respect to the second. Through these qualitative passages the elements of class composition are transformed into reality and tend toward political consciousness and will. The wealth of the working class becomes palpable and class consciousness takes its own development as its primary objective. Thus the bad characteristics of a dialectic that is otherwise always unfinished and inconclusive are resolved. Mediation and immediacy begin to approach one another when the material terrain of the mediations of consciousness is oriented toward the direct recuperation of wealth and power.

All of this has practical value to the extent that the social worker expands its power and that capitalist socialization is inverted in the social recomposition of the proletariat, through the subjectivization of abstract labor. There are also, however, a series of examples of the communist struggle over the social wage to be found in the large factories, amid the highest levels of proletarian consciousness and activity. Here the relationship between the social power of production and capitalist command is located along the axes of the organization of labor and the structure of fixed capital. In this case, too, during the most recent struggles and strikes in Italy, the collective will of reappropriation has managed to express itself in terms of power: taking control of the factories, putting them to work not to produce but to demonstrate positively the associative productive power of the working class in preparing the best possibilities of sabotage and struggle in the near future. This is what has been accomplished. Worker consciousness has not produced a fixed model but rather indicated a collective, mass path for deepening the struggle. At the social level and in the factories, the will for reappropriation realizes the worker tendency toward communism to the extent that through mass action it liquidates the implacably hostile power of the socialist mediation of social rule. When the single episodes of this project are consolidated in the field of appropriation, the struggle over the social wage demonstrates the worker tendency to transform the use of specific new contradictions of the capitalist mechanism of social accumulation in the struggle for power, in the struggle for communism.

Another element of the political and structural contradictions of public spending that is extremely important relates to the analysis of the State and the roles played by administrative employees in the management of spending. This involves a deepening of the critique of the political economy of administration. Given, as we have emphasized several times, that the role of the State becomes ever more internal and structural to the development of accumulation, we should investigate which contradictions are related to the State management of social capital. The tendency to define these administrative roles as productive was already indicated paradoxically by the heavy pressure capital placed on them to be productive. This is not simply bureaucratic rationalization. Here the functioning of the administration becomes indirectly productive (in the proper sense, that is, productive of surplus value), because the functioning of administration processes links social accumulation to processes of business legitimation. The role of the administrative employees becomes immediately contradictory at this point, because on one hand they constitute a moment of the process of social labor, but on the other hand they are required to manage that labor for profit. Expanding and ensuring the productivity of public administration means, in the final instance, solving this contradiction in completely capitalist terms of efficiency. The contradiction, however, is very large. In the first place, in fact, the awareness of being a participant in the productive social fabric assumes an always greater extension, driven by the effort to perfect the State machine. In the second place, however, the comprehensive lack of rationality in the capitalist command over the State apparatus brings on moments of crisis, and at times elements of insubordination. Certainly, the ideology of participation, technocracy, and reformist and bureaucratic socialism has a significant impact on employees in these social strata, but perhaps its influence is not complete, or perhaps it can be challenged and defeated on the basis of contradictions and antagonisms arising from capitalist socialization. This ideology is, in any case, vulnerable to being contested and, to a certain extent, overturned by the organization and action of the proletariat.

It makes no sense, however, to talk about reappropriation in this case. That would amount to proposing a socialist alternative that preserves State command! What must be accomplished at this level is rather the awareness of the participation of certain administrative sectors and employees in the social community of worker production, and thus the awareness of the possibilities of struggle even on the enemy's terrain. The struggles within the administration will be more like the activities of spies and informants, reporting on the movements of the enemy and provoking disruptions. This is the only way to avoid the socialist utopia that proposes "alternative" uses of State command and State apparatuses and thus to unveil the mystifications of the "revolution from above." What is proposed instead, then, is a strategy of the refusal of command and a tactic of the anomalous usage of administrative functions — as a practice of class struggle within the administration. All of this is only possible once it is recognized that administrative functions are in fact productive — indirectly productive, yes, but nonetheless productive of surplus value.

Last but not least, on the basis of an analysis of public spending, we can begin to bring political tactics together with lines of strategy, and, moreover, we can begin to propose a study of the political composition of the working class, with particular attention to the new strata that have come to be invested by the socialization of the mode of production and the proletarianization of their conditions of life and struggle. The politics of public spending, as it is further expanded as a system of social control, on one hand invests new social sectors, bringing them potentially into conflict with the State, and on the other hand creates class contradictions within the State machine, among the administrative employees of the State. Recognizing these phenomena clearly and proceeding in research and political practice — now more analytically than we were able to before — can bring about significant innovations in class analysis. The Marxian terms of the potential discussion are more or less given, but the creative deepening of the analysis still remains to be done. We must give the subjects of the State administration — those who work for the State, who are both subjects of exploitation and transmitters of capitalist command — the lead in this discussion. This project would involve an analysis of the State, a critique of politics and administration, and a new step forward in the analysis of the political composition of the working class — all of this against the reformist conceptions of power, the State, and administrative functions.

III

PART

S I X

Postmodern Law and the Withering of Civil Society

WITH THE end of the 1970s, there also ended particular conceptions of worker subjectivity, class struggle, and leftist politics in general. The 1980s seemed in many respects one long celebration of the definitive victory of capital over labor, from the neoliberal economic revolutions of Reagan and Thatcher in the early eighties to the "death of communism" dramatized by the fall of the Berlin Wall in 1989. Labor seemed to disappear from the scene while capital assumed the role of the primary productive force. The master had finally put an end to that annoying struggle and simply done away with the slave.

In many respects, the dialectic has indeed ended. We have undoubtedly entered a new era, one that perhaps was set irreversibly in motion by the uprisings of 1968, but that has revealed its particular forms increasingly clearly through the 1970s, 1980s, and early 1990s. That we have entered a new era, however (let us call it postmodern to at least mark its novelty), does not mean that every aspect of the social horizon has changed. It does not mean, for example, that labor has ceased to be the locus of social production or that class struggle has vanished. No one will deny that capitalist production still exploits labor-power; and in increasingly intense forms. Certainly, as long as there is exploitation of productive force, social antagonisms will emerge, link together in constellations of resistances, and tend toward the constitution of an alternative power. It is the primary challenge facing communist theory, then, a challenge we hope to begin to address in the remaining chapters of this work, to register the contours of this new era, mark the new locuses of social antagonism, highlight the figures of new subjectivities, and trace the lineages of the new emerging constituent power.

We begin our contribution to this task, however, not by leaping directly to the proposal of a project, but, as Marx did, by reading and critiquing the theory and practice of capital. Marx began by reading Smith and Ricardo and studying English factory legislation; in the previous chapters of this work, and in another era, we focused on the work of authors such as Keynes and Kelsen, analyzing the passage from the rights State to the social State; now, we propose to read the contemporary juridical and economic practices of the State in the context of the work of John Rawls, Richard Rorty, Charles Taylor, and others. We approach these authors not with any interest in exegesis, but rather to see what we can learn from them about the contemporary capitalist State-form, its deployments of power, its mechanisms of exploitation, and its production of social antagonisms. This will give us a solid standpoint from which to recognize the social subjectivities that emerge on this new terrain, and pose the contemporary potentialities of communism.

Rawls and the Revolution

John Rawls presents his work as a project to establish and articulate a reasonable and formal foundation for the theory of justice and democracy in such a way that the validity of his claims rests solely on the necessary connections in the unfolding of an ideal moral theory, a "moral geometry" (*A Theory of Justice*, p. 121). Rawls invites us to accept or reject his vision of the just basic structure of society on the basis of the philosophical coherence and moral necessity of the founding contractual moment and the procedure it puts in motion. Many of Rawls's critics focus on the philosophical inadequacy of this transcendental foundation by drawing into question the adequacy of a universal moral theory *sub specie aeternitatis*.[1] Other critics concentrate on the significant presuppositions that such a foundation hides: they argue that the founding rational principles only mask the relationships of force and domination that effectively organize society.[2] Although the critique of Rawls's idealist asceticism is certainly appropriate and important, what is compelling and exciting to us in Rawls's project, on the contrary, is precisely his *passion* for liberty and equality, a passion that often gets lost in the abstract passages of the argument. We propose reading *A Theory of Justice*, then, against the grain of Rawls's "moral geometry," treating it as a political project in step with the times and engaged in forging a feasible juridical arrangement to order the State. We want to read Rawls politically; that is, to bring to light the power relations suggested by his theory in the context of the political developments of recent decades.[3]

Once we pose Rawls's work on a political terrain, in fact, once we break the enchanting spell of its reasonable argument, we immediately recognize that the text is not of a piece, is not a geometrically ordered whole, but is rather comprised of an equivocal mixture of political directions and developments that can sustain diverse and often conflicting interpretations. We will focus in this chapter on two interpretations that have enjoyed particular prominence during the 1980s, both in Rawls's own writing[4] and in the work of his various critics: first, a postmodern interpretation that proposes the systematic juridical ordering of a thin State, abstracted from the differences and conflicts of society; and second, a communitarian interpretation that leads to a strong conception of the State, capable of effectively subsuming the social field within its order.

Let us begin with what might at first seem an obscure point in order to gain a fresh perspective on the system. At various points in the text Rawls relates his theory to the revolutionary proposition and articulation of justice. What Rawls wants to achieve in the act of choosing the principles of justice is the simulation or the subsumption of the revolutionary moment: "We can associate the traditional ideas of liberty, equality, and fraternity with the democratic interpretation of the two principles as follows: liberty corresponds to the first principle, equality to the idea of equality in the first principle together with equality of fair opportunity, and fraternity to the difference principle" (p. 106). The French Revolution takes form in the original position and, even though it is framed in terms of a rational choice, it appears as an intuition, an epiphany of social justice. The revolutionary moment is frozen as an image in the hypothetical context of the original position. This static moment is the core of Part I of *A Theory of Justice*, the ideal theory of justice.

In Part II, however, in order to set the revolution marching forward, to simulate its diachronic unfolding, Rawls moves from the French to the American experience. "The idea of a four-stage sequence is suggested by the United States Constitution and its history" (p. 196 n). The original position corresponds to the establishment of identity and principles, the Declaration of Independence and the Bill of Rights. At the second stage of the sequence the constituent assembly or the constitutional convention is convened. Here the constituent members choose the Constitution that best represents the principles of justice. In the next stage, the legislative stage, the social and economic policies of the nation are chosen. The final stage, then, is the application of rules to particular cases. With each stage in this sequence the veil of ignorance is partially lifted so that by the time we arrive at the direct application of the laws by judges and administrators to particular cases, no information is excluded. This description of the genetic mechanism of social institutions, tracing the development of the American Constitution, is designed to show the continuity of the complex passage from ideal and formal theory to real political practice.

As soon as Rawls invokes the French and the American experiences, however, he blunts their impact: the profound rupture of the revolutionary moment is flattened onto a formal structure and the historical displacements operated by dynamic practical forces are comprehended or subsumed within formal passages—in short, the constituent power of the revolution is normalized within an ideal formal procedure. The revolution is no longer an event. There is no explosion of antagonism, but rather the social conflicts are subsumed within the order of a stable equilibrium. Rawls detemporalizes the ruptures of innovative and creative forces, and formalizes them in a hypothetical or ideal contractual procedure: a passage without crisis. It is not a real social power that formulates the constitution and liberates society, but a formal dynamic of procedures, a depopulated constituent assembly—this is where the institutions are arranged.[5] The synchronic rupture of the revolution is deprived of its material contents and the diachronic dynamic is denied any real movement. The formal mechanisms of the constitutional procedure serve to tame the savage energy of the revolution and put them to work.

These specific references to the French and American revolutions may be casual and even incidental in Rawls's argument, but the relation between the theory of justice and the power and creativity of democratic social forces is necessary and central. Rawls recognizes the passional core of society in his conception of our "sense of justice," our common yearning for liberty, equality, and fraternity. Our sense of justice is the revolution latent in society, the motor that animates it as a living whole. The choice of the principles of justice and the subsequent procedural development, then, appear as a perpetual reenactment of the foundational moment and the historical unfolding of the revolutionary experience in the basic structure of society. This is not to claim that Rawls is revolutionary, but simply that his argument is supported by the idea or image of a democratic constituent power. Here lies the rhetorical force behind Rawls's appeal for social reform, for liberty and equality. Without the vision and dynamic of the democratic revolution at the heart of the theory, or at least as a foundational image integrated into the structure of its formal system, the rationalist arguments of right would carry no weight and the very aspirations that the project alludes to would fall flat. Through the subsumption of the constituent power of social forces into the constituted power of the juridical system, Rawls tries to pose an immanent solution to the traditional juridical problem of the sources of right. The theory of justice does not rely on a transcendental source of normative production; there is no unconditioned and categorical imperative nor any *Grundnorm* that founds the system; rather, through a generic and formalized reference to creative social forces, Rawls poses a system of right with an immanent source of production. The procedural system itself comprehends the productive dynamic, and then makes it disappear within its formal structure. (We will return to this process in more detail shortly in "The Genius of the System: Reflection and Equilibrium.")

As soon as we descend from the heights of ideal moral theory, however, and touch our feet back to earth, we see that the reality of the revolution cannot be swallowed whole and assimilated so easily. Rawls's system is destined to be plagued by indigestion. The conception of the revolution as the author of the just constitution, the reliance on our sense of justice, our passion for liberty, equality, and fraternity indicate that the juridical system is founded on creative social activity, on what Marx calls living labor. Living labor, however, poses a tragic dilemma for constitutionalism. On one hand, living labor is the constituent power of society. It presents itself as the creative, vital locus, a dynamic factory of values and norms. At the same time, however, living labor presents a critique of any constituted power, of any fixed constitutional order. In the production of new norms, living labor destabilizes the dead structures of society, devouring all of the existing norms that come in its path. Insofar as it is the source of right, living labor is, at its very essence, the radical critique of law. Constitutionalism has to regard such creative social activity as a savage force, a ferocious and powerful beast—a beast that, as Hegel pointed out, must be tamed.

This dilemma gives rise to an alternative in Rawls's work and in the various interpretations of it. We can identify one line of development that seeks progressively to exclude the social forces of living labor from the liberal juridical system and thus leads to a stable and functional machine of order, but lacks the social depth and subjective force required for State authority. On the other hand, a second tendency, arising partly in response to the inadequacies of the first, seeks not to avoid but to harness and tame the power of living labor within the confines of a more substantial State structure; this effort, however, brings back into play the dangerous and destabilizing powers of creative social forces. We will analyze the first tendency in terms of a postmodern interpretation of Rawls's liberalism, and the second in the context of a communitarian perspective on his theory. These various arguments will give us a window through which to see the strange journeys that living labor and constituent power went through in the 1980s, exiled from the realm of juridical order only to reappear, inevitably, at its very heart.

Postmodern Law and the Ghost of Labor in the Constitution

Locating *A Theory of Justice* as a defense of Welfare State policies has become a truism, an almost obligatory point of departure for any political analysis of Rawls's work. In contrast to Robert Nozick's market-based libertarian moral theory, this claim certainly seems to hold. When we look more closely, however, Rawls's theory occupies an ambiguous and even contradictory position with respect to the tendencies of the modern Welfare State. To the extent that Rawls presents a theory of distributive justice that poses questions of redress and desert as issues of public policy and morality it is true that his work constitutes a philosophical defense of a State-centered policy of social assistance. For example, Rawls describes four branches of government required for distributive justice (pp. 276–77). Distribution, of course, should be understood in a very broad sense in this context: at the same time that the State sets in motion an economic distribution of wealth and commodities, it also promotes both a specific moral distribution of rights, responsibilities, and obligations and a directly political distribution of advantages and disadvantages.[6] In this way, then, Rawls takes up the political tendency whereby the State constructs systems of public assistence, initiated to a certain extent by Bismarck, and raises it to the transcendental plane of moral theory: the role of the State in the systems of distribution is not based on a political choice located in a particular historical context, but a moral choice based on philosophical principle.[7] Rawls's vision of the just basic structure of society is realized in a State that distributes through a series of regular institutional procedures.

The distributive function, however, is not the exclusive, nor even the principal, element that constitutes the modern Welfare State. The Welfare State is defined by its intervention not only in the realm of distribution but more important in that of production. In this sense, Rawls's work seems to run counter to the historical movement of the Welfare State. The political institutions inaugurated with the New Deal and the Keynesian and Fordist mechanisms that have governed the evolutions of the State-form through much of the twentieth century pose production as the epicenter of the economic and political constitution of capitalist societies. The Welfare State must harness production within a stable process of social and economic development. As we hope to have made clear in chapter 3, the development of the Welfare State as a social State through the course of the twentieth century has involved primarily a process of the constitutionalization of labor, that is, the mediation and ordering of the productive and antagonistic forces of labor within the juridical constitution of the State while at the same time grounding that constitution on these very forces of labor. It is now widely recognized that this shift was so broad that in various countries from the 1930s or 1940s onward it effectively determined a new constitutional regime.[8]

Rawls, however, does not address the need of the State to engage labor and intervene in production. Robert Paul Wolff, in fact, locates the primary shortcoming of *A Theory of Justice* in Rawls's "failure to focus squarely on the structure of *production* in the economy [concentrating rather] on alternative patterns of *distribution*" (*Understanding Rawls*, p. 207). We can broaden Wolff's economic assertion by viewing production in the large sense, just as we posed distribution in a broad sense: Rawls equally neglects the economic production of commodities and the juridical production of rights and norms. He gives no consideration to the fundamental role of labor either in economic relationships or in the juridical constitution. Wolff considers this limitation of Rawls's focus a mystification: "By focusing exclusively on distribution rather than on production, Rawls obscures the real roots of that distribution" (p. 210). When Rawls ignores the productive base, then, he violates not only one of the primary precepts of traditional political economy, but also the fundamental principle of the political ordering of the Welfare State: he undercuts and mystifies the liberal theory of distribution by neglecting its productive source. In this sense, Rawls's theory represents a radical departure from the constitution of the Welfare State. Rather than presenting a defense, it appears to undermine the pillars of the Welfare State by ignoring the foundational role of labor and the necessity of the State to manage it. Therefore, when Wolff wants to characterize Rawls's work as "a philosophical apologia for an egalitarian brand of liberal Welfare-state capitalism," he also has to locate it "historically in the tradition of utopian political economy of the late nineteenth and early twentieth centuries" (p. 195), that is, before the actual creation of the modern Welfare State. We end up thus with a paradoxical vision of the theory of justice as directed both toward furthering and abandoning Welfare State principles.

Although Wolff views Rawls's partial departure from the traditional economic and juridical principles of the Welfare State as a historical regression, we are more inclined to consider it as being in step with some of the most advanced developments of capitalist society. In other words, while Wolff locates Rawls's work in the era preceding the Welfare State, we would situate it in the era that succeeds the Welfare State. In any case, the appropriate question for our study is, given the central role of the concept of labor in juridical theory for much of the twentieth century, why today can a theory of right such as Rawls's that makes no reference to labor and production become not only accepted but hegemonic? Our hypothesis is that to a significant degree the success of Rawls's theory of right, in Europe as well as the United States, is due to the fact that it is functionally adequate to the recent changes in the State-form, the form of social organization and subordination, and the conditions of capitalist accumulation that Marx calls the phase of the real subsumption of labor within capital.[9] In effect, we are saying that the dominance of Rawls's theory is in part a demonstration that the process Marx recognized as a tendency in the nineteenth century, from the formal subsumption to the real subsumption of labor within capital, is today a reality.

Before we proceed, then, we need to clarify the contemporary relevance of Marx's intuitions. According to Marx, in the first of these two phases, the formal subsumption, the labor process is subsumed under capital, that is, it is enveloped within the capitalist relations of production in such a way that capital intervenes as its director or manager. In this arrangement, however, capital subsumes labor the way it finds it; capital takes over existing labor processes that were developed in previous modes of production, or at any rate outside of capitalist production. This subsumption is *formal* insofar as the labor process exists within capital, subordinated to its command *as an imported foreign force*, born outside of capital's domain. Capital tends, however, through the socialization of production and through scientific and technological innovation, to create new labor processes and destroy old ones, transforming the situations of the various agents of production. Capital thus sets in motion a specifically capitalist mode of production. The subsumption of labor is said to be *real*, then, when the labor processes themselves are born within capital, and therefore when labor is incorporated not as an external but as an internal force, proper to capital itself. The historical transition between these phases is, of course, a slow and gradual tendency, which passes through various intermediary stages. In the nineteenth century, Marx recognized the characteristics of the real subsumption only in large-scale factory production, a very small portion of the economy at the time. Through the continuous technological advances and the socialization of these labor processes outside the walls of the factory, the characteristics of the real subsumption have come to fill larger and larger portions of the social domain. The factory-society has expanded in step with the real subsumption to the point where today social production is dominated by the specifically capitalist mode of production.

Marx's distinction between the two phases is important for our discussion because it gives us the terms to understand the different roles that labor plays in capitalist juridical constitutions of society. In the phase of the formal subsumption, labor, no matter how solidly it is internalized within capitalist relations, remains in essence foreign to capitalist development. The irreducibility of the foreignness of labor forces capital to recognize two distinct roles in production, with labor as the source and capital as the manager of social wealth. The formal subsumption of labor, then, corresponds in juridical theory to what we have called in chapter 3 the constitutionalization of labor in the social State, or rather the process whereby, on one hand, the category of labor is adopted by theories of right as the exclusive criterion of social valorization and normative production, and, on the other hand, the State deploys its mediatory juridical and economic structures to recuperate and tame the antagonisms born in the process of exploiting this labor. Labor functions as an antagonistic *Grundnorm*, a hostile but necessary point of support, originating outside the system but serving as a foundation for its articulation and legitimation. As we move to the phase of the real subsumption, however, Marx explains that the labor processes evolve so that, first of all, production is no longer a direct and individual activity but an immediately social activity:

As the basis on which large industry rests, the appropriation of alien labour time ceases, with its development, to make up or to create wealth; so does direct labour *as such cease to be the basis of production, since, in one respect, it is transformed more into a supervisory and regulatory activity; but then also because the product ceases to be the product of isolated direct labour, and the combination of social activity appears, rather, as the producer.* (Grundrisse, p. 709)

Furthermore, this socialized labor power itself seems to disappear as it is displaced from its position as the source of capitalist production:

This entire development of the productive forces of socialized labour *(in contrast to the more or less isolated labour of individuals), and together with it the* use of science *(the* general product of social development), in the immediate process of production, *takes the form of the* productive power of capital. *It does not appear as the productive power of labour, or even of that part of it that is identical with capital.* (Capital, vol. 1, p. 1024)

The source of capitalist production shifts from individual labor to social labor and finally to social capital, particularly in terms of its technological innovations: "The entire production process appears as not subsumed under the direct skilfulness of

ist theories, however, have proved vulnerable to charges that they are arbitrary, abstract, and impractical. On the other hand, another current in juridical formalism has argued that law can function as an adequate analytical grille for interpreting civil society, as a faithful representation of social forms. Here the formal system is grounded on a material foundation and articulated along its lines. This current, however, must struggle to create a certain detachment from the incoherent and inconstant elements of society, to give representation the relative autonomy that a formal system needs to propose the order of a juridical arrangement. Many of the most sophisticated elaborations of juridical formalism, of course, combine these two strategies—Hans Kelsen, for example, brackets the material foundation in the *Grundnorm* and then articulates it through a rational, scientific deduction—but this combination or mediation does not resolve the problem of the foundation.

An "antifoundationalist" theory of right represents, in effect, the adequate realization of these tendencies latent in the formalist juridical tradition. We will argue in the following section of this chapter that Rawls manages to navigate between the twin dangers of traditional foundationalist solutions: he avoids both the empirical foundation in the material constitution of society and the transcendental foundation in the precepts of reason. By rejecting these foundations and seeking support instead in a reasonable and circular network of procedures, Rawls constructs a formal system that is both autonomous and practical. Here the juridical form becomes a motor, an abstract schema of normative production and circulation. The concept of procedure is a perfect candidate to fill this role: a procedure is a form in motion, a dynamic schema. The procedural republic, then, provides us with a means of understanding how the basic structure of postmodern society—the simulacra of social reality detached from production and labor—can generate and maintain itself.

The Genius of the System: Reflection and Equilibrium

Although the postmodern interpretation of Rawls flattens the tension in the text we identified earlier, it does in fact find resonances in *A Theory of Justice* and particularly in some of his more recent articles, gathered together in *Political Liberalism*. Specifically, in Rawls the autonomy of the formal juridical system is supported by a line of development that extends from our sense of justice and our considered convictions to the idea of reflective equilibrium and finally to the notion of systemic stability. Circularity and reflection give the formal schema a depth and stability that serve to displace the problems of the foundation of the system and the sources of normative production. The genius of the system is its discovery of stability without foundations and procedure without movement, which effectively displace social antagonisms and conflict from the institutional arrangement. Circulation comes to replace production as the center of juridical theory, creating an overlapping system of supports and thus guaranteeing the security of a well-ordered democratic regime.

The circularity of the juridical system is announced, or perhaps prefigured, in Rawls's method of argumentation. The "moral geometry" (p. 121) that he presents in *A Theory of Justice* differs radically from traditional conceptions of geometric development. Seventeenth-century arguments in *more geometrico*, for example, base their validity on the unilinear line of deductive demonstrations from definitions and axioms to propositions and conclusions. Rawls's geometry, on the other hand, rests on a circular form of exposition in which the argument's point of departure and its conclusion presuppose one another. We get a hint of this circularity simply by looking at the progression of themes in Part I of the text. The argument unfolds in an unusually complex order. Rawls begins with a series of tentative propositions that gradually become less provisional through a process of adequation or adjustment until the point when these very same propositions, no longer tentative, constitute the conclusions of the argument. The network of hypotheses are "proven" by their mutual support. In effect, all of the theory must be laid out before any of its elements can hold; the argument must be finished before it can properly begin. Paul Ricoeur points out, for example, that the two principles of justice are formulated (section 11) and interpreted (section 12) before we have investigated the situation in which they would be chosen. Nearly one hundred pages later we are presented with the full description of the situation of the choice of the two principles (sections 20–25) and the reasoning that justifies that choice (sections 26–30). "How can one formulate and interpret the principles, precisely insofar as they are principles, before having articulated the argument that is supposed to establish that those are truly the principles, that is to say the first propositions?" ("Le cercle de la démonstration," pp. 81-82). Obviously, Rawls has a particular notion of what constitutes a principle.

Since Rawls's presentation refuses linearity, it in fact makes little sense to conceive of certain elements as prior or posterior to others. "We are not dealing with a linear argument, but with a development that consists rather in the progressive elucidation of that which is already anticipated" ("Le cercle de la démonstration," p. 83). Since this is not a rationalist geometry in any conventional sense, perhaps we should call it a *reasonable* argument. Rawls appeals to the Kantian distinction between the Rational and the Reasonable to emphasize that his argumentation is not metaphysical but political, in other words, that the theory does not refer to a transcendental order of reason but to a practical realm of convictions ("Justice as Fairness," p. 237 n. 20, and "Kantian Constructivism in Moral Theory," pp. 528–32). While rational development is described by a straight, unidirectional movement, reasonable argument is conducted through a back-and-forth motion, within the conditions of feasibility. In fact, the reasonable argument is characterized not so much by motion as by a balancing procedure that arrives at a point of stasis, in other words, by the gradual elimination of motion.

The particularity of Rawls's methodology should indicate to us that he not only has a special understanding of geometrical development in a theoretical arrangement, but also of contractual development in a social arrangement. Like many formulations in the contractarian tradition, Rawls's contractual procedure is purely hypothetical, but it is novel in the way he conceives the authorship of the contract and the relationship of the parties entering into it. At the scene of the contract, in the original position, there is not a plurality of persons, not even hypothetical or representative persons. The background for the contractual argument is not an image of social difference and conflict, such as, for example, the state of nature in many early modern contractual arguments. In fact, several commentators have pointed out, with a certain perplexity, that Rawls's contractual procedure does not deal with difference at all: it is "noninteractive" and does not involve any bargaining, negotiation, nor even any choice — in effect, it does not involve a contract in any conventional sense. (See Chandran Kukathas and Phillip Pettit, *Rawls: A Theory of Justice and its Critics*, p. 34, and Michael Sandel, *Liberalism and the Limits of Justice*, pp. 130–32.) In a first instance, then, Rawls's contractualism refers not to any actual or hypothetical agreement but to a *condition* of theoretical discussion. "It is at this point that the concept of a contract has a definite role: it suggests the condition of publicity and sets limits on what can be agreed to" (*A Theory of Justice*, p. 175). It thus seems that "what matters is not so much the actual contract that would be made as the contractual situation" (Kukathas and Pettit, p. 68). At the same time, the public nature of the contractual situation defines the agent in that situation. Even though Rawls himself notes that the term "contract" implies a plurality (p. 16), there is only one subject in the original position and this subject is public, not in the sense that it represents a social average, but in that it is generic. The subject in the contractual situation can be best conceived as a displaced social subject: the limitations on knowledge imagined with the veil of ignorance create a subject that belongs to a specific society but is ignorant of its place in that society. Insofar as it is displaced, the subject can be understood as a sort of Rousseauian general subject, as distinguished from either an individual subject, a subject of the many, or the subject of all. Insofar as Rousseau's conception of the general will is invoked by the subject in the original position, however, we should note that it is invoked not as a center of democratic will, or popular subjectivity, but rather as a center of logical imputation. It would be completely inappropriate, Rawls insists, to link the generality of the original position to the actual positions of social subjects, in the way that Rousseau at times seems to link the general will to the forces of democratic participation:

The original position is not to be thought of as a general assembly which includes at one moment everyone who will live at some time; or, much less, as an assembly of everyone who could live at some time. It is not a gathering of all actual or possible persons. To conceive of the original position in either of these ways is to stretch fantasy too far. (p. 139)

Seen in this light, Rawls's original position is perhaps very close to a European tradition of constitutional thought (following in part a particular interpretation of Rousseau) that also emphasized the logical (not subjective) quality of the general will as foundation of the system. The first element of Rawls's contractualism, then, is its positioning a single displaced subject in a contractual situation.

Once we have established this condition, we can recognize that there is, in fact, a procedure of negotiation and agreement involved in Rawls's argument, not between persons but within the single subject found in the contractual situation. The process is oriented toward finding a fit between our sense of justice on one hand and the available theoretical principles of justice on the other. The convergence of these two lines will allow the subject in the original position the necessary support for proposing fair terms of social cooperation and thus for designating a well-ordered and just basic structure of society. We should look more closely, however, at the movement or progression involved in this contractual procedure. First of all, Rawls describes our sense of justice as our common moral capacity. Like our sense of grammaticalness in Chomskian linguistics, our sense of justice fills the role of intuition in Rawls's system: it is our innate ability to grasp an underlying structure of justice in the social field of moral signs (p. 47). Our sense of justice provides the raw material for a moral theory, but it is not necessarily reasonable. Rawls presents a refined version of our sense of justice as our considered judgments, "those judgments in which our moral capacities are most likely to be displayed without distortion" (p. 47). These judgments represent our firmest convictions and reflect our innate capacities for justice under the best conditions. They form a sort of natural substrate, the "facts" (p. 51) that give a solid social foundation to the system. On the other side of the balance, we have the organizing alternatives of the possible theoretical descriptions of our conception of justice. From one side, then, these alternative principles are weighed against our judgments and selected on the basis of their agreement. From the other side, our judgments are modified to conform with the selected principles. Eventually, this back-and-forth movement achieves a balance. "This state of affairs I refer to as reflective equilibrium. It is an equilibrium because at last our principles and judgments coincide; and it is reflective since we know to what principles our judgments conform and the premises of their derivation" (p. 20). Reflective equilibrium is a sort of contract in which reasonable convictions and rational principles have settled their differences and come to terms. To say that a certain conception of justice would be chosen in the original position means simply that certain principles would agree with our considered judgments in reflective equilibrium (p. 138).

This particularly abstract notion of contract does not address the differences among persons, but nonetheless seems to indicate a movement toward social stability through the rationalization of our convictions in a reasonable agreement. This is what gives the appearance of contractual progression in Rawls's system. When we look more closely, however, this contractual procedure, like Rawls's argumentative procedure, is comprised of a perfectly circular movement. The circularity, in fact, is what guarantees the stability. At first sight, it appears that we are dealing with a process that engages the differences within an empirical substrate (our sense of justice), negotiates them through the contract of reflective equilibrium, and thus arrives at the consensual construction of an institutional structure. As we noted earlier, the term "contract" connotes a plurality of parties or agents, and in this specific case it seems that the term "sense of justice" is what characterizes the open field of plurality and differences that come to be organized in the contract. One might assume that the back-and-forth motion leading to reflective equilibrium would involve some adjudication or negotiation among different senses of justice. We find, however, that there is no real plurality of beliefs, but rather there is effectively only one sense of justice in the system, just as there was only one subject in the original position. To understand the function of the sense of justice in Rawls's system we should not consider it as related to the beliefs or desires of real individuals, or even hypothetical or representative social subjects. On the contrary, the sense of justice is grounded strictly in the institutions of a democratic regime: "given that a person's capacity for fellow feeling has been realized by his forming attachments ... and given that a society's institutions are just and are publicly known by all to the just, then *this person acquires the corre-sponding sense of justice* as he recognizes that he and those for whom he cares are beneficiaries of these arrangements" (p. 491, emphasis added). In a well-ordered society, the institutions effectively inculcate a sense of justice in the individuals (p. 515). The sense of justice, then, is not a reference to a social plurality outside the system, to external "facts" or inputs, but rather a unique derivation of the convictions already embedded in the institutional structure. The theory can thus take an analytical shortcut, ignoring the sense of justice in the person and focusing instead on the "corresponding sense of justice" embedded in the institutions.

At this point the circularity of the argument is perfect, completely insulated from the destabilizing influences of social difference and conflict. The sense of justice leads through the contractual procedure to the choice of the just social order, and the just social order, in turn, inculcates the sense of justice. As Ricoeur noted with respect to the method, we are not dealing with any sort of movement, but with "the progressive elucidation of that which is already anticipated." The democratic regime, or the well-ordered society, is not only the end point but also the point of departure for the contractual process. The circular movement of self-reference gives the system a perfect equilibrium and thus the idea of a social contract is reduced to tautology. The system manages to achieve autonomy by avoiding or excluding any external inputs. The appearance of negotiation, dialectic, and mediation in the contractual procedure is only an appearance. No difference, in fact, disturbs the equilibrium of the system. Reflective equilibrium, then, perhaps best describes the stability achieved when the system is reflected back onto itself. The regime is democratic precisely insofar as the system freely elects itself to power.

Weak Subjects and the Politics of Avoidance

The postmodern interpretation of Rawls's theory of justice gives us a simulation of social reality, a depopulated horizon, emptied of all social contents. The machine that would go of itself marches through the social simulacra. Two elements have emerged as central to the "decentered" postmodern juridical machine—two elements that are essential (paradoxically, since the concept of essence seems to be excluded here) for a system without foundations. First, even though the system often alludes to pluralities, it only accepts an abstract unitary subject within its bounds. A postmodern unity is not created by mediating or even coercing a multiplicity to order, but rather by abstracting from a field of differences to free the system and thus pose a generic unity. There is not a plurality of persons in the conthe "principle of toleration" to mean that the system includes conflicting views within its structure. Rorty, however, recognizes that a postmodern juridical system has no means for mediation or reconciliation. The language of inclusion, therefore, subtly shifts to that of exclusion. After all, the method of avoidance, which realizes the principle of toleration, is not a mechanism of inclusion but one of exclusion. In Rorty's hands, then, the realization of Rawls's tolerant system becomes dependent on its indifference to and avoidance of social conflicts.[12] Postmodern liberal tolerance is thus based not on the inclusion but actually the exclusion of social differences.

Rorty takes care to historicize this progression in liberal thought. Although in the eighteenth century religion was the field of social conflict that produced the most dangerous threat to stability, today all fields of social conflict need to be avoided in order to create and maintain a stable system of rule. This "will be a society that encourages the 'end of ideology,'" according to Rorty, "that takes reflective equilibrium as the only method needed in discussing social policy. When such a society deliberates, when it collects the principles and intuitions to be brought into equilibrium, it will tend *to discard* those drawn from philosophical accounts of the self or rationality" (p. 264, emphasis added). Expressions of social difference are simply ignored or discarded as matters of indifference to the public sphere; politics thus becomes the mechanical and pragmatic system of balancing abstract social inputs to establish the equilibrium necessary for order and legitimation. Just as a previous generation of democratic political scientists proposed that we escape from the premodern religious authority of the idea of God, today Rorty proposes we escape from the modern philosophical authority of the idea of a subject (p. 264). Questions of labor, production, gender difference, racial difference, sexual orientation, desire, value, and so forth are all discarded because they are personal affairs and thus matters of indifference for politics. Democracy keeps its hands clean. This follows, in Rorty's view, from the general position that liberal political theory is deontological in the sense that it is not founded in any transcendental conception of the social good or any necessary and teleological structure of the human subject and human action. In fact, he takes this negation to be an affirmation of its opposite: if liberal ethics and politics do not necessarily follow from a transcendental, ideal order, they must be posed as absolutely contingent, refusing any reference to the depth and weight of real social determinations. After excluding and neglecting the subjective field of social conflict as merely the affair of the private sphere, then, what remains is an antiseptic, mechanical, self-sufficient political system of equilibrium. As we have already seen,

Rawls's conception of reflective equilibrium can be adequate to this task, because, from a perspective abstracted from the plurality of actually existing persons (that is, the original position), reflective equilibrium balances the sense of justice embedded in the existing social system with the principles possible in that same system. The autonomy of the self-balancing system of right makes possible the avoidance or exclusion of social difference basic to Rorty's conception of democracy.

In Rorty's interpretation of Rawls, in effect, we can recognize the tendency of abstraction in the tradition of juridical formalism pushed to its extreme so that now it resembles the systematism of Niklas Luhmann. Society, according to Luhmann, should be read as a self-referential or autopoietic system that poses an "internal totality" and thus maintains a closure or autonomy from its environment:

Autopoietic systems ... are not only self-organizing systems, they not only produce and eventually change their own structures; their self-reference applies to the production of other components as well.... Even elements, that is, last components (in-dividuals) which are, at least for the system itself, undecomposable, are produced by the system itself. Thus, every thing that is used as a unit by the system is produced as a unit by the system itself. (Essays on Self-Reference, p. 3; but see also pp. 1–20, 145ff., and 228ff.)

Society is a system of communication that is not only self-regulating and self-organized but also self-produced. All that remains is to solve the problems of complexity of the infinite specularity in this circular, autonomous world. Systematism is, in effect, the logical extension of the tendency in Rawls's work to pose the priority of feasibility over desirability in moral theory; or rather, it makes this priority absolute by making feasibility the only possible issue in the context of the system. This focus on systematic maintenance can only view the social constituents as weak subjects. "Within the world created by the operations of this system every concrete item appears as *contingent*, as something that could be different" (p. 147). In this view of the liberal public realm, the system occupies the place of necessity and casts all of its components as contingent. The system is an equilibrium machine, abstracted from the passional field of social conflict and thus empty of all social contents.

Liberal governance is no longer an art but a science, a technical calculus of force designed to achieve a systematic equilibrium in a society without politics. The "deficit of politics" in postmodern liberal theory implies a reduction of the State structure to its bare bones, a mechanical skeleton of rule. Does it consequently no longer make sense to pose the issue of power relations in society as a

social agent disappears in the system, in the equilibrium mechanism. The State is finally just one weak subject among others, a neutral guardian of order. One has to marvel at the theoretical perfection of this postmodern liberal vision of rule, at its imperturbable circularity, at its crystalline simplicity. When we now look to the plane of practical politics, there too we find the thin State, as a dream of the neoliberalism of the 1980s and the rhetorical centerpiece of the Reagan revolution. Let us break somewhat rudely, then, the line of our theoretical arguments, so that we can try to bring these liberal theories back to social reality and evaluate to what extent they are indeed functional to the practical needs and developments of the contemporary State.

First of all, we should note a profound resonance between the interpretation of Rawls that we have conducted thus far and the crisis of the Welfare State in the 1980s. We have emphasized the exclusion of the categories of production and labor in Rawls's theory of right and the absence of any role for intersubjective bargaining or negotiation in his conception of the social contract. In a parallel fashion, the 1980s saw the end of corporatism and collective bargaining as methods of State legitimation and planning for social and economic stability. The traditional trinity of Welfare State political economy — Taylorism in production, Fordism in political planning, and Keynesianism in economic planning — was no longer able to guarantee political order and economic development.[14] The economic crisis was above all a crisis of capital's ability to master its conflictual relationship with labor through a social and political dialectic. Excessive demands of labor (whether recognized as high wages, insubordination in the processes of production, or refusal of the social mechanisms of command) pushed the dialectical process to a point of rupture, making mediation unfeasible. The strategies for crisis management, then, shifted from mediation to exclusion: both exclusion of the traditional processes of negotiation and the exclusion of labor itself from the site of production.

We can recognize the tendency toward exclusion of the mechanism of negotiation between capital and labor in part as the political project against corporatism, initiated in the United States in this phase perhaps by the Nixon administration and realized to a certain degree during the Reagan years. This project itself was composed principally of two efforts. First, there was an indirect campaign against corporatism, destabilizing the balance of the labor market and weakening the conditions of bargaining. As part of a campaign of retrenchment, social-assistance programs were reduced and the rate of unemployment was allowed to rise. The expansion of the impoverished portion of society and the increased precariousness of employment greatly weakened the collective bargaining power of workers with respect to employers. (See, for example, Frances Fox Piven and Richard Cloward, *The New Class War*, p. 13.) The Reagan administration's efforts to repeal antitrust laws and to deregulate and privatize industry contributed to the campaign to weaken the position of labor and upset the contractual balance that had existed in one form or another since the New Deal. Second, the State conducted a direct attack on corporatism, encouraging a complete refusal of collective bargaining with labor. Increasingly strikes have been met not with negotiations but a silent show of force and replacement workers, beginning perhaps most significantly with the strike of PATCO (Professional Air Traffic Controllers' Organization) and continuing with the workers of Eastern Airlines, the New York Daily News, Greyhound Bus Lines, and Caterpillar, among others. (See Samuel Bowles, David Gordon, and Thomas Weisskopf, *After the Waste Land*, pp. 125–27, and, more recently, Stanley Aronowitz, *The Politics of Identity*, pp. 1–9.) The power of organized labor and corporatist representation suffered a continual decline throughout the 1980s. The positive content of the new social contract heralded by the Reagan administration remained vague, but its negative content was very clear: the social contract will not be founded on collective bargaining or any mediated balance between capital and labor typical of the Fordist political equilibrium.

Complementary to these political mechanisms to weaken the position of labor as a bargaining partner there was also a tendency to reorganize the workplace through automation and computerization, and thereby actually exclude labor itself from the site of production. This involves both the mobility of capital and the tendency, in Marxist terminology, of the decreasing portion of variable capital and the increasing portion of fixed capital. In the course of this process, the previously existing balance between labor and capital is further tilted, or rather the question of balance itself becomes increasingly irrelevant when the worker is replaced in the production process by machinery. The transformation of the automobile industry provides an excellent example of how a once-powerful work force can be reduced, pacified, and defeated through automation. In Flint, Michigan, as in Turin, Italy, the historical sites of the explosions of workers' subjectivities and power have become what Marco Revelli calls "factory deserts."[15] All of this goes hand in hand with a decline of unionism in general.

Just as the category of labor has been excluded from the constitution of the juridical order in postmodern liberal theory, bargaining and negotiation with labor have tended to be marginalized from the constitution of a political order in neoliberal practice. The exclusion of labor in the former, of course, can appear as passive (as if it were a lacuna or oversight of liberal theory), but in the latter an active, sometimes brutal exclusion is required. Despite these very real differences, however, this correspondence in the exclusion of labor from the constitution is perhaps a central element that explains why the contemporary political context has afforded Rawls's theory, and particularly a postmodern interpretation of it, a certain dominance among juridical theories and how in turn this version of liberal theory can be employed to further the neoliberal political project. In both liberal theory and neoliberal practice, we want to emphasize, the displacement or dispersal rather than the engagement and mediation of social antagonisms functions through the image of a weak subject as the generic social actor.

      The Welfare State was seriously eroded in the 1980s, then, in the sense that labor was progressively excluded from the constitution and the State's efforts toward full employment came to an end. If we take another perspective, however, and view the Welfare State in terms of State spending and State intervention in economic and social mechanisms, it did not wither during this period but actually grew. The neoliberal project involved a substantial increase of the State in terms both of size and powers of intervention. The development of the neoliberal State did not lead toward a "thin" form of rule in the sense of the progressive dissipation or disappearance of the State as a social actor. On the contrary, the State did not become a weak but rather an increasingly strong subject. "Liberalization" was not a decentralization of power, not a reduction of the State—any reduction was perhaps closer to the heightened reassertion of the "essential" State powers that Vattimo celebrates. Despite appeals to the rhetoric of classical liberal economics, State spending (even in most areas of social-welfare provisions) and State intervention into market activity actually increased (J. LeGrand and D. Winter, "The Middle Classes and the Defence of the British Welfare State," p. 148). In this sense, the spending structures of the Welfare State showed signs of irreversibility and a remarkable resistance to the neoliberal attack (Piven and Cloward, *The New Class War*, pp. 157–58). Neoliberalism could not respond to the economic crisis through a dispersal and decentralization of State power, but required on the contrary a concentration and reinforcement of authority on social and economic issues. While the heralded reductions were minimal, the expansions of State spending in new areas were dramatic, particularly in terms of military spending (Bowles, Gordon, and Weisskopf, *After the Waste Land*, pp. 130ff.). The neoliberal State thus did not act to reduce the structures of the Welfare State, but rather to redirect or restructure them. In this way, the neoliberalism of the 1980s constituted a revolution from above that maintained the enormous economic powers and structures created by fifty years of Welfare State politics while diverting them to different ends.

This same process of maintaining and restructuring State powers also took place in the juridical realm, both through a direct appropriation of powers by the executive branch and through a complementary transformation of the judicial branch to bring it in line with the executive's initiatives. The "Reagan revolution" in constitutional law was conducted through a series of appointments to the Supreme Court, the Department of Justice, and to the federal courts at all levels. Despite the claims of Reagan administration rhetoric, these changes of personnel did not free the judiciary from politics nor re-create a dream of pure interpretation of the constitution, but only brought about a new paradigm of tendentious constitutional interpretation and "judicial activism": liberal judicial activism has simply been replaced by conservative judicial activism. (See Ronald Dworkin, "The Reagan Revolution and the Supreme Court.") Although this new activism often operates under the cloak of federalism, refusing to consider cases on the federal level and pushing them back to the jurisdiction of the states, the executive has been no less effective in its pursuit of coherent ideological projects through the judiciary. The most serious effects of this shift were felt in the realm of women's reproductive rights, from the gag rule on doctors giving information on abortions to the right of abortion itself. In this way, just as the economic structures of the Welfare State and public spending were maintained and redirected, so too the extensive judicial powers have been preserved and oriented toward new goals, despite the rhetoric about a thin, nonideological State.

The reinforcement of the State as a corpulent and strong subject, as the dominant social actor in both the economic and juridical realms, is a decidedly "illiberal" face of the neoliberal State. This is perhaps most clear in the significant reductions of civil liberties in recent years. Throughout the series of wars launched in the past decade, not only the external wars on Panama and Iraq but also the internal wars on drugs and gangs, the Bill of Rights has been one of the most serious casualties. The foreign wars brought the temporary impositions of a semimartial law, notably through curbs of the freedom of the press and the freedom of assembly, but the domestic wars have created a permanent state of semimartial law. For example, the Fourth Amendment to the Constitution, prohibiting the State from conducting "unreasonable" searches and seizures, has been dramatically curtailed while the powers of the police have been equally extended.

Drug- and gang-related "profiles" are now commonly accepted as sufficient criteria for the police to stop and search citizens.[16] Adequate suspicion has been defined almost exclusively along racial and cultural lines. There is thus an enormously disproportionate number of racial minorities, particularly blacks and Latinos, not only stopped and harassed by the police without reasonable cause, but also arrested, convicted, and executed for crimes. (See Manning Marable, "Black America," p. 12.) The attack on the Fourth Amendment, then, coincides to a certain extent with a (re)institutionalization of racism in America. In general, the recent decline of the Bill of Rights has served to reinforce the traditional federalist project to strengthen the powers of the State against the danger of social disorder. A rising militarism on both foreign and domestic soil, then, and increasing recourse to a politics of social alarm, fear, and racism show the emergence of some fascistic elements of the State and the tendency toward the institution of a police state: The movement from *Rechtsstaat* toward *Polizeistaat* has always been accomplished through fear, hatred, and racism.

A central problem facing the Reagan revolution, then, was how to give the powers of an autonomous and strong State a foothold in the material constitution of society, in order to create a real unity and consensus, in other words, in order to recuperate and tame the social base within its order. One contribution to this project was the movement to expand State intervention to include a moral plane. Much of the rhetoric of the Reagan and Bush administrations posed the contemporary crisis not principally as an economic crisis or even a crisis of law and order but as a crisis of values, of national direction, of the moral fabric. The intervention of the State, then, was increasingly conceived as an instrument for not only the economic welfare but also the moral welfare of the citizenry. Areas such as women's reproductive capacities, drug use, religious practices, family values, and sexual orientation became more and more important as sites for direct State involvement. The country needed moral leadership and moral education. The strong subject of the neoliberal State, then, was in part consolidated on a moral plane through attempts to impose a national moral unity. We should point out that this is another "illiberal" aspect of neoliberal practice that is particularly incompatible with liberal theory as we have presented it. The priority of right over good is the slogan that precludes the creation of such a moral unity in the context of Rawls's liberal argument, and it is precisely this freedom from a metaphysical foundation and from a moral teleology that allows writers such as Rorty to pose the confluence of the liberal and postmodern projects.

In summary, we can see that neoliberal political projects of the

1980s coincide with postmodern liberal theory in the attempt to exclude the category of labor from the constitution and thus displace the social contract of the Welfare State from its center on bargaining and negotiation. While this shift leads liberal theory to the proposition of a thin conception of the State and a weak subject of politics, however, neoliberal practice moves in the opposite direction to reinforce and expand the State as a strong and autonomous subject that dominates the social field, in the realm of public spending as in that of judicial and police activity. These widely divergent images of the subjective figure of the State should indicate to us that the line of postmodern liberal theory that we have developed thus far will not be sufficient to account for and further the practical needs of neoliberal practice. The practice of the State of the Reagan-Bush years to present itself as a moral authority, capable of uniting the country in moral (not economic nor strictly juridical) terms, will provide us with an initial line of inquiry in our attempt to grasp a more adequate figure of the contemporary State-form.

Common Good and the Subject of Community

With these needs of the contemporary State in mind, let us return to the line of our theoretical argument and the sphere of liberal theory to take now a fresh look at its development. This time, after having seen the practical pressures imposed on the State during the 1980s, we want to trace the emergence of a strong social subject as a theoretical project in the work of Rawls and his critics. Throughout the development of a conception of postmodern law and its corresponding juridical system we have been aware of a flattening of the tension in Rawls's argument and an instrumentalization of his theory of justice. In certain respects, this interpretation has emptied the principle of liberty of its social contents, translated the principle of equality into a principle of indifference, and on the basis of these principles founded a formal procedural framework that guarantees order at the same time that it denies social depth and movement. This particular development of postmodern law clearly does not account for the full thrust of Rawls's vision.

Continually in *A Theory of Justice*, Rawls attempts to give a real determination and content to social being through an appeal to equality, fraternity, and common good. The summit of this tendency, perhaps, is the proposition of the difference principle as a mechanism for the development of social equality. The difference principle, Rawls explains, is the principle of justice that expresses our desire for fraternity and thus the principle that most clearly founds a human community and constitutes social being with real determinations. Here we see most clearly Rawls's passion for democracy: "The higher expectations of those

argument. Reading Sandel, in fact, we have the impression of being thrown back in the history of philosophy: reading Rawls from Taylor's perspective unfolds as a repetition of Hegel's famous reading of Kant. "If contemporary liberals were led to rediscover Kant," one author writes, "the critics of liberalism were forced to reinvent Hegel" (Steven Smith, *Hegel's Critique of Liberalism*, p. 4). Sandel's Hegelian standpoint not only provides a ground for critique, but also carries a series of hidden consequences. In other words, Sandel not only takes up Taylor's terms to frame the analysis but, as we shall see, in presupposing a Hegelian standpoint he creates a context in which the subsequent antinomies of the argument proceed inevitably toward a predetermined solution: a Hegelian synthesis in the form of a universal community. The thin subject of liberalism is thus fleshed out in a robust conception of the State as subject.

The central question that Sandel poses for Rawls concerns the nature and capacities of the deontological subject of liberalism. He first tries to reveal the theory of the subject or the self implicit in Rawls's discourse and then attempts to evaluate its adequacy to the tasks of morality. This approach casts Rawls's arguments in a new light and makes the liberal theory of justice suddenly appear weak and precarious. The feeble state of the liberal subject is the primary concern and the leitmotif of Sandel's study: "The self threatens at different points in the argument either to dissolve into a radically disembodied subject or to collapse into a radically situated subject" (p. 138). Before we proceed to look more closely at this characterization of the Rawlsian subject, we should take a moment to flesh out the perspective from which Sandel proposes this critique. Sandel conceives the modern theory of the subject as a treacherous field threatened by twin dangers: moral philosophy is posed with a sort of passage through Scylla and Charybdis. On one side, the theory of the subject can err by conceiving the self from a primarily intellectual point of view — the "radically disembodied" and thus radically free subject — and, on the other side, it can go off course with an overly material perspective — the "radically situated" and thus determined subject. However, while this central dilemma for moral theory — the opposing conceptions of the self — plays a fundamental role in Sandel's study, it is taken for granted and never fully developed.

For a coherent development of this theory of the subject, in fact, we have to turn to the work of Charles Taylor. In his study of Hegel, Taylor poses the problematic in very grand and comprehensive terms: (1) the theory of the subject is the fundamental terrain of modern thought; (2) there are two major opposing trends of thought and sensibility that characterize modern philosophy and indeed modern civilization itself; and (3) Hegel presents the synthesis of these two trends in his theory of the subject as embodied spirit.[20] The first trend, which Taylor finds most coherently articulated in Herder, is concentrated in the Romantic idea of a cosmic expressive unity: "One of the central aspirations of the expressivist view was that man be united in communion with nature, that his self-feeling unite with a sympathy for all life, and for nature as living" (*Hegel*, p. 25). Man is thus not set against an objective world but rather included as part of a material cosmic subject. The other trend of modern thought, which finds its most complete formulation in Kant, focuses rather on the Enlightenment conception of human moral freedom and hence proposes an intellectual, rational subject. "In being determined by a purely formal law, binding on me simply *qua* rational will, I declare my independence, as it were, from all natural considerations and motives and from the natural causality which rules them" (*Hegel*, p. 31). The radical conception of human freedom poses humans as self-determining not insofar as they are material beings but insofar as they are intellectual beings constituted by a rational, moral will. These two trends, according to Taylor, these two conceptions of the subject, continue to constitute the defining parameters of modern thought and civilization into our time. Hegel's philosophy, then, is of fundamental importance and "perennial interest" because he manages better than any other thinker to overcome the oppositions combining "the rational, self-legislating freedom of the Kantian subject with the expressive unity within man and with nature for which the age longed" (*Hegel*, p. 539). Now, the most distinctive feature of Taylor's work is his focus on the centrality of the theory of the subject. His strategy of reading the history of modern thought as one all-encompassing contradiction between two partial subjects prepares the ground, or rather creates the necessity, for a Hegelian supersession in "a unity between radical freedom and integral expression" (*Hegel*, p. 43). Given the point of departure, any other solution could only be partial.

The important fact for our study is that in reading Rawls, Sandel adopts not only a Hegelian perspective, but a perspective specific to Taylor's interpretation of Hegel: he employs both Taylor's terminology and his strategy of reading the central problematic of modern thought as the contradiction between a subject defined by the freedom of rational thought and a subject grounded in the determinations of material reality. Given this framework, one might expect Sandel to critique the Kantian idealism of Rawls's liberal project. Sandel, however, is more subtle and recognizes that Rawls departs from the Kantian moral framework in some very important aspects: "Rawls takes as his project to preserve Kant's deontological teaching by replacing German obscurities with a domesticated metaphysic less vulnerable to the charge of arbitrariness and more congenial to the Anglo-American temper" (pp. 13–14). Rawls reforms Kantian morality, according to Sandel, by rejecting the transcendental foundation and adopting in its stead a reasonable empiricism. Sandel's argumentative strategy, then, cannot be simply to take up a Hegelian critique of Rawls's Kantianism, but rather must be more nuanced. Insofar as Rawls follows Kant in the development of an ideal moral theory, Sandel will apply the critique of the "radical freedom" of the "disembodied subject"; on the other hand, insofar as Rawls rejects the Kantian transcendental foundation for an empirical and procedural social system, Sandel will apply the critique of the "radically situated" or determined subject.

Sandel's analysis turns on his reconstruction of the "subject of possession" underlying Rawls's arguments, a subject that seeks to avoid the twin dangers of modern moral theory.[21] In effect, Sandel presents the Rawlsian subject as a weak combination of the two modern subjects and thus prepares the ground for a strong Hegelian synthesis. According to Sandel, the complexity of the liberal subject lies in the relationship between the self and its ends, between the right and the good. In the original position we are presented with a subject that is detached from or ignorant of its ends, and thus capable of making the rational moral choice of justice in the Kantian fashion. The liberal subject, however, is not simply a noumenal or unconditioned self, nor even the generic subject defined by the general knowledge of our contemporary society. When the veil of ignorance is lifted we find an empirical self with assets, attributes, and interests. The Rawlsian self, then, according to Sandel, possesses attributes but is not constituted or determined by them: "The possessive aspect of the self means that I can never fully be constituted by my attributes, that there must always be some attributes I *have* rather than *am*" (p. 20). Sandel credits Rawls with having recognized the poverty of Kant's noumenal foundation and the need for a Hegelian solution such as that found in Taylor. "In Rawls' view, any account of self and ends must tell us not one thing but two things: how the self is distinguished from its ends, and also how the self is connected to its ends. Without the first we are left with a radically situated subject; without the second, a radically disembodied subject" (p. 54). The subject of possession provides a solution, according to Sandel, in that the self is given a relative autonomy, distanced from its ends but not detached altogether: the subject would thus be simultaneously free and determined.

Once Sandel has succeeded in posing *A Theory of Justice* as a Hegelian project, his critique can unfold easily, without major obstacles, because Rawls's explanations will never go far enough to fulfill the Hegelian criteria. Rawls will always appear in this light as a weak version of Hegelianism.[22] For example, Sandel initially problematizes the subject of possession with respect to the concept of desert. The reformist social institutions aimed at equalizing the distribution of goods, as implied by the difference principle, require a justification in the notion of social desert. However, "on Rawls' conception, no one can properly be said to deserve anything because no one can properly be said to possess anything, at least not in the strong, constitutive sense of possession necessary to the notion of desert" (pp. 85–86). The combination of autonomy and embodiment effectuated in the "subject of possession" proves to be too weak a synthesis. When the Rawlsian subject asserts its autonomy it effectively dissolves any claim to its attributes and ends.

With the problem posed in these terms, Sandel recognizes two modifications that would make the liberal subject more adequate to the established criteria. First, the subject must discover a collective dimension, a communal identity that can support a more substantial notion of common assets and social desert (p. 103). Second, and perhaps more important, the ends and attributes of the subject must be internalized within, and in this sense constitutive of, the subject itself. Even though Rawls explicitly objects to this characterization of the subject, Sandel insists at length that this is the most coherent way to make sense of and complete Rawls's own project. This allows us to understand, for example, how behind the veil of ignorance there is not a plurality of persons but a single subject that makes a contract not through choice or bargaining but by recognition and consent to the law. "What goes on in the original position is not a contract after all, but the coming to self-awareness of an intersubjective being" (p. 132). Here we can clearly see that *A Theory of Justice* is actually a Hegelian phenomenological project aimed at self-recognition, but one that simply does not go far enough.

The strong, "constitutive" conception of community allows Sandel to pose the synthesis of the subject in a more substantial way. The possession of attributes or qualities becomes an ontological notion. "For [the members of a society], community describes not just what they *have* as fellow citizens but also what they *are*, not a relationship they choose (as in a voluntary association) but an attachment they discover, not merely an attribute but a constituent of their identity" (p. 150).[23] The constitution of the community and even the choice (or acceptance) of the principles of justice must be defined by a dialectic of "deep reflection" and self-recognition. "The relevant agency here [is] not voluntarist but cognitive; the self [comes] by its ends not by choice but by reflection, as knowing (or inquiring) subject to object of (self-)understanding" (p. 152). Sandel develops Rawls's

Kantianism toward the political vision of the young Hegel, to the threshold of the *Phenomenology*. He grasps the thrust of the abortive tendency in the theory of justice toward the common good and fraternity, and attempts to give it a more solid foundation and a stronger constitution: "character" and "friendship" (p. 180) will thus constitute the community as a strong social subject.

The Autonomy of the State: Moral Welfare

Once we have established and accepted the critical standpoint, Sandel's reading of Rawls unfolds with admirable clarity. What is less clear, however, is the alternative moral or social vision implicit in his critique of liberalism. Sandel emphasizes that in order to set liberalism on its feet we need to give an ontological dimension to the theory of right, giving substance to our notions of common good, identity, and community. Our theory of the social subject must concern not only what we *have* but also who we *are*. In other words, our discourse on *Sollen* must be united with the order of *Sein*. The process of deep reflection and the resultant collective self-understanding are the first steps toward the strong identity that we lack. Let us take a moment to develop this process further in social terms to see the real implications of this communitarian political ontology.

The social program is founded on a social critique. From the communitarian standpoint, the crisis of liberalism is not only a theoretical crisis but also a social crisis: a crisis of identity and a crisis of values that takes the form of both a homogenization and a fragmentation of the social fabric. Taylor describes one face of this crisis as the increasing lack of meaningful social differentiation in postindustrial democracies and the "increasing 'classlessness' of modern society" (*Hegel and Modern Society*, p. 111). Liberal democracies have destroyed the bases of community and thus leave the contemporary social subjects powerless, unable to realize strong identities. "Thus Hegel's dilemma for modern democracy, put at its simplest is this: the modern ideology of equality and of total participation leads to a homogenization of society. This shakes men loose from their traditional communities, but cannot replace them as a focus of identity" (p. 116). If postindustrial liberal society manages to present itself as a unity, it does so merely as an undifferentiated, homogeneous unity that lacks identity and thus remains powerless. Taylor conceives the Hegelian alternative as the coherent formation of different partial communities that can unite in a single, powerful totality: "One of the great needs of the modern democratic polity is to recover a sense of significant differentiation, so that its partial communities, be they geographical, or cultural, or occupational, can become again important centres of concern and activity for their

members in a way which connects them to the whole" (p. 118). While homogenization produces an empty whole in which there is a weak link between the particular and the general, then, social differentiation in partial communities provides
a mechanism of mediation to forge strong ties between individuals and the totality
of society.

In the communitarian analysis of liberalism, the homogeniza-
tion of social differences is always coupled with the fragmentation of the social
totality. Homogenization and fragmentation are two faces of the same crisis.
Sandel poses the fragmentation of American society in historical terms. The construction of the American liberal State, at least in its twentieth-century form, was
founded necessarily on "a strong sense of national community, morally and politically to underwrite the extended involvements of a modern industrial order" ("The
Procedural Republic and the Unencumbered Self," p. 93). The nation as a whole
must realize a coherent identity so as "to cultivate the shared self-understandings
necessary to community in the formative, or constitutive sense" (p. 93). The national community or national identity would pose the unity of society as a whole
and, through its projected image of a common good, individuals and groups would
be able to situate themselves as partial communities within a constituted order.
The historical developments of liberal society, however, have eroded and fragmented the bases for national identity and unity. "As the scale of social and political organization has become more comprehensive, the terms of our collective
identity have become more fragmented, and the forms of political life have outrun
the common purpose needed to sustain them" (pp. 94–95). The incoherence of the
social fabric is finally the cause of the impotence of the nation. Liberalism provides
us with a State that has lost its power, both internally in its capacity to form a
coherent community and externally in its ability to pursue its objectives in the face
of other nations: "despite its unprecedented role in the economy and society, the
modern State seems itself disempowered, unable effectively to control the domestic economy, to respond to persisting social ills, or to work America's will in the
world" (p. 92). Debilitated by a weak identity, by a weak constitution, the State
cannot play the role of a powerful actor on the national or international scene.
The project of the nation in response to the crisis, then, becomes one of moral
coherence and unity. This crisis of moral fabric that Taylor and Sandel note on a
theoretical plane certainly also finds resonances in communitarian sociological
work. "The fundamental question we posed, and that was repeatedly posed to us,"
Robert Bellah and his colleagues explain, "was how to preserve or create a morally
coherent life" (*Habits of the Heart*, p. vii).

1992 election campaigns demonstrated the strong continuity of this theme. Sandel argues that liberals have a great deal to learn from this "communal strand of conservative thought": "the most potent part of [Reagan's] appeal was his evocation of communal values—of family and neighborhood, religion and patriotism. What Reagan stirred was a yearning for a way of life that seems to be receding in recent times—a common life of larger meanings" ("Democrats and Community," p. 21). Taylor echoes this sentiment without referring directly to the Reagan project when he advocates a new spirit of "patriotic identification" to bring the nation together. (See "Cross-Purposes," pp. 165–76.) Although the Reagan rhetoric holds promise, however, these communitarians note that the policies of the administration favored individualism and thus were not sufficient to cultivate these "public virtues." (See Bellah et al., *Habits of the Heart*, p. 263, and Sandel, "Democrats and Community," p. 21.) The communitarians, then, envision a program that would finally make good on Reagan's promises of a national moral community.

These communitarian critiques of the crisis of liberal society slide along the passage from the *Phenomenology* to the *Philosophy of Right*. Just as the deep reflection of the subject leads to self-understanding, just as it leads the subject to realize what it really is, so too a developed *Sittlichkeit* enjoins us to realize the values of our society, to bring about the order that already is, so that there is no gap between what ought to be and what is, between *Sollen* and *Sein*. In both the psychological and the social versions, no transformation is called for but merely a process of recognition and ordering. The resulting subject (whether an individual consciousness or a State) is the realization of a preexisting identity. The solution to the theoretical search for a situated and autonomous subjectivity and the political quest for a coherent ethical life in society, a national community, fit together as homologous processes in a continually expansive dialectical argument. The notions of reflective, situated subjectivity and community that these communitarians propose lead finally to the proposition of the State as the fully realized subject. The community conceived on a local level cannot take on a full meaning. Communitarians continually postulate the community as the expression of who we are without giving any particular specifications of this "we." In fact, if one were to try to conceive the community in local terms based on specific commonalities— a community of autoworkers, a community of gay men, even a community of women—we would have to qualify this in Taylor's terms as a "partial community."[24] Such a community cannot assume the role of a fully realized subject, but can only discover (through reflection) its identity in the whole. This is why Sandel, when he tries to be more precise about the nature of community, speaks of the national community. The only way to qualify the "we" is through identification to the whole—we Americans, we members of the procedural republic. The State inheres in these arguments as a necessity, as the only veritable subject of community, as the full realization of embodied subjectivity. "Es ist der Gang Gottes in der Welt, dass der Staat ist." It is essential to God's march through the world that the State exist (*Philosophy of Right*, addition to §§ 258). In the final instance, the communitarian preoccupation with the theory of the subject leads to the proposition of the State as the only fully realized and autonomous subject.[25]

The Real Subsumption of Society in the State

We have traced two lines of interpretation inspired by Rawls's work that have each played particularly prominent roles in the last fifteen years. While the two diverge in important aspects, they share the common project of theorizing the marginalization of labor in the constitution and the real subsumption of society in the State. In the first version, the postmodern interpretation of Rawls, the autonomy of the juridical order of the State is established not through an engagement with social forces, but rather through a process of abstraction from them. The political method of avoidance separates the juridical system from social reality so that questions of right tend to be resolved in a mechanical process of balancing abstract inputs to achieve a global equilibrium. This abstract projection of society is subsumed within the State automatically because the modes of existence in the social simulacra are products of the system itself. The postmodern subsumption thus has an artificial, mechanical quality. The second tendency, however, gives a more substantial version, but one that points to the same process of subsumption. In this case, the juridical system is not abstracted from society but rather it is imagined to infuse society at all levels. Law constitutes social subjects in line with the order of the State, and thus society is created as a pacific order within the State arrangement. The various social subjects, the "partial communities," are merely modes of the State itself and can only recognize themselves or be recognized insofar as they are recognized in the whole, the total community, the State. In this case too the subsumption is pregiven, because the partial social subjects are merely products of the State itself. At first glance, then, the debate between liberals and communitarians seems to be repeating a historical conflict between supporters of the rights State and proponents of the social State, but on further reflection we find that the two positions are merely two strategies intent on the same project—the subsumption of society within the State.

Like the real subsumption of labor within capital that Marx

foresaw, this real subsumption of society within the State marks a new era of social relations and requires a new paradigm of social theory. The novelty of this theoretical situation is most clear, we think, when one recognizes how the concept of civil society no longer occupies the central position it held in so many modern theories of the State. The concept of civil society has been used in very different ways in the history of political theory, and this is not the place for us to trace its complex evolution.[26] It is sufficient for our purposes here to note some of the elements that Hegel brought to this concept. In Hegel's conception, civil society is the dynamic site where the unorganized social-economic and legal exchanges, antagonisms, and conflicts are expressed and organized. Most important, it is the site of the organization of labor power and the formation of laboring corporations (*Philosophy of Right*, §§ 250-56). Hegel casts such organization as immediately educative in the sense that the particular interests brought into relation will be able to enter into or be subsumed within the universal. This is the same educative process that Hegel saw in the Jena period as the movement from concrete labor to abstract labor, in which the wild beast of singular interests is domesticated within the universal so that its power could be put to work (*Jenenser Realphilosophie*, vol. 2, p. 268). Along with the processes of production, both the interchanges in the market and the application and enforcement of the law each carry out this educative function of bringing the individual in line with the universal. The juridical and economic institutions of civil society highlight the lines of articulation along which the State can engage and recuperate the antagonisms born of capitalist production and capitalist social relations; this is the public space of mediation that opens the social dialect that leads to the State. Civil society is thus the site where the State, as representative of the universal interest, subsumes the singular interests that are extraneous or foreign to its order. In this sense, then, civil society is the space of the formal subsumption, the site where the State mediates, disciplines, and recuperates the social antagonisms foreign to its rule.

As the postmodern and communitarian theories we have examined suggest, however, the State no longer engages social forces foreign to it through the institutions of civil society. This passage is obvious when we consider the fortunes of the institutional trade union, the most prominent element of civil society in Hegel's analysis. In many respects, throughout the first half of the twentieth century, institutional labor unions did constitute a fundamental point of mediation between labor and capital, and between society and the State. Collective bargaining mechanisms held a privileged position in the establishment and reproduction of the social contract. (See chapter 3, "The Conditions of the Concretization of the Model of Abstract Labor.") Institutional labor unions and the affiliated parties served the dual purpose of providing an avenue for worker interests to influence the State (thus helping to legitimate State rule) and at the same time deploying the discipline and control of the State and capital throughout the work force. In recent years, the dialectic between the State and institutional labor and also the mechanisms of collective bargaining have gradually faded from the scene. (See earlier in this chapter, "The Strong State of Neoliberalism.") In the society of the real subsumption this dialectic no longer holds the central role, and capital no longer needs to engage labor or represent labor at the heart of production. Social capital appears to reproduce itself autonomously, as if it were emancipated from the working class, and labor becomes invisible in the system. What is subsumed is really a simulacrum of society, produced by the State itself. The State no longer has a need for mediatory mechanisms of legitimation and discipline: antagonisms are absent (or invisible) and legitimation has become a tautology. The State of the real subsumption is no longer interested in mediation but separation, and thus the institutions of civil society as sites of the social dialectic gradually lose their importance.[27] Not the State, but civil society has withered away!

The State no longer rules primarily through disciplinary deployments, but through networks of control. In this regard, the contemporary shift from disciplinary societies to societies of control that Gilles Deleuze recognizes in the work of Michel Foucault corresponds very well to the Marxian historical passage from the formal to the real subsumption, or rather it shows another face of this same tendency. (See "Postscript on the Societies of Control.") Disciplinary societies are characterized by enclosures or institutions, which serve as the skeleton or backbone of civil society; these enclosures define the striae of social space. If in the previous paradigm, that of sovereignty, the State maintained a certain distance or distinction from social production—ruling, for example, by taxing production—in disciplinary societies the State rules by reducing any distance and integrating or subsuming social production—not by taxing, that is, but by organizing production. The factory is perhaps, from this point of view, the paradigmatic enclosure of civil society. The disciplinary deployments that constitute the factory simultaneously subjugate and subjectivize the factory worker as site of domination and resistance. This factory striation of society provides a channel for the State's organization and recuperation of external social productive forces within its structure. The striation defined by the institutions extends like tentacles throughout civil society, or, as Deleuze says, like a mole's tunnels through social space.

Deleuze points out, however, that these social enclosures or institutions are today everywhere in crisis. One might interpret the crisis of the factory, the family, and the other social enclosures as the progressive crumbling of various social walls, thus leaving a social void, as if the striated social space of civil society had been smoothed into a free space. Deleuze suggests that it is more adequate, however, to understand the collapse of the walls of the enclosures rather as the generalization of the logics that used to function within these limited domains across the entire society, spreading like a virus. The logic of capitalist production perfected in the factory now invests all forms of social production equally. The same might be said also for the school, the prison, the hospital, the other disciplinary institutions. Social space is smooth, not in the sense that it has been cleared of the disciplinary striation, but rather in that those striae have been uniformly generalized across society.[28] Social space has not been emptied of the disciplinary institutions, but completely filled with the modulations of control. The subsumption of society in the State is thus not formal but real; it no longer involves the mediation and organization of the institutions for discipline and rule but sets the State in motion directly through the perpetual circuitry of social production. We can no longer use the metaphor of structure and superstructure that was central to the conception of the mediating institutions of civil society. The image of the intersecting burrows of the mole that characterized the structures of disciplinary societies no longer holds in this new domain. Not the structured passages of the mole, Deleuze writes, but the infinite undulations of the snake are what characterize the smooth space of the societies of control. The resistances that moved through the passages of the striae of civil society will obviously have no place to gain a foothold on the slippery surfaces of this new model of rule.

One consequence of this new situation is that now more clearly than ever any strategy of socialist reformism is completely illusory. (See chapter 7, "The Illusions of Juridical Reformism.") Certain popular interpretations of Gramsci, for example, still view civil society as the space of liberation and the space from which to rein in and control the oppressive powers of the State for "popular" or "socialist" ends.[29] Gramsci's work is seen in this context as a development of the Hegelian conception of civil society that emphasizes not only the economic but the cultural exchanges that are opened in this realm. Gramsci's is not, however, a linear development of the Hegelian conception, but one that effectively inverts the Hegelian relationship between civil society and the State, so that civil society will no longer be subsumed within the State, but rather exert its hegemony over the State apparatus and thus corral the State within its rule. The Hegelian subordination of civil society to the State is stood on its head so that the State is preserved but now subordinated to the plurality of interactive interests in civil society. The resulting political pluralism would be a sort of cultural-ideological free market of social forces that thrive on the dynamics of exchange, while maintaining the structures of the State now subordinated to the popular will.

Leaving aside questions about how well this interpretation corresponds to the central thrust of Gramsci's thought, it should be clear, both from our theoretical discussions and from analysis of the practical state of political affairs in our world, that this reformist political vision is properly speaking utopian. There is no space, in other words, no topos on which it can exist. This is precisely the point on which the two liberal theories analyzed earlier (the postmodern and the communitarian) firmly agree in their conceptualization of the contemporary State-form: civil society no longer exists; the State no longer needs it as the terrain either to mediate and recuperate social antagonisms or to legitimate its rule. More precisely, in fact, if civil society can be said to exist, it does so only as a virtual projection cast within the circularity of the autopoietic State system, while real, antagonistic social referents that are external to the State are excluded by methods of avoidance. Civil society, that is to say, has been really subsumed within the State. The smooth spaces of the societies of control and the compact whole of the real subsumption have passed beyond the channels or mediatory institutions that gave socialist strategy a foothold, that made the idea of socialism possible.

When we claim the impossibility of socialist reformism, signal the increasing power and autonomy of the capitalist State, and trace the gradual emergence of the paradigm of control, we in no way mean to strike a note of despair. We have merely attempted, through interpretations of certain predominant contemporary theorists, to provide a lucid outline of the figure of the contemporary State-form. This is only one side of the equation. "Modern bourgeois society," Marx and Engels wrote, "a society that has conjured up such gigantic means of production and exchange, is like the sorcerer who is no longer able to control the powers of the nether world whom he has called up by his spells" (*Manifesto of the Communist Party*, p. 39). We have looked at the sorcerer's spells; now we must descend into the nether world and grasp the subjective and productive figure of the powers that have been unleashed from its depths.

point of view of the most radical anticapitalism and reactionary humanism. On the other hand, those who hold capitalist development as the only possible form of economic and political civilization cannot condemn the gulag in any absolute way. When they do criticize it, in fact, the apologists of capitalism risk conducting an enormous historical whitewash, forgetting both the history of capitalist accumulation and the present gulags of exploitation and segregation, the remains of Vietnam and Iraq, and the terrible desolate spaces of continents ravaged by the effects of capitalist development. Rostow did not forget this when he compared, with minute attention, the series of economic developments of primitive accumulation in Great Britain in the seventeenth century and those of the emergence from underdevelopment to the capitalist economic takeoff of the underdeveloped countries in the twentieth century. In terms of the damages wrought by economic development, too, the gap between the two competing systems has thus progressively narrowed.

   Given that the effect of real socialism was to close the gap between East and West, it is puzzling that it has become commonplace to interpret socialist regimes with the category of totalitarianism. A State is understood as totalitarian when it enlists a total mobilization of productive forces and when every social dialectic is made functional to this mobilization. In the totalitarian regime, civil society is completely absorbed and swallowed up by the State, so that all of its autonomous potentiality and any claim to freedom are not only repressed but negated. Through the course of symbiotic histories, real socialism and Nazism eminently represented the category of totalitarianism in the twentieth century. We should recognize, however, that while the phenomenological and descriptive capacities of this category are doubtful at best (it seems delirious, in fact, to identify the total mobilization of a population to embark on economic development with the total mobilization of a mature capitalist economy to conduct an expansionist war), the category has absolutely no heuristic value. In effect, real socialism, in the very process of its disintegration, has shown the theorists of totalitarianism that it is not, as they claimed, a civil society reduced to a concentration camp but on the contrary the emergence (in several cases the absolutely original emergence) of a complex, dynamic, and articulated (even if disorganized) civil society, of a productive and civil chaos giving rise to open, innovative, and constituent sequences and alternatives. In effect, even if the concept of totalitarianism was capable of grasping some of the repressive features of real socialism, it generalized those characteristics and was thus completely blind to the real points of movement and innovation that were really changing those societies.

Our thesis, then, is that real socialism represented a process of accession to the market, insofar as it was a process in which the market was constructed and civil society reached the point of opening up and blossoming, the point of éclat. It was an accelerated and dilated form of accomplishing the process of primitive accumulation, a powerful deployment of the "formal subsumption" of society under capital. In seventy years, without considering the violent civil and foreign wars that hindered and radically reduced the period dedicated to development, the countries of real socialism came out of the Third World and entered the First. A real, terrific success, an exploit of acceleration that no capitalist country can boast in its own history and one that capitalist economists and politicians must admire. Never was capitalism so efficient in constructing a market and a civil society as were the countries of "real socialism." In short periods, from the mid-twenties to the end of the thirties, and from the fifties to the mid-seventies, the countries of real socialism experienced rhythms of economic growth that, to give only one example, not even the so-called countries of the dragon could boast of in the seventies and eighties — even with levels of exploitation higher and salary levels (including welfare) much lower than those in the Soviet Union.

At this point we might not know whether to marvel or scream scandalized when we remember that in 1936, in the middle of the development of real socialism, the Vyshinsky reform acted to formally represent the Soviet juridical system as a rights State, a State of law. (See Andrei Vyshinsky, *The Law of the Soviet State*, in particular the Introduction by John Hazard, pp. vi–x.) Through the enormous political changes of those years, the Soviet leadership definitely cast aside the "illusions" and the "utopias" of those who, both before and after 1917, had in economics and law posed the logic of "communism" against that of socialism, and revolutionary constituent power against the logic of capitalist accumulation. Those "utopians" believed there was another means for resisting and struggling (in that mortal struggle that knew the desire for freedom) against the gulag. This means, however, was unknown to Solzhenitsyn, to the theoreticians of totalitarianism, and moreover to the philosophers, economists, politicians, and jurists of capitalism, of its triumphant development and of the rights State. It is precisely to the study of this "unknown" means of resistance and expression of freedom that this chapter will be dedicated — to the redefinition of the "unknown god" before its altar in the middle of the agora of Athenian democracy.

Our theses should not seem paradoxical. Really, when we consider the crisis of real socialism as a consequence of the constitution of a complex civil society in the accomplishment of accumulation (and this seems to us an effectual truth), we find ourselves facing equally central phenomena in the capitalist State in postmodernity, presented there, however, in the context of the decline of civil society: for example, the separation of the citizenry from politics, the definition of an alternative social space through the refusal to participate in the processes of representation and legitimation in the democratic State, proposals of new forms of self-valorization and different horizons for realizing processes of social cooperation. In other words, the development of real socialism has constructed a political and productive subjectivity that, closing the historical gap, registers the crisis of the system at the same level as that in the West, in the very heart of the State of law with its same problems. The new citizen of real socialism is the double, the doppelgänger of the old citizen of mature capitalism, in the crisis of both systems.

This convergence of real socialism with the capitalist democracies, beginning in the 1930s, was a linear even if contradictory process. The ambivalence of Soviet constituent power, determined on one side by the emergence from underdevelopment and on the other by the construction of a communist society, has been broken — due perhaps, at least in part, to betrayal by the leaders and the tiredness of the masses, the hatred of the enemy, civil and foreign wars, and the blackmail of the world market. The transition was considered no longer communist but socialist, and it was reduced to a simple challenge of underdevelopment against mature capitalism. Communism, through the blows of the penal code and the gulag system, was thrown off the utopian course. Although in the early part of this century the Soviet State anticipated the developments of the capitalist State and presented itself as a planner-State, casting the hopes of the revolution on this anticipation, today it is the capitalist State of postmodernity that anticipates and challenges the former Soviet States in crisis. In any case, within this renewed confrontation, there is a full equivalence of problems and coincidence of situations. What is recast and what exceeds the framework of stabilization is the general problem of the revolution, which long ago ceased to have anything to do with the conflict between the regimes and was renewed within each of the two social situations.

In order to evaluate properly this passage and this tendential equivalence, however, we must better define the common nature of the problems that are posed in both the East and the West, that is, clarify what emerged in our analysis of postmodern law as the theme of separation and autonomy. (See chapter 6.) The social struggles in Eastern Europe were the foundation, the motor, and the decisive factor in the crisis of the system. Those societies were so little "totalitarian" (even if dictatorial) that the social struggles pushed them to the brink of catastrophe, and perhaps innovation. We mean by this that we should begin to understand the crisis by first recognizing that the social movements expressed their subversive power through new and atypical practices: through absence and refusal, flight and exodus. The resistance, which in other periods emerged actively and was subsequently defeated (for example, in 1956 and 1968), became invincible in the mass organization of refusal and exodus. It did not designate alternative positive forms in the traditional sense. The effectiveness of the struggles was demonstrated in the destabilizing and destructuring power of independence and separation. Against real socialism appeared a communism without memory, without ideology. A movement of mass cooperation was organized in the absence of memory, through the decision of exodus, through a practical clandestinity of liberation. Subtraction, flight, and refusal made the Berlin Wall fall. That was the social strike that upset the bureaucratic organization and shook the Kremlin towers. The regime imploded when its core was evacuated and proletarian independence took the form of exodus.

In this context, socialist theories and myths of transition completely broke down, precisely because they were based on a continuous trajectory of capitalist development in the productive process; the revolution was conceived as a substitution of one class (and/or its representatives) for another in the management of power and capital in the interest of development. From this point of view (exactly as was expressed in the Soviet Union by Vyshinsky's constitutional reform in 1936 or in the republics between 1945 and 1948), the revolution could be represented juridically as a modification of the material constitution (the dictatorship of the proletariat) without change to the formal constitution of the State (the dictatorship of the bourgeoisie). The claim in later years that this continuity was not linear but dialectical, or rather the emphasis (in terms of the supersession of the negation) that every modification of the social bases of legitimation kept whole the nature of the State, was simply rhetorical window dressing. This last mystification posed by the juridical theory and practice of the socialist transition was supported by another dialectical presupposition: the proletariat (endowed with universality and hegemonic capabilities) served as an active motor, that is, a participatory agent of reform and development. At this point, however, the overburdened mule collapsed—at the point when the hegemonic capacity of the proletariat expressed itself not as a will to participation but rather as the independence of self-valorization and consequently as a process of separation. This proletariat affirms not the participatory transition toward the shining horizons of socialism but the rupture, the denouncement of participation as mystification, the declaration of autonomy, and the constituent will of a radically new world.

If we look now at what is happening in the West, in the countries of mature capitalism, the scene is not too different. In this case too the dialectic of participation that until recently was felicitously represented in the relationship between the institutional workers' movement and the capitalist institutions, which imposed a strong reformist dynamic on the transformation of the State policies, has come to an end. The ritualistic repetitions of social "collective bargaining" are at this point only melancholic. The very definitions of "right" and "left" as political parties dialectically constitutive of a constitutional equilibrium appear only as obscurities and are completely useless. Keynesianism, the last idol of reformism and the democratic transition to socialism, is defunct. The participatory models of both economic life and political representation have been totally destroyed. Paradoxically, once again China is very close: Tiananmen and its cardboard statue of Liberty that, through separation, resisted power and its violence are more symbolic of and closer to our situation than are (or could be) any "refoundation" of old hopes, any Keynesian revival, and any socialist proposal. The catastrophe of socialism touches not only the countries of the East, but also the very theme of democratic participation. The reformist mechanisms of legitimation were constructed in response to socialism, from 1917 onward, even in the countries of mature capitalism. (See chapter 2.) The movement of separation destroys not only the present application, but even the very possibility of a dialectical definition of the State.

Postmodern theories of the State, as we argued in the previous chapter, are just as implicated in this predicament as Keynesian theories. The perception of an epocal passage that they interpret in terms of the search for an equilibrium based on weak subjects, with recourse to the techniques of systematism, does not in fact hold in the face of the solidity of the figures of the exodus that the crisis of real socialism has revealed. The weak practices of legitimation are now confronted with the exodus — migration, chaotic dynamics of transformation, and mass refusal. Here they clearly show the precariousness of their theoretical scaffolding.

Let us break the rhythm of this initial perception of a movement "beyond socialism," then, both in the former socialist States of Eastern Europe and in the Western capitalist democracies. Escaping from the crisis of the modern State, historically and theoretically constructed on the organization of the dialectic between the State and the constituent power of the multitude, can only consist in the State's attempt to reconstruct this dialectic. What happens, however, when for once the instigator of crisis is not a constituted power but a constituent power, one that refuses development and does not call for the dialectic? What does it mean that the masses have destroyed the socialist illusion and positioned themselves as a force of separation and self-valorization in the face of the State? When this emergence of constituent power is not episodic and insurrectional but continuous, ontological, and irreversible, what does this catastrophe mean with respect to law and the State? We understand exodus as a fundamental political reality of the present. As the Founding Fathers teach us, an enormous creative energy is accumulated in the exodus. Could we recognize the positive content, the creative energy of the exodus as a new constituent power? What does the exercise of constituent power mean today?

Real socialism, through its rise and crisis, carried the world of the East to the heart of the West and consequently cut through a fundamental mystification about the definition of the possible alternatives of freedom. The form of the present crisis in the East and the West is defined as an exodus from the political, as separation and social self-valorization. Finally, there exists a positive determination of the exodus and it can be defined on the juridical terrain: it is constituent power, the organization and the institution of the exodus. The crisis of real socialism thus opens a space of freedom that invests also and primarily the rights State and the capitalist democracies. We must now explore this new terrain.

Paradoxes of the Postmodern State

In order to address the problematic we have begun to outline, it will be useful first of all to grasp some paradoxes of the postmodern State. The first and fundamental paradox (from which all of the others derive) consists in the fact that, in the ideal type of this figure of the State, the hegemony of civil society is made to serve in the absence of civil society itself. Even while the real elements of civil society wither, as we claimed earlier, its image is reproposed at a higher level. In order to affirm the preeminence of an idea of the image of civil society, the postmodern State takes away any social dialectic that might constitute an actual civil society. By making every relationship of power horizontal, the postmodern State both annuls every social power and obliges it to find meaning only in the form of the State.

The postmodern State, as we saw in chapter 6, presents itself as the horizon of the most perfect democracy in the circularity of all the constitutive elements of its structure. These elements would be weak enough to be continually recomposed and re-formed in the circularity of the institutional functioning. It follows that every dialectical opposition between the material constitution (as the set of physical and political conditions that are presupposed by the historical Constitution) and the formal constitution (that is, the legal and juridical structure of the State) is taken away. Analogically, all sequences of contractual procedures of equilibrium in society and between the State and social bodies are considered to be exhausted. Postmodern politics and law take away the dialectic and remove any form of crisis from the horizon of the material functioning of the State-form. Hence, as every reality or even semblance of social dialectic disappears, the autonomy of the political from the social becomes total. Civil society can only exist in the figure of the political. Although this passage may be experienced as melancholy (Lyotard) or play (Baudrillard), the extinction of the social and the totalization of the political are given as a definitive result of capitalist development. From this point of view, postmodernity presents an odd and unexpected repetition of the traditional Marxist vision in that it sees the withering away of the State in the society of mature capitalism—or better, the transformation of civil society into a pacified political form.

The central paradox of the postmodern State is repeated in each of the single concepts that define the State-form. This is true both for the State presented in a systematic (or neocontractual) form or the State presented in communitarian form—in either case the concepts of "legitimacy," "representation," and "responsibility" are submitted to an operation of maximum flattening, maneuvered on a purely horizontal level and therefore reduced to functions of a circular and self-centering mechanism. Every social dialectic is taken away; democracy is realized; history is over.

In the postmodern phase of the theory of the State and law, the concept of legitimacy appears as an extreme figure of the rationalization of power (in the Weberian sense). Every residual of traditional (or rather, corporatist and contractual) legitimacy along with every charismatic (or rather, regal and plebiscitary) character are considered to be obsolete. The juridical obligation, which in the history of political thought is always formed as a mediation of consensus and authority, no longer constitutes the problem: postmodern democratic legitimation is the perfect synthesis of consensus and authority. If deviant or antagonistic social practices emerge, they are included in the notion of criminality. Outside of the law of the pacified society, they are only pathology and terror. As for power, it can only be defined in a democratic sense, simply democratic; nothing exceeds, nothing can exceed the democratic rationality.

The same is true for the concept of representation. The two

systems that the mature capitalist State has known for organizing popular representation, the system of party representation and the system of corporatist representation, have been effectively nullified. Political representation by means of the social mediation of parties is considered obsolete in the sense that it looks toward a mechanism of delegation that is formed in society (as a reality different than the State), that is verticalized in the State (as a reality different than society), and that selected political personnel (as a reality different than the rational administrative mechanism). This type of representation was adequate to a modern liberal society in which the subsumption of society under capital was not yet accomplished. Political representation by means of the social mediation of the corporations, the trade unions, the lobbies, and so forth, is also considered obsolete in the sense that it looked to a contractual mechanism that traversed society and the State in a linear way, politically (and not only administratively) articulating the representative relationship. This type of representation was adequate to a social-democratic society in which the subsumption of society under capital and the State was still only formal and incomplete (in other words, society was not prefigured by capital and the State). Corporatist representation still incites vertical dimensions in the relationship between society and the State; that is, the political has not been erased fully in the systematic, rational, and administrative horizon of postmodernity. This, however, is in the process of disappearing.

The concept of responsibility is transformed along analogous lines. Along with the concept of legitimacy, it too must now be formed on a rational horizon completely flattened and centripetal. Responsibility, in the systematic and communitarian sense, does not look toward the outside, it does not confront socially determined factual or ethical horizons with a polytheistic heaven, but looks only toward the inside of the system and the community, and it is posed in conformity with the rules of this internal realm. The ethics of responsibility is completely subjugated to the system of administrative coherence and instrumental logical consequences. In all of these cases, therefore, the maximum power of the political goes hand in hand with the extreme neutralization of social space. The concept of social equilibrium becomes normative and is presented as a fully realized political space. The absorption of the social in the political becomes the evacuation of the space of the social.

We will have to develop our analysis of these phenomena later, but we can observe here nonetheless some consequences of these mechanisms, primarily in relation to the theme of representation. The withering away of "social space" and the continually stronger tendency of the contemporary "political market" to be resolved in the hard necessities of management both demand solutions of substitution, or more exactly of the overdetermination and simulation of representation. If political representation continues to function while lacking any solid foundation in society, this void must be covered over by the construction of an artificial world that substitutes for the dynamics of civil society. The new communicational processes of the so-called information society contribute to this end. A mechanism familiar to the development of democratic society is repeated here: the passage from the democratic representation of the masses to the representatives' production of their own voters. Through the mediatic manipulation of society, conducted through enhanced polling techniques, social mechanisms of surveillance and control, and so forth, power tries to prefigure its social base. Society is made aseptic through mediatic and communicative operations designed to dominate the dynamics of transformation and simplify the complexity of reality. The crisis of collective identities is in this way pushed to the extreme; individualism is maintained as the supreme value and the antagonisms are manipulated by the mechanisms of compensation that participate in the repression or eclipsing of the historical and social events. Society has to dance according to the rhythm of power and every dissonance, every instance of cacophony must be reduced to the heart of the harmony in which power invents the rules in every case. The passivity of consensus becomes the fundamental rule; the reduction of social space is the norm of political space; political space produces the social event, which produces the social dynamics and creates consensus; and finally the social is annulled through communicative overdetermination and substitution. The concepts of legitimation and administrative and political responsibility are ground up in this same mill.

In summary, the postmodern schema of law and the State is a powerful means of the mystification of democracy. In the moment when it pretends to immerse power in the social and assume the market as an exclusive basis of the political, the postmodern schema radicalizes power in the highest figure of the State. At this point we need to investigate further to discover how this efficient mystification is possible, recognizing which social bases produce it and how they make it effective.

The Social Bases of the Postmodern State and the Existing Prerequisites of Communism

Which social transformations are at the base of these phenomena? How can we understand the proletarian exodus and the postmodern form of the State? Is there a single root that links the transformation of the class composition with the transformation of the State-form? In order to respond to these questions we must take a few steps backward and look at the historical process that has led us to the present situation, on the terrain of the struggle between the classes and the transformation of the social composition.

The history of the recent transformations should be centered, we believe, around the events of 1968. In that year the workers' attack against the organization of factory labor and against the social division of labor reached its summit. Through their struggles, the workers, up until then regimented in the factory and in society in the Taylorist, Fordist, and Keynesian mode of production, shattered the compatibilities and the equilibria of the capitalist reproduction of society en masse through successive waves of extended struggles on an international level. To reformulate a Hegelian phrase, in 1968 the ferocious beast of living labor smashed every disciplinary limit. It was necessary, therefore, to tame it. In the years immediately after 1968, then, a new era of relationships began between capital (along with its State, be it bourgeois or socialist) and labor. This new era was characterized by four factors.

1. Norms of consumption tended away from Fordist wage planning and led back to the laws of the market. In this sense a new type of individualism was launched—an individualism in the choice of the goods of reproduction, but strongly conditioned by the collective structure of the social organization of production and communication in which this new individualism was nurtured and recognized.

2. Models of regulation extended beyond the national boundaries that were at the base of Keynesian policies of planning. They were extended along multinational lines and continually more regulated by monetary policies throughout the world market.

3. Laboring processes were radically modified by the automation of factories and by the computerization of society. Immediately productive labor was displaced from the central position it had occupied during the entire previous history of the capitalist organization of society.

4. Within this set of mechanisms the composition of labor-power was completely modified. Workers were no longer individuals bought by a capitalist to be submitted to the collective process

labor, interest, and language). We call them irreversible insofar as they constitute conditions of social life that have become unavoidable, even in the case of catastrophe. In this way, an element of historical collective aggregation becomes a profound institutional moment, and a cluster of contradictory and conflictive collective wills becomes ontological, a part of being. These determinations, however, even though they are ontologically solid, remain contradictory. The struggle against exploitation continues to cut across them, just as it produced them. It keeps them open and even goes so far as to propose potential crises on the horizon of the entire system.

We can see an elementary example of the functioning of a prerequisite in the institutions of the Welfare State. As we have argued in the earlier chapters of this book, the social institutions of the Welfare State are the product of social struggles that forced the State, through an institutional compromise, to accept at its heart the representation of organized collective interests, sometimes antagonistic to the State itself.[3] This representation, which was posed in the service of a tendency toward an egalitarian redistribution of social income, always under more comprehensive pressure of collective interests, has become a solid institutional reality. The resistance of these institutional phenomena to reduction is further reinforced by the griddings of power relations that ran throughout its beginnings, by the repeated conflicts of interest, and paradoxically by the inertia of the institutions themselves. This, in short, is an effect of the comprehensiveness of the apparatuses across the entire system. We have witnessed this irreversibility in the capitalist countries during these twenty years of neoliberal counterrevolution (see chapter 6, "The Strong State of Neoliberalism"), and we can also recognize it in the crisis of real socialism. Political science and the study of civil and constitutional law have had to alter their own scientific statute in relation to these phenomena, abandoning traditional formalism and subordinating the analytical procedure to the continual permeability of struggles and institutions. The consequent dynamics of control have been forced onto a terrain that privileges the interchangeability and indistinguishability of the social and the political. Political science is thus limited to the intersection between the social mobility of individual and collective subjects and the institutional ontology of the results that derive from them — the processes of government are grounded on this foundation. Comprehensiveness and rigidity are wedded together; every act of governance risks modifying the entire system of social production and reproduction. This is precisely the movement that continually reopens the crisis and defines sequences of growing contradictions. In effect, the determinate contradiction of collective interests, irreversibly grounded on the institutional level, can only be resolved by collective means.

In the terms of classical economics and its critics, one could say that in this phase of development of the mode of production, every attempt to maneuver or control the proportion of necessary labor comes back in the reproduction costs of socially consolidated fixed capital. This rigidity, then, is irreversible. Certainly, this claim is *beyond* Marx's analysis (even if we can recognize it perhaps in his conception of the tendency), but it is even further outside contemporary economic thought, either in its neoliberal or its neo-Keynesian form. In these schools, the mobility of all social and economic factors is assumed, in more or less intensive form, as a condition of government. Our claim, however, translated in terms of the critique of political institutions and thus in terms of the analysis of the Welfare State, is that the government of social reproduction is only possible in terms of the collective management of capital. In fact, the conditions of the existence of capital are no longer only implicitly but explicitly collective. They are no longer, that is, simply linked to the abstraction of collective capital, but are part of the empirical, historical existence of the collective worker.

The Welfare State and its irreversibility (just like, at first sight, the irreversibility of certain fundamental determinations of real socialism) do not represent, therefore, deviations in capitalist development; on the contrary, they constitute real islands of new social cooperation, new and intense collective conditions of production, recognized as such on the institutional level itself. Hence the crisis that the mere continued existence of the Welfare State continually provokes in the liberal-democratic State. Hence also the dynamics of rupture that this irreversibility continually breaks open in the present State-form, because the determinations of the Welfare State are both necessary for social consensus and required for economic stability. Are these active prerequisites of communism? It would be stupid to simply suppose that they were. They are, however, undeniable prerequisites of a permanent destabilization of the systematic axes of the liberal or socialist management of the State. They are prerequisites of a passive revolution.

Much more important, though, are the prerequisites of communism that can be identified in the contemporary evolution of the form and organization of labor. We find the second existing prerequisite in the new capacities of productive cooperation in the laboring subject. In preceding periods of capitalist evolution, both in the phases of primitive accumulation and "manufacturing" (represented constitutionally by the State of the ancien régime) and in the successive phases of the organization of "large-scale industry" (represented constitutionally both by the evolving modern democratic State from its liberal to its social-democratic form and in Eastern Europe, through the acceleration of rhythms of development, by the socialist form of the State), the history of capitalism and its historical merit were characterized by the process of successive abstractions of labor. In the most recent period, Taylorism determined the process of the abstraction of labor-power; Fordism made this abstract subjectivity available to the mechanisms of the collective negotiation of consumption, posing the bases of the State (and its public expenditures) within the productive mechanism; and Keynesianism proposed a progressive schema of proportions between socially necessary labor and surplus value, thus accomplishing the State's enormous task of organizing continuous compromises between antagonistic social subjects. Today, in the field of organized labor, these relationships have been overthrown. In effect, in the development of struggles in the 1960s and 1970s, the abstraction of labor went beyond its subjective dimensions and spilled over to the terrain of subversion. The subsequent capitalist reaction had to try to reduce this new subject to an objective quality of the labor process by means of economic restructuring that would move beyond the abstraction of labor.

Today we are in the midst of this process of restructuring. In the passage from Taylorism to post-Taylorism and from Fordism to post-Fordism, subjectivity and productive cooperation are posed as *conditions* not results of labor processes. The Fordist relationship between production and consumption has been internalized in order to optimize the logic of production, the logic of circulation, and the realization of the value of the product. New mass production certainly requires total flexibility, and similarly the "self-making" of the working class has to be reduced to the immediate element of production and circulation. In this process, however, productive efficiency is actually subordinated to the autonomy and the self-activation of the working class. The thousands of varieties of "the Japanese model" and its fortunes throughout the world all reduce in the final analysis to the most explicit recognition of the immediately valorizing function of workers' subjectivity. Throughout the period of the hegemony of Taylorism, in stark contrast, subjectivity could only be recognized as antagonistic estrangement. It is quite true that this acceptance of the productive function of the subject within the organization of labor does not go without some peremptory conditions. This productive function can be recognized from the capitalist point of view, that is, only in terms of industrial integration and the negation of the traditional workers' subject, in both its syndicalist and class form. Only those, however, with an incurable fetish for the past (to the extent that the past can be seen as glorious) can deny the determinant positive modification that is brought about by the transformation of the workers' subject. This new workers' figure is the fruit of a historic defeat, following the cycle of struggles in the sixties and seventies, but nonetheless in labor processes and in laboring cooperation it already demonstrates a high degree of the consolidation of collective subjectivity.

Without overlooking the undeniable passive aspects, we can follow the progression of laboring cooperation from the antagonism of abstract labor-power to the concreteness of a collective labor-power — not yet antagonistic but subjectively active. The working class has maintained in its daily existence the values of cooperation — experienced in previous phases — on the terrain of abstract antagonism. Today this cooperating and subjective activity is carried, as if in a latent state, within the labor process. The contradiction is acute and can only become more powerful as the process of restructuring is developed. In general terms, we can conclude that living labor is organized within the capitalist enterprise independently from capitalist command; it is only afterward, and formally, that this cooperation becomes systematized in command. Productive cooperation is posed as prior to and independent of the entrepreneurial function. Consequently, capital is not presented in the role of organizing labor-power, but rather in that of registering and managing the autonomous self-organization of labor-power. In this sense the progressive function of capital has come to an end.

In this case, too, we are well beyond the terms of classical economics (and even those of its critics) that recognize as productive only the labor incorporated within capital. It is interesting to note how all the schools of economic thought turn impotently around this unheard-of truth of post-Fordism: living labor is organized independently of the capitalist organization of labor. And even when this new determination seems to be grasped, such as in the regulation school, it lacks the capacity to be developed further, to understand the inversion of the theory of industrial integration in the theory of the developed antagonism. In blind objectivism, some economists continue to wait for some miraculous power to transform living labor "in itself" into the working class "in and for itself" — as if this transformation were a mythical event and not instead what it really is, a process. On the other hand, it is the intelligence of this process that keeps theory out of the only terrain on which we can explain the permanence of the crisis that began in the early 1970s (parallel, therefore, to the restructuring): the terrain on which the process of the political liberation of labor emerges. It is here, and only here, that all the production of value is accumulated. The figure of the capitalist entrepreneur withdraws into always more external and parasitic activities, and thus in the final analysis the collective capitalist is not able to intervene in the crisis. Although in previous periods the development of the abstraction of labor and the formation of processes of social cooperation of the productive forces were consequences of the development of the productive and political capitalist machine, today cooperation is posed prior to the capitalist machine as an independent condition of development. The new era of the organization of capitalist production and reproduction of society is dominated by the emergence of the laboring subjectivity that claims its mass autonomy, its own independent capacity of collective valorization, that is, its self-valorization with respect to capital.

To analyze the third prerequisite of communism we must move directly onto the terrain of subjectivity and touch on a higher degree of connection between the passive aspects of the process of transformation of the mode of production and the potentialities that come alive within this process. The processes of the creation of value, as we all know, are no longer centered on factory work. The dictatorship of the factory over society, its position at the crossroads of all processes of the formation of value, and therefore the objective centrality of directly productive (male, manual, and waged) labor are all disappearing. Capitalist production is not enclosed by the factory walls and neither are the forces that resist it. Recognizing these obvious facts does not mean renouncing the labor theory of value; it means, on the contrary, reexamining its validity by means of an analysis that grasps the radical transformation in its functioning. Moreover, recognizing these obvious facts does not mean mocking the reality of exploitation, pretending that in a so-called postindustrial society exploitation has been removed from our experience — on the contrary, it means locating the new forms in which exploitation is practiced today and therefore identifying the new configurations of class struggle. It means asking ourselves, first of all, if the transformation deals not so much with the nature of exploitation as with its extension and the quality of the terrain on which it is put into play. Only on this horizon can we witness the eventual modification of the nature of exploitation, almost as a passage from quantity to quality.

The fundamental characteristic of the new mode of production seems to consist in the fact that the principal productive force is technico-scientific labor, insofar as it is a comprehensive and qualitatively superior form of the synthesis of social labor. In other words, living labor is manifest above all as abstract and immaterial labor (with regard to quality), as complex and cooperative labor (with regard to quantity), and as continually more intellectual and scientific labor (with regard to form). This is not reducible to simple labor — on the contrary, there is an always greater convergence in technico-scientific labor of artificial languages, complex articulations of cybernetic appendages, new epistemological paradigms, immaterial determinations, and communicative machines. The subject of this labor, the social worker, is a cyborg, a hybrid of machine and organism that continually crosses the boundaries between material and immaterial labor.[4] The labor of this worker should be defined as social because the general conditions of the vital processes of production and reproduction pass under its control and are remodeled in conformity with it. The entire society is invested and recomposed in the process of the production of value by this new configuration of living labor: invested to the point that, within this process, exploitation seems to have disappeared — or better, seems to have been restricted to irremediably backward zones of contemporary society. This appearance, however, is easily swept away. In reality, capitalist power dramatically controls the new configurations of living labor, but it can only control them from the outside, because it is not allowed to invade them in a disciplinary way. The contradiction of exploitation is thus displaced onto a very high level where the subject who is principally exploited (the technico-scientific subject, the cyborg, the social worker) is recognized in its creative subjectivity but controlled in the management of the power that it expresses. It is from this very high point of command that the contradiction spills over into the entire society. And it is therefore with respect to this very high point of command that the entire social horizon of exploitation tends to unify, situating within the antagonist relationship all the elements of self-valorization, at whichever level they arise.

The conflict, then, is social precisely because technico-scientific living labor is a massified quality of the laboring intelligensia, of cyborgs and hackers. This "intelligensia" is not, however, some recomposed vanguard or leading sector; rather, it is a quality and a subjectivity that extends horizontally across the spectrum of social production and through the various sectors of production. The conflict is social, then, because all of the efforts of the refusal of work of all the other exploited social strata tend to be identified with and converge toward technico-scientific labor in an antagonistic way. New cultural models and new social movements are constituted in this flux in the place of old workers' subjectivities, and the old emancipation *through* labor is replaced by the liberation *from* waged and manual labor. Finally, the conflict is social because more and more it is situated on the general linguistic terrain, or rather on the terrain of the production of subjectivity. In the domain of the social worker there is no room left for capitalist command. The space that capital has won is simply that of the control of language, both scientific and common language. This is not an irrelevant space. It is

activity, to which was opposed the forces of expropriation, private wealth, and instrumental rationality. Translated into Machiavellian terms, the universality of "virtue" was opposed by the despotic particularity of "fortune." Translated instead into Spinozian terms, the *potentia* (power) of the multitude is opposed by the *potestas* (Power) of the State.[5] Modern rationalism is not a continuity that can be described on the basis of scientific progress; it is a contradictory product of different rationalities, one insistent on the productive capacity of human cooperation in the construction of history and life itself, and the other insistent instead on the order of power and the organization of a social division of labor directed toward the reproduction of that power. Modernity should be defined within this struggle, this logical and ethical struggle over human destiny itself, over freedom and subjugation. In its most mature form, this is defined as a dialectic, or really as a systematic form of the instrumental utilization of freedom for the construction of structures of the organization of power that are continually more inclusive and efficient. The dialectic is the imposition of the transcendental supersession on the continuous conflict that the collective constituent power of the masses, of associative labor, imposes on constituted power. The dialectic understands modernity as a state of crisis that it sublimates transcendentally.

We have to return instead to the crisis, where we can recognize the effectiveness of its transcendental solution in continual decline. We must refer to the modern metaphysics of politics, because this domain allows us to grasp in its diverse figures the inconclusiveness of the very definition of modernity. In the theory of the State developed from Machiavelli to Hobbes, from Spinoza to Rousseau, and from Hegel to Marx, modernity appears precisely as an alternative between one line that, standing on the ontological power of living labor, sees in democracy (understood in absolute terms) the only political form adequate to the process of productive socialization developing in history and another line that seeks to expropriate in the transcendental realm (be it the divinity of the sovereign, the impersonality of the juridical general will, or the dialectical absolute) the living productivity of human cooperation. This logical struggle is a real struggle. Cooperation and democracy are really opposed to command and sovereignty. In the modern era the victory of the transcendental alternative, both in the form of the authoritarian State and in that of the liberal State, still has never succeeded in eliminating the substantial crisis that runs throughout history: the other alternative, although continually defeated, is nonetheless present. It is continually reborn from its ashes and imposes an irreducible discontinuity on the development of the modern sovereign State of capitalism. Every victory of the line of sovereignty is forced to concede always more space to cooperation. From one revolution to the next, the critical process of modernity was played out in its alternatives. Every victory of capital has had to leave more space to associative living labor as its essential alternative. The socialist revolution represents the emblematic and highest point of this process: here the productive masses are conceded sovereignty, not democracy—and this is equally true for the socialism of Eastern Europe and the social democracy of the West. Finally, it is democracy against sovereignty that is the order of the day, today, in the crisis of modernity. This crisis does not negate modernity but definitively liberates one of its potentialities, its living productive alternative. The postmodern State, insofar as it is a renewed apologia of constituted power and sovereignty, is capitalism's attempt to acknowledge the definitive conditions of its crisis without paying the price; it is the attempt to evade the consequences of a lost war. In reality, in this crisis *another postmodern* is unleashed: the power of living labor, the productivity of a cooperation that finds in immanence and the immediacy of its logics the force to develop itself. This is the autonomy of the masses and at the same time a set of productive and political subjectivities.

Although the history of modernity and our various conceptualizations of it allow us to understand this alternative, it seems nonetheless difficult to grasp the event, the critical point in which the democratic, productive, and cooperative alternative would be released. In our opinion, attention should be focused on two social explosions: the explosion of 1968 that upset the Western world, putting in motion the present capitalist restructuring, and twenty years later the explosion of 1989 that, through the Soviet process of restructuring, toppled the socialist world. In both of these events, three-quarters of a century of the history of modernity was precipitated, showing the rupture of the two ideal alternatives, bringing to light definitively the emergence of the new political subject: the social proletariat organized through immaterial labor and made productive through cooperation. This is a subject that is consequently capable of being free, of exercising a democracy without sovereignty—without a constitution that organizes freedom, because freedom is continuously and always a constituent power. It is without mystifications that are inverted on the capacity of collective rationality to make itself freedom—because rationality is experienced in cooperation and in the continuous construction of the conditions of collective freedom. Machiavelli describes the movement of communal democracy; Spinoza conceived of democracy as an absolute, completely immanent government, free from any transcendent norm; Marx, in his historical writings, but above all in the *Grundrisse*, identified the new political subjectivity in the intellectual cooperation of a labor power that

opacity of reality is not absolutely taken away; the era of utopia is long gone. The process, however, that poses the subject in relation to the common, the common in relation to the transcendental, the transcendental in relation to the imagination, and the imagination in relation to the ethical constitution is not utopian, but rather very real. Democracy may be primary to philosophy, just as Rorty claims, but not in the sense that it affirms a contingent and relativist criterion against the universality of philosophy—on the contrary, because it affirms the ontological weight of the desires and practices of existing subjects and develops this social being through an indefatigable and irreducible process of the constitution of community, cooperation, and collectivism. Ontology is a development of democracy and democracy is a line of conduct, a practice of ontology.

The proposition of an ontological theory of constitution, then, disrupts the conventional sets of alternatives that dominate much of the discourse in political theory: if we try to situate it in the polemics between liberals and communitarians or between modernists and postmodernists, we have to recognize that the theory of constitution is *au milieu*, not as a compromise but as an objection to the terms of the debate—it effectively displaces the discussion. We can perhaps most clearly recognize the political methodology of constitution in the tradition of critical Marxist analysis. The problem of constitution became part of the Marxist discussion primarily in the 1970s. In the English tradition that centered around the work of E. P. Thompson with its methodological focus on the self-making of the working class, the work of Hans-Jürgen Krahl in Germany, and also the emerging workerist tradition in Italy, the problem of constitution was posed as a new synthesis of the project of communist democracy and the analysis of the transformation of the working class and productive labor.[7] In each of these traditions the refusal of all the dialectical methodologies (especially that of dialectical materialism in its orthodox form) was accompanied by the attempt to grasp in the development of the struggles not only the motor of the transformations of the capitalist system but moreover and primarily the construction of a historic, concrete, and determinate alternative to the capitalist system.

Two problematic lines of inquiry were simultaneously put in motion. The first was one that critiques the discourse on the socialist transition, a discourse that involved considering socialism as a stage of development toward communism. The political critique of real socialism was just as important, from this point of view, as the critique of social democracy in the countries of mature capitalism. The socialist transition was, in this respect, nothing other than a variant on capitalist development. The second problematic line was intended to recuperate the active element of the thematic of transition. The methodological discussion arrived at this point by considering the power of living labor as the only basis of wealth, as the only form of the expression of desire, as the only means of democratic construction. When living labor was recognized as immaterial labor, as a cooperative force par excellence, and as a strong residual of subjectivization, it was clear that the global methodological point of view could be cast as the perspective of communism. Communism has no need of agents external to the productivity of cooperative, immaterial, living labor. The transition has no need of the State. The critical Marxism of the 1970s gave only one response to the problem of the transition: there is nothing by which to transfer, there is only the force of construction, constituent power. The juridical forms of communist society will not be, in any case, projections or residuals of bourgeois law — they can only be constructions of a new constituent power, the same that is manifested in the struggles, that is exercised in the democracy of the agentic singularities and in the constructive relationship of the collectivities.

Although this first mass experiment of a new Marxist methodology was defeated after the 1970s (defeated on a political, not a theoretical, terrain), the methodology of constitution has been continually developed in political philosophy, in various terms and contexts. The "ontological history of ourselves" and the philosophical-social research it involves, as we said earlier, have led in the work of many authors to an ethical and political project. The analysis of the mechanisms of the constitution of social being presents us with a myriad of possibilities to intervene in the process of ontological constitution: recognizing how we are constituted as subjects leads us to see how and to what extent we can constitute ourselves as subjects. Deleuze and Guattari have traced the nomadic movement of singular subjects, the deterritorializing flows of desire, and the processes of political assemblage in immanent planes of consistency. (See *A Thousand Plateaus*, in particular pp. 351–500.) These constituent forces never fully escape the striated space and territorializing apparatuses of capture of the State machine, but they nonetheless continually shatter the constituted world of the State and work with the creativity and innovation of their own free activity, their own constituent powers. Subjective assemblages constitute the mechanisms of their own social organization, their own singular communities from below, drawing exclusively from the immanent social plane. They pose a vision of democracy as in an absolutely horizontal social plane on which social bodies are set loose to destroy the strictures of predetermined social forms and discover their own ends, invent their own constitution. The horizontal society is the open site that fosters practical creation and

represent its own power and the powerlessness of its opponent, the State. The representational plane holds nonviolent action and terrorism together at opposite poles.

The second problem raised by the discourse of nonviolent action, which is closely related to the first, is the critique of violence and the proposition of justice it assumes at its foundation. There is clearly a strong vein in this tradition, which includes an undeniable religious component in the thinking of those such as Gandhi, Thomas Merton, and Martin Luther King, Jr., that assumes the inherent injustice of the violent and the corresponding justice of the nonviolent. This moral perspective must concentrate on the purity of nonviolent activists to insure that they adequately represent the just position. Gandhi argues strenuously, for example, that one must adopt nonviolence not because it is politically effective (and thus might be discarded in cases when it is seen as ineffective), but because it is right and thus applicable universally, in all situations and throughout one's life. This attitude of purity from violence is widespread in the various U.S. activist communities (often without its religious component), and often dovetails with what is conceived as politically correct in various activities, such as diet, movie watching, sexual relationships, and so forth. From this point of view any form of violence is inherently unjust and would cast the protesters in the same moral category as the State whose actions they are attempting to oppose.

On a theoretical level, it should be obvious that attempts to critique violence by posing oneself as completely outside of it are precarious at best. One could cite numerous authors who have investigated the forms of violence that are not easily isolatable but infuse our entire world and ourselves: James Baldwin and Frantz Fanon on race, Marx on class, Ivan Illich on poverty, Catharine MacKinnon on sexuality, and so forth. It would take a very reduced notion of what constitutes violence to be able to consider ourselves pure from it: our complicity is a condition of our social existence. Furthermore, it is highly untenable to sustain the moral equivalence between violence and injustice. The materialist tradition has long conceived the exertion of power, which is the essence of the world, as a form of violence. In authors such as Spinoza and Nietzsche, life itself involves violence and it would make no sense to pose any notion of the right, the just, or the good outside of the context of the exertion of our power. All that could result is a sort of morality or asceticism that denies life, or more specifically denies our power. The ressentiment involved in this sort of representational politics is precisely what links nonviolence with terrorism, casting it together with what it so adamantly tries to oppose. (The nonviolent critique of terrorism is weak, then, both because in attempting to oppose violence *tout court* it fails to recognize the specificity of terrorist violence and because it is fundamentally linked with terrorism on the plane of representational politics, posing an external relationship between performative practices and their ends.)

Although it is untenable in this theoretical context, it should nonetheless be understandable why nonviolent action has recently spread so widely among activist groups. It is symptomatic, above all, of the dearth of legitimated forms of political action that has resulted from the withering of civil society. The institutions of civil society provided channels for legitimate political contestation and legitimated different forms of political violence. The most prominent example is the right to strike granted to the institutional trade unions. With the right to organize and strike, codified in the United States by the Wagner Act and the National Industrial Recovery Act in the 1930s, the labor union became the largest institution outside the State legally licensed to wield violence. The forms of political contestation channeled through all the institutions of civil society involved the legitimation of violence in some form or other. With the withering of civil society, however, the structures that legitimated violent political contestation have equally withered, so that now it appears that no contestational violence can be legitimated. The horizon of contestational practice appears as barren between the two poles, with nonviolent action on one side and terrorism on the other. There seems to be nowhere left for us to stand between these two unacceptable positions.

Clearly, the terms of political practice and violence must be rethought so that we can move to a different plane with richer possibilities. The critique of violence should not be conceived as an operation that delimits from the outset the boundaries of violence in life or in our world, but rather as an effort to discern from an internal perspective the differentiations within violence and within the exercise of power. In his critique of power, Foucault insists repeatedly that he is not arguing for a society without power relations but simply for an analysis that from the beginning brings into question all forms of power: "I am not saying that all forms of power are unacceptable but that no power is necessarily acceptable or unacceptable. This is anarchism. But since anarchism is not acceptable these days, I will call it anarcheology—the method that takes no power as necessarily acceptable" ("Du Gouvernement des Vivants"). Using Foucault's anarcheology as a methodological basis, we can begin to conceive a critique of violence that takes no violence as necessarily acceptable or unacceptable but rather looks to the different forms and instances of violence in our lives to differentiate among them.

This is the spirit in which Walter Benjamin sets out on his cri-

tique of violence. Benjamin's criterion of differentiation is the relationship between violence and the law. The predominant form of violence that we experience
in our world is one that is intimately related to the law, serving one of two functions: the lawmaking function or the law-preserving function. The various apparatuses of the State (the police, the army, the judiciary, and so forth) are all involved
in one or both of these functions, but so too are many forms of violence that
oppose the State or seek to achieve ends different than those of the State. These
forms of violence too seek to pose a law, even if that be a new law that destroys the
present one. "All violence as a means is either lawmaking or law-preserving. If it
lays claim to neither of these predicates, it forfeits all validity" ("Critique of Violence," p. 287). The logic that legitimates this form of violence involves relating
means to ends, causes to effects. Benjamin is not referring here to all forms of
causality but to a specifically *external* relationship—an effect external to its cause,
an end external to its means. This type of violence involves constructing an external relation between an action (violence) and its representation (the law). Benjamin
gives this lawmaking and law-preserving violence the name mythical violence,
using the notion of myth to capture the ruling effects of representations.

The question obviously arises for Benjamin as to how we might
conceive other kinds of violence than those that pose and support the law. How
can we understand a violence that is not a means external to its end? How can we
conceive a nonrepresentational or unrepresentable violence? Benjamin begins by
citing the difference between the conception of a revolutionary movement that
seeks to take control of the State and the movement that seeks rather to destroy
State power altogether and refuse any relation to the law (pp. 291–92). This second form of violence, revolutionary violence, is "unalloyed" or "immediate" in the
sense that it does not look to anything external to itself, to any representations, for
its effects. This proposition of anarchism as an alternative form of violence, however, only poses a negative definition. Benjamin tries to grasp this second form
of violence positively in terms of divine violence. "Mythical violence is bloody
power over mere life for its own sake, divine violence pure power over all life for
the sake of the living" (p. 297). The mythical performs the law and thus represents
its rule of mere life; divine violence expresses life in itself in a nonmediate way,
outside of law, in the form of the living. "One must reject all mythical violence,
lawmaking violence, which we may call governing violence. One must also reject
law-preserving violence, the governed violence in the service of the governing.
Divine violence … is the sign and seal but never the means of sacred execution"
(p. 300). We call this divine violence constituent power.

The constitutive practice of the multitude is not the means to anything but its own power. This practice is not a performance; it does not look to its representations for effects, nor focus its energies on sending a message. This alternative practice operates on an entirely different plane than that of representation. (Constitutive practice thus gives us the tools for the most powerful and adequate critique of the performance of terrorism, and of the entire plane of representational politics.) Deleuze would say that this constitutive practice poses a power not separated from but internal to what it can do; means and ends are posed in an internal relationship of efficient causality. The only logic constituent practice follows is the expansive rhythm of the power of the multitude. This practice is divine precisely in the Spinozian sense that its savage action destroys and constitutes being.[8] It is unalloyed and unrepresentable, affirming its own power. Constitutive practice is precisely what we earlier saw emerging in the prerequisites of communism. The exodus of the multitude from the strictures of State order is the march of an unrepresentable community. The productive cooperation of the social worker, through its technico-scientific, immaterial, and affective labor, creates the networks of self-valorization that animate constituent power. (We will return to develop this theme in terms of the genealogy of the constituent subject.)

The Normative Development and Consolidation of the Postmodern State

Now that we have fleshed out some of the theoretical and practical bases of the potentialities for a communist alternative existing today, we can turn back once again to our analysis of the contemporary State-form. The postmodern State presents itself as the paroxysmal figure of the dialectical conception of modernity, normativity, and sovereignty. In its effort to overcome the permanent crisis, it appears as the sublimation of the modern.

We have already emphasized, in our analysis of the paradoxes of the postmodern State, how (1) the conception of legitimation has been led back to a centralized, centripetal criterion of sovereignty and normative production, (2) the conception of political representation similarly has been reduced to the category of simulated representation, and (3) the conception and practice of responsibility continually have become more functional in the sense that they have become reinforced by systematism. On the basis of this analysis of the social bases of postmodernity (and the postmodern State that both interprets it and is produced by it) we can now hazard the thesis that the postmodern State absolutizes separation as a

Grundnorm of the constitution, as a legitimizing and functional foundation of its reality. The postmodern State appears as a paroxysmal figure of the dialectical conception of modernity because in normativity and sovereignty it pushes to an extreme the rupture of the dialectic through the fiction of its sublimation, its supersession: the postmodern State organizes the separation of the State from society, pretending that this separation does not exist. The withering of civil society we spoke of earlier is precisely the withering of the connective tissue, the web of mediations that have served to link the State to productive social forces. With the decline of civil society this separation becomes inevitable. The assumption of this separation coupled with the fiction that it does not exist is what defines the category of postmodernity and its State.

The material bases of the constitution of postmodernity, insofar as it is a political and governmental reality, result from the fact that capital no longer has anything to do with social production. The concept of the postmodern State with respect to social production can be defined as the production of commodities through command. In other words, in the terms of the critique of political economy, the postmodern State goes beyond the general definition of the modern State (the production of commodities through the exploitation of labor) just as it goes beyond the definition of the Keynesian State (the production of commodities through economic planning and regulation, the equivalence of supply and demand, of wage and investment, the reformist relationship between the capitalist State and organized labor-power). The postmodern State poses its interests in social production as an external observer, only concerned with the fact that autonomous social production reproduces (or is forced to reproduce) the conditions of command, or rather the conditions of the reproduction of the State and capital as purely autonomous powers of disposition over society.

If we pass now from the categories of the critique of political economy to those of the critique of the State-form and critically observe the modifications of the structure of the postmodern State, we can clearly identify the tendencies that are set in motion. The new form of the State — or rather, the new formal constitution of material relationships of separation between the State and society — is represented in a tendentially homogeneous way on the terrain of international law, in the new communitary ordering of markets, in domestic constitutional law, and in social law. In each case, the tendencies that emerge show the same formal characteristics.

International law is presented as a new order. A process of the unification of global command, brought about in large part through the imposition of the economic norm (principally through the World Bank and the International Monetary Fund), initially on the capitalist countries of the First and Third Worlds and finally, after the crisis of real socialism, extended on a truly global scale. The acceptance of Russia and the former Soviet republics into the World Bank and the IMF is one of the final pieces in the puzzle. Economic command over the First, Second, and Third Worlds can now be presented as global political command. Once the application of the economic norm has sufficiently weakened and eroded it, international law, conceived as the rights of formally equal subjects, can be completely overturned. The right of capital to intervene at a world level, after having been demonstrated through the power of international economic organisms and camouflaged behind the humanitarian interests of governmental and nongovernmental programs (such as the Alliance for Progress), can now be posed as a juridical power. The contractual structure of international relationships is brought back to a single source of juridical production, one in which juridical command can organize both capitalist logic and the maximum concentration of bellical means. The separation of the central command of capital from the process of political and social organization of peoples, from the singular expressions of the struggles and constituent powers, is here at an extreme. The foundation of international law and the logic of the new world order are represented on one hand by the capitalist necessity to arrange the world market and on the other by the lethal power (lethal for all of humanity) of nuclear arms. The world has been juridically unified. The dream of the Enlightenment, of *Aufklärung*—alas, what a heterogenesis of ends!—is magnificently realized. Never before has the category of "production of commodities through command" found a more perfect realization. Through global command the international order reproduces both the organization of production and the division of labor on an international scale. Never before has the process been juridically regulated, becoming an instrument of the police, and an administrative organ. Nuclear power represents sacredness, the final decision on life and death, the power over the new world order. Never before has the separation of power from the dialectic with society become so enormous. Legitimation, representation, and responsibility of the single systems of government and the single constitutions are defined only in relation to their positions within the new world order. The central displacement of the juridical *Grundnorm* defines a new spatiality of the juridical ordering in all its aspects, formal and material, and characterizes it through an absolute predominance of the rule of the separation between command and self-valorization, between State and society, between capital and the proletariat. From this fact follows an enormous series of consequences the opposition between the technical norm and authority on one side and social collective bargaining on the other becomes extreme. Here the two aspects of the "social contract"—the associative moment and the authoritarian moment—are separated in the clearest form. The fundamental point is the negation of civil society (conceived as laboring society) through the negation of the activity of the labor force as a source of social wealth. In the postmodern State, labor has become once again, as it was before Marx, the enigma of civil society. The real and complete subsumption of society under capital has repercussions on the entire system of social relations—as a clouding of the social relationships, as the collapse or exhaustion of the relationship of exploitation. From the juridical point of view, the law of capitalist reproduction has become natural, in its most abstract, most normal aspects. Money has been substituted for the juridical norm. Civil society has been reduced to an administrative mechanism, to a system of the reproductive compensations of cooperation that is purely and only technical—directed toward the reproduction of social relationships in their present identity. Law, specifically, is presented in two forms: either as a set of procedural norms that regulate the normality of the process of reproduction or as the set of exceptional rules that restabilize the normality of the process of production. Between procedure and exceptionality, the juridical existence of civil society itself and its participation in the juridical mechanism as a means of the formation of legitimate authority are negated. In the postmodern State the separation of the constitutive terms of society between who obeys and who commands becomes total, just as the ancient and traditional definitions of authority would have it (and in this regard postmodernity looks surprisingly premodern). Never before has the modern State reached such a point of radical separation, nor has there ever been such sophistication in the suitable normative terms to impose it. The juridical innovations of the Keynesian State, from the recognition of social subjects as immediately agentic subjects on the juridical level to the proceduralization of normative relationships, are eclipsed and suspended through the crushing blows of the emergency policies and the exceptional interventions that effectively transfer the procedural techniques of the formation and execution of the law from the social and contractual terrain to the administrative, State terrain. The weakening of social subjects goes hand in hand with the reinforcement of an administrative arrangement of society that while presenting itself as procedural is really systemic. In social law the postmodern State appears increasingly as a true and proper police State while the police appear as the supreme administrative system.

The Illusions of Juridical Reformism

We said at the beginning of our consideration of social law, however, that even though this evolution of social law is coherent and totalitarian it also opens up new potentialities: by eliminating the social space of contradiction it recasts the contradiction itself back toward the juridical system, to all of its levels and to the interior of all the relationships that it organizes. The anarchic and corporatist dispersal of social subjectivities, the atypical search for identity, the increase of corruption and mafia activity, along with the emergence of self-valorization and singularity, all appear mixed together at this point and plague the legal system, from bottom to top, with violent seizures, pressures that are both consistent with and contradictory to exodus and reterritorialization — undiagnosable convulsions. The real subsumption of society under capital separates society from the State: what is subsumed is merely a simulacrum of civil society produced by the State itself, and separate from the real plane of social forces. At the same time, however, this separation exposes the State to all levels of contradiction in society.

This framework, which is defined linearly by the development of the postmodern State over the entire set of contradictions embedded in its structure, is the focus of a great deal of contemporary legal studies. The progressive currents of legal studies, which are the only ones that interest us here, attempt to counter the effects of the desocialization of law and the State and thus reconstruct within the constitution of postmodernity spaces in which law can be reappropriated by society. It is not immediately clear, however, if this project can actually be accomplished. Is it still possible in the situation that we have described to conceive an effective juridical reformism? Or, instead, given contemporary conditions, is every alternative, reformist juridical endeavor completely illusory? In an effort to respond to these questions, let us consider the work of four currents of contemporary legal studies that we define in order of greater radicalism: (1) democratic evolutionary schools; (2) neo-Marxist and neocorporatist schools; (3) deconstructive approaches; and (4) critical approaches.

The democratic evolutionary schools are active primarily in Europe. Since the Second World War they have represented the reformist current of European juridical thought in reference to two fundamental problems: (1) the transition from fascist regimes to constitutional State structures and (2) the compromise between the constitutional State and the (syndicalist and socialist) forces of renewal that emerged in the postwar period from the new free organization of the world of labor. The antifascist thrust central to this current of juridical thought has been adopted directly as an element of democratization and a means of opening the dialectic of the juridical and administrative horizon to include also the social horizon. The social horizon is defined (in this historical framework) as a source of transformation for social egalitarianism. The rights of citizenship and liberty must, from this perspective, be made adequate to the rights of equality and solidarity. The logic of juridical thought thus takes inspiration from jurisprudential methods, believing these to be driven by a progressive tendency. In this way, these schools played a significant role in sustaining and developing the Welfare State throughout Europe after the Second World War. On this same terrain, then, we have seen the development of juridical sociology and the theory of constitutional and administrative right.[9]

In recent years, the democratic evolutionary schools have reacted to the transformation of the modern constitutional State, the rights State, into a postmodern State by focusing on the circularity of the normative and sociological aspects of law. The premise of this perspective, in other words, consists in considering as definitively over the era in which the sociological fact (the claim of the citizen to be recognized by the law) could only be considered juridically relevant after being formally inserted into the constitutional structure. The evolution of law should now be conceived from within a functional continuity between the emergence of always new sociological facts (the claims of citizens) and the institutionalization of these facts. The normative mechanism is socially open: the State must guarantee it and the administration must continually explain and formalize it.

The neo-Marxist and neocorporatist schools have also held an important position in the development of European juridical theory. Postwar Marxist juridical theories were born primarily of the Soviet polemics of the 1920s and the discussion about the nature of right in a socialist society. (Eugenii Pashukanis is the emblematic theorist of the communist critique of the Stalinist State structure, and it was primarily his point of view that was revived in the years surrounding 1968.) From this perspective the construction of right and thus the theory of right itself were oriented toward the withering away of the State and the establishment of always more vast and effective subjective public rights.[10] In the 1970s, however, the revolutionary thrust of the Marxist theories of right came to an end. With the crisis of the 1980s and the general decline of the communist perspective that characterized the intellectual consciousness of that period, neocorporatist positions began to take hold. Seen from the perspective of the crisis of Marxism, their logic can be explained in this way: even though the organizations and the social forces that sustained the push for a revolutionary project have declined, there still exist subjects that have an interest in modifying the situation of class relations (even on a minoritarian, contractual, and compromised basis); even though the hegemony of the proletariat has come to an end and the proletariat is no longer able to impose a majoritarian position, there can still be a sort of worker resistance based on subjects that really exist and thus are able to condition, even in a minoritarian way, the development of juridical systems in pluralistic constitutional regimes. The term "corporation" (which generically refers to workers' corporations) poses a residual but symbolically strong sense of resistance and alludes to the capacity of the "disadvantaged" classes to condition the dialectic of forces in the liberal system. Many diverse social groups have thus found in neocorporatism a terrain on which to express their claim to specific rights and engage the jurisprudential system.[11]

In response to the formation of the postmodern State, neo-Marxist and neocorporatist schools set out from the same premise operative in the democratic evolutionary perspective, that is, from a dynamic conception of the juridical norm in the institutional continuum of the postmodern State structure. Different than the democratic evolutionary schools, however, which conceive a center of equilibrium for the transformative dynamics and the normative arrangements of the State, the neocorporatist schools insist instead on the subjective nature of the transformations and thus on the need to find the point of normative equilibrium within the contractual relationships that define the subjects and organize their claims. The weakening of the class description of society (which neo-Marxist schools take as a point of departure) does not imply the weakening of the contractual and interactive structure of social subjects. Even if communism is over, they seem to say, historical materialism lives on. If the reformism of the working class, considered the motor of juridical reformism from Hugo Sinzheimer to the progressive jurists of the New Deal, has reached its historical limit, the dynamic of social subjects (as carriers of juridical claims organized by interests) will nonetheless continue to be the site to which juridical development and, more important, the systematic equilibrium of the Constitution will be practically entrusted and theoretically validated.

It should be obvious from our earlier analysis that these two jurisprudential positions only beg the question of the new configuration of law in the postmodern State. They both assume, even if in different forms, the possibility of a theory of juridical norms *au milieu* between society and the State. They do not recognize that the postmodern reconstruction of this *milieu* is purely simulated. The foundation has in effect been pulled out from under this traditional conception of juridical reformism. The confusion of sociological and normative phenomena is not an effect of the reduction of the normative to the social, but on the contrary the product of the subsumption of the social within the normative. The relative indetermination of the circulation of facts, values, and social subjects does not negate but rather affirms and reinforces the State's exclusive power to determine their "value" and generate norms. The relative oscillation of normative behaviors, between society and the State, does not in any way hinder the concentration of the determination of the systemic equilibrium (and thus of the possibility to decide the normative quality, to put in motion the normative character) toward a State center of gravity. The more it is dynamic, the more the constitution of the postmodern State is an equilibrium internal to the State, to the logics of command for the reproduction of capital. The democratic evolutionary schools and the neo-Marxist corporatist schools, from this perspective, are presented as late, outdated theories of the juridical market. The market is at this point only the simulacrum of the freedom of individual and collective subjects, the hollow image of a civil society granted by the State. We are thus on the terrain of a pure and simple mystification: jurisprudence pretends an autonomy of civil society and its juridical and normative power that does not and cannot exist given the autonomy of the State. These schools are built on an illusion—an illusion that supports a traditional conception of law and the State while forgetting or ignoring the essential transformation that the postmodern State has set in motion.

The various poststructuralist currents of jurisprudence denounce these perversions of juridical reformism, and, as we have seen, rightly so. What remains to be seen, however, is if they are able to take juridical theory beyond the plane of reformism and the mystificatory effects that follow from it, giving juridical theory a new and powerful statute. The practitioners of both deconstructive juridical theory and critical legal studies continually refuse to be linked together as schools or methods of legal interpretation and practice, but nearly all of their work shares a common point of departure in a radical antiformalism.[12] Let us use this common initial project to link these two approaches tentatively for the sake of our analysis. The unifying program they share involves the recognition of the distance posed in the dominant juridical conceptions between text and context, that is, between the system of norms and the fabric of social and political expression. There is no meaning, they claim, outside the context or free from interpretation; or, in other words, all legal forms and actions must be understood as inextricably embedded within social and political frameworks.[13] The deconstruction or subversion of the distance posed by juridical formalism between the legal text and its context is the first order of business that defines both deconstructive and critical legal approaches.

These approaches pose a critical condition, one that we think is essential for setting in motion a process that demystifies the juridical nature of the postmodern State. In many cases, by demystifying the autonomy of the text and the normative system, these authors manage to grasp an adequate definition of the real structures of postmodern society and thus present a radical methodological denunciation of the continual circulation of the text and the context, of the normative and the social, which is illusory when not actually prefigured. In the process of this methodological denunciation, the critical viewpoint becomes effective. Efforts to define the autonomy of contexts, break away from the dictatorship of the normative, and free from the State new spaces of social expression arise as real possibilities. These operations are accomplished with no illusion of determining new (and at this point impossible) normative processes but simply with the idea of claiming new horizons of freedom. The theory of juridical norms itself is, from this point of view, radically brought into question. What is contested is the very possibility of translating the social into the normative, and what is affirmed is the continual deficit of the normative with respect to the social.

It is not by chance that, while the democratic evolutionary and neocorporatist conceptions are proposed primarily within the closed juridical systems of continental Europe, the poststructuralist and deconstructionist perspectives manage to influence juridical methodology principally in Anglo-Saxon countries with open (that is, jurisprudential) juridical structures. In the countries with the tradition of closed juridical systems, the poststructuralist perspective in legal studies — after having contested the postmodern system on the philosophical level — has been relegated to the postulation of a juridical anthropology that is posed outside of the positive juridical terrain. In this situation, European juridical poststructuralism often appears as something like a theory of natural law, or rather an alternative phenomenological juridical terrain, which although effective as critique is ineffective on the constructive terrain. On the contrary, in the countries with open juridical structures, the "liberal" deconstructionist currents manage incursions on the terrain of positive law. In this context, the system of norms is considered historically equivocal, the system of sources continually open, and the method of interpretation potentially constructive. A fundamental ruse of the alternative logic is alive in this perspective, which grasps and actively utilizes the post-

words, the proposition of a radical alterity is not a matter of advocating the cause of the weak against the powerful, nor of calling for the intervention of a third power (at this point a completely illusory notion of reformism), but rather a matter of affirming one type of power over another: the constituent power of the multitude against the constituted power of the State. There exists no real alternative that does not pose as the central and exclusive problematic the alternative production of subjectivity and the alternative constitution of power. The critical perspective must grasp the genealogy of social movements and emerging subjectivities not as reformist pressures on the existing order, but as elements of a new constituent power.

Along with the definitive crisis of "real socialism," then, so too are over the adventures of juridical socialism and liberal reformism in all their variants. There is no longer the space to conceive this type of alternative as effective. The system of power has attained such high levels of command, globally over the world market and internally over the social production of subjectivity, that it is able to separate itself and legitimate autonomously the new social order. We can regain an adequate, reconstructive juridical perspective only by going back down to the materialist metaphysical matrixes of modernity, to its radical anthropological alternatives, and thus producing a critique of the postmodern order on the terrain of the formation of its structure and the consolidation of its force. Only by reinterpreting the social dimensions of separation in the postmodern State can we grasp those mechanisms of the production of subjectivity that, in separation, are posed against the independence of the sovereign. The powerful subject that poses a total critique of the juridical State is the constituent subject that, on the plane of separation, poses a radical and effective alternative.

Genealogy of the Constituent Subject

Within the history of modern thought there has lived, against the normative line — of which the postmodern conception of law and its State are the final exasperated expressions — a constituent, libertarian, and productive line. It has continually posed a series of questions: Is it possible to conceive community outside of sovereignty as a separate and autonomous entity? Is a juridical and political theory possible that takes away the necessity of the one as foundation of the multitude? Is a juridical and political theory possible, therefore, that assumes the one as a simple surface on which the multitude expresses itself? Today, in the situation that we have been describing, where both the crisis of capitalism and the end of the socialist transition are evident, these questions become central once again. In reality, it seems here that the widespread chaos of the crisis cannot but relaunch political reasoning toward an absolutely originary point of foundation, of continual refoundation, a *ritorno ai principî*. As we have seen, it is no longer sufficient at this point to try to impress new meanings on an indefinite, perverse circulation. The only possibility of reconstructing meaning is that of refounding the process, reconstructing it *ex novo*. Our problem is no longer that of demonstrating that reformism is impossible — it is not only impossible, but also boring, perverse, repetitive, and cruel. The State is no longer defensible, not even with irony. On the other hand, if the constituent, libertarian, and productive line is now theoretically hegemonic, if only — on both the epistemological and the juridical terrains — this can give meaning to the events, how is it possible to show this line in action? How is it possible to recognize it not only as theoretical line and project but also as subject and power? How is it possible at this point, once and for all, to abandon the conception of constituent power as necessarily negating itself in posing the constitution, and recognize a constituent power that no longer produces constitutions separate from itself, but rather is itself constitution? The critical elements of the interpretation of the postmodern State we have proposed precipitate now toward the possibility of positively constructing this alternative.

We can only begin to formulate a response to the problems we have raised by going down again toward the social terrain and there beginning to describe the genealogy of a constituent subject, operating in the contemporary, postmodern world. This subject is a laboring subject — a creative, productive, affirmative subject. Its social existence is outlined by the considerations that we developed earlier about the subjective synthesis of immaterial labor and the cooperative essence of production. In the developments we discern in contemporary society, productive labor tends to propose completely immanent social dimensions of meaning, independent of any coercion to cooperate that could be posed outside labor itself. The increasingly immaterial dimensions of labor pose the terms and the networks of the laboring cooperation at the heart of social production. Capital, displaced from its traditional role as orchestrator of productive cooperation, thus tends to take the form of an apparatus of capture. Productive social labor moves historically toward becoming independent from any form of direct capitalist command — and therefore even more clearly independent from the indirect form of capitalist command over labor that is represented by State normativity. The role of capital and the capitalist State is thus reduced to one of preying on and controlling the essentially autonomous flows of social production. As a result, once the State has posed sovereignty in the most extreme form of autonomy and separation, any

in their action, in the whole of their procedural agreements, and only in this framework does it become possible for the exercise of force to be legitimate. Constituent power is democratic communication within which the institutions of society's reproduction are continually formed and re-formed.

This analysis and this perspective are rooted in the real self-making of productive society. When the subjects have become autonomous producers of wealth, knowledge, and cooperation, without the need of external command, when they organize production itself and social reproduction, there is no reason for an overarching, sovereign power external to their own power. There is no reason for something that hinders their construction or that commands the meaning of the constitutive power of the new subjects. In this situation the institutional processes that organize the life of the multitude can only be internal to the life of the multitude itself. Constituent power is the only form in which democracy can be understood so as not to be, in its very definition, negated.

We are not proposing a utopia. Our analysis and our research, like the political will that animates them, are conscious that this definition of democracy as constituent process is a path that must be traveled, and that the multitude of subjects must construct its institutionality. We also know that the liberation of constituent power, and therefore the real constructive processes of democracy, go hand in hand with the destructuring of constituted power, that is, the actual scaffolding of the constitutional, social, and economic enslavement of the multitude. Precisely because this process is not teleological, but rather a continuous, metaphysical construction of the conditions of freedom, we know that the relationship between processes of liberation and processes of destructuring is not mechanical, nor negatively complementary. In fact, in the separation that distinguishes immanent, constituent power from sovereign, constituted power, there is no longer a dialectic, not even a negative dialectic. A productive exodus characterizes the constituent process of the multitude: the institutional construction and constitution of cooperation are pursued independent from the processes of the extinction of constituted power. These two lines move on the horizon of the world as an ungraspable alterity. There will nonetheless be a moment in which the two independent processes will come to confront one another, because there will be a moment in which the implosion of the postmodern State into the vacuousness of its ontological referent will threaten the entire world with a moment of destruction and death. There is no guarantee that this threat will be made powerless; and, in any case, the construction of democracy by the multitude develops in this shadow of death. This shadow of death pushes and accelerates the processes of constitution—to break the linguistic and communicational codes that give birth to its hegemonic power, to demand that the event be determined. We are living a revolution that is already developed and only a death threat stops it from being declared. If there is a dialectic — the only dialectic possible — between the delirium of the power of the postmodern State and the construction of the democracy of the multitude, then it resides in this death threat.

This is perhaps the point on which the genealogy of the new subject, after being shown in its autonomy, its productivity, and its extended democratic plurality, is definitively given; in other words, when faced with death, it shows both its finitude and the insuppressible desire for life that animates it. The power of finitude is revealed therefore in this implacable struggle against death, against finitude itself. In this collective existence, the new subject comprehends the autonomy and productivity of its action confronting its limit — a limit that is always solid but beyond which the new subject must always go.

Today, in the assumption of this catastrophe, communism is revived — in the *ritorno ai principî* of a radical constructivity, stripped of the illusion that socialism or mature capitalism can interpret the path of freedom. Freedom can be realized only by breaking apart the alternatives of modernity and choosing the mortal risk implied in this break. No juridical ordering is possible outside of this choice of the disutopia, outside of this renewal of human constructivity in the autonomy, productivity, and plurality of the constitutive process. Constituent power is this process — absolute immanence on the surfaces of potentiality. The only power that can be transcendent is that of human finitude, rich with all its powers. There, in finitude, the form of the constituent process and the subject of constituent power coincide.

economists, in chapter 5, "First Analytical Approach." Michael Lebowitz gives a clear summary of the problems presented by the "one-sidedness" of the productive labor debate in *Beyond Capital*, pp. 100–103. Finally, for a discussion of the need to reconsider several central categories of Marx's analysis in light of the contemporary social situation, see Antonio Negri, "Interpretation of the Class Situation Today: Methodological Aspects," pp. 78ff.

8. See, for example, Danièle Kergoat, "L'infirmière coordonnée." More generally, on the specificity of the struggles of female workers in France, "the internal logic of their practices," and the subjective figures they give rise to, see Danièle Kergoat, *Les Ouvrières*, in particular, Part IV, "Les Pratiques Sociales des Ouvrières," pp. 107–31.

9. Donna Haraway's "Cyborg Manifesto" has already been taken up by a variety of scholars in different directions. For one of the many examples, see Celeste Olalquiaga, *Megalopolis*, in particular pp. 10–17. We will elaborate the connection between the cyborg and the social worker in chapter 7, "The Social Bases of the Postmodern State and the Existing Prerequisites of Communism."

Chapter 2. Keynes and the Capitalist Theory of the State

1. The trade-union and political movement outside Russia, following the October Revolution, can be summed up as a homogeneous movement based essentially on "self-management," generally expressed and led by working-class aristocracies, even in those instances where the movement was of a mass nature. Sergio Bologna's essay "Composizione di classe e teoria del partito alle origini del movimento consiliare" is devoted to defining the movement's homogeneity. For a general introduction to the problematic, see also, A. S. Ryder, *The German Revolution*; A. Rosenberg, *Histoire du bolchevisme*; Branko Pribicevic, *The Shop Steward Movement in England*; Theodore Draper, *American Communism and Soviet Russia*; and Gaspare de Caro, "L'esperienza torinese dei consigli operai."

2. See, for example, the charges of "totalitarian fascism" that some sectors of big business leveled against the New Deal in the United States.

3. This is true of the working-class struggles in the United States. On the homogeneity between forms of behavior of the American and European working classes in struggle during the years immediately after the First World War, see the essays by Sergio Bologna and George Rawick contained in *Operai e Stato*. In particular, it should be remembered that between 1914 and 1920, membership of the AFL rose from two to four million, a level of trade-union membership unsurpassed until the 1930s. For useful data, see also Irving Bernstein, *The*

Lean Years: A History of the American Worker, 1920–1933, and the essay by W. Galenson in *Mouvements ouvriers et dépression économique*, edited by Domenico Demarco et al., pp. 124–43.

4. Keynes's political objective in this phase was to reunify the two lines of the capitalist system's defense — with the corollary that this defense could only be organized around the fulcrum of Germany. This perspective remained one of the fundamental elements in Keynes's political thinking. In 1922, with *A Revision of the Treaty*, Keynes repeated to the point of boredom that idea that "Germany's future is now towards the East and all its resurgent hopes and ambitions will certainly turn in that direction." Keynes's alleged "pro-Germanism," which brought him much criticism even as late as Étienne Mantoux's *The Carthaginian Peace, or the Economic Consequences of Mr. Keynes*, thus has a much deeper class significance than his critics were ever prepared to see. It is an approach that offers a perfect parallel to the best of bourgeois political thinking in Weimar Germany. For example, it is not difficult to find identical intuitions during these years in Max Weber. (See Wolfgang J. Mommsen, *Max Weber und die Deutsche Politik, 1890–1920*, pp. 280ff.) Also, Keynes never concealed his deep sympathy with the Weimar intellectuals and their political groups. In his essay "Dr. Melchior: A Defeated Enemy" he gives a picture of this circle that comes close to apologetics.

5. For a good treatment of the problem, see Robert Lekachman's Introduction to the volume edited by him, *Keynes' General Theory: Reports of Three Decades*, pp. 1–10. Logically enough, R. F. Harrod's hagiographic *Life of John Maynard Keynes* is in agreement. For Paul A. Samuelson the road that leads to the General Theory is a "road to Damascus." See his article, "The General Theory," p. 330.

6. See particularly Bertil Ohlin's articles "Mr. Keynes' Views on the Transfer Problem" and "The Reparation Problem."

7. This is a remark of Keynes cited by E. A. G. Robinson in his essay "John Maynard Keynes 1883–1946," p. 34.

8. Reviewing this volume, Keynes admits the correctness of Churchill's political line at the peace conference, but at the same time, he makes the by no means light criticism that he failed to grasp the central importance of the Soviet revolution: "[Churchill] fails to see — or at least to set — in perspective the bigness of the events in their due relations, or to disentangle the essential from casual episodes.... the Bolsheviks remain for him, in spite of his tribute to the greatness of Lenin, nothing more than an imbecile atrocity" (*Essays in Biography*, pp. 72–73).

9. The biographers have rightly stressed the effect of the continuous stimulus of English political events on

Keynes's development during the 1920s. See R. F. Harrod, *The Life of John Maynard Keynes*, pp. 331ff., and E. A. G. Robinson, "John Maynard Keynes 1883–1946," pp. 41ff.

10. On how the problem appeared to Keynes, see E. A. G. Robinson, "John Maynard Keynes 1883–1946," pp. 41ff., and Claudio Napoleoni, *Economic Thought of the Twentieth Century*.

11. In addition to Branko Pribicevic's *The Shop Steward Movement in England*, see also Mauro Gobbini's article on the 1926 English General Strike contained in *Operai e Stato*.

12. See R. F. Harrod, *The Life of John Maynard Keynes*, pp. 375ff.

13. "But if our central controls succeed in establishing an aggregate volume of output corresponding to full employment as nearly as is practicable, the classical theory comes into its own again from this point on" (Keynes, *The General Theory of Employment, Interest and Money*, p. 378).

14. In his essay "Newton the Man," Keynes contrives to move via the identification of a secret, magic moment, and a comparison of this with the triumphant Enlightenment aspects of the Cambridge physicist/mathematician's thinking, to a model of scientific knowledge in which both aspects coexist, but the former has greater authenticity. Indeed, creative genius is sustained by irrational interests. This is the fascination of Newton, that he still managed to view the universe as an enigma. It is interesting to ask how far this image of Newton defines Keynes's awareness of his own scientific development.

15. For a good account of this long polemic, see R. F. Harrod, *The Life of John Maynard Keynes*, pp. 338ff.

16. A good account of the political and cultural climate in which Keynes arrived at these conclusions can be found in Paul Sweezy's essay, "John Maynard Keynes." Sweezy gives a much broader treatment to this issue in *The Present as History*, pp. 189–96.

17. In the essays written in 1926, "Liberalism and Labour" and "The End of Laissez-Faire," this viewpoint receives special emphasis, especially in reference to the political necessities that emerged after the General Strike.

18. For this, and many other aspects of the economic analysis of the 1930s, I follow the investigations of Heinz Wolfgang Arndt, *The Economic Lessons of the Nineteen-Thirties*.

19. The importance of all this for American society, at the heart of the economic crisis, is highlighted by Arthur M. Schlesinger, Jr., *The Crisis of the Old Order 1919–1933*, and by Mario Einaudi, *La rivoluzione di Roosevelt*, pp. 51 and 90. Significant data are also quoted by Peter G. Filene, *Americans and the Soviet Experiment 1917–1933*.

20. See Keynes, *The General Theory*, in particular pp. 99–104, 218–20, and 322–25. Note that as early as May 10, 1930, Keynes warned of the gravity of the situation in an article for the *Nation*. "The fact is — a fact not yet recognised by the great public — that we are now in the depths of a very severe international slump, a slump which will take its place in history amongst the most acute ever experienced. It will require not merely passive movements of bank-rates to lift us out of a depression of this order, but a very active and determined policy" (cited by R. F. Harrod, *The Life of John Maynard Keynes*, p. 398).

21. In this connection, W. B. Reddaway makes an excellent analysis of the inclusion of the State in the Keynesian analysis — excellent particularly because it stresses the internal and "structural" nature of State action. (See his "Keynesian Analysis and a Managed Economy.") As we shall see, this is where the Keynesian economic analysis begins to become particularly important for the definition of the new model of the State.

22. Georges Burdeau, in "Le plan comme mythe," has offered perhaps the best analysis of how the future is absorbed or incorporated in the present within the perspective of economic planning. He also clarifies important implications for the conception of constitutional right.

23. W. B. Reddaway rightly notes how the State's internalization within economic life takes place essentially as regards investment. At the limit, its function is directly productive. See his essay "Keynesian Analysis and a Managed Economy."

24. Of course, despite all the efforts of Keynes and his school to analyze this situation, the best description remains Marx's account of the formation of "social capital." See, for example, *Capital*, vol. 2, pp. 103ff.

25. On capital as a focus of "social imputation," see once again Marx's chapters on "The three formulas of the circuit" in *Capital*, vol. 2, chapters 1–4.

26. The essays by Paul Sweezy, "John Maynard Keynes" and "The First Quarter Century," lay appropriate stress on this point.

27. The concept of effective demand is defined and developed in *The General Theory*, pp. 23–32, 55, 89, 97–98, 245–54, and 280–91.

28. The mutual interdependence of the entire system is evidenced particularly by "orthodox" interpreters of Keynes, though. For a review, see R. F. Harrod, "Mr. Keynes and Traditional Theory."

10. See Mortati, *La Costituzione in senso materiale*, chapter 2. See also Georg Jellinek, *Gesetz und Verordnung, staatsrechtliche Untersuchungene auf rechtsgeschichtlicher und rechtsvergleichender Grundlage*, pp. 262ff.

11. Franco Pierandrei has further developed the analysis of the inherence of fact and normativity in the material constitution of the ordering. This argument and an ample bibliography of the relevant literature can be found in his article "La corte costituzionale e le 'modificazioni tacite' della Costituzione," in particular pp. 334ff.

12. It is useful here to keep in mind that this formal conception of power has a long tradition in Italy and reached its apex in the so-called sociological school, in the work of authors such as Pareto, Mosca, and Michels. This school is indeed plagued by the very same contradiction. We should be careful to point out, however, that there is no reason to suppose that this school directly influenced the work of Mortati, who in fact at times pushes his definition of "dominant political force" to extreme points of relativism.

13. This conception is characteristic primarily of the constitutions of the Central European countries between the wars. See Rudolf Schlesinger, *Central European Democracy and Its Background*.

14. For example, Giuseppe Grosso writes: "The problem of the adequation of juridical norms to economic facts can be seen from two different perspectives: one related to the economic needs and oriented toward what appears to be the economic solution and the other related, as a means, toward the goal of organizing the economic facts in the sense desired by the legislator" ("Distinti complessi giuridici e varietà di rapporti fra norma giuridica e fatto economico," p. 811). This methodological alternative also comes to be configured in the ambiguity of the definition of the so-called right of economics. See, in particular, Enrico Allorio, "Intervento al convegno degli amici del diritto dell'economia," which contains an extensive bibliography on this theme. Allorio claims, for example, that the field of the right of economics is "the study either of the interpretation of the norms that govern these materials in constant development ... or of the formulation of an adequate reformist politics" (p. 1211).

15. It is not by chance that the direct object of Weber's critique is R. Stammler's formalist proposal. We will demonstrate, however, that this Weberian critique only addresses the issues that are linked to the Engelsian conception of the problem of the "superstructure"—a problem that never had any place in Marx's thought and that survives as a "commonplace" only thanks to the desperate scholasticism of certain strains of Marxism, in particular Second Internationalist and Stalinist currents.

16. This recognition is a mark common to the best constitutionalist theories. Before 1906 Georg Jellinek, for example, showed ample awareness of this need in *Verfassungsänderung und Verfassungswandlung*. Pierandrei relates Jellinek's analysis to the Italian Constitution in his "La corte costituzionale e le 'modificazaioni tacite' della Costituzione," p. 338. In any case, we will return to this problem later in this chapter, in the section titled "Critique of the Model of the Bourgeois Theory of Authority."

17. There is a rich literature on the relationship between the rights State and the social State, but we will limit ourselves here to citing the work of two authors: Ernst Forsthoff, "La Repubblica federale tedesca come Stato di diritto," pp. 551ff., and Tullio Ascarelli, "Ordinamento giuridico e processo economico," pp. 59–60.

18. See Forsthoff, "La Repubblica federale tedesca come Stato di diritto," pp. 553–54 and p. 560, and Ascarelli, "Ordinamento giuridico e processo economico," pp. 59–60 and p. 65.

19. Gerard Lyon-Caen and Giannini have adequately described this phase in historical terms. See Lyon-Caen, "Fondamenti storici e razionali del diritto del lavoro," and Giannini, "Profili costituzionali della protezione sociale."

20. The articles by Lyon-Caen and Giannini also elaborate this second phase.

21. Lyon-Caen emphasizes the "transitory" or "unstable" character of the right of labor. (See "Fondamenti storici e razionali del diritto del lavoro," p. 78.) The author then dwells on the analysis of the rational bases of the right of labor, and, arguing against several other definitions (such as those of Capitant-André, Amiaud, Scelle, Mossé, Rouast, and Durand), seeks to establish the coherence of the right of labor with the entire structure of right in the capitalist State, in the various phases of its development but particularly in the most recent phase. (See in particular p. 81.) His conclusions, although very summary and at times overly ideological, are fundamentally correct.

22. It should be enough, in this regard, to refer to the passage from the conception and system of corporatism to the system installed by the Italian Constitution to recognize two pertinent facts: the phases of the workers' struggle are linked to the development of legislation regarding labor in a direct way, determining its timing and transformations; and in recent Italian history the act of regaining the freedom for unions to organize, gaining freedom in the factories, and so forth, are direct results of the workers' struggle (whatever uses capital might subsequently put these gains to). In any case, on the principal differences between the system of the "labor charter" and the system installed by the Italian Constitution, see Giuliano Mazzoni, "Intervento al convegno degli amici del diritto dell'economia," in particular pp. 1226–27.

23. In this regard, see the significant article by Barna Horvath, "Les sources du droit positif." Horvath claims, for example, that "the source of right is nothing other than right itself in transition between two states or situations, its passage from a state of fluidity and subterranean indivisibility to the state of evident certainty." This is clearly an absolutely idealistic position, and this position is echoed by several other articles appearing together with that of Horvath in the same collection, *Le problème des sources du droit positif.* It is interesting to note, however, that several other positions, which are much more positively founded and which are based on substantially realistic philosophical premises, end up creating a concept of source with the same systemic illusion. See, for example, Mircea Djuvara, "Sources et normes du droit positif," or in a very different vein, Ferruccio Pergolesi, *Saggi sulle fonti normative,* in particular pp. 1–28. We will return to the work of Pergolesi later to investigate a series of positive contributions in relation to gradualist theory.

24. For one example of this argument, see Ernst Swoboda, "Les diverses sources du droit: leur équilibre et leur hiérarchie dans les divers systèmes juridiques." Here the system of sources, with equilibrium (harmony) and the hierarchy (from freedom to society) of its elements, is seen as constituted by a series of regulative principles that the juridicism constitutes according to a rational plane. The neo-Kantian foundation of Swoboda's position is entirely clear, and it serves to show in general the philosophical premises of such theories.

25. For a useful and carefully prepared literature review of the Italian jurisprudence of this period on the theme of the sources of right, see Lorenza Carlassare Caiani, "Sulla natura giuridica dei testi unici." The author presents positions that in general take the view opposing the one I have presented here, clarifying the distinctions that arise at the heart of this substantially homogeneous reference of the foundation of right to the underlying reality. She makes clear too the severity of the critique of Hans Kelsen proposed by these authors. For our purposes, however, it is sufficient to recognize the general proposition.

26. See Bobbio, *Lezioni di Filosofia di diritto,* p. 52, and Francesco Carnelutti, *Sistema di diritto processuale civile,* vol. 1, paragraph 25.

27. Bobbio provides definitions of the two types of sources. "By defining [productive] source we understand the source by which the juridical norms, even those deriving from cognitive sources, carry their obligatory force.... By cognitive source we understand the source that gives rise to the knowledge of the juridical norms" (*Lezioni di Filosofia di diritto,* p. 61). Carlassare Caiani adds: "By cognitive sources we understand the modes that make possible the knowledge of the rules, which have themselves derived from a productive source" ("Sulla natura giuridica dei testi unici," p. 45). On this question in general, see Giuseppe Codacci-Pisanelli, "Fonti di cognizione e fonti di produzione."

28. This dualism is discussed at length by Mortati, *La Costituzione in senso materiale,* pp. 35ff. In a strictly sociological sense, A. M. Koulicher maintains precisely the multiplicity of the underlying constitutional arrangements that naturally accompanies "the multiplicity of sources in constitutional right" even though he himself subsequently demands the continual reconciliation of the dualism ("La multiplicité des sources, en droit constitutionnel").

29. It is no coincidence that the origin of the distinction between productive sources and cognitive sources is canonical. (See Codacci-Pisanelli, "Fonti di cognizione e fonti di produzione," pp. 230–32.) Since the source of right is directly divine, it is a matter of identifying the "documents" of its expression. Hence we arrive at a distinction between *fontes essendi* and *fontes cognoscendi.* This explains how the distinction could then be adequate to the expression of the effects of the mysterious development of the *Volksgeist.* It is certainly no coincidence, finally, that the systematic madness of idealist theorists gravitated toward this distinction.

30. The clearest demonstration of this claim that we have seen is contained in Vezio Crisafulli, "Gerarchia e competenza nel sistema costituzionale delle fonti." On this topic, see also Crisafulli, *Lezioni di diritto costituzionale,* vol. 1, pp. 192ff. and 285ff.

31. A fundamental moment in the contemporary problematic of the crisis of sources is demonstrated in both *Le problème des sources du droit positif* and *Recueil d'études sur les sources du droit en l'honneur de G. Geny.* Characteristically, the crisis of sources is presented in these texts as a crisis of legalism, in other words, a crisis of the dogma of the exclusivity of the law as source and a recognition of a series of new sources that contest the traditional theory of juridical positivism.

32. On the reconstruction of juridical positivism, see Erich Neuy, *Das rechtsphilosophische Relativismusproblem in der Sicht des Neopositivismus.*

33. For a general description of this process, see, in addition to the work of Forsthoff, the beautiful analysis of Kurt Ballerstedt, "Über wirtschaftliche Massnahmegesetze," and the essays of Giuseppe Guarino collected in *Scritti di diritto pubblico dell'economia e di diritto dell'energia.*

34. For an example of this position in constitutional law, particularly in relation to the problem of the division of powers, see the important analysis of Giorgio Balladore-Pallieri, "Appunti sulla divisione dei poteri nella vigente Costituzione." For a comparative discussion of the various postwar juridical arrangements, see Enzo Cheli, "L'ampliamento dei poteri normativi dell'esecutivo nei principali ordinamenti occidentali." Finally, with respect to administrative law, see Forsthoff, *Lehrbuch des Verwaltungsrechts*, vol. 1, *Allgemeiner Teil*, which, in our opinion, is the most perceptive and exhaustive compendium of the contemporary problematic.

35. We should keep in mind that the process of the dissolution of the dogma of the sovereignty of the law developed not only through the debate over the sources of right but also through debate over interpretation. This is not the place, however, to address more fully that polemic.

36. "This is the fact that, in this as in other spheres of life, it is the conflict itself which gives rise to the formation and consolidation of groups and to the establishment of the relevant social relations as group relations. To be sure, conflicts develop out of group relations, but at the same time, group relations develop out of conflicts, and it is more correct to say that labour-management disputes tend to develop into intergroup conflicts than that they have that character from the outset" (Otto Kahn-Freund, "Intergroup Conflicts and their Settlement," p. 194).

37. See Kahn-Freund, "Intergroup Conflicts and their Settlement," pp. 202ff., and Gino Giugni, *Introduzione allo studio dell'autonomia collettiva*, pp. 11–12.

38. In this regard, see the interesting analysis of Walter Bogs, "Autonomie und verbändliche Selbstverwaltung im modernen Arbeits- und Sozialrecht," pp. 1–9, in particular p. 5. It should come as no surprise that after setting out from these premises Bogs arrives at the same definition of the social State proposed by Forsthoff.

39. Among the many studies that affirm this point, see Ubaldo Prosperetti, "Preliminari sull'autonomia sindacale." Prosperetti's study is very good, even though it maintains certain privatistic tendencies.

40. See Hugo Sinzheimer, "La théorie des sources du droit et le droit ouvrier," which summarizes this argument and demonstrates the author's proximity to the school of "social right," including authors such as Gurvitch.

41. This process, which shows also the profound ambiguity of the socialist reformism that developed between the wars, is perfectly grasped and described by Schlesinger, *Central European Democracy and Its Background*.

42. See, for example, Francesco Carnelutti's celebrated definition of the collective contract: "The collective contract, however, is a hybrid that has the body of the contract and the soul of the law; the contractual mechanism brings into play a force that transcends subjective right and unleashes a movement that goes beyond the juridical relation between the parties" (*Teoria del regolamento collettivo dei rapporti di lavoro*, p. 108).

43. See, for example, Francesco Santoro Passarelli, *Saggi di diritto civile*, in particular pp. 264–65, and Bruno Mazzarelli, *La norma collettiva nella teoria generale del diritto*, pp. 103–4.

44. See Ascarelli's excellent contribution to the convention proceedings of *Diritto dell'economia*, 1956, p. 1254.

45. L. A. Miglioranzi expresses this position clearly: "The labor relationship is not therefore purely and simply an institutional relationship, but an institutional relationship that is necessarily dependent, at least in normal circumstances, on a preceding contractual agreement" ("Il rapporto di lavoro nella sua evoluzione").

46. See primarily Max Weber, *Economy and Society*, vol. 1, pp. 319ff.; Adolf Merkl, *Allgemeines Verwaltungsrecht*, pp. 104ff.; and Giovanni Miele, "Profilo della consuetudine nel sistema delle fonti di diritto interno."

47. With regard to the "decentralized" creation of right (from an international perspective), see Hans Kelsen, "Théorie du droit international coutumier," pp. 266ff. With regard to the passage from the negotiation of agreements to the procedural institution, both in domestic and international law, see Giuseppe Guarino, *Scritti di diritto pubblico dell'economia e di diritto dell'energia*, pp. 56–59.

48. On the relationship between the concept of labor and the (hidden or explicit) conditions of the relationship of exploitation, see Karl Marx, "Critique of the Gotha Program," in particular Part I.

49. A comparison between Kelsen's positions and those of the many authors who wrote about the *Grundnorm* before him would be enough to demonstrate the importance of Kelsen's work. In the work of these other authors, the "fundamental norm" is generally given an abstract meaning, exemplifying the condition of the imperativeness of the juridical ordering. See, for example, Walter Jellinek, *Gesetz, Gesetzesanwendung und Zweckmässigkeitserwägung*, p. 27.

50. See Adolf Merkl's classic *Allgemeines Verwaltungsrecht*, in particular his definition of the administration and administrative function, pp. 1–44, and his theory of the administrative act, pp. 177ff. For an excellent analysis of Merkl's thought, see Roger Bonnard, "La théorie de la formation du droit par degrés dans l'œuvre d'Adolf Merkl."

51. In this regard, F. Wehr seems to us to make an important contribution in his article "La notion de 'processus juridique' dans la théorie pure du droit."

52. It is no coincidence that precisely these historical movements of the formation of the right of labor are subsequently found to be included in modern Constitutions as diverse but linked moments of the juridical discipline of labor. The Italian Constitution is perhaps exemplary in this regard. See Mortati, "Il lavoro nella Costituzione," pp. 160ff. and 180ff., and Giannini, "Rilevanza costituzionale del lavoro."

53. This project seems to have been most fully applied in British legislation regarding labor and in the strategies to calm the controversies that derive from it. See Mario Grandi, "La risoluzione delle controversie di lavoro in Gran Bretagna."

54. From the juridical point of view, the most suggestive proposal in this regard is that of Ernst Herz in *Anspruch und Norm in Arbeitsrecht.* Herz's analysis quickly succeeds in going beyond the limits of the labor-right approach and grasps the permanent elements in which process is introduced into the life of the State.

55. From this point of view, then, the theme of the expansion of the contract becomes the inverse analogue to the theme of the spread of the process, insofar as the necessity of recomposition is directly proportional to the intensity of the conflict. See the excellent analysis of Rudolf Reinhardt, "Die Vereinigung subjektiver und objektiver Gestaltungskräfte in Verträge."

56. We use the terms "planning," "programming," and so forth interchangeably here despite the efforts of some (which are useless, in our opinion) to pose a distinction among them.

57. We have already cited the literature on the importance of the State's assumption of planning decisions for the form of the State itself. See, for example, Crisafulli, "Appunti preliminari sul diritto del lavoro nella Costituzione," p. 163, and Predieri, *Pianificazione e costituzione,* pp. 35ff. and 323ff.

58. For an analogous discussion focusing on conflict among political parties, see Antonio Negri, "Lo Stato dei partiti."

59. For an example of the debate over the private or public juridical character of trade unions, see the lively polemic between Esposito (*La Costituzione italiana,* pp. 151–79) and Mortati ("Il lavoro nella Costituzione," p. 197). Predieri demonstrates how the debate in this form has recently declined in importance and been redefined instead with regard to the situation of the union within the schema of the planned functioning of the State. See *Pianificazione e costituzione,* pp. 437ff.

60. This conclusion is stated with great authority by Luigi Mengoni in his analysis of the problem of business controls. See "Recenti mutamenti nella struttura e nella gerarchia dell'impresa," in particular pp. 694–99.

61. See Alf Ross, *Towards a Realistic Jurisprudence,* in particular on the antimony in the theory of the sources of right, Part V, sections 2–4, and on the antinomies in the theory of validity, Part III, sections 2–3. In the case of the theory of sources, the antinomy that interests us most is the third one that Ross presents: the antinomy of unity and multiplicity. With respect to the theory of validity, we are most interested in the second, that is, the antinomy between the validity among juridical rules as imperatives and the validity among juridical rules as hypothetical judgments.

62. See Ilmar Tammelo, "Contemporary Developments of the Imperative Theory of Law, A Survey and Appraisal," and Felice Battaglia, "Alcune osservazioni sulla struttura e sulla funzione del diritto," in particular pp. 513–14 and 517. Even though these two authors set out from different, and sometimes even opposite, perspectives, they both arrive at the declaration of a revival of imperativist theories.

63. This position is given its clearest expression in the Scandinavian school. See, for example, Karl Olivecrona, *Der Imperativ des Gesetzes.* In his "Contemporary Developments of the Imperative Theory of Law," Tammelo highlights the coincidence of the positions regarding the nature of normative judgment espoused by the Scandinavians, the English, and—more interestingly—analytical philosophers such as Hare.

64. Marx reminded his contemporaries of this fact, and this is why it is important to study the aspects of his thought that relate to the theory of the crisis and the tendential fall of the rate of profit.

Chapter 4. Communist State Theory

1. See *Imperialismus heute* and *Der Imperialismus der BRD,* edited by the Institut für Gesellschaftswissenschaften beim ZK der SED; Rudi Gündel et al., *Zur Theorie des staatsmonopolistischen Kapitalismus*; *Le capitalisme monopoliste d'Etat,* edited by the Comité Central PCF.

2. Georg Lukács clearly demonstrated the structural and objective intensity of the mechanisms of legality in *History and Class Consciousness.*

3. For a critique of the theory of State monopoly capitalism, see Margaret Wirth, *Kapitalismustheorie in der DDR,* and R. Ebbinghausen, ed., *Monopol und Staat* (in particular the articles by R. Winkelmann, pp. 45–97, and W. Tristram, pp. 98–136).

4. Hence the terribly repressive effect exercised by theories of State monopoly capitalism in the socialist countries. See Margaret Wirth, *Kapitalismustheorie in der DDR*, pp. 27ff.

5. See Wygodski, *Der gegenwärtige Kapitalismus*, but primarily the references cited by Wirth in *Kapitalismustheorie in der DDR*.

6. It is interesting in this regard to consider the debate that surrounded the 1974 congress of the French Communist party, in which there arose a new opposition to the theories of State monopoly capitalism (and thus to the directing line of the party) mounted by sectors more closely linked to working-class organization. The Althusserian left put forward an interpretation of this polemical position, attacking what was taken to be the orthodoxy of Althusser himself. See Etienne Balibar, "Plus-value et classes sociales."

7. In general, see Riccardo Guastini, *Marx, dalla filosofia del diritto alla scienza della società*.

8. See also Ralph Miliband, "The Capitalist State: Reply to Nicos Poulantzas," and H. B. Haupt and Stephan Leibfried, "Anmerkung zur Kontroverse Poulantzas-Miliband."

9. On this methodology, see Louis Althusser and Etienne Balibar, *Reading Capital*, and Louis Althusser, *For Marx*.

10. On theories of the forms of the State, see Gerhard Leibholz, *Staatsformen*.

11. For critiques of Althusser's methodology, see Pier Aldo Rovatti, *Critica e scientificità in Marx*, and Jacques Rancière, *L'ideologia politica di Althusser*.

12. For a critique of Gramsci's theory of civil society "from a Marxian perspective," see Norberto Bobbio, "Gramsci and the Conception of Civil Society."

13. Among the radical journals that appeared in Italy during this period, see *Classe Operaia* (1964–67), *Contropiano* (1968 onward), *Potere Operaio* (1969–73), and the monthly edition of *Il Manifesto*.

14. Unfortunately, because of the lack of more recent analyses of this problematic, we must refer again here to Marx's *Grundrisse* and to *Capital*, vol. 1, pp. 943–1084.

15. See Hans-Jürgen Krahl, *Konstitution und Klassenkampf*, and Uwe Bergmann et al., *Die Rebellion der Studenten oder Die neue Opposition*.

16. In particular, see the authors of the so-called pessimistic school, such as Peter Bachrach and Morton Baratz, *Power and Poverty*, and E. E. Schattscheider, *The Semi-sovereign People*.

17. For an explicit analysis of the class nature of these phenomena from the perspective of this methodological framework, see Jorg Huffschmid, *Die Politik des Kapitals*.

18. See Johannes Agnoli and Peter Brückner, *Die Transformation der Demokratie*; Johannes Agnoli, "Die bürgerliche Gesellschaft und ihr Staat"; and Johannes Agnoli, "Strategia rivoluzionaria e parlamentarismo."

19. Despite the significant methodological differences between our analysis and his, Louis Althusser confronts an analogous problematic and also resolves it in an analogous manner in his "Ideology and State Ideological Apparatuses."

20. This critique is indebted to the analysis by S. Sardei-Biermann, J. Christiansen, and K. Dohlse, "Class Domination and the Political System: A Critical Interpretation of Recent Contributions by Claus Offe."

21. See Elmar Altvater, "Notes on Some Problems of State Intervention"; Sybille von Flatow and Freerk Huisken, "Zum Problem der Ableitung des bürgerlichen Staates"; and Margaret Wirth, "Towards a Critique of the Theory of State Monopoly Capitalism."

22. The first steps in this direction were taken in Italy by works such as *L'operaio multinazionale*, edited by Alessandro Serafini, and *Imperialismo e classe operaia multinazionale*, edited by Luciano Ferrari Bravo.

23. In addition to the Italian authors, notable exceptions to this claim include E. P. Thompson and Hans-Jürgen Krahl. See chapter 7, "Ontology and Constitution."

24. See Sergio Bologna et al. *Operai e Stato*, and *The Great Depression Revisited: Essays on the Economics of the Thirties*, edited by Herman van der Wee.

25. See G. L. S. Shackle, *The Years of High Theory: Invention and Tradition in Economic Thought, 1926–1939*; Heinz Wolfgang Arndt, *Economic Lessons of the Nineteen-Thirties*; Alvin Harvey Hansen, *Full Recovery of Stagnation?* and *Fiscal Policy and Business Cycles*.

26. On the fortunes of decisionism, see George Schwab, *The Challenge of the Exception*, and Julien Freund, *L'essence du politique*.

27. On the crisis of State planning, see James O'Connor, *The Fiscal Crisis of the State*; P. Brachet, *L'État-Patron*; Pierre Dubois, *La mort de l'État-Patron*; and Mario Cogoy, "Werttheorie und Staatsausgaben."

28. In addition to the fundamental declarations of the Italian Communist party, see Luciano Cafagna, "Classe e Stato nello stato di transizione leninista."

Chapter 5. The State and Public Spending

1. See the review of this literature in chapter 4, "Developments of the Structural Analysis of the State: The State in the Theory of Crisis." The article by Sybille von Flatow and Freerk Huisken, in particular, has engendered a large debate in Germany. See Helmut Reichelt, "Some Comments on Sybille von Flatow and

Freerk Huisken's Essay"; Hunno Hochberger, "Probleme einer materialistischen Bestimmung des Staates"; and Heide Gerstenberger, "Class Conflict, Competition, and State Functions."

2. David Yaffe, following the work of Manel, makes this argument. See "The Crisis of Profitability" and "The Marxian Theory of Crisis, Capital and State." Joachim Hirsch also seems to fall into this ambiguity. See his "Zur Analyse des politischen Systems," in particular pp. 95 and 97. Hirsch's work, however, represents nonetheless an enormous contribution that pushes forward the Marxist theory of the State, and we will consider it greater in detail.

3. Many authors have recently expressed reservations regarding Roman Rosdolsky's interpretation of the *Grundrisse* in *The Making of Marx's 'Capital,'* in particular with respect to the concept of "comprehensive capital." See, for example, W. Schwarz, "Das 'Kapital im Allgemeinen' und die 'Konkurrenz' in ökonomischen Werk von Karl Marx." According to these authors, Rosdolsky confused Marx's different levels of scientific abstraction, failing to distinguish between "comprehensive capital" as a simple logical category and "comprehensive capital" as the level on which competition comes into play, which is not a logical but a historical category. It is certainly necessary that studies of the *Grundrisse* be evaluated on the basis of central aspects of Marx's analysis, and certain passages of Rosdolsky's work should indeed be revised, but in my opinion this is not the case with his conception of "comprehensive capital," a concept fundamental to Marx's thought. Rosdolsky clarifies the fact that this is a tendential category that only today begins to approach its real effectiveness. On the other hand, it does not seem that Schwarz has fully appreciated the complexity of the relationship between logical categories and historical categories in Marx's thought.

4. The U.S. literature on this crisis is already enormous. Allow me to refer only to Peter Bachrach and Morton Baratz, *Power and Poverty,* and Francis Fox Piven and Richard Cloward, *Regulating the Poor.*

5. For these problems in general, see James O'Connor, *The Fiscal Crisis of the State,* in particular p. 9 and the final chapters.

6. O'Connor may have developed these distinctions on the basis of the Claus Offe's analyses of the political structures of the State. For a development of these themes, see Offe's *Strukturprobleme des kapitalistischen Staates,* pp. 27ff. and 123ff., and "Crisis of Crisis Management," pp. 57ff.

7. Marx's definition of productive labor runs throughout his mature work in a coherent series of passages. See, for example, *Grundrisse,* pp. 266–73, 293–95, 304–18, 699–716, *Capital,* vol. 1, pp. 643–44, and *Theories of Surplus Value,* Part I, pp. 152–304.

8. See also Ian Gough, "Marx's Theory of Productive and Unproductive Labour"; J. Harrison, "Productive and Unproductive Labour in Marx's Political Economy"; B. Fine, "A Note on Productive and Unproductive Labour"; and P. Bullock, "Categories of Labour Power for Capital" and "Defining Productive Labour for Capital."

9. See Marx's investigations and conclusions about the public debt in private accumulation.

10. The extension of the concept of productive labor to the domain of domestic labor has proved to be a particularly interesting point in the debate among English economists. See J. Harrison, "The Political Economy of Housework," and Ian Gough and J. Harrison, "Unproductive Labour and Housework, Again."

11. Joachim Hirsch argues convincingly that there is an inherent continuity between the processes of socialization and the structure of the contemporary State. See "Zur Analyse des politischen Systems," in particular pp. 89, 91, 93, and 103. On this line, see also Johannes Agnoli, *Überlegungen zum bürgerlichen Staat,* in particular the chapter titled "Der Staat des Kapitals."

12. Confronting the difficulties posed by State administration on this terrain, it is useful to keep in mind the writings of Claus Offe discussed in chapter 4, *Strukturprobleme des kapitalistischen Staates* and "Crisis of Crisis Management." For a good critique of Offe's sociological and structural objectivism and an evaluation of the positive contributions of "Crisis Theory" to this field in Germany, see Josef Esser, *Einführung in die materialistische Staatsanalyse.*

13. See Antonio Negri, "Crisis of the Planner-State" and "Partito operaio contro il lavoro."

14. Hirsch provides a very clear example of the attempt to refer the fundamental problems of political science and the theory of planning to the fundamental antagonisms of the socialization of production. See "Zur Analyse des politischen Systems," pp. 85, 128–30.

15. The contributions to the so-called *Planungsdiskussion* that has developed in West Germany testify to this "negative" consciousness. Hirsch provides a bibliography of these sources in "Zur Analyse des politischen Systems," pp. 88, 93–94.

16. See Rosdolsky's critical reconstruction of the Marxian theory of the wage in *The Making of Marx's 'Capital',* pp. 282ff.

17. For an extension of this analysis, see Antonio Negri, *Proletari e Stato.*

18. See, for example, the documentation on the German situation provided by H. J. Weissbach in *Planungswissenschaft.*

find resonances with the neo-Kantian formalist tradition, which emphasizes formalist logic and a kind of schematism of reason. Eminent proponents of this tradition include Hermann Cohen and Paul Natorp.

12. If one were to consider *A Theory of Justice* alone, one would have to object that Rorty is stretching Rawls's argument to the point of distortion. In fact, we can find several passages in that text that are in patent contradiction with Rorty's thesis. For example: "liberty of conscience and freedom of thought should not be founded on philosophical or ethical skepticism, nor on indifference to religious and moral interests. The principles of justice define an appropriate path between dogmatism and intolerance on the one side, and a reductionism which regards religion and morality as mere preferences on the other" (p. 243). However, in Rawls's subsequent articles (such as "Justice as Fairness," "The Idea of an Overlapping Consensus," "The Priority of Right and Ideas of the Good," and "The Domain of the Political and Overlapping Consensus"), his position is much less clear and does in certain respects support Rorty's reading. For a summary and analysis of this phase of Rawls's work, see Kukathas and Pettit, *Rawls*, pp. 133–41 and particularly pp. 148–50.

13. For a practical analysis of this "method of avoidance" in relation to the urban development and the 1992 riots in Los Angeles, see Michael Hardt, "Los Angeles Novos." The architecture and territorial arrangement of Los Angeles provides a particularly clear example for investigating the practical relation between avoidance and exclusion. See Mike Davis, *The City of Quartz: Excavating the Future in Los Angeles*, in particular pp. 223–63.

14. The studies of the recent collapse of the Welfare State trinity—Taylorism, Fordism, and Keynesianism—are too numerous to cite here. For one widely read example, see Michael Piore and Charles Sabel, *The Second Industrial Divide*.

15. For the history of the restructuring of the FIAT plant in Turin, see Marco Revelli, *Lavorare in FIAT*. Benjamin Coriat has also done excellent work on the effects of industrial automation and the so-called Japanese model of production. See *L'atelier et le robot* and *Penser à l'envers: Travail et organisation dans l'entreprise japonaise*.

16. For a good discussion of the recent shrinking of civil liberties, particularly the Fourth Amendment, as a result of the war on drugs, see Stephen Saltzburg, "Another Victim of Illegal Narcotics: The Fourth Amendment." Mike Davis discusses the results of the Los Angeles Police Department's war on gangs for civil liberties in chapter 5 of *The City of Quartz*, "The Hammer and the Rock," pp. 265–322.

17. Even brief attention to a few examples of possible implementations of the difference principle makes clear its practical ineffectiveness when posed in terms of advocacy. Michael Sandel evaluates the difference principle in the context of affirmative-action policies to show that even when it furnishes a theoretical vision of equality it provides an inadequate practical basis for an institutional mechanism to diminish social inequalities. The difference principle invokes a conception of the communal ownership of social assets, he argues, but is grounded in no concept of community and therefore carries no practical weight in the debate about practical policy decisions of social desert (*Liberalism and the Limits of Justice*, pp. 135–47 and more generally chapter 2). Even more revealing, perhaps, is an example Rawls gives us of the strategic invocation of the difference principle in the thought of John M. Keynes that sheds light on its theoretical pallor. In the late nineteenth and early twentieth centuries, Rawls explains, "it was precisely the inequality of the distribution of wealth which made possible the rapid build-up of capital and the more or less steady improvement in the general standard of living of everyone. It is this fact, in Keynes's opinion, that provided the main justification of the capitalist system. . . . the essential point here is that Keynes's justification, whether or not its premises are sound, can be made to turn solely on improving the situation of the working class" (*A Theory of Justice*, p. 299). After the succession of arguments on priority have marginalized the question of social equality in the system of justice, the generalized system to reproduce inequality is justified and rationalized—and, to add insult to injury, it is supported in the name of the least advantaged! Here we can see that through a series of subordinations Rawls succeeds in eliminating the tension of the system and reduces the democratic and egalitarian tendency to a mere appearance.

18. Even though communitarianism is a phenomenon too diverse to call a movement or a school, it contains a certain coherence when it is positioned as a critique of a specific version of Rawls and liberal social theory. In contrast to the formalist conception of right, the individualist basis of morality, and the resulting weak social subjectivity, the communitarian concerns stand out clearly as a strong and solid theoretical position. If in the late 1960s and early 1970s, at the time of Rawls's writing, the debate in moral theory centered on the polemic between Welfare State liberalism and conservative libertarianism, since that time the focus has shifted radically toward a polemic between liberal theories of right and communitarian conceptions of virtue and common good. We should emphasize, however, that communitarians should not thus be conceived as antiliberals: the communitarian position presents itself as a critique not in the sense that it refutes liberalism but in that it "completes" liberalism, just as the Hegelian critique of Kant completed the ideal system.

19. We will focus on Michael Sandel, Charles Taylor, and a particularly Hegelian version of communitarianism in this discussion, not because this line can be said to be representative (indeed, it would be difficult to claim any position as representative in such a diverse group of scholars) but because we find it the most coherent and fully articulated challenge to Rawls and liberal theory. Many attempt to characterize the field of communitarians by their philosophical heritage: a Hegelian school inspired by Taylor, an Aristotelian school represented by Alasdair MacIntyre, and a civic republican line led by Quentin Skinner. This is convenient shorthand, but it may be misleading because the boundaries are not so clear. MacIntyre, for example, is a fine Hegel scholar himself and his reading of Aristotle in *After Virtue: A Study in Moral Theory* is certainly deeply influenced by Hegel; Taylor, for his part, is often an ardent proponent of civic republicanism. (See, for example, "Cross-Purposes: The Liberal-Communitarian Debate," pp. 165ff.) We hope, then, that our reading of a Hegelian version of communitarianism here, while it cannot claim to be representative, will at least shed light on the other lines of communitarian thought. Other scholars often cited as being communitarians, though they do not necessarily claim the label for themselves, are Roberto Unger, Robert Bellah, William Sullivan, and Michael Walzer. Critical reviews of the literature that we have found helpful include Chantal Mouffe, "Le libéralisme américain et ses critiques"; Amy Gutmann, "Communitarian Critics of Liberalism"; Michael Walzer, "The Communitarian Critique of Liberalism"; Michael Sandel, Introduction to *Liberalism and its Critics*; Charles Taylor, "Cross-Purposes"; and Nancy Rosenblum, Introduction to *Liberalism and the Moral Life*.

20. Taylor complicates this problematic considerably in his *Sources of the Self: The Making of Modern Identity*. He considers a much broader historical period, deals with many more authors, and gives greater nuance to the historical trends he proposes. In particular, Hegel is no longer posed as the dominant figure on the modern horizon. Despite these shifts, however, Taylor's argument remains focused on the synthesis between a subject of expressive unity and a subject of disengaged reason as the central project of modernity.

21. It is certainly debatable whether this characterization is adequate to Rawls's presentation. Sandel's reading of the subject of possession has been carefully critiqued by Thomas Pogge, *Realizing Rawls*, chapter 2.

22. Kukathas and Pettit also insist on the Hegelian tendency in Rawls's work, noting its classically conservative aspects. "The Hegelian character of Rawls' philosophy lies in his understanding of his project not as a bid to re-model his society in the image of some rational ideal, but as an attempt to understand liberal democratic America by eliciting the principles latent in the (reasonable) institutions of its public political culture" (Rawls, p. 145).

23. Charles Taylor echoes this critique that Rawlsian morality lacks attention to ontology and extends it to the contemporary field of moral philosophy in general: "This moral philosophy has tended to focus on what it is right to do rather than what it is good to be" (*Sources of the Self*, p. 3; see also pp. 88–89).

24. We should keep in mind, of course, that this is not the only way to employ the term "community." Consider, for example, how the "Black community" (which Taylor would qualify as a partial community) is posed as a powerful subject with a certain autonomy, or possibility for separation, in the discourse of Malcolm X. We will return to this issue in the next chapter.

25. This tendency in moral and political theory dovetails with the studies in comparative politics that center around the work of Theda Skocpol. The (relative) autonomy of the State as a historical social actor is posed by Skocpol as a methodological axiom for empirical research, without normative or political value. Her work never questions whether the State should or should not be autonomous from social forces, whether it should be the primary social actor, but merely claims that by considering the State as an autonomous subject we are able to construct better explanatory models for the historical transformations of societies. According to Skocpol, the proposition of State autonomy is not a political question, or rather it is a politically neutral question of scientific research that can be tested and verified with empirical data. Even if one were to accept this claim, the coincidence between Skocpol's work and the Hegelian propositions that the State be the autonomous and primary social actor cannot but create an atmosphere of mutual support. For a summary of Skocpol's position, see "Bringing the State Back In: Strategies of Analysis in Current Research."

26. For more extensive discussions of the concept of civil society in the history of political theory, see Antonio Negri, "Journeys Through Civil Society," in *The Politics of Subversion: A Manifesto for the Twenty-First Century*, pp. 169–76, and *The Savage Anomaly*, pp. 136–43. Also useful in this regard is Norberto Bobbio, "Gramsci and the Conception of Civil Society."

27. Paradoxically, the real subsumption always implies a radical separation. In the process of real rather than formal subsumption what is subsumed is not foreign but proper to the system itself. The process deprives the system of mechanisms for engaging what is external to it and thus increases the autonomy or separation of the system. We will return to the connection between the real subsumption and separation at several points in chapter 7.

28. Deleuze and Guattari are careful to point out that the smoothing of social space does not bring an end to social striation; on the contrary, within the process of smoothing, elements of social striation reappear "in the

Works Cited

Ackerman, Bruce. *We The People: Foundations.* Harvard University Press, Cambridge, 1991.

Agnoli, Johannes. "Die bürgerliche Gesellschaft und ihr Staat." *Das Argument*, Berlin, no. 6, 1970.

———. "Strategia rivoluzionaria e parlamentarismo." *Sviluppo economico e rivoluzione.* De Donato, Bari, 1969.

———. *Überlegungen zum bürgerlichen Staat.* Wagenbach, Berlin, 1975.

Agnoli, Johannes, and Peter Brückner. *Die Transformation der Demokratie.* Voltaire Verlag, Berlin, 1967.

Allorio, Enrico. "Intervento al convegno degli amici del diritto dell'economia." *Diritto dell'economia*, no. 3, 1956, pp. 1198–1213.

Alquati, Romano. *Sindacato e partito.* Edizioni Stampatori, Turin, 1974.

———. *Sulla FIAT e altri scritti.* Feltrinelli, Milan, 1975.

Althusser, Louis. *For Marx*, translated by Ben Brewster. Vintage Books, New York, 1969.

———. "Ideology and State Ideological Apparatuses." *Lenin and Philosophy.* Monthly Review Press, New York, 1971.

Althusser, Louis, and Etienne Balibar. *Reading Capital*, translated by Ben Brewster. New Left Books, London, 1970.

Altvater, Elmar. "Notes on Some Problems of State Intervention." *Kapitalistate*, no. 1, 1973, pp. 96–116, and no. 2, 1973, pp. 76–83. A shorter version appears as "Some Problems of State Intervention," in *State and Capital*, edited by John Holloway and Sol Picciotto, University of Texas Press, Austin, 1978, pp. 40–42.

Arendt, Hannah. *The Human Condition.* University of Chicago Press, Chicago, 1958.

Arndt, Heinz Wolfgang. *Economic Lessons of the Nineteen-Thirties.* F. Cass, London, 1963.

Aronowitz, Stanley. *The Politics of Identity: Class, Culture, Social Movements.* Routledge, New York, 1992.

Ascarelli, Tullio. "Intervento." *Diritto dell'economia*, no. 3, 1956.

———. "Ordinamento giuridico e processo economico." *Rivista trimestrale di diritto pubblico.* A. Giuffrè, Milan, 1956.

———. *Autonomia: Post-Political Politics.* Semiotext(e), vol. 3, no. 3, 1980.

Azzariti, Giuseppe. "La nuova costituzione e le leggi anteriori." *Foro Italiano*, vol. 4. Rome, 1948.

Bachrach, Peter, and Morton Baratz. *Power and Poverty.* Oxford University Press, Oxford, 1970.

Balibar, Etienne. "Plus-value et classes sociales." *Cinq études du matérialisme historique.* Maspero, Paris, 1974.

Rosenfeld, and David Gray Carlson. Routledge, New York, 1992, pp. 3–67.

Di Leonardo, Micaela. "The Female World of Cards and Holidays: Women, Families, and the Work of Kinship." *Signs*, vol. 12, no. 3, 1987, pp. 440–53.

Djuvara, Mircea. "Sources et normes du droit positif." *Le problème des sources du droit positif.* Annuaire de l'Institut de Philosophie du droit et de sociologie juridique, first session, 1934–35, Sirey, Paris, pp. 82–101.

Draper, Theodore. *American Communism and Soviet Russia.* Viking Press, New York, 1960.

Dubois, Pierre. *La mort de l'État-Patron.* Editions Ouvrières, Paris, 1974.

Dworkin, Ronald. "The Reagan Revolution and the Supreme Court." *The New York Review of Books*, July 18, 1991, pp. 23–27.

Ebbighausen, Rolf, ed. *Monopol und Staat. Zur Marx-Rezeption in der Theorie des staats-monopolistischen Kapitalismus.* Suhrkamp Verlag, Frankfurt, 1974.

Eckart, Christel, et al. "Arbeiterbewusstsein, Klassenzusammensetzung und ökonomische Entwicklung. Empirische Thesen zum 'instrumentellen Bewusstsein.'" *Gesellschaft*, no. 4, pp. 7–64.

Ehlert, Willi. "Politische Planung — und was davon übrig bleibt." *Leviathan*, Düsseldorf, no. 1, 1975.

Einaudi, Mario. *La rivoluzione di Roosevelt.* Einaudi, Turin, 1959.

Eisenstein, Zillah. "Developing a Theory of Capitalist Patriarchy and Socialist Feminism." In *Capitalist Patriarchy and the Case for Socialist Feminism*, edited by Zillah Einsenstein. Monthly Review Press, New York, 1979, pp. 5–40.

Elson, Diane. "The Value Theory of Labour." In *Value: The Representation of Labour in Capitalism*, edited by Diane Elson. Humanities Press, Atlantic Highlands, N.J., 1979, pp. 115–80.

Emenlauer, Rainer, ed. *Die Kommune in der Staatsorganisation.* Suhrkamp Verlag, Frankfurt, 1974.

Emmanuel, Arghiri. "Le taux de profit et les incompatibilités Marx-Keynes." *Annales, économies, sociétés, civilisations*, vol. 21, A. Colin, Paris, 1966, pp. 1189–1211.

Engels, Friedrich. *Anti-Dühring.* Progress Publishers, Moscow, 1969.

Epstein, Steven. "Democratic Science? AIDS Activism and the Contested Construction of Knowledge." *Socialist Review*, vol. 21, no. 2, 1991, pp. 35–64.

Esposito, Carlo. *La Costituzione italiana.* CEDAM, Padua, 1954.

Esser, Josef. *Einführung in die materialistische Staatsanalyse.* Campus Verlag, Frankfurt and New York, 1975.

Euchner, Walter. "Zur Lage des Parlamentarismus." In *Der CDU-Staat. Analysen zur Verfassungswirklichkeit der Bundesrepublik*, edited by Gert Schäfer and Carl Nedelmann. Suhrkamp Verlag, Frankfurt, 1967, vol. 1, pp. 105–32.

Evans, P., D. Rueschemeyer, and Theda Skocpol, eds. *Bringing the State Back In.* Cambridge University Press, Cambridge, 1985.

Fabra, Paul. "25 ans après Bretton Woods." *Le monde de l'économie*, July 8, 1969.

Fauvel-Rouif, Denise, ed. *Mouvements ouvriers et dépression économique.* Van Gorcum, Assen, 1966.

Fechner, Erich. *Rechtsphilosophie.* Mohr, Tübingen, 1956.

Ferrari Bravo, Luciano, ed. *Imperialismo e classe operaia multinazionale.* Feltrinelli, Milan, 1975.

Filene, Peter G. *Americans and the Soviet Experiment 1917–1933.* Harvard University Press, Cambridge, 1967.

Fine, Ben. "A Note on Productive and Unproductive Labour." *Conference of Socialist Economists Bulletin.* London, Fall 1973.

Finzi, Roberto. "Lo Stato del capitale, un problema aperto." *Studi Storici.* Rome, 1970, no. 3.

Fish, Stanley. *Doing What Comes Naturally: Change, Rhetoric, and the Practice of Theory in Literary and Legal Studies.* Duke University Press, Durham, N.C., 1989.

Flatow, Sybille von, and Freerk Huisken. "Zum Problem der Ableitung des bürgerlichen Staates." *Probleme des Klassenkampfs*, no. 7, 1973, pp. 83–153.

Forsthoff, Ernst. "La Repubblica federale tedesca come Stato di diritto." *Rivista trimestrale di diritto pubblico.* A. Giuffrè, Milan, vol. 6, 1956.

———. *Lehrbuch des Verwaltungsrechts*, vol. 1. C. H. Beck, Munich and Berlin, 1951.

———. *Rechtsstaat im Wandel: verfassungsrechtliche Abhandlungen, 1950–1964.* Kohlhammer, Stuttgart, 1964.

———. "Über Massnahme-Gesetze." *Gedächtnisschrift für Walter Jellinek*, edited by Otto Bachhof, Isar Verlag, Munich, 1955.

Foucault, Michel. "Du Gouvernement des Vivants." Course given at the Collège de France, January 30, 1980; cassette recording available at the Bibliothèque du Saulchoir, Paris.

———. "What is Enlightenment?" In *The Foucault Reader*, edited by Paul Rabinow. Pantheon Books, New York, 1984.

Freiburghaus, Dieter, and G. Schmid. "Techniken politischer Planung: vom Markekalkül zum Plankalkul?" *Leviathan*, Düsseldorf, no. 3, 1974.

———. "Theorie der Segmentierung von Arbeitsmärkten." *Leviathan*, Düsseldorf, no. 3, 1975.

Freund, Julien. *L'essence du politique*. Sirey, Paris, 1965.

Galgano, Francesco. *Le istituzioni dell'economia capitalistica*. Zanichelli, Bologna, 1974.

Galston, William. "Pluralism and Social Unity." *Ethics* 99, 1989, pp. 711–26.

Gerstenberger, F. "Produktion und Qualifikation." *Leviathan*, Düsseldorf, no. 2, 1975.

Gerstenberger, Heide. "Class Conflict, Competition, and State Functions." In *State and Capital*, edited by John Holloway and Sol Picciotto. University of Texas Press, Austin, 1978, pp. 148–59.

Giannini, Massimo-Severo. "Profili costituzionali della protezione sociale." *Rivista giuridica del lavoro*, Rome, 1951.

———. "Rilevanza costituzionale del lavoro." *Rivista giuridica del lavoro*, Rome, 1949–50, no. 1, pp. 1–20.

Giddens, Anthony. *Central Problems in Social Theory: Action, Structure, and Contradiction in Social Analysis*. University of California Press, Berkeley, 1979.

Giugni, Gino. *Introduzione allo studio dell'autonomia collettiva*. A. Giuffrè, Milan, 1960.

Goldfield, Michael. "Worker Insurgency, Radical Organization, and New Deal Labor Legislation." *American Political Science Review*, vol. 83, no. 4, December 1989, pp. 1257–82.

Goldthorpe, John H., David Lockwood, Frank Bechhofer, and Jennifer Platt. *The Affluent Worker*. 3 vols., Cambridge University Press, London, 1968–69.

Gough, Ian. "Marx's Theory of Productive and Unproductive Labour." *New Left Review*, no. 76, November–December 1972.

———. "State Expenditure in Advanced Capitalism." *New Left Review*, no. 92, July–August 1975.

Gough, Ian, and J. Harrison. "Unproductive Labour and Housework, Again." *Conference of Socialist Economists Bulletin*, London, February 1975.

Grandi, Mario. "La risoluzione delle controversie di lavoro in Gran Bretagna." *Rivista di diritto del lavoro*, Milan, vol. 11, 1959, Part I, pp. 42–104.

Grosso, Giuseppe. "Distinti complessi giuridici e varietà di rapporti fra norma giuridica e fatto economico." *Diritto dell'economia*. A. Giuffrè, Milan, 1955.

Guarino, Giuseppe. *Scritti di diritto pubblico dell'economia e di diritto dell'energia*. A. Giuffrè, Milan, 1962.

Guastini, Riccardo. *Marx, dalla filosofia del diritto alla scienza della società*. Il Mulino, Bologna, 1974.

———. "Teoria e fenomenologia dello Stato capitalistico." *Politica del diritto*, December 1971, no. 6, pp. 781–806.

Gündel, Rudi, Horst Heininger, Peter Hess, and Kurt Zieschang. *Zur Theorie des staatsmonopolistischen Kapitalismus*. Akademie-Verlag, Berlin, 1967.

Gutmann, Amy. "Communitarian Critics of Liberalism." *Philosophy and Public Affairs*, Summer 1985, pp. 308–22.

Haberler, Gottfried. "Sixteen Years Later." In *Keynes' General Theory*, edited by Robert Lekachman. St. Martin's Press, New York, 1964, pp. 289–96.

Habermas, Jürgen. *Legitimation Crisis*, translated by Thomas McCarthy. Beacon Press, Boston, 1975.

———. *Strukturwandel der Öffentlichkeit: Untersuchungen zu einer Kategorie der bürgerlichen Gesellschaft*. Luchterhand, Berlin, 1962.

Hansen, Alvin Harvey. *Fiscal Policy and Business Cycles*. Norton, New York, 1941.

———. *Full Recovery of Stagnation?* Norton, New York, 1938.

Haraway, Donna. "A Cyborg Manifesto: Science, Technology, and Socialist-Feminism in the Late Twentieth Century." In *Simians, Cyborgs, and Women: The Reinvention of Nature*. Routledge, New York, 1991.

Hardt, Michael. *Gilles Deleuze: An Apprenticeship in Philosophy*. University of Minnesota Press, Minneapolis, 1993.

———. "Los Angeles Novos." *Futur antérieur*, Paris, nos. 12–13, 1992, pp. 12–26.

Harrison, J. "The Political Economy of Housework." *Conference of Socialist Economists Bulletin*, London, Winter 1973.

———. "Productive and Unproductive Labour in Marx's Political Economy." *Conference of Socialist Economists Bulletin*, London, Fall 1973.

Harrod, R. F. *The Life of John Maynard Keynes*. Macmillan, London, 1951.

———. "Mr. Keynes and Traditional Theory." In *Keynes' General Theory*, edited by Robert Lekachman. St. Martin's Press, New York, 1964, pp. 124–38.

Hartsock, Nancy. *Money, Sex, and Power: Towards a Feminist Historical Materialism*. Northeastern University Press, Boston, 1985.

Mazzarelli, Bruno. *La norma collettiva nella teoria generale del diritto.* A. Giuffrè, Milan, 1957.

Mazzoni, Giuliano. "Intervento al convegno degli amici del diritto dell'economia." *Diritto dell'economia,* Milan, 1956.

Mediobanca, ed. *La finanza pubblica.* 2 vols. Mediobanca, Milan, 1968–1972.

Mendner, J. H. *Technologische Entwicklung und Arbeitsprozess.* Fischer, Frankfurt, 1975.

Mengoni, Luigi. "Recenti mutamenti nella struttura e nella gerarchia dell'impresa." *Rivista delle società.* A. Giuffrè, Milan, 1958, pp. 689–724.

Merkl, Adolf. *Allgemeines Verwaltungsrecht.* J. Springer, Vienna and Berlin, 1937.

Miele, Giovanni. "Profilo della consuetudine nel sistema delle fonti di diritto interno." *Stato e diritto,* vol. 4, no. 1, 1943, pp. 24–29.

Miglioranzi, L. A. "Il rapporto di lavoro nella sua evoluzione." *Scritti giuridici in onore di Antonio Scialoja,* vol. 4. N. Zanichelli, Bologna, 1953, pp. 291–306.

Miliband, Ralph. "The Capitalist State: Reply to Nicos Poulantzas." *New Left Review,* no. 59, January–February 1970, pp. 53–60.

———. *The State in Capitalist Society.* Basic Books, New York, 1969.

Mishra, Ramesh. *The Welfare State in Capitalist Society.* University of Toronto Press, Toronto, 1990.

Mommsen, Wolfgang J. *Max Weber und die Deutsche Politik, 1890–1920.* Mohr, Tübingen, 1959.

Morishima, Michio. *Marx's Economics: A Dual Theory of Value and Growth.* Cambridge University Press, London, 1973.

Mortati, Costantino. "Il lavoro nella Costituzione." *Il diritto del lavoro,* Milan, 1954, pp. 149–212.

———. *La Costituzione in senso materiale.* Milan, 1940.

———. *Istituzioni di diritto pubblico.* CEDAM, Padua, 1969.

Mouffe, Chantal. "Le libéralisme américain et ses critiques." *Esprit,* March 1987, p. 100–114.

Moulier, Yann. "Introduction." In *The Politics of Subversion: A Manifesto for the Twenty-First Century* by Antonio Negri, translated by James Newell. Polity Press, Cambridge, 1989, pp. 1–44.

Müller, Wolfgang. "Die Grenzen der Sozialpolitik in der Marktwirtschaft." In *Der CDU-Staat. Analysen zur Verfassungswirklichkeit der Bundesrepublik,* edited by Gert Schäfer and Carl Nedelmann, Suhrkamp Verlag, Frankfurt, 1967, vol. 1, pp. 14–47.

Müller, Wolfgang, and Christel Neusüss. "The Illusion of State Socialism." *Telos,* no. 25, Fall 1975, pp. 13–90. A shorter version appears as "The 'Welfare-State Illusion' and the Contradiction between Wage Labour and Capital," in *State and Capital,* edited by John Holloway and Sol Picciotto, University of Texas Press, Austin, 1978, pp. 32–39.

Musil, Robert. *The Man Without Qualities.* 3 vols. Picador Classics, London, 1988.

Napoleoni, Claudio. *Economic Thought of the Twentieth Century.* Wiley, New York, 1972.

———. "Sulla teoria della produzione come processo circolare." In *Il dibattito su Sraffa,* edited by Franco Botta. De Donato, Bari, 1974, pp. 37–62.

Navarra, A. "Le speranze (sinora) deluse." *Rivista di diritto del lavoro,* Milan, 1953, pp. 139–57.

Negri, Antonio. *Alle origini del formalismo giuridico.* CEDAM, Padua, 1962.

———. "L'antimodernité de Spinoza." *Les Temps Modernes,* no. 539, June 1991, pp. 43–61. An Italian version appears in *Spinoza Sovversivo: Variazioni (in)attuali,* Antonio Pellicani Editore, Rome, 1992, pp. 129–51.

———. "Archaeology and Project: The Mass Worker and the Social Worker." In *Revolution Retrieved.* Red Notes, London, 1988, pp. 203–28.

———. *Constituent Power.* University of Minnesota Press, Minneapolis, forthcoming.

———. "Crisis of the Planner-State: Communism and Revolutionary Organisation." In *Revolution Retrieved.* Red Notes, London, 1988, pp. 94–148.

———. "Interpretation of the Class Situation Today: Methodological Aspects." In *Open Marxism,* vol. 2, edited by Werner Bonefeld, Richard Gunn, and Kosmas Psychopedis, Pluto Press, London, 1992, pp. 69–105. Also appears as "Twenty Theses on Marx: Interpretation of the Class Situation Today," *Polygraph,* no. 5, 1992, pp. 136–70.

———. "Is There a Marxist Doctrine of the State?" In Noberto Bobbio, *Which Socialism?* University of Minnesota Press, Minneapolis, 1987, pp. 121–38.

———. "Lo Stato dei partiti." In *La forma Stato.* Feltrinelli, Milan, 1977, pp. 111–49.

———. *Marx Beyond Marx: Lessons on the Grundrisse,* translated by Harry Cleaver, Michael Ryan, and Maurizio Viano. Bergin and Garvey, South Hadley, 1984.

———. "Marx on Cycle and Crisis." In *Revolution Retrieved.* Red Notes, London, 1988, pp. 47–90.

———. "Partito operaio contro il lavoro." In *Crisi e organizzazione operaia*. Feltrinelli, Milan, 1974.

———. *The Politics of Subversion: A Manifesto for the Twenty-First Century*, translated by James Newell, introduction by Yann Moulier. Polity Press, Cambridge, 1989.

———. *Proletari e Stato*. Feltrinelli, Milan, 1976.

———. *Revolution Retrieved*. Red Notes, London, 1988.

———. "Rileggendo Pasukanis: note di discussione." In *La forma Stato*. Feltrinelli, Milan, 1977, pp. 161–95.

———. *The Savage Anomaly: The Power of Spinoza's Metaphysics and Politics*, translated by Michael Hardt. University of Minnesota Press, Minneapolis, 1991.

Negt, Oskar. *Soziologische Phantasie und exemplarisches Lernen*. Europäische Verlagsanstalt, Frankfurt, 1968.

Neumann, Franz. *The Democratic and the Authoritarian State*. Free Press, Glencoe, Ill., 1957.

Neuy, Erich. *Das rechtsphilosophische Relativismusproblem in der Sicht des Neupositivismus*. Dissertation, Mainz, 1951.

Nietzsche, Frederick. *The Will to Power*, translated by Walter Kaufman. Vintage Books, New York, 1967.

Nuti, Domenico Mario. "Economia volgare e distribuzione del reddito." In *Il dibattito su Sraffa*, edited by Franco Botta. De Donato, Bari, 1974, pp. 261–71.

O'Connor, James. *The Fiscal Crisis of the State*. St. Martin's Press, New York, 1973.

Offe, Claus. *Berufsbildungsreform. Eine Fallstudie über Reformpolitik*. Suhrkamp Verlag, Frankfurt, 1975.

———. "Crisis of Crisis Management: Elements of a Political Crisis Theory." In *Contradictions of the Welfare State*. MIT Press, Cambridge, 1984.

———. "Dominio politico e struttura di classe." *Rassegna Italiana di Sociologia*, vol. 12, no. 1, 1971, pp. 47–82.

———. *Industry and Inequality: The Achievement Principle in Work and Social Status*, translated by James Wickham. St. Martin's Press, New York, 1977.

———. "Rationalitätskriterien und Funktionsprobleme politisch-administrativen Handelns." *Leviathan*, Düsseldorf, no. 3, 1974.

———. *Strukturprobleme des kapitalistischen Staates, Aufsätze zur politischen Soziologie*. Suhrkamp Verlag, Frankfurt, 1972.

Offe, Claus, and Wolf-Dieter Narr, eds. *Wohlfahrtsstaat und Massenloyalität*. Kiepenheuer und Witsch, Cologne, 1975.

Ohlin, Bertil. "Mr. Keynes' Views on the Transfer Problem." *The Economic Journal*, vol. 39, September 1925.

———. "The Reparation Problem." *The Economic Journal*, vol. 39, June 1925.

Olalquiaga, Celeste. *Megalopolis: Contemporary Cultural Sensibilities*. University of Minnesota Press, Minneapolis, 1992.

Olivecrona, Karl. *Der Imperativ des Gesetzes*. Munksgaard, Copenhagen, 1942.

Paci, Massimo. *Mercato del lavoro e classi sociali in Italia*. Il Mulino, Bologna, 1973.

Panzieri, Raniero. *La ripresa del marxismo-leninismo in Italia*, edited by D. Lanzardo. Sapere, Milan, 1972.

Pashukanis, Eugenii. *Law and Marxism: A General Theory*, translated by Christopher Aurther. Ink Links, London, 1978.

Pateman, Carol. *The Sexual Contract*. Polity Press, Cambridge, 1988.

Pergolesi, Ferruccio. *Saggi sulle fonti normative*. A Giuffrè, Milan, 1943.

Pierandrei, Franco. "La corte costituzionale e le 'modificazioni tacite' della Costituzione." *Scritti giuridici in onore di Antonio Scialoja*, vol. 4. N. Zanichelli, Bologna, 1953, pp. 315–62.

Piore, Michael, and Charles Sabel. *The Second Industrial Divide*. Basic Books, New York, 1984.

Piven, Frances Fox, and Richard Cloward. *The New Class War*. Pantheon, New York, 1982.

———. *Regulating the Poor*. Random House, New York, 1972.

Pizzorno, Alessandro. "Sul metodo di Gramsci (dalla storiografia alla scienza politica)." *Quaderni di sociologia*, vol. 16, no. 4, Turin, 1967.

Pogge, Thomas. *Realizing Rawls*. Cornell University Press, Ithaca, 1989.

Poulantzas, Nicos. *Political Power and Social Classes*, translated by Timothy O'Hagan. New Left Books, London, 1973.

———. "Préliminaires à l'étude de l'hégémonie dans l'Etat." *Les Temps Modernes*, nos. 234–35, 1965.

———. "The Problem of the Capitalist State." *New Left Review*, no. 58, 1969, pp. 67–78.

Predieri, Alberto. *Pianificazione e costituzione*. Edizioni di comunità, Milan, 1963.

Preuss, Ulrich Klaus. *Legalität und Pluralismus, Beiträge zum Verfassungsrecht der BRD*. Suhrkamp Verlag, Frankfurt, 1973.

Pribicevic, Branko. *The Shop Steward Movement in England*. Oxford University Press, Oxford, 1955.

————. *Intellectual and Manual Labor: A Critique of Epistemology*. Humanities Press, Atlantic Highlands, N.J., 1978.

————. *Materialistische Erkenntnistheorie und Vergesellschaftung der Arbeit*. Merve Verlag, Berlin, 1971.

————. "Technische Intelligenz zwischen Kapitalismus und Sozialismus." In *Technologie und Kapital*, edited by B. Vahrenkamp, Suhrkamp Verlag, Frankfurt, 1973.

————. *Warenform und Denkform, Aufsätze*. Europa Verlag, Vienna and Frankfurt, 1971.

Sraffa, Piero. *Production of Commodities by Means of Commodities*. Cambridge University Press, Cambridge, 1960.

Sweezy, Paul M. "The First Quarter Century." In *Keynes' General Theory*, edited by Robert Lekachman. St. Martin's Press, New York, 1964, pp. 305–14.

————. "John Maynard Keynes." In *Keynes' General Theory*, edited by Robert Lekachman. St. Martin's Press, New York, 1964, pp. 297–304.

————. *The Present as History*. Monthly Review Press, New York, 1953.

Swoboda, Ernst. "Les diverses sources du droit: leur équilibre et leur hiérarchie dans les divers systèmes juridiques." *Archives de philosophie du droit*, Sirey, Paris, 1934, nos. 1–2, pp. 197–207.

Tammelo, Ilmar. "Contemporary Developments of the Imperative Theory of Law, A Survey and Appraisal." *Archiv für Rechts- und Sozialphilosophie*, vol. 41, nos. 2–3, 1963, pp. 255–77.

Taylor, Charles. "Cross-Purposes: The Liberal-Communitarian Debate." In *Liberalism and the Moral Life*, edited by Nancy Rosenblum. Harvard University Press, Cambridge, 1989, pp. 159–82.

————. *Hegel*. Cambridge University Press, Cambridge, 1975.

————. *Hegel and Modern Society*. Cambridge University Press, Cambridge, 1979.

————. *Sources of the Self: The Making of Modern Identity*. Harvard University Press, Cambridge, 1989.

Theobald, Robert. *The Guaranteed Income: Next Step in Economic Evolution?* Doubleday, Garden City, N.Y., 1966.

Thompson, E. P. *The Making of the English Working Class*. Vintage Books, New York, 1963.

Treichler, Paula. "How to Have Theory in an Epidemic: The Evolution of AIDS Treatment Activism." In *Technoculture*, edited by Constance Penley and Andrew Ross. University of Minnesota Press, Minneapolis, 1991.

Tronti, Mario. *Operai e capitale*. Einaudi, Turin, 1966.

Unger, Roberto. *The Critical Legal Studies Movement*. Harvard University Press, Cambridge, 1986.

Vahrenkamp, B., ed. *Technologie und Kapital*. Suhrkamp Verlag, Frankfurt, 1973.

Varga, Eugen. *Die Krise des Kapitalismus und ihre politischen Folgen*, edited by E. Altvater. Europäische Verlagsanstalt, Frankfurt, 1969.

————. *Politico-Economic Problems of Capitalism*, translated by Don Danemanis. Progress Publishers, Moscow, 1968.

Vattimo, Gianni. "Senza Polizia Non C'è Uno Stato." *La Stampa*, September 22, 1991.

————. *The Transparent Society*, translated by David Webb. Polity Press, Oxford, 1992.

Vyshinsky, Andrei. *The Law of the Soviet State*, translated by Hugh Babb, introduction by John Hazard. Macmillan, New York, 1948.

Wahl, Nicholas. "Aux origines de la nouvelle Constitution." *Revue Française de Science Politique*, 1959, no. 1, pp. 30–66.

Walzer, Michael. "Philosophy and Democracy." *Political Theory* 9, 1981, pp. 379–99.

————. "The Communitarian Critique of Liberalism." *Political Theory*, February 1990, pp. 6–23.

Weber, Max. *Economy and Society*, edited by Guenther Roth and Claus Wittich. 2 vols. University of California Press, Berkeley, 1968.

Wee, Herman van der, ed. *The Great Depression Revisited: Essays on the Economics of the Thirties*. Marinus Nijhoff, The Hague, 1972.

Wehr, F. "La doctrine de M. Adolphe Merkl." *Revue internationale de la théorie du droit*, vol. 2, 1927–28, pp. 215–31.

————. "La notion de 'processus juridique' dans la théorie pure du droit." *Studi filosofico-giuridici per Del Vecchio*, vol. 2. Società tipografica modenese, Modena, 1931.

Weissbach, H. J. *Planungswissenschaft. Eine Analyse der Entwicklungsbedingungen und Entwicklungsformen der Arbeitsmarkt*. Achenbach, Biessen-Lollar, 1975.

Wirth, Margaret. *Kapitalismustheorie in der DDR, Entstehung und Entwicklung der Theorie des staatsmonopolistischen Kapitalismus*. Suhrkamp Verlag, Frankfurt, 1972.

————. "Towards a Critique of the Theory of State Monopoly Capitalism." *Economy and Society*, vol. 6, no. 3, August 1977, pp. 284–313.

Wolff, Robert Paul. *Understanding Rawls*. Princeton University Press, Princeton, 1977.

Wygodski, S. L. *Der gegenwärtige Kapitalismus, Versuch einer theoretischen Analyse*. Pahl-Rugenstein Verlag, Cologne, 1972.

Yaffe, David. "The Crisis of Profitability." *New Left Review*, no. 80, 1973.

———. "The Marxian Theory of Crisis, Capital and State." *Conference of Socialist Economists Bulletin*, London, Winter 1972.

Zolo, Danilo. *La teoria comunista dell'estinzione dello Stato*. De Donato, Bari, 1974.